THE
CORRUPTION
CHRONICLES

OBAMA'S BIG SECRECY,
BIG CORRUPTION,
AND BIG GOVERNMENT

TOM FITTON

THRESHOLD EDITIONS
New York London Toronto Sydney New Delhi

Threshold Editions
A Division of Simon & Schuster, Inc.
1230 Avenue of the Americas
New York, NY 10020

First Threshold Editions hardcover edition July 2012

THRESHOLD EDITIONS and colophon are trademarks of
Simon & Schuster, Inc.

For information about special discounts for bulk purchases,
please contact Simon & Schuster Special Sales at 1-866-506-1949
or business@simonandschuster.com.

The Simon & Schuster Speakers Bureau can bring authors
to your live event. For more information or to book an event,
contact the Simon & Schuster Speakers Bureau at 1-866-248-3049
or visit our website at www.simonspeakers.com.

Designed by Renata Di Biase

Manufactured in the United States of America

10 9 8 7 6 5 4 3

Library of Congress Cataloging-in-Publication Data

Fitton, Thomas.
   The corruption chronicles : Obama's big secrecy, big corruption, and big
government / Tom Fitton.
       p.   cm.
    1. Political corruption—United States—History—20th century.   2. Obama,
Barack.   3. Judicial Watch, Inc.   I. Title.
   JK2249.F57   2012
   364.1'3230973—dc23   2012014647

ISBN 978-1-4516-7787-4
ISBN 978-1-4516-7789-8 (ebook)

CONTENTS

THE
CORRUPTION
CHRONICLES

Introduction

THE MISSION OF JUDICIAL WATCH

Judicial Watch was established in 1994 to fight for transparency, honesty, accountability, and integrity in government, politics, and the law. Our conservative, nonpartisan educational foundation promotes high standards of ethics and morality in our nation's public life. We stand watch to ensure that our elected officials and judicial officials don't abuse the powers we entrust to them. Our motto is "Because no one is above the law!"

Judicial Watch fulfills its mission through litigation, investigations, and public outreach. We don't take "no" for an answer, and we will sue whomever and wherever necessary to enforce the rule of law. That means that we sometimes stand out alone on the battlements—but we don't mind, since that's what we're here to do. But we never sue just for the sake of suing. We often sue to gain access to information that can educate the American people about the operations of our government. And we sometimes even sue politicians directly to hold them accountable. All of our lawsuits, whether they are against the government or to protect innocents, are designed to uphold the rule of law.

Our chief methods of pursuing our mission are via open records and freedom of information laws. Litigation and the civil discovery process not only uncover information for the education of the American people on anticorruption issues, but can also put a stop to corruption by public officials and government agencies. In other words, we're doing the work that the government will not do itself.

We provide the information and the impetus to enforcement of law designed to promote honest and open government.

And, yes, Judicial Watch "watches" the judiciary. We take on the important job of ensuring high ethical standards in the judiciary itself. Unfortunately, our judiciary is plagued by many of the same problems as the rest of our federal government—it requires constant oversight, just like everything else government does. By monitoring judges and using the judicial ethics process to hold judges to account, we can make sure that the third branch of government does its important job untainted by corruption or even the appearance of corruption.

Our investigative, legal, and judicial activities provide the basis for our educational outreach, which includes speeches, op-eds, publications, educational conferences, media outreach, radio and news television appearances, and direct radio outreach through informational commercials and public service announcements. Judicial Watch is a long-standing member of the media. Our flagship publication, *The Verdict,* and other investigative pieces educate the public about abuses and misconduct by political and judicial officials, and advocate for the need for an ethical, law-abiding, and moral civic culture. Our website, www.judicialwatch.org, is specifically designed to make our open records documents, legal filings, and other educational materials accessible to the public and the media. We consider ourselves the "wiki" of government corruption. We know that the media drives the American public debate, and we have no intention of allowing that debate to be defined by the apologists for corrupt politicians and corrupted government in the media establishment.

We also provide legal services to other conservatives (and train "regular" citizen-activists) so they can use the Freedom of Information Act (FOIA) and other open records laws to obtain information and accountability on various issues. FOIA and the Privacy Act deserve more detailed explanation. FOIA especially is a tool that Judicial Watch uses regularly, and one that you too can use to help carry through the vision of the Founders and protect your government from corrupt insiders.

Think of Judicial Watch as your anticorruption watchdog in Washington, D.C., and in any state where we can leverage our investigatory and legal expertise to hold corrupt politicians and governments accountable to the rule of law.

We are America's largest and most effective government watchdog group, and we are both proudly conservative and proudly nonpartisan—which means that neither Democratic nor Republican corruption escapes our scrutiny. Our motto still stands: "Because no one is above the law!"

We use the open records and freedom of information laws to uncover corruption from federal, state, and local governments, but when government agencies don't follow the law and turn over documents as they are supposed to—we sue in court to get them. We sue local governments, too, when they violate the law—whether it is for ignoring federal immigration law and providing sanctuary for illegal alien lawbreakers or for illegally spending tax dollars to line politicians' pockets. We also go to court to protect the rule of law from a rampaging federal government that is attacking the sovereign rights of the states to protect their citizens.

When Judicial Watch was founded in 1994 it was during the dark days of the Clinton administration—when we had what we considered the most corrupt president and First Lady in the history of our country. Judicial Watch took on a leadership role in investigating, uncovering, and suing in the courts over Clinton corruption.

But we didn't close up shop when Bill Clinton left town. We took on Bush administration corruption and secrecy. We sought to hold the Bush administration accountable for secretive "energy policy" meetings similar to the corrupt Health Care Task Force meetings that Hillary ran in her failed effort to have the government run your health care. And we took on corrupt Republican politicians who traded access for political contributions. The former Republican majority, allegedly conservative, was elected in 1994 by a public fed up by a Congress where corruption seemingly ruled.

Rather than change the regime and create a rigorous ethics system as promised, Republicans eviscerated the congressional ethics process and actually curtailed some of the minor ethics reforms they did institute. As Republican leaders now acknowledge, the party of small government became, in many ways, the party of big corruption, or at least a party that countenanced big corruption.

Meanwhile, Democrats also put politics ahead of principle, agreeing to a congressional ethics process that protected Republicans (and themselves) in the short term and one that would protect Democrats in the long term if and when they regained the majority.

But when Democrats took control again, they simply repeated history; they didn't seem to care that corruption matters to the voting public. Most notably, House Speaker Nancy Pelosi quickly became an ethics disaster. Pelosi (and too many other members of Congress from both parties) use luxury travel provided by our military to go on junkets far and wide. Who pays for it? You do. We found that "Air Pelosi" cost over $2 million in just two years.

Why is Nancy Pelosi now in the House minority? Because she couldn't be bothered to keep her promises for "the most open, most honest, and most ethical Congress in history."

Do those promises remind you of President Obama's promises: Transparency? Forget about that. Health-care negotiations on C-SPAN? Forget about that. No lobbyists in the White House? Forget about that. Posting a bill on the Internet at least five days before signing? Forget about that, too.

Even before President Obama was sworn into office, he was interviewed by the FBI for a criminal investigation of former Illinois governor Rod Blagojevich's scheme to sell the president's former U.S. Senate seat to the highest bidder. He got involved with Tony Rezko in a serious real estate scandal. He signed up with the Big Labor and ACORN election-thwarters.

Once he entered office, it got even worse. The Obama administration made the startling claim that "the Privacy Act does not apply to the White House." The Obama White House believes it can violate the privacy rights of American citizens without any legal consequences or accountability. Unfortunately, courts ultimately agreed with Obama—leaving a gaping hole in the protections Americans thought they had to protect their government files from White House abuse.

President Obama boldly proclaimed that "transparency and the rule of law will be the touchstones of this presidency," but his administration is addicted to secrecy, stonewalling far too many of Judicial Watch's more than eight hundred Freedom of Information Act requests, and refusing to make public White House visitor logs as federal law requires.

The Obama administration turned the National Endowment for the Arts (as well as the agency that runs the AmeriCorps program) into propaganda machines, using tax dollars to persuade "artists" to promote the Obama agenda. President Obama has installed a record number of "czars" in positions of power. Too many of these individuals are leftist radicals who answer to no one but the president. And too many of the czars are not subject to Senate confirmation and seem to exercise unprecedented authority (which raises serious constitutional questions).

Under the president's bailout schemes, the federal government continues to appropriate or control—through fiat and threats—large sectors of the private economy.

And the list goes on . . .

Government-run health care and car companies, White House coercion, uninvestigated ACORN corruption, debasing his office to help Chicago cronies, Solyndra, attacks on conservative media and the private sector, unprecedented and dangerous new rights for terrorists, perks for campaign donors—this is Obama's "ethics" record.

And it's that ethics record—along with the big government and big secrecy that accompanied it—that led to the rise of the Tea Party movement. The billions of dollars in bailouts and the $24 trillion in new taxpayer liability are an affront to the notion of constitutional, limited government. And we now know the Fannie and Freddie fraud had a lot of corrupt support in Congress. Barack Obama, who had only four years in the Senate under his belt, was a top recipient of Fannie and Freddie cash. We've sued, so far unsuccessfully, to get access to the Fannie/Freddie documents concerning political contributions to Obama and others. The "transparent" Obama White House says no one should be able to see these documents.

Despite their well-known accounting fraud problems and dire warnings of crisis, these "government-sponsored enterprises," with the support and protection of liberals in Congress and their special-interest group allies—like ACORN—pushed for more subprime lending for their politically correct constituencies. And calculating financial institutions (too many of which had corrupt relationships with these very same politicians) were happy to play along.

Any lessons learned? Not in Washington, D.C. Fannie Mae and Freddie Mac continue to subsidize the ruinous business of making subprime loans to those who can't handle them. The Obama administration has put taxpayers on the hook for upwards of $400 billion for these subsidies—which has resulted in a potential liability of $6.5 trillion for the American taxpayer.

Most Americans are not fools. Our polling shows large majorities believe political corruption played a "major role" in the financial crisis. (President Obama recently suggested "fat cat bankers" were the chief cause of the crisis.)

Let me tell you something about that. Judicial Watch sued the Obama Treasury Department in order to obtain documents regarding the historic 2008 meeting held by former Treasury secretary "Hank" Paulson with top bank executives. The documents show that Paulson and other officials—including then–head of the New York Federal Reserve and current Treasury secretary and tax cheat Timothy Geithner—forced the executives to take the government's $125 billion "investment" (and resulting government control).

So in the Obama world, you force banks to take government investment, the banks pay it back with interest, and then you tax these same banks as punishment!

Arguably, the financial crisis is part of the biggest government corruption scandal in our nation's history. But the Obama administration stands like a stone wall against releasing information about the bailouts.

And again, that's just the beginning. The breakdown in our immigration system and the resulting lawlessness is also a crisis. Communities across America are wrestling with the local consequences of the illegal immigration crisis. Drugs, violent crime, overcrowded schools, and an overburdened health-care system are just a few of the social problems caused by rampant illegal immigration.

As the federal government continues to fail in one of its most basic functions—to protect our borders—local officials are increasingly being left to clean up the mess. Some local governments and states rely on the rule of law and place a priority on the rights of American citizens. Far too many other states and localities, unfortunately, flout the law and place a priority on the needs of illegal aliens. So we sue them in court. For too long, politicians have cowered in the face of threats of litigation by the American Civil Liberties Union. Judicial Watch is the conservative answer to the ACLU. It is about time these politicians learn to be afraid of a conservative group of citizens who want to protect the Constitution and their tax dollars and uphold the rule of law.

For decades, the ACLU and other leftists tried to gain credibility with Americans by pretending to challenge the government on behalf of the "oppressed." Conservatives ceded the field of government-watchdog work to those whose idea of government oversight was making sure that regulations were being expanded and more government money was being spent. Judicial Watch is the first conservative group to use on behalf of conservative principles tools that the left developed.

We're conservative in that we generally believe in limited government, individual liberty, the free market, traditional values, and a strong national defense. We also know that corruption is nonpartisan and nonideological. During the Clinton years, Judicial Watch was a hero to conservatives as we took on that administration. The liberal media was less supportive of us. During the subsequent Bush administration, by contrast, liberals (especially in the media) loved us as we took on Bush secrecy.

Our supporters are Republican, Democrat, and independent and comprise a grassroots army that makes us one of the largest conservative groups in the country—and certainly the most widely supported government watchdog group in the world.

One of the chief tools we use in our work is requests made under the Freedom of Information Act. Here's some background.

The Freedom of Information Act (5 U.S.C. § 552) was enacted by Congress and signed into law by President Lyndon Johnson in 1966. The manner in which Johnson signed the law shows just how much those in power were uncomfortable with it. LBJ didn't write about the signing in his daily diary. He wouldn't hold a formal ceremony for the signing and made sure he put into force a signing statement attempting to undercut the law. Interestingly, then-congressman Donald Rumsfeld (R-IL) was a big backer of FOIA, bashing the Johnson administration's "continuing tendency toward managed news and suppression of public information that the people are entitled to have." Johnson was so ticked at the prospect of the bill that he reportedly said of Representative John Moss (R-CA), one of the chief supporters of the legislation, "What is Moss trying to do, screw me? I thought he was one of our boys, but the Justice Department tells me his goddamn bill will screw the Johnson administration." Johnson tried to stall the bill. He then slashed strong transparency language from his press statement, striking the following line: "I signed this measure with a deep sense of pride that the United States is an open society in which the decisions and policies—as well as the mistakes—of public officials are always subjected to the scrutiny and judgment of the people." Bill Moyers, Johnson's White House aide, said that LBJ had to "be dragged kicking and screaming to the signing. . . . He hated the very idea of the Freedom of Information Act; hated the thought of journalists rummaging in government closets and opening government files; hated them challenging the official view of reality. He dug in his heels and even threatened to pocket veto the bill after it reached the White House. And he might have followed through if Moss . . . and other[s] hadn't barraged him with pleas and petitions. He relented and signed 'the damned thing,' as he called it." [1]

FOIA gave the public the right to obtain and access information from federal government agencies. Before that, the government actually put the burden on the individual making a request to prove a right to examine the documents. The enactment of FOIA reversed this process, placing the burden upon the government to justify withholding the documents. While FOIA doesn't require that the government create any documents regarding an information request, it does require that the agency release any document, file, or other record that already exists pertaining to the request.

FOIA was amended in 1996 to include electronic information. It was expanded again in a revision signed by, of all people, President George W. Bush; it allowed more people to be considered representatives of the news media, making more people eligible to get information free from the feds. (Every state has its own freedom of information laws that provide access to operations of state and local government.)

FOIA does not apply to the entire federal government, only to executive branch "agencies." This generally means cabinet agencies and other independent government agencies outside the White House. It doesn't apply to Congress or the federal courts, including the Supreme Court, or to what the lawyers refer to as the "Executive Office of the President" or the White House Office. In other words, one can't FOIA President Obama directly—as his office and most White House offices that directly support the president are exempt from FOIA.

For the most part, FOIA applies to any federal agency records that are either created or obtained by an agency and under the agency's control at the time of the request. Anybody can make a FOIA request: individuals, partnerships, corporations, associations, or even foreign governments.

One of the great benefits of FOIA is its statutory "turnaround time." Once an agency receives a FOIA request, the agency has twenty business days to determine whether to comply. Most importantly, FOIA allows requesters to sue noncomplying government agencies to try to force compliance with the law.

FOIA requests can take years to be answered or completed,

especially if the requester does not follow up or file a lawsuit over the request. In our experience, lawsuits are effective in prying loose documents from an unwilling government. For those who need immediate answers—as we at Judicial Watch so often do—FOIA requests aren't automatically granted in short order. The news cycle moves too fast. But in Washington, there is nothing new under the sun in terms of public policy controversy and scandals. So if it takes months—or even years—to get the government to disgorge information, there still is a public benefit. I can't tell you the number of dormant scandals that Judicial Watch revived with the public as a result of new FOIA documents uncovered after a lengthy and persistent fight in court.

Despite the Freedom of Information Act, secrecy too often reigns supreme in Washington, D.C. That is why Judicial Watch remains such a vital institution. I can think of no one else doing more to pry loose government secrets about corruption and abuse. Judicial Watch is quite simply the most active FOIA requestor and litigator in operation today. We've had significant victories over the past two decades, and there will be significant victories in years to come. Open government is honest government. This is a principle the American people instinctively understand. Yet as you will see in *The Corruption Chronicles,* secret government leads to corrupt government as surely as night follows day.

We are prepared to take on the Obama machine, or whatever the big government proponent happens to be, to protect our freedom and the rule of law.

And, citizen reader, I ask you to join our fight. Please take up the cause of holding government to account. You can file FOIAs. You can demand your political leaders make enforcing the rule of law a priority. And you can provide and demand leadership to the rampant government corruption in Washington, D.C., and in your state. Let's combat the czars, revive legitimate congressional oversight, cut back our government to a manageable size, protect our national security, take back control of the private sector from federal takeovers, and secure our borders. That will have to be done no matter what happens in 2012. A clean, transparent government run by ethical politicians is essential to the future of our republic.

As you fight these battles to secure our nation's promise for the rising generations, you can count on Judicial Watch to give you the facts and do its best to promote the return of ethics and morality to our nation's public life.

PART 1

JUDICIAL WATCH BEFORE OBAMA

1.

THE CLINTON MACHINE

To understand our current crisis of government in these times, it is useful to go back to the 1990s. The liberal media constantly lectures Americans about the alleged crimes of the Nixon administration. They would have you think that Richard M. Nixon was the first and last corrupt president of the twentieth century.

Far from it. It is certainly ironic that one of the young prosecutors on the congressional impeachment team was Hillary Rodham, who would later become Hillary Rodham Clinton, the First Lady, U.S. senator, and current secretary of state—yet Nixon's hallmarks, including dirty tricks, abuse of office, misuse of the FBI, crony politics, intimidation, and cover-ups, became hallmarks of the Clinton presidency. While the heart of this book lies in the secrets of the Obama administration, I want to be clear from the outset: corruption and secrecy didn't start with President Obama.

Judicial Watch was established in 1994, in the aftermath of the election of President William Jefferson Clinton. Judicial Watch became nationally known during the Clinton administration for its use of FOIA requests and other legal actions to hold corrupt politicians like Bill and Hillary Clinton to account. Of course, if the Clinton administration had been full of misunderstood innocents, we'd have gotten no attention. But because the Clinton administration was the most corrupt since Nixon's, our watchdog group, the first from the right to take on government corruption in a serious and sustained way, gained a national following.

Every day seemed to bring new information linking the Clinton administration to abuse of power. Undergirding the corruption was cover-up culture that gave new meaning to the term made famous by Nixon: *stonewalling*. We made it our mission to hold the Clinton administration accountable to the law—we weren't afraid of the Clinton administration, and we wouldn't be intimidated.

Abuse of Power

President Bill Clinton was, above all, a bully. He used the power of his office to intimidate those who disagreed with his political agenda, and he wasn't shy about doing it—and he couldn't do it without the cover of secrecy. If the public had known about the tactics the Clinton administration was using to silence its critics and opponents, the public could have held Clinton accountable, which was the last thing he wanted. As always, the more powerful the person—or the more power he or she seeks—the more they are interested in avoiding transparency. The goal of law is to be both regular and proper; bypassing rules, abusing the law, is neither regular nor proper.

In 1996, the Internal Revenue Service audited Joseph Farah's Western Center for Journalism (WCJ), which had led the way in investigating the death of Clinton deputy White House counsel Vince Foster. In 1998, we helped the WCJ sue the IRS for what we alleged was its retaliatory audit—the audit itself, by the way, came to nothing, and the WCJ was found to be in total compliance. "When IRS field agent Thomas Cederquist first visited our accountant in 1996 to announce the audit, he told us that this was a 'political case' and the decision about our fate would be made 'at the national level,' " reported Farah. "In America, things like this are not supposed to happen—especially to journalists simply doing their job reporting on corruption in government." Farah said that by early 1996, he was hearing rumors that WCJ had been fingered by the IRS. Farah stated that the IRS was asking why WCJ had been investigating White House corruption, why they were working on the Vince Foster case, and what the center was doing to "balance" their stories.[1]

Sure enough, we found that the audit originated with a complaint forwarded to the IRS by the White House. The White House had forwarded it after Bill Clinton himself received it from a California resident. According to the Treasury Department, "the audit originated from a taxpayer who faxed a letter to the White House expressing his concern over a one-page advertisement paid for by WCJ [Western Center for Journalism] that asked for contributions to investigate Foster's death. The fax was forwarded to the EO (Exempt Organizations) National Office and then to the respective Key District Office for appropriate action."[2]

Other Clinton enemies felt the brunt of the administration's secret manipulation of the IRS, too. Juanita Broaddrick's nursing home business was audited in 2000, just after she filed a lawsuit against the White House. Broaddrick, a Judicial Watch client, had alleged that Bill Clinton had raped her. Gennifer Flowers, too, was audited by the IRS following a lawsuit we helped her file against James Carville, George Stephanopoulos, Little Brown & Company, and Hillary Rodham Clinton based on the Clinton administration's ongoing attempts to defame her. Carville had famously told the press, "you all are more interested in putting some bimbo on the air than in getting at the truth. And the truth is that this is just sleazy tabloid trash and you all should be ashamed of yourselves." In the book he wrote with his wife, Mary Matalin, Carville bragged, "I was the first surrogate to go after her. By going with the *Star*, taking the money, playing the aggrieved lover, she put herself in the line of fire, she was fair game. I thought, 'Just don't call her a whore—but short of that, let 'er rip.' "[3]

Paula Jones, too, was audited by the IRS, shortly after announcing her historic lawsuit against Clinton and then rejecting a settlement. In fact, the White House actually declined to comment when the *Washington Post* asked if they had any role in the IRS audit.[4] Former White House Travel Office director Billy Dale was audited shortly after Travelgate came to light—a White House lawyer apparently told friends that the IRS commissioner was "on top of it."[5] Elizabeth Ward Gracen, an actress who had an affair with Clinton, was audited. So was Katherine Prudhomme, a concerned citizen who at a public forum in New Hampshire grilled Vice President Al Gore about Clinton's Broaddrick assault.

When it came to conservative 501(c)(3) organizations, Clinton's IRS was even more active with regard to his perceived enemies. During his tenure, the Heritage Foundation, Concerned Women for America, National Rifle Association, and *National Review,* among others, were all audited.[6]

One reason we were so determined is that we knew that IRS-gate was real, since it had happened to us. Judicial Watch felt the sting of IRS-gate directly in 1998, when the IRS sent us an audit letter. The letter told us to provide "the names and addresses of the directors and their relationship to any political party or political groups." Was this a politically motivated siccing of the IRS on one of the president's political opponents? The answer came just a few months later, in January 1999, when a senior IRS official admitted to me and my colleagues during a meeting at IRS offices, "What do you expect when you sue the president?"

It turns out that our claims that the IRS's moves against us were politically motivated weren't just speculation—in July 2002, after the IRS finally responded to our FOIA requests, columnist Robert Novak reported that the Clinton White House had received an email in September 1998 from an unspecified sender stating, "[Judicial Watch has] obviously targeted you and the vice president. My question is how can this obviously partisan organization be classified as tax-exempt." One month later, the White House sent the message on to the IRS, and two weeks later, Judicial Watch found itself on the receiving end of the IRS audit. Several Democratic politicians, including Representatives Charlie Rangel (D-NY), Martin Frost (D-TX), Jim Moran (D-VA), Tom Harkin (D-IA), John Lewis (D-GA), and Richard Neal (D-MA), were linked to requests that the IRS check out our nonprofit status. "The mystery surrounding Internal Revenue Service tax audits against critics of President Bill Clinton during his administration has been cracked," Novak announced. "The unmistakable evidence is that the supposedly nonpolitical tax agency responds to complaints by prominent politicians."[7]

Former commissioner of the IRS Donald Alexander stated, "the circumstances surrounding the IRS's audit of Judicial Watch are unusual and deviate from the procedures and practices normally followed by the IRS when investigating and auditing 501(c)(3) tax-exempt organizations."[8] In the end, we were given a clean bill of health. So now the IRS is going after Tea Party organizations. Executive branch corruption never dies—it just fades in and out.

The Clinton Payoff Administration

When it came to secrecy and corruption, the Clinton administration didn't limit itself to tracking down its political opponents—they also used the instruments of government to both create and cover up completely inappropriate deals designed to bulk up Clinton's campaign finance coffers. Nowhere is it more important for the American people to know about the actions of their politicians than with regard to campaign finance, since the potential for abuse of office is so high. That's why Judicial Watch made it one of its key missions during the Clinton administration to rip the cover off any campaign finance improprieties. The most famous of these cases was Chinagate.

As David Limbaugh wrote in *Absolute Power,* "Of the innumerable scandals of the Clinton administration, none is more shocking and disturbing than the campaign finance scandal. None is more far-reaching or complex."[9] During the 1996 election cycle, according to the Senate Governmental Affairs Committee report, Clinton spent endless amounts of time campaigning; in the ten months before the 1996 election, Clinton attended no fewer than 230 campaign functions, bringing in almost $120 million. In order to end-run around campaign finance regulations, Clinton softened the line between hard money (which generally meant contributions made specifically to a candidate) and soft money (more lightly regulated expenditures by political parties and entities "independent" of the candidate) by taking control of Democratic National Committee operations.[10]

The worst sort of corruption started in 1995, however, when former Commerce Department official John Huang, who had worked for the huge Indonesian finance company and Clinton donor the Lippo Group, joined the DNC. At Commerce, Huang was a regular at the Clinton White House—visiting seventy-eight times between July 1, 1995, and October 3, 1996. With Huang at the DNC, his top-secret clearance should have been revoked, but it wasn't. Huang was in charge of Asian outreach for the 1996 Clinton campaign. He funneled immense sums to the Clinton campaign, and seemingly in return, the Clinton administration shifted its positions on issues ranging from Taiwan to Indonesia. Meanwhile, Clinton was also fund-raising from a Miami drug kingpin (who had a picture taken with Hillary) and from a front company for the Russian KGB.[11] Judicial Watch deposed Huang five times in the course of FOIA litigation that investigated cash for seats on Commerce Department international trade trips, and this deposition testimony remains Huang's most detailed account of his close ties to Clinton (which went back to Clinton's tenure as Arkansas governor).

Through Huang's testimony, we exposed that the scandal was bipartisan. In fact, Republican senator Mitch McConnell (now the leader of the Senate Republicans) was forced to return a contribution from Huang as a result of our discovery.

That was just the beginning. In December 1996, it came out that the head of a weapons company owned by the Chinese military was invited to have coffee with Clinton. The meet-up was brokered by Yah Lin "Charlie" Trie, a "Friend of Bill," an American citizen who had raised in excess of $600,000 in illicit money for Clinton's legal defense fund. That was only the beginning: in February 1997, Bob Woodward reported that the Justice Department was looking into information that the Chinese embassy had tried to fund Clinton's reelection effort. The Chinese had already funneled cash to the campaign accounts of several major congressional leaders who oversaw trade standards with China. It turns out that the contacts between the Chinese and the Clinton administration ran wide and deep, and the cash flowed freely—as did the policy promises. Eventually, the Democrats were forced to return $3.2 million in tainted cash.[12] Meanwhile, Clinton's attorney general, Janet Reno, with the full-throated supported of her then-deputy Eric Holder, did everything in her power to stonewall a serious investigation by refusing to appoint an independent counsel.

Another key player in the Clinton-China fund-raising scandal was Johnny Chung, a contributor who signed checks worth $360,000 to the DNC while visiting the White House in excess of fifty times. Chung, who became Judicial Watch's client, rocked Washington when he testified that an officer in China's military and an executive for a Chinese government–run aerospace company had arranged for a $300,000 donation to the DNC. "I see the White House is like a subway," Chung told the *Los Angeles Times*. "You have to put in coins to open gates."[13]

Chung's turning state's evidence changed the entire complexion of the case. He said that the DNC knew full well what was going on, and that a DNC finance director asked him personally for a $125,000 donation, already aware that Chung was a middleman for the Chinese. As for that $300,000 donation, Chung now testified that China's military intelligence chief was behind it, and quoted him as saying, "We really like your president." Chung also said that after turning state's evidence, his life was threatened.[14]

The most deeply troubling element here was the Clinton administration's lackadaisical approach to national security and the Chinese government. Loral Space and Communications CEO Bernard Schwartz was the single biggest individual contributor to the DNC in 1997, and had opened up his wallet to the tune of over $1 million since 1995. Loral had an interest in having the Chinese launch its satellites into space, but such business had to be approved by the State Department, which had to approve sensitive exports under law. The State Department, with the support of the Defense Department, wanted to make sure that sensitive technology on U.S. commercial satellites did not fall into the wrong hands. At Loral's request, Clinton overruled his national security establishment by transferring satellite licensing authority from State to a more export friendly Commerce Department. Another law designed to punish the Chinese after the Tiananmen Square massacre required Clinton to also approve waivers for the Loral satellite launches with the Chinese regime. Clinton signed the necessary waivers. When one of these Clinton-approved Chinese launches failed, Loral tried to help the Chinese figure out what went wrong. In 1996, Loral and another company allegedly gave the Chinese assistance that could have been used to make Chinese intercontinental ballistic missiles more accurate. This assistance was a potential violation of law and a Justice Department criminal investigation was launched. Nevertheless Clinton approved another waiver allowing Loral to launch another communications satellite a Chinese missile—even as his own Justice Department was investigating Loral for its alleged earlier illicit assistance to China.[15] A special congressional investigation, the results of which was published as the Cox Report, disclosed that government reviews concluded that Chinese ICBM's were made more reliable thanks to Loral's help and were "likely to lead to improvements in the overall reliability of [Chinese rockets] and ballistic missiles and in particular their guidance systems."[16] In other words, the Chinese could better aim their nuclear missiles at us.

This is where Judicial Watch came in. We came up with a creative strategy to uncover the corruption that had resulted in the transfer of crucial missile assistance to the communist Chinese: we filed a lawsuit seeking to hold Schwartz and the Clinton administration accountable under federal racketeering law, arguing that the campaign contributions from Schwartz were a sort of bribery. As far as Schwartz's China mission went, he told the *Washington Post* that meetings Ron Brown (the former head of the DNC that Clinton installed as commerce secretary) had put together for him "helped open doors that were not open before." Schwartz also told the *Wall Street Journal*, "I think that political involvement does enhance the visibility of a corporate executive, and to the extent that visibility is enhanced, access is enhanced as well." Schwartz went even further with *BusinessWeek*: "I can open any door I want as chairman of a $6 billion company." No wonder Deputy White House Chief of Staff Harold Ickes told Clinton to call Schwartz for donations, explaining, "I have it on good authority that Mr. Schwartz is prepared to do anything he can for the administration."[17] (As you might imagine, the courts weren't too thrilled by Judicial Watch's suggesting that the Clinton White House was run as a racketeering operation that benefitted the Chinese missile program and our lawsuit was dismissed.) In 2002, the Bush administration let Loral off with a fine $14 million for helping China. Loral paid the fine without admitting or denying the government's charges.[18]

Our work left little doubt that the Clinton administration used the Commerce Department as a payoff center for large campaign contributors. Clinton appointed his 1992 chairman of the DNC, Ron Brown, to secretary of commerce; Melissa Moss, a former top DNC fund-raiser, became director of the Commerce Department's Office of Business Liaison; Alexis Herman, a DNC fund-raiser, became director of public liaison for the White House before becoming secretary of labor. Under Brown, many of Clinton's biggest contributors were granted seats on government-sponsored trade missions, including Schwartz, who received a Commerce Department Trade Mission slot to China. According to a DNC brochure, contributors of more than $100,000 to the DNC were "invited to participate in foreign trade missions, which affords opportunities to join Party leaders in meeting with business leaders abroad."

On this score, Judicial Watch secured testimony from Nolanda Hill, business partner and friend of Ron Brown, stating that Hillary Clinton was behind the fund-raising scheme involving the sale of seats on official trade missions—and that she had the support of both her husband and Vice President Al Gore.

Our work prompted court findings that stuck against the Clinton administration. Judicial Watch "got the ball rolling" with its FOIA requests on the Commerce Department. We obtained a court judgment against the Clinton-Gore Commerce Department, finding that evidence had been destroyed and testimony falsified. In our lawsuits related to Commerce Department trade missions, we were awarded just under $900,000 for attorney fees and costs. The judge noted in his ruling that Judicial Watch's efforts prompted two congressional committees and the Federal Election Commission to investigate, and that the Commerce Department thereafter changed its policy for selecting participants in trade missions.

Perhaps the most obvious patronage scandal of all was yet another -gate, this time Travelgate. When the Clintons entered the White

House, they quickly decided to fire several members of the nonpolitical White House Travel Office. One of those was Billy Dale, head
of the office. In place of Dale and his employees, the Clintons put in
place several of their buddies, including major campaign donors as
the associated travel planning company, World Wide Travel. Hollywood producer Harry Thomason also attempted to get the Clintons
to use their air charter business to book presidential travel. Hillary
Clinton stood behind the moves, utilizing the FBI to investigate the
Travel Office employees. Billy Dale was wrongly tried for embezzlement of $68,000 in news media cash. A year afterward, the General
Accounting Office (GAO) released a report ripping the Clintons'
handling of the Travel Office, and, according to the *Washington Post*,
"the appearance of improper influence because of easy White House
access by Clinton friends." [19]

Hints of What Was to Come

It would be almost a decade before the American people became
aware of the implications of what seemed to be a small-scale scandal,
at least for the Clintons. That scandal broke in 1999, when Judicial
Watch brought a shareholder lawsuit against Deutsche Bank specifically to stop the bank from giving special treatment to the Clintons
on a home loan. In September 1999, we sent a letter to Deutsche
Bank and its subsidiary, Bankers Trust Company, about recent reports that Deutsche Bank and Bankers Trust were going to give a
cozy home mortgage deal to the Clintons. Collateral for the deal was
to be provided by a $1.35 million guarantee from future Democratic
National Committee chairman Terry McAuliffe, at the time chairman of Clinton's 53rd Presidential Inaugural Committee and chairman of the White House Millennium Celebration.

The loan would have violated the law. Under federal campaign
finance laws at the time, campaign contributions in the amount
of $1,000 or more were illegal. Further, gratuities are obviously il-
legal under federal law. Since Hillary Clinton was then running for
U.S. senator from New York and seeking to establish residency in

the State of New York, the loan guarantees counted as campaign contributions—what else would you call it when someone puts up the collateral for a multimillion-dollar home, freeing up cash for you to use yourself for other purposes, including campaigning?

We threatened to sue the bank to stop the loan, and when they refused, we went ahead with the lawsuit. In it, we noted that McAuliffe seems to have made it his personal mission to back the Clintons with copious piles of money, raising nearly $5 million for Clinton's legal defense fund and raising $150,000 for Hillary's Senate campaign. As far as the loan itself, Bill and Hillary were well over $5 million in debt, Hillary was unemployed, and Bill was making only $200,000 as president. How could they afford a $1.35 million loan, even with a below-market rate? They couldn't without McAuliffe's help.

Meanwhile, New York mayor Rudy Giuliani made hay out of the budding scandal, wryly noting, "People are trying to figure out how they can get someone to give them $1.3 million to buy a house."[20] Again, the court was not too keen to intervene in the Clintons' fraudulent mortgage deal because doing so might make the Clintons look like "crooks." To this day, I can think of no worse example of court justice being cowed by political power.

At the time, this seemed like a relatively minor scandal, at least on the Clinton scale, but it presaged a series of scandals that would rock the U.S. economy down to its foundations in 2008, as we'll discuss. The close dealings between the congressmen charged with oversight of the mortgage industry and the mortgage lenders themselves resulted in financial disaster for virtually all Americans. The Clintons led the way here, and it's not surprising that Deutsche Bank would later be called on the carpet for home loan fraud. One government lawsuit alleged that Deutsche Bank "lied to be included in a Government program to select mortgages that violated program rules in blatant disregard of whether borrowers could make mortgage payments. While Deutsche Bank . . . profited from the resale of these Government-insured mortgages, thousands of American homeowners have faced default and eviction, and the Government has paid hundreds of millions of dollars in insurance claims, with hundreds of millions of dollars more expected to be paid in the future."[21] Countrywide Financial, a major player in the subprime mortgage market, had an official VIP program that provided special discounts and services to politicians on the Hill, both Democrat and Republicans. Sweetheart mortgage loans for politicians by banks implicated in the subprime mortgage crisis is a near-perfect example of the everyday corruption in Washington that sets many Americans seething.

Of course, President Clinton affected the mortgage market in more ways than simply getting a personal favor from Deutsche Bank. In September 1999, the *New York Times* reported that Fannie Mae, the biggest mortgage underwriter in the country and a government-sponsored entity, was "under increasing pressure from the Clinton administration to expand mortgage loans among low and moderate income people and felt pressure from stockholders to maintain its phenomenal growth in profits. In addition, banks, thrift institutions and mortgage companies have been pressing Fannie Mae to help them make more loans to so-called subprime borrowers." Clinton's former budget director, Franklin Raines, was running Fannie Mae at the time; he was also allegedly receiving a nice benefit from Countrywide in the form of a sweetheart mortgage deal. "Fannie Mae has expanded home ownership for millions of families in the 1990s by reducing down payment requirements," said Raines. "Yet there remain too many borrowers whose credit is just a notch below what our underwriting has required who have been relegated to paying significantly higher mortgage rates in the so-called subprime market."[22] Woe for those newly underwritten borrowers ended up as woe for millions more Americans as the real estate market tanked a decade later.

The financial crisis helped set in motion by the Clinton administration wouldn't happen until 2008. But the Clinton administration's failure to pursue Osama bin Laden began impacting America almost immediately.

On December 11, 2001, we used FOIA to request documents concerning the government of Sudan's reported offer to share intelligence files on bin Laden. The Clinton administration had supposedly rebuffed an offer by Sudanese officials to turn bin Laden over to the United States. In August 2005, we finally got the documents we'd been seeking: two declassified "Top Secret" State Department documents showing that Clinton administration officials were warned of the activities of bin Laden following his expulsion from Sudan in May 1996. "Bin Ladin," the report noted, "seemingly should be on the run. But his willingness to speak more openly to the press about his militant opposition to the Saudi regime and the West suggests more a man emboldened by recent events, whether or not he was involved in them. He may believe tensions in Saudi Arabia are ripe for exploiting through increased terrorism. Keeping bin Ladin on the move by reducing his haven options will inconvenience him, but his informal and transnational network of businesses and associates will remain resilient. Even a bin Ladin on the move can retain the capability to support individuals and groups who have the motive and wherewithal to attack U.S. interest almost worldwide." This wasn't hindsight being twenty-twenty—these documents showed that the Clinton administration knew the danger bin Laden posed back in 1996 and failed to take any meaningful action to stop him.[23]

In 2008, Judicial Watch obtained access to the redacted portions of the document, and they were even more shocking. The document stated, "[redacted] . . . indicated bin Ladin planned to sponsor suicide car bombings against US interests in the UK, in part to punish London for 'submitting' to US pressure to bar his entry into the UK." Other information in the documents showed that the leadership of Sudan, President Omar Al Bashir and Hassan Turabi, had ties with bin Laden. The Clinton administration also rebuffed an offer by Sudanese officials to turn bin Laden over to the United States. Bin Laden's many passports, his private plane, and the backing he received from foreign sponsors allowed him to travel freely "with little fear of being intercepted or tracked," the report said. The report even warned that bin Laden's prolonged stay in Afghanistan "could prove more dangerous to U.S. interests in the long run than his three-year liaison with Khartoum," and predicted that even if bin Laden were forced to move from place to place, it wouldn't be anything more than an inconvenience, since "his informal and transnational network of businesses and associates remain resilient." Bin

Laden, the report said, wouldn't be stopped from pursuing his activities while on the move: "[he] can retain the capability to support individuals and groups who have the motive and wherewithal to attack U.S. interests almost worldwide." The document showed that well over five years before 9/11, and four years before the USS *Cole*, the Clinton administration was warned in full about bin Laden's murderous intent, including specific threats to attack U.S. interests, but took no meaningful action against bin Laden. As a result, thousands of Americans were murdered in New York, Washington, D.C., and Pennsylvania.[24]

Clinton's inaction with regard to Sudan had other ramifications, too—when he finally bombed the al-Shifa plant in Sudan in 1998, most experts thought it had been a mistake. Judicial Watch made a FOIA request in January 2000 to the CIA on this topic, and only two years later did they respond. They provided a set of heavily redacted documents, including a September 21, 1998, Senior Executive Intelligence Brief, titled "Middle East: Currents Favor Saddam." That document stated that "Arab anger over the US military strike in Sudan . . . added momentum to regional trends benefitting Saddam. . . . [The strike] has fueled Arab perceptions of US hostility toward Muslims, increasing the political risk to US allies of siding with Washington to renew pressure against Saddam." At the time, Clinton's Sudan strike was seen as a "wag the dog" distraction, as it came shortly after Clinton appeared before a federal grand jury about the Lewinsky scandal. (*Wag the Dog* was a movie that year in which a fictional presidential administration made up a war against Albania in order to cover up a presidential sex scandal.[25]) The "wag the dog" Sudan strike didn't do any damage to bin Laden, but it did create support for Saddam Hussein.[26]

On the Way Out

The Clintons hadn't entered the White House with any sense of honor, and they left it the same way: by pilfering the silverware and pardoning criminals in the dead of night. To the last minute and beyond, we knew we would have to stay on top of them, ripping away the mask of secrecy and power behind which they hid.

One might not think it possible that an impeached president, implicated in selling his office to foreign interests, could top this corrupt record on his final day in office, but Clinton managed to end his presidency on a truly infamous note. On the last possible day of his administration, Clinton issued an unbelievable 140 pardons, commuting thirty-six sentences; in full compliance with established Clinton precedent, many of those pardons went to convicted felons who had paid large fees to Clinton's associates. One of them was Marc Rich, whose wife, Denise, had donated over $1 million to Democratic Party causes and the Clinton Library.

This Pardongate scandal also caught Hillary Clinton, who had just been elected to the U.S. Senate to help represent New York. It turns out that Hugh Rodham, Hillary's brother, took a payoff of $400,000 from associates of two felons who successfully used Hugh to lobby Bill for their pardons.[27] He later supposedly had to return the money in order to avoid the fallout. And were pardons exchanged for votes? Years later, in 2008, our investigators obtained thirty-four photos from the Clinton Presidential Library of Hillary Rodham Clinton, then-president Bill Clinton, and Grand Rabbi David Twersky at a White House meeting during which the grand rabbi and other community leaders allegedly lobbied the Clintons to commute the jail sentences of four Hasidic men convicted of stealing $30 million in government education aid. The meeting took place in December 2000, just after the New York–based Hasidim sect delivered 1,400 votes to Hillary Clinton's Senate 2000 campaign and only twelve to her opponent, Rick Lazio.

This was the second meeting between Hillary Clinton and representatives of the Hasidic men. Prior to the election, in August 2000, Hillary Clinton visited New Square, the Hasidic community just outside New York City.[28]

Our FOIA requests for the Clinton pardon documents were initially stonewalled by the Bush administration, so we had to file one of our first lawsuits against the Bush administration—about a Clinton scandal!

Clearly the case began as an investigation into corruption, but it quickly became a fight against government secrecy. The Bush administration tried to stop us in our tracks by suggesting that the pardon recommendations of the Justice Department's Office of the Pardon Attorney (which never were reviewed by Clinton!) were subject to the presidential communications privilege—a presidential executive privilege recognized by the courts to protect the confidentiality of communications between the president and his closest advisors.

The second most important federal court in the country, the U.S. Court of Appeals for the District of Columbia Circuit, rejected that Bush secrecy gambit in 2004. To allow the presidential communications privilege to govern the pardon documents from the Justice Department "would be both contrary to executive privilege precedent and considerably undermine the purposes of FOIA to foster openness and accountability in government," said the court. "Indeed, a bright-line rule expanding the privilege could have the effect of inviting use of the presidential privilege to shield communications on which the President has no intention of relying in exercising his pardon duties, for the sole purpose of raising the burden for those who seek their disclosure." [29] When the department finally released some 915 pages of documents in May 2005, they blacked out virtually everything. The text of the recommendations was completely covered by black ink. Since the presidential communications privilege was not available to them, the Bush Justice Department invoked the deliberative process privilege, which can allow the government to keep secret pre-decisional material. So, since all the pardon recommendations were "pre-decisional," the Bush administration wouldn't offer anything of importance in the end and gave us 915 blacked-out pages. [30] This smarmy contempt for the people's right to know is a good illustration of Washington corruption in the Clinton-Bush era.

The Bush administration's protection of Clinton through a narrow reading of FOIA proves that government secrecy can be part of the governing platforms of both political parties.

2.

THE BUSH FOG

President George W. Bush's administration began full of high hopes and grand promises. But the American people came to see an arrogance and contempt for accountability that led to repudiations of the Bush legacy at the ballot box in 2006 and 2008. At a minimum, the Bush crowd thought that since they were not Bill Clinton, they could do no wrong and shouldn't be questioned. And they had an ideological hostility to governmental transparency and openness that served to undermine the people's confidence in the administration from the beginning.

Immediately upon his election, President Bush made clear that he wasn't interested in pursuing any of the investigations of the Clinton years. "I think it's time to get all of this business behind us," he said. "I think it's time to allow the president to finish his term, and let him move on and enjoy life and become an active participant in the American system. And I think we've had enough focus on the past. It's time to move forward."[1] At the same time, Bush used the rhetoric of honesty and transparency, issuing a memo to his executive branch employees that read, "Everyone who enters into public service for the United States has a duty to the American people to maintain the highest standards of integrity in Government."

A president who was elected as an antidote to the corruption of his predecessor quickly brought into Establishment Washington an arrogance that saw anticorruption efforts and the Clinton impeachment as déclassé. The Bush people also made the political calculation that the American people were tired of so-called scandal politics. This meant that the rule of law would take a backseat to politics as usual. And I'm sure the Bush people were more than a little afraid of the Clinton gang—with their FBI files, private investigators, etc. The Clinton impeachment, they surely took note of, did not result in Clinton's removal from office—but in the removal of one Republican House Speaker: Newt Gingrich; and one Republican House Speaker-designate: Bob Livingston.

Whatever the motive, it was no excuse for ignoring the rule of law.

The Bush administration started protecting the Clinton corruption at the expense of the taxpayer literally from day one. After the departing Clinton staff vandalized the White House, the Bush folks had ample reason to be angry and upset, and to hold the Clintons accountable. But after a few brief remarks by Bush officials about the bad manners of the Clinton staff, the Bush White House tried to spin away the entire story. Press Secretary Ari Fleischer, in an attempt to undercut the reports, said that the damage wasn't officially catalogued: "The cataloguing that I mentioned, frankly, that's one person in our administrative offices who is really just keeping track in his head about things that may have taken place. . . . As far as we're concerned, it's over." Bush distanced himself from any implication that there was something worth investigating—as there clearly was: "There might have been a prank or two. Maybe somebody put a cartoon on the wall, but that's OK. It's time now to move forward." Meanwhile, former Clinton White House administrator Mark Lindsay was falsely claiming that there was not "one instance of vandalism, not a single one."[2]

The *Washington Times* reported that the Bush White House was actually calling up members of Congress to try to stop them from investigating the vandalism.

This was especially problematic, since it revealed not just the Bush administration's desire to stifle any public knowledge of the true costs to the taxpayer of the vandalism, but also the Bush administration's dismissive attitude toward the *real* damage: the destruction of computer hard drives, the theft of laptops, and the deletion of emails. As one anonymous Bush official put it, "We just were pleased to let the matter fade so that people could return to the focus on policy."[3]

Then there was the Clintons' outright theft of White House furniture to stock their new home in Chappaqua, New York. On January 4, 2000, Hillary brought a moving van to 1600 Pennsylvania Avenue to start the move. We suspected at the time that Hillary was looting the White House in order to fill up her new house. Sure enough the Associated Press reported that White House property had indeed been removed. One year later, the *Washington Post* reported similarly, "President Bill Clinton and his wife started shipping furniture from the White House to the Clintons' newly purchased home in New York more than a year ago, despite questions at the time by the chief usher about whether they were entitled to remove the items. . . . [The chief usher] believed [the items] were government property donated as part of a [$396,000] White House redecoration project in 1993, during Clinton's first year in office."[4] In the end, the Clintons—who had filched an iron and glass coffee table, a TV armoire, and a custom gaming table, among other high-end furniture—had to return $28,000 in furniture to the White House. If that doesn't tell you about the petty criminality of the Clintons, I don't know what will.

So what did Bush do to track down the Clintons for their violation of law in simply walking off with taxpayer-bought accoutrements? Once again, he ignored it. At the swearing-in of Secretary of Commerce Donald Evans, he stated, "It's important for all the facts to be laid out on the table and I'm confident that the President—the former President and First Lady will make the right decision."[5] As if that weren't vague enough, Bush reemphasized his usual "time to move on" language a few days later.

When it came to Pardongate, the Bush administration was just as willing to stall any investigation whatsoever. As the *New York Times* editorial board, surprisingly getting it right, wrote, "Mr. Clinton does not have many friends . . . unless you count President Bush, who said yesterday it was time to move on."[6] Despite mountains of evidence against the Clintons in the Pardongate scandal, the Bush administration shut down the investigation of the issue. In February 2001, just as congressional and Justice Department inquiries heated up, Bush was asked aboard Air Force One about the scandals. "Do you think it's a good idea for Congress to be investigating pardons, or for the Justice Department to do that?" Bush's answer: "I think it's time to move on."[7]

It was only natural, then, that with this kind of tepid response from the Bush administration, his political appointees at Justice were only too eager to shove the scandal back into the closet. Instead of pursuing the matter themselves, they allowed Mary Jo White, a Clinton appointee and U.S. attorney for the Southern District of New York (White had killed a major scandal involving the Teamsters and Democrats), to open an investigation. White supposedly didn't like the pardon of Marc Rich, since her office wanted to prosecute Rich, but even the liberal *Los Angeles Times* recognized that her newfound involvement had only occurred because "Bush's remark dampened interest within the Justice Department for a criminal investigation, said one source familiar with the matter."[8]

And just as with the vandalism scandal, the Bush administration took active steps to shut down the investigation of Pardongate by Congress. According to *Newsweek* magazine, "White House administration officials are quietly pressuring GOP Congressional investigators to end the probe of former President Bill Clinton's pardons as quickly as possible. . . . 'Everybody's not real happy with us over there,' says one Republican staffer. 'I've been getting calls from the White House saying, "Hey, what are you guys doing?" ' "[9]

Again, the kindhearted reading was that the Bush administration wanted to move on without distractions that could be caused by full-scale investigations of the Clintons. But a more base reason was suggested by *Newsweek*: the Bush team didn't want to implicate I. Lewis "Scooter" Libby, who had tried to aid Rich in obtaining the pardon. Said *Newsweek*, "In private, Bush White House officials worry about a political backlash from Democrats if the pardon investigation drags on much longer. For more than 10 years, Rich's chief American lawyer and advocate was Lewis (Scooter) Libby, now Vice President Cheney's chief of staff. Last week Democrats on the Burton committee fired a political warning shot, insisting that Libby, who worked for Rich until last year, be called as a witness." Libby apparently admitted that his law firm had billed Rich for some $2 million in legal fees, and that he called Rich a couple of days after the pardon from Clinton to congratulate him. "The revelation," reported *Newsweek*, "delighted Democrats, who have been dying to inflict a little political pain themselves." Unsurprisingly, congressional hearings came to a quiet end, smothered by soon-to-be Senate Minority Leader Trent Lott.

We wouldn't stand for either the Bush administration or its allies in Congress ignoring Clinton's pardon outrages. Working with Congressman Bob Barr (R-GA), we made an innovative legal claim, arguing that the pardons themselves were not in compliance with law and that Bush should declare them void. Specifically, the problem was that Clinton's last-minute pardons all stated that the pardons were for offenses specified in the pardon applications. Here's the actual text of Clinton's pardons: "AFTER CONSIDERING THE REQUESTS for executive clemency of the following named persons, I hereby grant full and unconditional pardons to the following named persons for those offenses against the United States described in each such request."

There was only one issue: there were no formal applications filed by many of the applicants, since they were working illicit back channels to obtain their pardons. In fact, 44 of the 138 individuals Clinton pardoned had no requests pending before the Office of Pardon Attorney. Court precedent suggested that pardons are valid only if they clearly state the offenses being pardoned. This would prevent blanket pardons for any crimes in the past. Say, for example, that Clinton had written a pardon for all offenses previously committed by Rich, and then a year later, the police had found that Rich committed murder. The pardon shouldn't be effective as to the murder, since the crime wasn't known at the time. That's why pardons should name specifically the crimes at issue. As a matter of law, until a pardon is delivered, a president may cancel it as well.

In Clinton's rush to issue pardons, he didn't deliver them—he needed the Bush Justice Department to deliver them for him.

Thankfully for Clinton and for Clinton's corrupt and criminal pardon recipients, Bush did just that. All President Bush had to do was refuse to deliver the pardons. Wanting to protect himself politically and wanting to delink his staff from the scandal, Bush chose not to. The Pardongate scandal ended up being a bust.

Of all the Clinton scandals, the worst was Chinagate. So of course that is where the Bush administration worked hardest to end any substantive investigations. Here the Bush gang was just following in the footsteps of Janet Reno's Justice Department—she had refused six times to appoint an independent counsel to investigate violations of campaign finance law, including the alleged approval by Clinton of technology transfers to China in return for political donations. Many crucial figures fled the country rather than testify against the Clintons.

So what did the Bush administration do? You guessed it: they stymied the investigation. Even during the presidential campaign, Bush said he would do nothing about Chinagate. "While it's clear that Al Gore engaged in a number of fund-raising activities and gave the FBI statements that continue to raise the issue of credibility, the American people are sick and tired of all these scandals and investigations," Bush said. "The best way to put all these scandals and investigations behind us is to elect someone new."[10] It was a point Bush made at the Republican National Convention as well. This prompted conservative columnist par excellence (and old Nixon hand) William Safire of the *New York Times* to comment, "Republicans on the unpopular ramparts of the rule of law were coolly informed he preferred 'civility and respect.' "[11]

In March 2001, Bush and company had a chance to truly implement justice in Chinagate, without even getting their hands dirty. It would have been tough, but the new Bush team could have worked to dismantle a sweetheart plea agreement for James Riady and his Lippo Group. Riady had made Clinton a personal promise to raise a million dollars for the 1992 campaign—and everyone knew Riady was a foreign national. Riady also installed John Huang, his agent, in the executive branch at the Commerce Department, where Huang had high-level access and helped funnel cash to the Clinton reelection campaign. Riady's goals were to attain Most Favored Nation trade status for China, get rid of trade barriers with Indonesia, and normalize relations with Vietnam—all three of which Clinton accomplished on his behalf.[12] Just days before Clinton left office, Riady reached a plea agreement with the Clinton Justice Department but his sentencing was delayed until March 2001, which meant that it had to be blessed by Bush Justice Department. What was Riady's penalty for this blatant buying of the White House? A ridiculous four hundred hours of community service, to be served, in all places, in Indonesia. The fantastic plea bargain for Riady, who was believed by a Senate committee "to have had a long-term relationship with a Chinese intelligence agency," meant that he would not have any incentive at all to testify about what he knew.[13]

We were prepared to oppose the plea agreement in court. What we didn't expect was that John Ashcroft's Justice Department would go along with the sleazily generous deal from the Reno Justice Department. We argued at the sentencing hearing that four hundred hours was ludicrous, especially in light of the fact that another witness in the case—a friendly, cooperative witness, no less—received three thousand hours of community service. Incredibly, the Chinagate cover-up didn't end there.

What of Loral, the company that Clinton helped to aid the Chinese missile program, putting American lives at risk? Again, the Bush administration allowed Loral to pay a $14 million civil fine, and didn't force Loral to admit improprieties. Loral was allowed to go on its merry way (and keep its business dealings with the Chinese government).[14]

Not one official from the Clinton administration was ever indicted concerning campaign finance law violations.

The Bush administration saw the selling of the White House and the related missile technology assistance to Communist China as political problems to be put to bed. In fact, the disgraced Bill Clinton and George H. W. Bush became informal ambassadors-at-large for the Bush administration. It seems no one person did more to rehabilitate the image of the impeached Bill Clinton than his Republican successor. The abrogation of President Bush's duty to uphold the law kept the Clintons off Bush's back but did nothing to vindicate the rule of law from Clinton's historic abuse of office.

The Bush Ethical Blind Spot

President George W. Bush prized loyalty and valued his friends, characteristics which are virtues—to a point. Bush passed that point when his loyalty to his friends led to some truly awful appointments. Bush's first questionable appointment was his Commerce secretary, Don Evans. Evans, like his predecessors Malcolm Baldridge, Robert Mosbacher, Ron Brown, Mickey Kantor, and Bill Daley, was a major fund-raiser for the man who nominated him for his position. Evans was personally close to President Bush and had served as Bush's finance chairman during the 2000 campaign. We understood at the time that putting a fund-raiser at the head of Commerce would prove to be—as it has in the past—a whole lot of trouble.

Within months, we found out we were right. It turns out that Bush friend and donor Ken Lay of Enron called up Evans and asked him to use his influence with Moody's, the credit ratings agency, to prevent Moody's from continuing to downgrade Enron's debt. By downgrading Enron's debt, Moody's would prevent Enron from being able to raise cash to pay off Enron's debts. Evans said he didn't do as Lay requested because that would have been an abuse of office. We first ran into Enron during the Clinton administration. I remember being surprised when Enron became popularly known as a Bush corporate crony, since we knew about their coziness with the Clinton cash-for-favors regime. In 1995, Ken Lay joined Clinton's commerce secretary, Ron Brown, on a trade trip to India. Enron also got hundreds of millions in government support from the Clinton administration for Enron's energy projects in India, and even attempted to enter into joint ventures with John Huang's Lippo Group.

It got worse. Bush's transportation secretary was Norman Mineta, whom he had retained from the Clinton administration. That decision was absolutely outrageous. When Mineta was first nominated by Clinton, we protested strongly—Mineta had been involved in the Clinton Commerce Department trade mission scandal, in which we found that seats on trade missions had been sold in exchange for campaign contributions. Mineta participated in the Commerce Department trade mission to Indonesia, which involved the ubiquitous Huang and other Chinagate participants. News outlets also reported that Mineta was an emissary on behalf of Clinton to accused Chinese spy Wen Ho Lee's family during an active federal espionage investigation, Mineta supposedly helped Lee as part of an effort to turn out Asian votes for Democrats. The Bush administration ignored all of that and placed Mineta in the Bush cabinet to give it the appearance of bipartisanship. He would turn out to be one of Bush's most controversial picks.

The Bush administration courted controversy by nominating Elaine Chao as secretary of labor. John Huang revealed under deposition that Elaine Chao hadn't just asked him for political contributions for former senator Alfonse D'Amato, but that her husband, Senator Mitch McConnell (R-KY), had also received contributions from Huang and the Lippo Group. Huang testified that the money he funneled to McConnell and D'Amato was actually laundered illegally from overseas bank accounts. Huang took the Fifth Amendment when asked if he had donated more than $2,000 to McConnell during the 1990s. It took Bob Novak's syndicated column reporting the testimony in order for McConnell to return the contribution.[15]

Chao was actually Bush's second choice—his first choice, Linda Chavez, had been embroiled in a "scandal" surrounding providing shelter to an illegal immigrant. Now, in retrospect, conservatives had good reason to like Chao's policies at Labor, as she was an effective leader that used the law to hold labor unions accountable in ways never seen before in the history of her department. Nevertheless, her role in shepherding money from a man believed to on the payroll of a foreign government should have been fully explored before she was allowed to serve in the Bush cabinet.[16]

The Bush administration also kept on IRS Commissioner Charles O. Rossotti. IRS commissioner Rossotti allowed his agency to be used by the Clinton administration to audit and intimidate the latter's perceived adversaries. On top of this, as commissioner, Rossotti oversaw the awarding of IRS contracts to AMS, a company he founded and in which he had a major financial interest. In 2002, AMS was supposed to make at least $17 million from its IRS contracts. Rossotti's wife served as outside counsel for AMS. Just before Clinton left office, he granted Rossotti a waiver for his conflict of interest.

Unfortunately, the Bush administration, which should have known better, was untroubled by these conflicts of interest and by Rossotti's IRS being used as a club against Clinton's opponents. But at least the Bush administration did force Rossotti to sell his interests in AMS, but only after we filed complaints over this conflict of interest (and prompted over 25,000 citizen petitions to Bush requesting he fire Rossotti).

What about the FBI, another Clinton tool? Bush left it in the hands of another Clinton appointee, Louis B. Freeh. Under Freeh's watch, the FBI sent Republican FBI files to political operatives at the Clinton White House, including Craig Livingstone. Freeh's FBI was also responsible for the fiascos at Waco, Ruby Ridge, the Atlanta Olympic bombing investigation, and other scandals where cover-ups and obstruction of evidence took place. Freeh's FBI took no action as Chinese agents waltzed through the Oval Office and White House to drop off laundered fund-raising cash. Only when Freeh resigned did he leave office in June 2001.

The Bush Justice Department

At first glance, Bush's appointment of Attorney General John Ashcroft seemed terrific. Ashcroft was an honest man, committed to cleaning up the devastated Reno Justice Department, and able to restore trust in the institution. We looked forward to working with him.

He wasn't so eager to work with us. We tried again and again to set meetings with him to offer our help in ferreting out government corruption. He ignored our requests. Within the first year, it was clear that the Justice Department wasn't interested in changing the way business was done. As it turned out, although we couldn't swing a meeting with Attorney General Ashcroft, big-time donors could.

On September 20, 2001, we identified the Holy Land Foundation (HLF) and nineteen other organizations as money laundering fronts for Islamic terrorists. We wrote up the case against the groups and sent copies of our complaint to Ashcroft, his assistant attorney general (and future secretary of homeland security) Michael Chertoff, Secretary of the Treasury Paul H. O'Neill, Rossotti, and President Bush. One month after that, the *Washington Post* reported that Ashcroft and other members of the Justice Department actually met with legal counsel for the HLF, an organization that allegedly has directly financed the murder of Americans. Ashcroft actually met with their attorney, George Salem of Akin Gump Strauss Hauer & Feld, along with three of his fellow HLF-hired attorneys. HLF wanted the Justice Department to write a favorable amicus brief—a friend-of-the-court brief, filed by a third party to help one of the parties to the case—on behalf of HLF in a case related to the death of an American at the hands of Hamas. So why would Ashcroft meet with these lawyers? Did it have something to do with the fact that Salem helped raise $3 million for the Bush-Cheney campaign as chairman of Arab Americans for Bush-Cheney 2000?

When the Bush team entered office, we also hoped that their professed desire to restore honor to the White House would extend far enough to cover reasonable treatment of FOIA requests. Instead of ratcheting down the Clinton White House's FOIA obstructionism, the Bush administration ratcheted it *up*. However disingenuous they were, Janet Reno's actual guidelines on FOIA were very reasonable, with federal agencies being told to err on the side of disclosure. But now, Attorney General Ashcroft told federal agencies to consider all possible exemptions before releasing documents under FOIA, essentially creating a presumption that documents shouldn't be released. "When you carefully consider FOIA requests and decide to withhold records, in whole or in part, you can be assured that the Department of Justice will defend your decisions unless they lack a sound legal basis or present an unwarranted risk of adverse impact on the ability of other agencies to protect other important records," the memo said.[17] The Bush administration policy now seemed to be to err on the side of secrecy. So it wasn't surprising to find out that when we sought documents from the IRS, the Commerce Department, the State Department, and other agencies, we had to face off in court with the Bush administration.

The Bush attack on transparency continued with a new Bush administration interpretation of the Presidential Records Act. In November 2001, Bush issued an executive order allowing himself or *former presidents* to veto the release of presidential papers. Even the family of a deceased president could on occasion prevent the release of presidential papers. This executive order was so overreaching that it stated that a former president could override a sitting president as to whether his papers were released. As usual, the Bush administration cited national security as the chief concern. Some analysts at the time thought that the executive order wasn't designed to protect Clinton but another former president—George W. Bush's father, George H. W. Bush. They posited that records under the Reagan administration could have damaged H.W.'s reputation.

As a general rule, though, the Bush administration actually wanted to defend all presidents and former presidents from public scrutiny. This broad assertion of executive power to protect the executive from public scrutiny came from the highest levels—in fact, it had the strong support of the man a heartbeat away from the presidency.

The Vice President

Vice President Dick Cheney was a true believer in the executive branch's prerogative to keep more of its operations immune from oversight—whether from Congress or from the American people. An honorable man on national security matters, the problem with Cheney was that as a career politician who spent an inordinate amount of time in the executive branch (he served as chief of staff to President Ford, defense secretary to George H. W. Bush, and vice president), he was used to the Washington, D.C., way of doing things: secrecy, secrecy, and more secrecy. That's why perhaps our biggest all-out brawl during the Bush administration wasn't with President Bush, but with the office of Vice President Cheney.

Early in his tenure, President Bush, in response to a media-fantasy "energy crisis," decided on a review of U.S. energy policy. Presumably the review was to be a bit more industry-friendly, which had not been the case during the Clinton years, largely due to the impact of the environmentalist lobby and its acolytes at the Environmental Protection Agency (Carol Browner) and Department of Energy (Hazel O'Leary). Vice President Cheney was tasked with reviewing policy, meeting with the interested parties, and formulating policy and legislative recommendations.

The energy sector is an area particularly subject to government abuse. Because government works so closely with the companies it regulates, we wanted to shine a light into the nature of the Bush administration's energy policies. We were concerned that energy policy was being made in secret by individuals and interests with a financial and political stake in particular policies. We felt that if the vice president wanted to involve the oil industry or environmentalists in his Energy Task Force deliberations, that was his right, but the law required that the American people be kept abreast of the deliberations. Cheney felt differently. I recall thinking that this task force was just like Hillary Clinton's Health Care Task Force, which conservatives had objected to on grounds of secrecy. Unfortunately, for too many conservatives (and Republicans), a Republican administration could do all sorts of things that conservatives had objected to under Clinton. We thought that the rule of law should apply to both Democrats and Republicans equally.

We felt that the law was on our side—under the Federal Advisory Committee Act (FACA), government task forces that have private individuals as members must file a charter, allow for input from interested people, comply with FOIA and the Government in the Sunshine Act, publish meeting notices in the Federal Register, and provide balance on its board. As the government itself recognizes, the point of FACA was to "ensure that advice by the various advisory committees formed over the years is objective and accessible to the public." [18] Our contention was that those private individuals meeting with Cheney's Energy Task Force became in fact members providing valuable advice to the group. Conservatives had rightly accused Hillary Clinton of violating open meetings law in the operations of her Health Care Task Force. This Energy Task Force was no different.

Vice President Cheney's counsel told us that he rejected our view of the law, prompting *New York Times* columnist Paul Krugman to write, "What Mr. Cheney is defending, in other words, is a doctrine that makes the United States a sort of elected dictatorship: a system in which the president, once in office, can do whatever he likes, and isn't obliged to consult or inform either Congress or the public." [19] Cheney's view was only expressed in detail recently in his memoir, *In My Time*:

> We said no, not because we had anything to hide. Every recommendation we made was publicly available, as was the legislation we put forward based on the report. But I believed, and the president backed me up, that we had the right to consult with whomever we chose—and no obligation to tell the press or Congress or anybody else whom we were talking to. . . . There were plenty of people, including some in the White House, who thought we should just turn over the lists. Since there were no nefarious secrets hidden in them, they argued, all we were doing was creating a real political headache for ourselves by refusing to give them up. But I believed something larger was at stake: the power of the presidency and the ability of the president and vice president to carry out their constitutional duties. [20]

It was a basic conflict of visions. Our vision was one of transparency; Cheney's was one of secretive executive power. To be clear: we were not fighting to see who was visiting the Oval Office, but to uncover information on lobbyists and special interests seeking taxpayer support who were visiting task force members, such as the head of the EPA or the secretary of interior. The Cheney vision of secrecy extended certain privileges afforded the president to virtually every agency head in the federal government.

So we sued. The General Accounting Office, which also tried to get the information we sought, was stonewalled, too. The case ended up riding the escalators of the judicial process—up to the Supreme Court and back down again—and finally ended with the U.S. Court of Appeals for the District of Columbia ruling that the task force didn't have to comply with FACA. Not before we had a series of victories, however, culminating in forty thousand pages of documents being released from the Energy and Commerce departments and the EPA as a result of our separate freedom of information lawsuit.

The documents showed that the Energy Task Force was the typical Washington bazaar. Every energy interest with an idea for taxpayer funding, tax breaks, or other government support came hat-in-hand to friendly agencies. The oil lobby went to Interior and the environmentalists went to their buddies at EPA. Despite the media's attempt to paint the task force as a vehicle for the oil lobby, the truth was that other interests got a seat at the table.

Back during the Clinton years, we had to work hard to get our anticorruption activities covered by an often-hostile media. Our work on the Cheney Energy Task Force was different. Reporters loved it. When the first major release of documents came out, we had over a dozen reporters from every major media organization in our office working as a team to cull important documents for news value. It was an extraordinary scene. I recall helping write the resulting news story with reporters for one national newspaper.

The ridiculous part of the situation was that had Cheney merely released the records, the scrutiny wouldn't have been half as great—the findings of the Energy Task Force were typical Washington, more money for favored energy interests and a few commonsense, obvious proposals. But Cheney made it impossible to defend the task force, because the environmentalists and their allies in the media now had a secrecy club with which to beat the Bush administration. It was a pyrrhic victory for Vice President Cheney's secrecy policies. The American people began to sour on this obsessive Bush administration secrecy.

One interesting side story: I recall chatting with a lawyer for the Bush administration while we sat next to each other waiting for the Supreme Court to hear our Energy Task Force case. The lawyer told me that "they"—the Bush administration—opposed all of FOIA in principle. Of course, that wasn't "official" Bush administration policy but I had to laugh at his honesty and shook my head.

The Energy Task Force issue didn't die. Some of the biggest players in the Energy Task Force, the *Washington Post* reported in July 2007, were James J. Rouse, vice president of Exxon Mobil and a big Bush donor, and Ken Lay, head of Enron (who met with the task force not once, but at least twice).[21]

The Bush administration's cozy relationship with Enron in particular followed in the footsteps of the Clinton administration's. Despite our FOIA requests, the Bush administration refused to turn over Enron-related documents concerning the company's contacts with the Bush administration, denying that Enron (which at the time was under investigation for fraud) received any favors due to campaign contributions. Ari Fleischer even suggested that there was no need to investigate the Enron scandal and its close connections with the Clinton administration, and that the American public was tired of "political witch-hunts." The appearance of impropriety wasn't helped when Bush himself implied that Ken Lay hadn't supported his run for governor of Texas, when in fact he had. The *New York Times* even reported that White House advisor Karl Rove had Enron hire former Christian Coalition executive director Ralph Reed in 1997 in order to cement Reed's ties to Bush. We went ahead and filed a Federal Election Commission complaint demanding an investigation on this score. In fact, Ken Lay was the first and last name actually released by the White House voluntarily in connection with the Task Force—after the furor he caused, they didn't want to grant any more access.

When the full list of participants in the Energy Task Force was finally released, years later, Vice President Cheney's office denied comment. "The vice president has respectfully but resolutely maintained the importance of protecting the ability of the president and vice president to receive candid advice on important national policy matters in confidence, a principle affirmed by the Supreme Court," insisted Cheney's spokeswoman. A Cheney political enemy, Representative Henry Waxman (D-CA) was far less politic. He said that the stonewalling was "ridiculous," and that Cheney's unwillingness to allow transparency to the task force showed "how secretively Vice President Cheney wanted to act." [22]

The Energy Task Force wasn't the only area in which Cheney's behavior was questionable. On May 20, 2001, the vice president hosted four hundred Republican donors for a Republican National Committee party at his government residence in the Naval Observatory complex. Most of these donors had given or pledged at least $100,000 to the Republican Party. This gathering probably violated the law, since government resources cannot be used for political fund-raising—violations similar to those alleged against Clinton and Gore, and for which Clinton and Gore were rightly raked over the coals. Spinning wildly, the Bush administration spokesman called the party a "thank-you" rather than a blatantly political fund-raising event, which it truly was. As usual, we weren't going to take such lack of transparency sitting down, and so we requested the names of the donors who attended the event. And, as usual, Vice President Cheney simply refused to release the names.

You can see why I find hypocrisy in some of the Republicans today attacking Obama secrecy. We were virtually alone in going after Bush secrecy—there was not a Republican cricket to be heard in those transparency fights. I hear they quietly were concerned about Bush's politically counterproductive secrecy, but, in cowardly fashion, refused to take a public stand.

Corruption within organizations influenced by Cheney dated back to his days in the private sector with Halliburton. During Cheney's tenure with Halliburton, the company and its accounting firm, Arthur Andersen, allegedly participated in fraudulent accounting practices. In typical Cheney fashion, he refused to answer questions from the press about his role as chief executive in Halliburton's bookkeeping. He wouldn't say whether Halliburton's accounting practices would hold up under investigation, and he declined further comment, stating that if he did comment, it would look as though he was attempting to pressure the Securities and Exchange Commission. But President Bush had already made statements exonerating Cheney from wrongdoing. Originally, Halliburton's executives had maintained that Cheney knew about the accounting changes that put Halliburton into dicey territory, but they later recanted.

While we don't believe the radical claims that Cheney was personally profiteering from his association with Halliburton during the war on terror—he did divest all of his holdings in Halliburton after being elected vice president—his association with Halliburton did raise some questions. In 2003, Kellogg Brown & Root, a Halliburton subsidiary, won a $7 billion sole-source contract to provide services to Iraq. There was no competitive bidding process, something that we found problematic and suspicious. We used FOIA to seek information regarding how contracts related to Iraq were allocated. The Department of the Army refused to comply with the FOIA request, stating that to do so would harm national security. We were given no alternative but to file a lawsuit, which we did. During that lawsuit, we obtained an email showing possible involvement of Vice President Cheney's office in awarding the contract—the email said that the Pentagon was fine with the contract going to Kellogg Brown & Root "contingent on informing" the White House. It continued, "We anticipate no issue; since action has been coordinated w VP's office." In September 2004, Reuters reported that the Department of the Army would rescind the contract and open the work to competitive bidding. The Department of the Army agreed to pay us $24,000 in legal fees and costs for the lengths we had to go to get the full truth.

We didn't pursue cases like this because we were trying to undermine the wars in Iraq and Afghanistan. In point of fact, the issue of Halliburton and favoritism was an unnecessary distraction from the war effort. The Bush administration's obliviousness to the public perception of Halliburton's "most favored" contractor status was a significant propaganda gift for the anti-American left and our enemies abroad.

The corruption of the Bush critics also needed exposing. When Judge Anna Diggs Taylor, a federal court judge in Michigan, ruled the government's warrantless wiretapping program unconstitutional in 2006, for example, we uncovered her significant conflict of interest, one that arguably should have barred her from trying the case, *ACLU et al. v. National Security Agency.* It turns out that Judge Taylor was secretary and trustee for the Community Foundation for Southeastern Michigan, which made a huge grant to the ACLU of Michigan, a plaintiff in the case. How did we figure this out? Because it was nearly impossible for everyday litigants to get the financial disclosure forms of federal judges, we created a program to get each and every form for every federal judge every year. When Judge Diggs Taylor's ruling came down, one of our investigators (an intern) looked at her form out of curiosity and discovered the connection. For us, it is all about full disclosure and transparency, not about "getting" anyone. Judge Taylor's ruling, which was terribly weak, subsequently was overturned by her appellate colleagues.

The truth is that Cheney's secrecy push was hardly the only problem in the Bush administration, especially with regard to fundraising. Through a FOIA lawsuit, we uncovered documents showing that Secretary of Health and Human Services Tommy Thompson met with Republican donors—many of whom were connected to industries impacted by his decisions—in his government offices. According to certain reports, members of the "Presidential Roundtable," a group of contributors whose minimum donation was $5,000, got to attend a briefing by Cheney at the Pentagon. Both the National Republican Senatorial Committee and the National Republican Congressional Committee sold access to Bush cabinet officials, Bush foreign policy officials, foreign ambassadors, and other federal employees. After our attention to these issues brought them to light, in fact, Republican House Speaker Denny Hastert and Republican senator Peter Fitzgerald, among other Republican heavy hitters, were forced to repudiate these fund-raising tactics. House Majority Whip Tom Delay, however, refused to budge—a refusal that was unsurprising in light of his suspect ethics.

The 9/11 Attacks

Government secrecy can produce the worst results imaginable: the deaths of Americans. Prior to the attacks of September 11, 2001, few in the general public knew what was going on in terms of tracking down Osama bin Laden until it was too late; four separate times (the Khobar Towers bombing, the bombings of the American embassies in Tanzania and Kenya, and the bombing of the USS *Cole*) bin Laden attacked U.S. interests, and the public remained in the dark. Instead of tracking down the problems inside the American national security infrastructure that may have allowed the 9/11 attacks to happen, the Bush administration made a point of preventing any significant "after-action" analysis of the 9/11 attacks. In fact, President Bush and Vice President Cheney tried to convince Congress not to hold any public hearings in the first place.

Louis Freeh, head of the FBI until June 2001, certainly bore some of the responsibility for failing to prevent the attacks of September 11, especially since, as the 9/11 Commission found, a lack of coordination between the FBI and CIA helped prevent the government from stopping the September 11 catastrophe. Freeh, of course, disclaimed any and all responsibility. "Analyzing intelligence information can be like trying to take a sip of water coming out of a fire hydrant," he complained. "The FBI was focused on preventing domestic and foreign attacks, and I take exception to the finding that we were not sufficiently paying attention to terrorism at home. . . . Al-Qaeda type organizations, state sponsors of terrorism like Iran and the threats they pose to America are beyond the competence of the FBI and the CIA to address." If the FBI and CIA can't handle these threats, who should? Freeh didn't say.[23]

One continuing area of controversy is whether Saudi interests had anything to do with 9/11. We might know more if the Bush administration had not allowed a host of well-connected Saudis to use chartered jets to flee the United States in the days following 9/11, during a time when it was mostly impossible for anyone else to fly.

The Saudi flight story began when Judicial Watch sued and finally obtained records from U.S. Customs and Border Protection (CBP) under FOIA detailing the departure of 160 subjects of the Kingdom of Saudi Arabia, "including but not limited to members of the House of Saud and/or members of the Bin Laden family," between September 11, 2001, and September 15, 2001.

The CBP document, dated February 24, 2004, listed the birth date, visa status, citizenship, date of departure, port of departure, departing airline code, and flight number for each Saudi subject who left the country at a time when the U.S. government had supposedly restricted all commercial and private air traffic through U.S. airspace. Notably, the names were not provided.

Judicial Watch filed its FOIA request on October 7, 2003, with the Department of Homeland Security, the Central Intelligence Agency, the Federal Aviation Administration, the State Department, the Federal Bureau of Investigation, the Justice Department, and the Department of Transportation.

In the October 2003 issue of *Vanity Fair* magazine, accusations were leveled against the FBI that the bureau considered unfair and led to an internal FBI investigation that the agency named "VANITYBOM." In the days after the 9/11 attacks, the FBI gave personal airport escorts to two prominent Saudi families who fled the United States, and several other Saudis were allowed to leave the country without first being interviewed, suggesting that Saudis had received preferential treatment in leaving the country.

Saudi families in Los Angeles and Orlando requested FBI escorts, saying they were concerned for their safety in the wake of the attacks. The FBI arranged to have agents escort them to their local airports, the documents show. Prominent Saudi subjects left the United States on several flights that had not been previously disclosed in public accounts, including a chartered flight from Providence, Rhode Island, on September 14, 2001, that included at least one member of the Saudi royal family, and three flights from Las Vegas between September 19 and September 24, also carrying members of the Saudi royal family. The government began to slowly reopen airspace on September 13, but most flights remained grounded for days afterward.

Emails from 2003 obtained by Judicial Watch show that the FBI employees referred to themselves as "fellow VANITYBOM victims." One email from an unnamed FBI intelligence analyst coordinating a draft of the report notes "snide remarks encouraged." Once the Saudis arranged chartered flights out of the country, an unidentified prince in the Las Vegas group "thanked the FBI for their assistance," according to one internal report. The records show that in several cases, Saudi travelers were not interviewed before departing the country, and FBI officials sought to determine how these apparent lapses had occurred. The FBI went back to Caesars Palace and the Four Seasons hotels with subpoenas five days after the initial flight had departed to collect further information on the Saudi royal guests, the documents show. The FBI documents left open the possibility that some departing Saudis had information relevant to the September 11 investigation.

"Although the FBI took all possible steps to prevent any individuals who were involved in or had knowledge of the 9/11/2001 attacks from leaving the U.S. before they could be interviewed," a 2003 memo said, "it is not possible to state conclusively that no such individuals left the U.S. without FBI knowledge."

In June 2004, Judicial Watch provided the 9/11 Commission with previously unreported documents from U.S. Customs and Border Protection showing that 160 Saudis were allowed to leave on fifty-five commercial flights from airports around the country between September 11 and September 15, 2001. The documents represent the first admission by the government that the flights occurred at all. Judicial Watch asked the 9/11 Commission to investigate and reconcile previous contradictory testimony about Saudis being allowed to leave the country. Although the FBI says that it checked the manifests of the flights taken by the Saudis against its terror watch list, the 9/11 Commission has indicated that there is no evidence that happened.

Additional information detailing flights of Saudis out of the United States from Las Vegas and Providence revealed FBI procedures in processing the Saudi flights. It was apparent from the report that bin Laden family members and Saudi royals were subject to only cursory, pro forma questioning by the FBI. Experienced investigators suggest that detailed counterterrorism interviews would have taken a minimum of two hours per passenger. There is no evidence offered that any such efforts were made by the FBI. Author Craig Unger, in a June 1, 2004, *New York Times* opinion piece, pointed out that the 9/11 Commission investigated only the departure of 142 Saudis on six charter flights. The commission was never told about the additional 160 Saudis who left.

The Saudi flight documents contain many redactions that the Justice Department claims were made in the privacy interests of the Saudi subjects identified in the report. It is not clear how the Justice Department concluded that the alleged privacy privileges of non-U.S. persons trump the public's interest in obtaining full information about the government's investigative response to the 9/11 terrorist attacks. Redactions were claimed for law enforcement investigative purposes even though the report claims that "no information of investigative value" was learned from interviews of bin Laden family members and Saudi royals.

In April 2007 the FBI made a final—court-ordered—production of records responsive to our FOIA request and lawsuit.

The report is silent as to whether National Security Council staff member Richard Clarke or other White House officials approved any of the flights.

It seems as if the FBI was more interested in achieving diplomatic success than investigative success.

The Bush administration's penchant for secrecy even held up the work of the 9/11 Commission itself. As representatives of survivors of the 9/11 terror attacks in lawsuits against bin Laden, Al Qaeda, and the Taliban and their state sponsors, we felt it necessary to call on the Bush administration to release all the requisite documents so that the commission could get to the bottom of its work. Their foot-dragging was a troubling addition to their record of unwarranted secrecy.

We didn't need 9/11 to know that the Middle East was a sensitive area of concern for our nation's security. That's why in March 2001 we called on former president George H. W. Bush to resign from the Carlyle Group, a major private equity firm, while his son was in office. The *New York Times* reported that H.W. was allowed to buy a stake in the Carlyle Group investments, including 164 companies throughout the world. James Baker III, who had been secretary of state under George H. W. Bush, was a partner at the Carlyle Group. As we said at the time, "This is simply inappropriate. Former President Bush should immediately resign from the Carlyle Group because it is an obvious conflict of interest. Any foreign government or foreign investor trying to curry favor with the current Bush administration is sure to throw business to the Carlyle Group." As we headlined, the conflict of interest would pose significant problems for American Middle East policy.

As it turns out, we were exactly right. Less than three weeks after the September 11 attacks, the *Wall Street Journal* reported that George H. W. Bush worked with the bin Laden family business in Saudi Arabia through the Carlyle Group. Bush had met with the bin Laden family at least twice. While Osama was reported to have been disowned by his Saudi family, those reports were far from conclusive. The FBI at the time actually subpoenaed the bin Laden family business bank records.

In the wake of September 11, the Carlyle Group cut off relations with the bin Laden family, but it maintained close relations with the Saudi royal family. Documents we uncovered in late 2001 via a FOIA request to the Defense Department showed that the Carlyle Group had high-level access to the U.S. government, including contact with Secretary of Defense Rumsfeld. The letters between the group and Rumsfeld showed that the two were discussing the restructuring of the Defense Department. Not coincidentally, the Carlyle Group was listed in the Pentagon documents as a Defense Department contractor. (We successfully FOIA'd a list of every single Carlyle-related contract from the Pentagon.)

Another nasty scandal emerged a few months after 9/11. In the aftermath of the September 11 attacks, letters containing anthrax were mailed to media offices and two senators. Five people were killed and seventeen were injured. Two of the employees at the Brentwood Road mail facility in Washington, D.C., died of anthrax poisoning. As representatives of hundreds of postal workers and a grassroots postal workers support group organized as "Brentwood Exposed," we forced the postal service to turn over documents by court order, after the agency failed to comply with FOIA requests.

The documents were stunning. One of them was a diary or log written by a senior Brentwood postal official. The diary showed that U.S. Postal Service and government officials knew as early as October 18, 2001, that "mail was leaking" anthrax spores into the Brentwood facility, and that an anthrax spore swab test confirmed that the swabs "tested hot." Despite this knowledge, the postal service kept the Brentwood facility open in violation of their own written emergency regulations for four days—until news broke of the two dead postal workers. Even after the facility was closed, postal officials ordered workers to push out truckloads of potentially contaminated mail to the American people. The bottom line is this: when government secrecy is allowed to prevail, lives are put in danger. If the government had been transparent about what it knew up front, postal workers' lives may never have been endangered (and some might have been saved).

The subsequent investigation of the anthrax attacks was another debacle. We never found out who the true culprits were; the federal government, based on flimsy circumstantial evidence, suggested that the case was closed after their suspect du jour, Bruce Ivins, killed himself. Only then—not before—did a judge mandate the release of documents related to the FBI's by-now seven-year-old investigation. The documents may have settled the case for some, but the problem is that the government's theory of Ivins as the sole culprit could now never be tested in court. The anthrax attacker may now never be conclusively known. And our attempts to get justice for those postal workers hurt by the anthrax attacks were turned away.

Eventually, the Bush administration's focus on secrecy became a knee-jerk habit rather than a rationally calculated tactic. After September 11, we FOIA'd the Department of Defense for any tapes it had of the Flight 77 attack on the Pentagon. I had been approached by a longtime acquaintance of mine in the conservative movement who was convinced that a missile had hit the Pentagon and that the Twin Towers had been brought down through explosive charges. I politely tried to steer him away from that conspiracy theory. "Then why don't they [the Bush Defense Department] release the tapes?" he asked accusatorily. I didn't know that there were tapes of the 9/11 attacks on the Pentagon. So I thought by releasing the tapes, we could complete the historic record and shut down the conspiracy theories that 9/11 was an "inside job."

Nothing is easy. The Bush administration refused to turn over those tapes, citing national security issues and the fact that the federal government still had a case open against the so-called twentieth hijacker, Zacarias Moussaoui. In response, we filed a federal lawsuit against the Department of Defense in order to get the tapes released, pointing out that there was really no justification or excuse for the government's failure to allow their release. Once again, the Bush administration fought us, even though our only goal was to complete the public record of that horrible day. It took over eighteen months of waiting, but the video footage depicting the attack on the Pentagon was released to us in May 2006, more than four years after the attack. The choppy video, taken from a parking lot security camera, shows the American Airlines Flight 77 airliner hitting the Pentagon, leading to a fiery explosion. The world's media converged on our offices. We posted the video immediately to our Internet site, which was overwhelmed by the resulting traffic. Even the Pentagon's servers reportedly couldn't handle the traffic once they posted the video. I shouldn't have been surprised by the interest, but I remain surprised to this day that it was left to our relatively small outfit to force the release of video of the worst attack in American history.

The conspiracy theorists were not convinced but the release of the video certainly accelerated and confirmed their fall to the fringe of popular consciousness. (Until one of their own, Van Jones, was appointed to a position in the Obama White House!)

The most unbelievable example of the Bush administration's misguided secrecy was the FBI's invocation of the right to privacy on behalf of Osama bin Laden. Yes, you read that right—the FBI wanted to protect bin Laden's right to privacy. In a September 24, 2003, declassified "Secret" FBI report we obtained via FOIA, we found out that the FBI invoked Exemption 6 under FOIA law—the privacy exemption that allows the government to withhold all information about U.S. persons in "personnel and medical files and similar files" when the disclosure of such information "would constitute a clearly unwarranted invasion of personal privacy." The FBI should have conducted a basic "balancing test," weighing the public's right to know against the individual's right to privacy. Obviously when it came to bin Laden, any such test would have come out in the public's favor. Many of the references in the FBI document cited publicly available news articles from sources such as the *Washington Post* and Associated Press. Based on analysis of the news stories cited in the FBI report (by analysis, I mean we read the headlines), it didn't take a genius to figure out that it was bin Laden's name that was redacted from the document, including newspaper headlines in the footnoted citations. My colleagues and I had seen some audacious assertions of government secrecy, but I must say that I think that was (and is to this day) the absolute worst. Our publicizing of the insulting absurdity of the Bush administration's seeking to protect bin Laden—the most wanted man in American history—from "an unwarranted invasion of privacy" forced the Bush administration to do the right thing and back off their offensive legal position.

The 9/11 attack on America became another excuse for the Bush administration to ratchet up its policy of secrecy with regard to the American public. According to a study by the Coalition of Journalists for Open Government about FOIA exemptions—cases in which the government claimed that FOIA didn't apply—less information was released via FOIA in 2004 than in 2000. Even though agencies processed *fewer* requests in 2004 than in 2000, the overall use of exemptions rose by 22 percent. Bizarrely enough, most of those exemption uses were not related to national security. In fact, said the coalition, "the analysis found a marked decline in the use of the exemption for information classified in the interest of national security, even though national security has been regularly cited since September 11, 2001 as justification for the increased safeguarding of records."[24] National security was the excuse for the Bush

administration to continue in the footsteps of the Clinton administration, undermining the trust of the American people by rejecting
transparency.

White House Visitor Logs—
the Beginning of the Battle

Perhaps that rejection of transparency was because there were also
severe fund-raising improprieties going on within the Bush administration, a fact we sensed as soon as we got a whiff of their knee-jerk
position toward secrecy in government. In 2002, we heard rumors
about corruption at the Bureau of Indian Affairs (BIA) involving a
lobbyist named Jack Abramoff. The *Wall Street Journal* reported in
April that wealthy tribes were giving increased amounts of money
to the GOP in order to procure tax breaks. Ivan Makil, president
of the Salt River tribe, told the *Journal* that he had to increase their
political spending by a factor of five since "if we don't ante up and
play the game, we'll get left in the dust." [25] A few days later, *Time* reported that a representative of the Chinook Indian tribe gave Wayne
Smith, the second in command at BIA, her business card, and that
two weeks later, the representative was contacted by Phil Bersinger,
Smith's former business partner, who offered to influence decisions
at BIA for a fee. The representative told *Time* that the scam was so
obvious she thought perhaps it was an FBI sting operation. [26]

The *Journal* also reported that Secretary of the Interior Gale
Norton had met with the Mississippi Band of Choctaw, as well as
the Coushatta and Chitimacha from Louisiana, at a home in the
Georgetown section of Washington, D.C. Those tribes were represented by Abramoff, a fund-raiser for Bush. Each tribe agreed to
contribute at least $1 million to Republican campaigns. Another
such meeting with Bush and some tribal leaders was arranged by
Grover Norquist of Americans for Tax Reform. (Grover has ada-
mantly denied doing anything wrong.)

It turns out that Abramoff wasn't linked only to the Bush administration, but to politicians on both sides of the aisle, including

Senate Majority Leader Harry Reid (D-NV) and Senator Conrad Burns (R-MT).[27] Two Burns aides took a trip to the 2001 Super Bowl in Abramoff's jet, and in 2003, Burns, who is now retired from the Senate, got the Interior Department to make a $3 million grant to a Michigan-based tribal client of Abramoff's.

Most important to us, we wanted the White House visitor logs showing Abramoff's contact with President Bush and his team. Our FOIA request rightly stated, "the taxpaying American public deserves full disclosure of the entry and exit of Jack Abramoff from the White House. According to press reports, President Bush stated initially that he did not know controversial lobbyist Jack Abramoff, however the two might have met at holiday parties. However, the White House also admitted that indeed Abramoff had attended White House staff meetings. The public deserves to know the level of contact that Abramoff had with the White House."[28] As usual, the White House stonewalled. And as usual, we had to bring a lawsuit, this time against the Secret Service, to compel them to release the information. We were successful in getting the U.S. District Court for the District of Columbia to compel release of the White House logs. They showed two documented visits by Abramoff to the White House, but they also appeared to be incomplete, especially when compared against Clinton White House visitor logs. One could argue they didn't show much, but then why the big fight in federal court over a lousy two visits to the White House?

Citizens for Responsibility and Ethics in Washington (CREW) was founded during the Bush administration to serve as a left-wing version of Judicial Watch. Hillary Clinton and her supporters saw how devastatingly effective we were, and they decided to copy us (CREW received big money from George Soros and other major-league Democrat supporters). CREW was interested in the Abramoff logs and visits of social conservatives to the White House. Tired of the Abramoff controversy, the Bush administration went dark on White House visitors altogether. In a transparent attempt to get around FOIA, the White House signed an agreement with the Secret Service. That agreement sought to move entry and exit logs from the Secret Service to the White House, where the records would not be subject to immediate disclosure under FOIA.[29] CREW fought this cause until Obama was elected—at which point, they conveniently "settled," forcing us to take up the baton.

And congressional Republicans didn't wait long to try to mimic Bill Clinton's system of selling public office for campaign contributions. Some of the most well-known Republican corruption was linked to House Majority Leader Tom DeLay (R-TX). DeLay was a hero to many social conservatives—but that didn't stop us from seeking to hold him to account. Some of our erstwhile conservative friends were horrified and angry at our criticism of DeLay. Our view was that those who held conservative public policy views needed to ensure that "conservative" politicians be above reproach. Liberal activists learned that with Bill Clinton. Liberals lost the presidency in the 2000 election and set their cause back as a result of Clinton corruption. Despite railing against Clinton corruption for years, however, Republicans got right into the Clintonesque groove after the 2000 elections.

In early 2002, the press reported that DeLay had promised "meetings with top Bush officials to small business owners whose donations would underwrite a GOP ad campaign promoting the president's tax plan." He actually made recorded telephone calls around the country asking small business owners "to serve as an honorary member of our new Business Advisory Council," and telling them that they would be "invited to meetings with top Bush administration officials." This scheme was seemingly in violation of federal laws that bar bribery of public officials—more exactly, it bars payment in exchange for "being induced to do or omit to do any act in violation of the official duty of such official or person." While DeLay and others said that brokering such meetings didn't violate the bribery provision since they weren't done in the course of lawmaking, the courts had already interpreted the antibribery law to mean that congressmen and senators could not sell official acts, including "all of the acts normally thought to constitute a congressman's legitimate use of his office."[30] Brokering meetings with the president and top administration officials to influence policy seemed to be illegal on its face.

The NRCC had already attempted to dismiss this obviously illegal conduct by stating that "no contributor to this Committee is receiving any sort of official, government reward, position or privilege for their contribution, nor is there any official action taking place." But even DeLay's fellow Republicans were aghast at the behavior. "In the final waning days of the Roman Republic," ranted then-representative Mark Kirk (R-IL), "in ancient times, public office was auctioned and that led directly to the destruction of the Roman Republic. The United States government is the greatest force for the good that mankind has ever designed. But our offices cannot be led out for auction." (Kirk now sits in Barack Obama's Illinois seat in the U.S. Senate.) Then-representative Adam Putnam (R-FL) agreed, saying, "It's clearly not appropriate."[31]

But the Bush administration Department of Justice felt differently. In response to our demand that the department initiate proceedings against DeLay, they sent us a letter stating that they would "not conduct the investigations you requested." The Justice Department maintained, like the NRCC, that banning payment in exchange for meetings with high-ranking officials ("pay to play") didn't count as an "official act." In fact, a Justice bureaucrat wrote us that Illinois Republican congressman Henry Hyde (now deceased) had similarly complained about Bill Clinton's fund-raising activities, but that no investigation took place; the same lack of investigation would help cover up Republican fund-raising practices. Clearly the lawlessness Bill Clinton brought to town had infected both parties.

That didn't deter us from fighting such improprieties. DeLay wasn't the only one committing them, or being protected by the Department of Justice in doing so. In April 2001, the press reported that "[f]or $10,000 each, or $15,000 per couple, GOP faithful can become life members of the Republican Senatorial Inner Circle, an adjunct of the National Republican Senatorial Committee, and spend three days rubbing shoulders with senators, Cabinet officials and diplomats. . . ."[32] Attendees from the administration included Commerce Secretary Don Evans, Education Secretary Rod Paige, Energy Secretary Spencer Abraham and Secretary of Health Tommy Thompson. The reports prompted Senator Peter Fitzgerald (R-IL) to quit his job with the Republican campaign fund-raising committee, and forced House Speaker Denny Hastert to skip a tax-reform briefing for GOP contributors.[33] As we said in our complaint to the Federal Election Commission and the Public Integrity Section of the Criminal Division of the Justice Department, "When this was done in the universally corrupt Clinton administration, Judicial Watch took legal action. It cannot look the other way for the Republican Congress and the Bush administration."[34]

In 2004, the House Ethics Committee released a report stating that DeLay had offered Representative Nick Smith (R-MI) an endorsement for Smith's son's congressional campaign in exchange for Smith's yes vote on the massive Medicare drug expansion plan.[35]

That same year, then-representative Chris Bell (D-TX), working with the left-wing CREW, levied similar charges against DeLay. In a complaint to the House Committee on Standards of Official Conduct (the so-called House Ethics Committee), Bell alleged that DeLay had violated both state and federal law by laundering corporate cash in order to impact Texas state races. Eventually, a Texas prosecutor indicted DeLay for violating Texas campaign finance laws. It was all too much, and DeLay resigned from Congress in 2005. But Bell's charges eventually ended in DeLay's conviction on state charges in Texas in November 2010 for "illegally funneling corporate money to Texas candidates in 2002," according to the Associated Press. DeLay was sentenced to three years in prison on the charges.[36] DeLay strongly denies wrongdoing and is appealing the verdict.

Sure enough, Democrats (the party that rallied around the despicable Bill Clinton) were able to win back the House in 2006 thanks in significant part to voters' disgust with Abramoff, Delay, and the arrogant corruption of Bush-era Republicans.

The Ethics Gap

In 2004, as Republicans on the Hill were facing significant pressure on ethics, the House Republican leadership desperately attempted to curtail the power of the House Ethics Committee. Judicial Watch joined a coalition of mostly liberal good-government groups to try to uphold the ethics process. Our alliance was called the Congressional Ethics Coalition. We knew that most of the groups disliked Republicans and conservatives and probably had ulterior motives to go after a lack of ethics in a Republican-led Congress. But principle trumped politics for us.

Unfortunately, since 1994, there had been a "Mutually Assured Destruction" pact between Democrats and Republicans not to use the House Ethics Committee for cross-party complaints, especially against House leaders. By 2005, despite a number of scandals involving members of both parties, the Ethics Committee effectively ceased to function. This was because after Ethics Committee members "reprimanded" Tom DeLay for misconduct in 2004, the Republican leadership purged the committee.

Republicans in the White House and on the Hill, incredibly, had managed to hand the Democrats (who rallied around the disgraced Bill Clinton at the White House on the day he was impeached!) the issue of government reform and corruption. After all the scandals that plagued the House and Senate during the Clinton and Bush administrations, Nancy Pelosi and her colleagues smartly campaigned on the promise to "drain the swamp" of corruption in Washington, D.C. Pelosi told NBC, " 'Drain the swamp' means to turn this Congress into the most honest and open Congress in history. That's my pledge—that is what I intend to do." The new Democratic majority in the House tried to take advantage of their majority by reforming its internal ethics process.

The new Speaker appointed a "Special Task Force on Ethics Enforcement," led by her blunt-talking lieutenant, Representative Mike Capuano (D-MA). The new Republican minority appointed conservative stalwart Representative Lamar Smith (R-TX) to represent their interests; despite their shellacking at the polls, Republicans were still skeptical of "ethics reform." I met a few times with Capuano, who knew he had little shot of initiating true reform in the face of opposition from colleagues on both sides of the aisle. Representative Smith clearly opposed any significant strengthening of the process, though he seemed resigned that *something* would happen. A Republican member of the Task Force, then-representative Todd Tiahrt (from Kansas) expressed worry in one meeting about being held to account for innocently not filling out a form correctly. Of course, that wasn't the issue (though it is an issue for citizens who deal with government regulations every day). Of course, no member of Congress was going to be called to account for not dotting an *i* or crossing a *t* on some obscure form. The goal was to catch real corruption, not some "gotcha" game over someone innocently failing to fill out a required disclosure form correctly.

In April 2007, I testified on behalf of Judicial Watch before Pelosi's Ethics Task Force. I suggested their reforms be guided by three major principles:

- **Accountability**—In the end, Members should be responsible for upholding the ethics rules of the House. Any inspector general or office of public integrity must be answerable to an ethics committee of some sort. An unaccountable and unelected official or body conducting ethics investigations of House members would lead to problems. A strong Ethics Committee that supports independent investigations of ethical violations—while ensuring the rights of Members are protected—is essential. Accountability also means being answerable to the public. Whether the Ethics Committee retains complete jurisdiction or works with a congressional watchdog agency, the process needs to be opened up so that complaints from individuals or groups can be formally considered.

- **Integrity**—There needs to be a regular and fair process for handling ethics complaints and investigations. A process should be put in place to summarily dismiss frivolous complaints or complaints without any factual foundation. There needs to be a regular and timely investigative process for any complaints that are pursued by the Ethics Committee or other entity. It is not fair to Members or to the public to conduct investigations that may last years or even many election cycles. Certainly, the vast majority of ethics investigations should last no longer than six months.

The leadership of both parties must repudiate the ethics truce and make it clear that ethics enforcement is a top priority and no Member or outside entity will be retaliated against for filing or pursuing non-frivolous ethics charges. In the past, outside groups have been pressured and Ethics Committee members punished for pursuing ethics charges. A "non-interference" pledge by the House leadership is key to fixing the House ethics process. To help rebuild public confidence in the institution of Congress, it is imperative that any ethics body not only maintain the appearance of independence, but be independent in practice.

- **Transparency**—The process must be open. Not only should citizens and groups be able to file ethics complaints, but there must be mandatory reporting on the disposition of any complaints. This has to be true for the Ethics Committee and for any new office of inspector general or office of public integrity. The Senate's ethics committee allows for the filing of outside complaints, but there is no requirement that it publicly inform anyone about the outcome of the complaints. Both the House and the Senate should do better. It is only fair to Members that any ethics body alert the public if a complaint is summarily dismissed, or dismissed after a thorough investigation. And the public must certainly know if an investigation concludes that there is misconduct.

For too long, the ethics process in the House has been broken. The process can be fixed by following certain principles—accountability, integrity, transparency, and independence. No matter one's party, no matter one's political ideology, these are principles upon which we should all be able to agree.

In the end, the House took some of our advice. The House passed an ethics rules change creating the Office of Congressional Ethics (OCE), with only thirty-three House Republicans supporting it.[37] Members of the OCE are not current members of Congress and can refer ethics matters to the full House Ethics Committee. The OCE, though it lacks subpoena power, has been the most successful ethics reform in the House in a generation. Between October 9, 2009, and January 2012, the OCE has made twenty-seven referrals to the House Ethics Committee regarding alleged unethical acts by House members.[38] The public disclosure of these referrals embarrassed the House Ethics Committee into taking action on many of them.

Pelosi has probably come to regret her creation. Many members of the Congressional Black Caucus have been caught up in OCE investigations. Most notably, in 2008, Representative Charlie Rangel (D-NY) came under fire for excluding rental income—$75,000 in twenty years—from his tax forms. He also had rent-stabilized apartments in New York in violation of state and city regulations and House ethics rules. Rangel had even used his office to solicit millions of dollars in donations from corporations with business interests before his panel. The $30 million he raised was supposed to be used for a new academic center to be named after him. The project was started with a $1.9 million check signed by the taxpayers in an earmark. As a result of the OCE's initial referral on the matter, Rangel was reprimanded by the full House (though he should have been expelled). Some suggested that the OCE was racially profiling Rangel and other black members of the House.[39] In 2010, twenty members of Black Caucus sought to weaken the OCE by, among other changes, restricting the ability of the OCE to publicize its investigative reports.[40]

So with the Black Caucus, and so many of its compromised members, beginning to play the race card against the OCE, and with Republicans eager to kill it, there were many long knives out for OCE.

That's why we joined with the ethics coalition again for a major press conference on Capitol Hill just after the November 2010 elections to help defend the Pelosi ethics reforms. I told the press that it would be a test for the new Tea Party Congress—would it stand up for the Office of Congressional Ethics? If the new majority didn't, it would show their supporters that the party of small government was really a party of big corruption. The fact was, I pointed out, that a vast majority of Americans thought that corruption in Washington, D.C., had increased—and a vast majority of Americans also thought it would continue to increase. The Tea Party Congress had a lot of work to do.

Speaker John Boehner and his leadership team got the message: the OCE was reauthorized by the new Tea Party Congress, with efforts by the Congressional Black Caucus to weaken the OCE going nowhere. On a positive note, the *Washington Times* reports that the OCE "has conducted more investigations in three years than the full [House Ethics] committee has in more than a decade. . . ."[41]

3

THE FINANCIAL MELTDOWN: FROM CLINTON TO BUSH TO OBAMA

In September 2008, the American economy imploded. That implosion came as a shock to virtually everyone, including the so-called experts who had predicted for years that the economy would continue climbing indefinitely. A short time later, President George W. Bush and the Republican and Democratic leadership in Congress (including the two then-candidates for the presidency, Barack Obama and John McCain) all eventually signed on to what was called a bailout—the Troubled Asset Relief Program (TARP). The financial crisis that hit our nation resulted in a greatly increased role of government in the financial sector.

Even we were stunned, though, by the sheer amount of corruption and scandal involved in the financial meltdown and the response to it. Since the collapse, we have actively pursued documents regarding the unprecedented explosion in the size and reach of the government through its use of $24 trillion for TARP, "bank rescues," stealth financial sector subsidies and the Obama administration's misguided economic "stimulus" plan, which failed to stimulate anything other than Obama's union buddies (as we'll discuss).[1]

From the get-go, TARP was administered in a way that confounded all attempts at accountability. Neil Barofsky, the former special inspector general of TARP, admitted that the Treasury Department had "repeatedly failed to adopt recommendations [to allow] the highest degree of accountability and transparency." As

Representative Edolphus Towns (D-NY) said, "If the banks can't tell us how they're spending TARP money, then maybe they shouldn't have it. How can Treasury commit billions—and potentially trillions—of taxpayer dollars but not ask recipients what they're doing with the money? That takes 'burying your head in the sand' to a new level."[2] The $150 billion (and counting) taxpayer bailout of Fannie Mae and Freddie Mac was arguably the worst of these boondoggles—and it was certainly the biggest government corruption scandal in our history.

Over the course of the years since the meltdown, our efforts in uncovering what really goes on behind the closed doors of government have revealed key documents showing Congress's awareness of the poor business practices of Fannie and Freddie at the same time as key members of Congress continued to block attempts to regulate the two government-sponsored entities (GSEs). A FOIA lawsuit we filed against the Department of the Treasury resulted in documents that revealed details of how the government forced CEOs of several major banks, in tyrannical fashion, to accept TARP funds. We have dozens of FOIA requests and several lawsuits still pending.

Here's the real story of what happened, the behind-the-scenes story, showing the bipartisan corruption and secrecy that spanned from the Clinton administration to the Bush administration to the Obama administration.

Fannie Mae and Freddie Mac

The financial meltdown was caused by the collapse of the American mortgage market. In 2007, the real estate market crashed, thanks to inflated real estate prices. Up until 2007, banks had been creating mortgages at record rates for borrowers who had absolutely zero shot at paying them back. Their logic was simple: if they lent money to borrowers who defaulted on their mortgage, there was really no problem at all, since with a rising real estate market, the borrowers (or a bank that had to foreclose) could just sell the property and pay off the mortgage. The problem arose, however, when property values tanked. Now all those risky borrowers, known as subprime borrowers—for the most part borrowers who had borrowed with little cash down and had low credit scores—couldn't sell. When their houses went underwater—meaning that they owed more on the house than the house was worth—many of these folks simply stopped paying the mortgages. The banks couldn't sell the houses at prices that would cover the outstanding mortgage debt, so the banks were stuck with nonperforming mortgages backed by a glut of foreclosed-upon properties.

It turns out that the banks hadn't just picked up the mortgages and stuck them in a safety deposit box. They securitized the mortgages. That means lenders grouped mortgages together to provide investment-grade mortgage-backed securities that were sold and resold. To provide additional security for investors, some of these mortgage-backed securities were insured under products called "credit default swaps." When the mortgage-backed securities *did* go bad, it was like a shock wave to the entire financial structure, blasting through banks, insurance companies like American International Group (AIG), investment firms, and, most of all, Fannie Mae and Freddie Mac.

As it turns out, Fannie Mae and Freddie Mac were backstopping the vast majority of mortgages put out by banks. That means they were actually buying the mortgages or mortgage-backed securities from the private mortgage lenders. And since Fannie and Freddie are government-sponsored enterprises, what that *really* means is that the taxpayer was put on the hook for all those mortgage-related investments. When the housing market went south (and called into question the value of many of the mortgage-backed assets that lenders and Fannie/Freddie held), investors were devastated and taxpayers had to pick up the tab. The federal government seized control of Fannie and Freddie, TARP was passed, and other bailout programs commenced. So when the collapse of the housing market led to the collapse of Fannie and Freddie, the federal government takeover of those enterprises saddled taxpayers with over $6.5 trillion in attendant liabilities.

But what led up to the housing crisis? Many blame Uncle Sam for pushing precisely the sorts of mortgages that went bad. Using the Community Reinvestment Act, a federal law that tacitly encouraged quotas for lenders, the Clinton administration and Congress ratcheted up pressure on lenders and Fannie/Freddie to make more loans available to the disadvantaged and minorities. So follow the money trail back about eleven years and you'll find that Fannie Mae was throwing out sensible credit requirements on mortgage loans that it was buying up from other banks and lenders. As the *New York Times* reported, "The action, which will begin as a pilot program involving 24 banks in 15 markets—including the New York metropolitan region—will encourage those banks to extend home mortgages to individuals whose credit is generally not good enough to qualify for conventional loans. Fannie Mae officials say they hope to make it a nationwide program by next spring." Why would they do that? According to the *Times*, they were receiving pressure from the Clinton administration "to expand mortgage loans among low and moderate income people and felt pressure from stock holders to maintain its phenomenal growth in profits."[3] The article went on to predict, quite presciently, that such a strategy wouldn't cause problems during times of economic prosperity, but that Fannie Mae could run into serious financial trouble during an economic downturn.

While the Clinton administration was certainly culpable for getting the ball rolling on these high-risk loans, there was plenty of blame to go around. Overall, Fannie and Freddie spent more than $180 million from 1998 to 2008 to lobby their friends in Congress, making sure that nothing happened in Washington that they didn't want to happen. According to Politico, "The two government-chartered companies run a highly sophisticated lobbying operation, with deep-pocketed lobbyists in Washington and scores of local Fannie- and Freddie-sponsored homeowner groups ready to pressure lawmakers back home."[4] Fannie Mae was also nabbed in an all-too-familiar accounting scheme where the company's profits were overstated so that top executives could reap huge cash bonuses.

The tentacles of the Fannie and Freddie debacle reach deep into Washington and both political parties. Again, from Politico:

Franklin D. Raines, a former budget director in the Clinton White House, was paid $90 million in the five years he served as Fannie's CEO. He resigned amid an accounting scandal in 2004 with a $19 million severance package, though it was later whittled down after court challenges. Former Clinton FBI Director Louis Freeh sits on Fannie's board today. Bush White House veteran Stephen Friedman was once a board member, and former Bush trade representative and State Department official Robert Zoellick did a tour as a Fannie executive vice president.

Freddie's foundation has its own list of heavy hitters. Among its former board members are Rep. Rahm Emanuel (D-Ill.), a confidant of Democratic nominee Barack Obama, and Harold Ickes, a senior adviser to both President Clinton and Sen. Hillary Rodham Clinton (D-N.Y.). From the Republican side, David Gribbin, an aide to Vice President Cheney, once sat on the board, and Robert Glauber, a former Treasury undersecretary, is on the board.[5]

Working at Fannie alongside Raines was future Obama campaign advisor Jim Johnson. Those two allegedly cooked the books at Fannie, set policies that encouraged the issuance of countless dubious mortgages, and then took huge bonuses before leaving the company. Both were also accused of accepting special mortgage deals from Countrywide Financial, a chief mortgage player in this mess.

Politicians on Capitol Hill were no better. For example, Senate Banking Committee chairman Chris Dodd (D-CT) took more money in campaign contributions from Fannie Mae and Freddie Mac than anyone else in the U.S. Senate (Barack Obama, with only four years in the Senate under his belt, was close behind). When reform proposals for Fannie and Freddie were put before Dodd, he called them "ill advised."

Dodd, of course, was more than familiar with the ins and outs of government corruption. Senator Dodd appeared at a hearing on behalf of Edward Downe Jr. in 1993 to help Downe obtain a reduced sentence for violations involving tax and securities laws. In 2001, on President Clinton's last day in office, Dodd ultimately helped Downe secure a full presidential pardon for his crimes, bypassing the normal pardon vetting process. In 2002, Dodd allegedly received a gift in the form of a significantly reduced, below-market sales price, for a two-thirds interest in a property located in County Galway, Ireland, from Downe's associate William Kessinger. (Dodd already owned a one-third interest in the property.) Downe's signature appears on the property transfer documents. He is listed as a witness. Dodd, chairman of the Senate Banking, Housing and Urban Affairs Committee, allegedly failed to report the discounted real estate gift in 2002 and may have filed inaccurate Senate financial disclosure forms related to the property in subsequent years, in violation of the 1978 Ethics in Government Act. The penalty for filing false financial disclosure forms is $50,000 and up to one year in prison. Dodd received no punishment.

A few years later, Dodd received a special mortgage deal from Countrywide Financial—their CEO, Angelo Mozilo, reportedly gave Dodd the sweetheart mortgage as part of his "Friends of Angelo" VIP program. A few years after that, Dodd tried to create a program that would bail out Countrywide after the housing crisis began.

We filed a complaint with the Senate Ethics Committee about these Dodd dealings. The Ethics Committee, chaired by Senator Barbara Boxer (D-CA), sat on the complaint for nearly two years. Then they rejected it out of hand, stating, "The Committee has carefully evaluated the allegations and information in your complaint. . . . After considering all of the information before it, the Committee has determined that there is not sufficient substantial credible evidence of improper conduct or violation within its jurisdiction to warrant further action by the Committee." This was, simply put, a pathetic joke. Dodd's Senate colleagues were giving him a retirement present. And signing the card in big, loopy handwriting was Barbara Boxer, a fellow Countrywide client with no fewer than seven mortgages with the company. As Leslie Merritt of the Foundation for Ethics in Public Service said, Boxer was "less than candid, if not lying," about her connections with Countrywide.[6] Dodd, predictably enough, crowed over his colleagues' whitewashing, falsely claiming that our complaint was "baseless" and "politically motivated."

Our "baseless" complaint caused Dodd to amend his disclosure forms and the stench of corruption forced him into retirement. It is the tired defense of politicians like Dodd to cry "politics" whenever someone calls them out for ethical transgressions and corruption.

Then there was Barney Frank (D-MA). Frank's boyfriend, Herb Moses, was the assistant director for product initiatives at Fannie Mae. At the same time, Frank was on the House Banking Committee . . . which has oversight power over Fannie Mae. "It's absolutely a conflict," Dan Gainor, vice president of the Business & Media Institute, rightly pointed out. "He was voting on Fannie Mae at a time when he was involved with a Fannie Mae executive. How is that not germane? If this had been his ex-wife and he was Republican, I would bet every penny I have—or at least what's not in the stock market—that this would be considered germane. But everybody wants to avoid it because he's gay. It's the quintessential double standard." For years, Frank used Herculean efforts to stop Republican colleagues from placing stricter regulations on Fannie and Freddie. Bill Sammon of Fox News reported, "In 1991, the year Moses was hired by Fannie, the *Boston Globe* reported that Frank pushed the agency to loosen regulations on mortgages for two- and three-family homes, even though they were defaulting at twice and five times the rate of single homes, respectively. Three years later, President Clinton's Department of Housing and Urban Development tried to impose a new regulation on Fannie, but was thwarted by Frank. Clinton now blames such Democrats for planting the seeds of today's economic crisis."[7]

Frank's allegiance to these policies at Fannie and Freddie continued after he broke up with Moses. When members of the Bush administration proposed more regulation of the GSEs, Frank said, "I want to begin by saying that I am glad to consider the legislation, but I do not think we are facing any kind of a crisis. That is, in my view, the two government-sponsored enterprises we are talking about here, Fannie Mae and Freddie Mac, are not in a crisis. We have recently had an accounting problem with Freddie Mac that has led to people being dismissed, as appears to be appropriate. I do not think at this point there is a problem with a threat to the Treasury."

Again in 2003, he said that Fannie and Freddie were doing just fine—and then he went on to say, "even if there were problems, the federal government doesn't bail them out."[8]

Encouraged by Fannie and Freddie—both of which were free to mess around, with Frank's protection—banks began making tens of thousands of "subprime" loans to individuals who under prudent lending rules never would have qualified for them. This ruinous game was played for ten years under both the Clinton and George W. Bush administrations. As the *Washington Post* noted in a December 9, 2008, story: "These new products included home loans made to people with blemished credit histories, called subprime loans, and mortgages made without verification of income, assets or employment. . . . The loans required borrowers to state their incomes and assets, but not prove them."

The decision to violate sound lending principles to advance the Clinton administration's politically correct agenda was bad enough.

But that's not all.

Executives at Fannie and Freddie received huge bonuses if "loan targets," including targets for subprime loans, were met. Franklin Raines earned more than $90 million and Jamie Gorelick, another former Clinton administration official, earned more than $26 million in compensation and bonuses from Fannie Mae!

In other words, these "government-sponsored entities" not only trashed well-established lending standards—they also encouraged their executives to hustle as many bad loans as possible. In fact, we now know that at Fannie Mae in 1998, its then-head Franklin Raines allegedly cooked the books by deferring $200 million in expenses in order to fraudulently inflate profits so he and other senior Fannie executives could receive massive bonuses that year.

Despite their accounting problems and warnings of crisis, Fannie and Freddie, with the full support of liberals in Congress and their special-interest community organizing friends like ACORN, pushed for even *more* subprime lending. And calculating financial institutions (too many of which had corrupt relationships with these very same politicians) were happy to play along.

When the GOP took over the White House and Congress, the

folks at Fannie and Freddie moved fast to protect their cash cows by putting key Republicans on their boards and payrolls, including former Bush trade representative Robert Zoellick, who served a tour as Fannie's executive vice president, and former Cheney aide David Gribbin, who sat on Freddie's board.

The main objective of the Fannie and Freddie racket was to make sure that no one in Washington would hold them to account—and they certainly succeeded. Fannie and Freddie contributed lavishly to the politicians who chaired or had senior positions on the committees that had oversight responsibility for their institutions.

Fannie Mae alone contributed to the campaigns of 354 congressmen and senators, from both parties. The top four recipients of money from Fannie in order of cash magnitude were:

Senator Christopher Dodd (D-CT), the chairman of the Senate Banking, Housing and Urban Affairs Committee; Dodd would continue to oversee our financial sector until scandal forced him into retirement.

Senator Barack Obama (D-IL), a member of the Federal Financial Management, Government Information, Federal Services and International Security Subcommittee and now our president;

Senator Chuck Schumer (D-NY), chairman of the Senate Finance Committee;

Representative Barney Frank (D-MA), chairman of the House Financial Services Committee. Like Dodd, Frank remained a key player until his retirement this year.

Now, that's campaign money well spent!

Even after a 2004 government investigation found massive fraudulent bookkeeping at Fannie Mae, Congress held no hearings, no one went to jail, and business went on as usual, including aggressively marketing more loans to unqualified buyers. Incredible!

Now, of course, our country is facing financial ruin. But Barney

Frank had the gall to tell the American public that he was shocked—shocked!—when the mortgage market collapsed. Not many people buy those lies anymore. In July 2008, then–secretary of the Treasury Hank Paulson told Frank that the government required "billions of taxpayer dollars to backstop the institutions from catastrophic failure." That's according to Paulson himself. Frank then went on national TV and said that Fannie and Freddie were "fundamentally sound, not in danger of going under." He later said, "It was part of a conscious strategy to say to people, 'Hey, look, we think we can handle this.' It didn't work."[9] It is ridiculous and insulting that Frank, the consummate Washington insider, would try to "play dumb" with respect to corruption and the resulting financial catastrophe at Fannie and Freddie. He knew what was happening at Fannie and Freddie. He actively blocked attempts to reform the institutions and then lied, by his own admission, to the American people about the whole sordid affair. Frank's unwillingness to hold Fannie and Freddie accountable has nothing to do with wearing "ideological blinders." It has to do with Frank's "ethical blinders." Just last year, Frank finally admitted in the book *Reckless Endangerment* that he helped his friend (Mr. Moses) gain his lucrative position with Fannie. With his typical arrogance, Frank dismissed his abuse of office with a lame joke. Frank said, "If it is a [conflict of interest] then much of Washington is involved in [conflicts]."

Sure enough, these conflicts weren't limited to Barney Frank and Chris Dodd. On December 4, 2008, we sent a FOIA request to the Federal Housing Finance Agency (FHFA), requesting records related to congressional activity regarding the policy of Fannie Mae and Freddie Mac to increase lending to individuals with poor credit ratings, as well as all correspondence between FHFA and Fannie and Freddie. What we received stunned us: document after document showing that members of Congress were aware for years that Fannie and Freddie were playing fast and loose with accounting issues, risk assessment issues, and executive compensation issues, even as liberals in Congress tried to block attempts to regulate them more closely.

One letter, dated March 26, 2007, from the director of the Office of Housing Enterprise Oversight (OHFEO) to Republican senators Elizabeth Dole (NC), Chuck Hagel (NE), Mel Martinez (FL), and John Sununu (NH), stated, "This is a very serious issue. Freddie Mac's inadequate systems and controls make it a significant supervisory concern. Furthermore, its lack of timely public disclosures deny market participants the essential financial information made available by all other publicly traded companies so that investors may make informed judgments." The letter pointed out that "Fannie Mae still has not filed financial statements for 2005 and 2006 and thus, they are not timely filers either." In December 2004, Frank was told that Fannie and Freddie would be unable to complete their reviews of financial statements and said that they could have lost up to $9 billion dating back to 2001. In another letter dated June 16, 2006, from OHFEO director James Lockhart to Senator Hagel, Lockhart stated,

> In January 1999, Chairman and CEO Franklin Raines approved a recommendation made by the Chief Financial Officer (CFO) (Tom Howard) and the Controller (Leanne Spencer) to defer recognition of $200 million in amortization expense. This deferral, along with other accounting decisions made at that time relating to provisions for loan losses and the recognition of low-income housing tax credits, allowed management to meet the EPS threshold for maximum bonuses.

In other words, manipulation of the accounting allowed everybody to get the bonus that they wanted. This is government corruption at its finest.

When Fannie and Freddie started to implode, the federal government put them into conservatorship—Fannie/Freddie came under full federal control. Hank Paulson, then–secretary of the Treasury, held a joint press conference with Director Lockhart, in which Paulson said that after looking at "all options available," they had decided that conservatorship was the best option. "Based on what we have learned about these institutions over the last four weeks—including what we learned about their capital requirements—and given the condition of financial markets today, I concluded that it would not have been in the best interest of the taxpayers for Treasury to simply make an equity investment in these enterprises in their current form," Paulson said. Lockhart expressed support for the Treasury secretary's decision, indicating that he told the Treasury secretary that "conservatorship was the only form in which I would commit taxpayer money to [Fannie and Freddie]."

How much taxpayer cash did they pour into Fannie and Freddie? Overall, taxpayers put over *$150 billion* into the institutions.

Meanwhile, because of the government's mortgage programs designed to keep underwater borrowers in their houses, Fannie and Freddie now own 65 percent of the mortgages in the entire country—which means that the taxpayers are potentially on the hook for all of them. Between Fannie/Freddie and the Federal Housing Administration, nearly every new mortgage in the United States is ultimately backed through the federal government. Our nation has nationalized mortgage financing by government fiat. No laws explicitly authorized this—it was done through policy decisions and the power of government spending, which crowded out private financing from the housing market. Generally speaking, private mortgage lenders conform their mortgages to the standards set by the federal government, which in turn ultimately buys about 9 out of 10 mortgage loans issued today.[10]

The Bush administration's decision to place Fannie and Freddie into conservatorship was arguably as momentous as any that occurred during the financial crisis. But we heard nothing from the Bush administration about the rationale behind the conservatorship/government takeover versus a simple bailout—or as we were told would be done with TARP money, a targeted buying up of the "bad" mortgages to get them off Fannie and Freddie's books, turning the institutions profitable overnight. Or, even better than that, we could have placed Fannie and Freddie into receivership, selling off their assets, liquidating the companies, and getting the government out of the mortgage business. That could have cost far less than simply taking over the institutions. Was it considered? We have no idea. Nothing had been detailed regarding why the option of conservatorship was chosen. In December 2009, the Obama administration pledged an unlimited amount of taxpayer dollars to keep Fannie and Freddie afloat. Right now, there is no ceiling to how much taxpayer money (again, $150 billion and counting) could go to prop up the mortgage sisters. Because of the lack of transparency surrounding the decision to place the GSEs into conservatorship, we filed a lawsuit against FHFA on behalf of former Fed analyst Vern McKinley that sought documents detailing the rationale to keep Freddie and Fannie on life support through conservatorship. (As you'll see below, Judicial Watch and McKinley had partnered on several efforts related to bailout transparency.)

We already had filed another lawsuit against FHFA to obtain documents related to political contributions made by the GSEs. According to the FHFA, Fannie and Freddie might well possess documents responsive to Judicial Watch's initial FOIA request. However, the agency claimed it was not obligated to release such documents; we contended that since the GSEs are now run by the feds, they're subject to FOIA law. Obviously, this issue in particular goes to the very heart of government corruption—it involves one agency being overseen by another part of the government potentially giving political contributions to members of the government. Overall, members of Congress received more than $4.8 million in political contributions between 1998 and 2008. The top ten recipients were:

Senator Dodd (D-CT)
Senator Obama (D-IL)
Senator Kerry (D-MA)
Senator Bennett (R-UT)
Representative Bachus (R-AL)
Representative Blunt (R-MO)
Representative Kanjorski (D-PA)
Senator Bond (R-MO)
Senator Shelby (R-AL)
Senator Reed (D-RI)

Dodd was chairman of the Senate Banking Committee responsible for regulating the mortgage industry. Obama's future corruption was presaged here—he was the second-largest recipient of campaign cash from the agencies, even though he had only been in the Senate for three years—which made him, effectively, the number-one recipient of Fannie/Freddie campaign cash.[11]

During the 2008 election cycle alone, the securities, banking, and mortgage sector gave Obama $22.5 million, Senator Hillary Clinton $21.5 million, and John McCain $19.6 million. Chris Dodd received $6 million and Barney Frank got $720,000. The second-ranking Democrat on the House Financial Services Committee, Representative Paul Kanjorski (D-PA), received $755,000, and Representative Spencer Bachus (R-AL) also pulled down $704,000.

The decision to keep Fannie and Freddie's political contribution records secret obviously protected President Obama, Chief of Staff Rahm Emanuel, and his top party allies on the Hill—and many Republicans, too. Fannie and Freddie funneled "profits" from backing risky mortgages to politicians like Dodd and Obama. These politicians then prevented proper oversight of the agencies. This fundamentally corrupt scheme led to the collapse of the housing market and the subsequent financial crisis.

Unfortunately, the appellate court sided with the government, ruling that Fannie's and Freddie's secrets were not really subject to FOIA since "no one at the FHFA has ever read or relied upon any such documents. The district court held that the documents are not agency records subject to FOIA, and we agree." In other words, because no one at the FHFA, the agency in charge of Fannie Mae and Freddie Mac, has "read or relied upon" the documents, they are not considered agency records under FOIA, and cannot be released. Here's an idea. Maybe someone at FHFA *should* read the documents so someone in the government might have a clue as to why these two institutions failed so miserably. We strenuously disagree with the court's Alice-in-Wonderland logic, as we explained in our appellate brief: "In every meaningful way, the FHFA is lawfully in control of these records. There is nothing contingent, hypothetical, indefinite, or limiting about this plain statutory language vesting the FHFA with both legal custody and lawful control over the records."

The decision to keep these Fannie/Freddie records secret is the most significant antitransparency decision of the Obama administration. You can obtain documents from the Central Intelligence Agency, the National Security Agency, and other "secretive" government agencies that deal with life-and-death matters. But, if the Obama administration continues to get its way, not one document from the government Fannie and Freddie mortgage monsters will *ever* be given to you under the freedom of information law that governs most every other executive branch agency. We continue to try to extract documents from them but remember the Fannie/Freddie secrets Obama's keeping the next time you hear him or one of his mouthpieces highlight the administration's supposed transparency achievements.

We didn't just foot the bill for Fannie's and Freddie's massive mishandling. We actually ended up paying the *legal bills* of the executives who led that botchery. According to the *New York Times*, "Since the government took over Fannie Mae and Freddie Mac, taxpayers have spent more than $160 million defending the mortgage finance companies and their former top executives in civil lawsuits accusing them of fraud. The cost was a closely guarded secret until [early last year], when the companies and their regulator produced an accounting at the request of Congress. The bulk of those expenditures—$132 million—went to defend Fannie Mae and its officials in various securities suits and government investigations into accounting irregularities that occurred years before the subprime lending crisis erupted. The legal payments show no sign of abating." [12]

One of the controversial executives specifically referenced by the *Times* is none other than Franklin Raines, Bill Clinton's former budget director, who held the job of chairman and chief executive officer of Fannie Mae from 1999 to 2004. He is one of three executives who divvied up a tidy $24.2 million from the taxpayers to defend themselves in court. When asked why on earth the FHFA agreed to continue paying the outrageous legal fees for Fannie and Freddie executives, Edward J. DeMarco, acting director of the FHFA, simply said in a statement, "I have concluded that the advancement of such fees is in the best interest of the conservatorship." He provided no further explanation. How's that for accountability?

Of course this incestuous deal to pay massive legal fees was a "closely guarded secret," as the *Times* characterized it. Fannie, Freddie, and their friends in government knew the public would never knowingly get behind a bailout that would pay the legal defense bills of executives who got us into this financial mess. Most Americans oppose the bailouts on principle alone—never mind the flagrant corruption that helped lead to them. Let's face it. You don't broker a deal like this without being well connected in Washington, D.C.

But the Obama administration has made the argument that *no* Fannie or Freddie documents are subject to disclosure to the American people under FOIA. What other bombshells are they hiding in their files? We know, for instance, that President Obama himself was a top recipient of political contributions from these two agencies. As the *Times* points out, there is no end in sight for these taxpayer-funded legal payments. So the Obama administration wants more money from you but doesn't want to answer any of your questions through the direct accountability of FOIA about how or why that money is being spent.

And Obama is not only protecting himself with his illicit secrecy; he's also helping those seeking to oust him from office.

During the 2012 presidential campaign, former House Speaker Newt Gingrich has continuously misled the American people about how he, like many retired politicians, participated in D.C.'s lucrative influence-peddling industry.

Gingrich insinuated during one presidential debate that some members of Congress who took money from Fannie and Freddie should go to jail. And yet, over a span of eight years, according to Bloomberg News, the Gingrich Group was paid between $1.6 million and $1.8 million by the Freddie Mac. At the same time, Freddie Mac was engaged in massive fraud. Gingrich suggested he was a "historian" for Freddie Mac. But the evidence clearly shows he was "throwing his weight" behind the two government-sponsored enterprises to prop them up, saying in one interview that Fannie and Freddie provided a more "liquid and stable housing finance system than we would have" without them.

We've asked the FHFA again for documents, this time about Newt Gingrich, and we're still getting stonewalled. It is unbelievable—though so typically "Washington"—that Obama protects his campaign opponent Gingrich through unprecedented assertions of government secrecy.

And now the Obama administration is using Fannie and Freddie secrecy to advance its gangster government ways. On September 2, 2011, the FHFA, which oversees Fannie and Freddie, announced that it had filed a lawsuit on their behalf against seventeen financial institutions, including Bank of America, Countrywide, Citigroup, Morgan Stanley and JPMorgan Chase, among others. With its lawsuit, the FHFA alleges "some portion of the losses that Fannie Mae and Freddie Mac incurred on private-label mortgage-backed securities are attributable to misrepresentations and other improper actions by the firms and individuals named in these filings." (Private-label mortgage-backed securities were allegedly sold and marketed to Fannie Mae and Freddie Mac.)

FHFA contends that these institutions misrepresented the level of risk associated with these financial instruments when selling them to Fannie and Freddie. According to the *New York Times,* "financial service industry executives argue that the losses on the mortgage-backed securities were caused by a broader downturn in the economy and the housing market, not by how the mortgages were originated or packaged into securities. In addition, they contend that investors like . . . Fannie and Freddie were sophisticated and knew the securities were not without risk."

The notion that these financial institutions somehow duped Fannie and Freddie is ludicrous. Again, Fannie and Freddie (and federal housing policy, generally) helped created the mortgage-backed securities and secondary mortgage markets that collapsed in 2008 because of the loss of confidence in the subprime mortgage market—which was also pushed along by the federal government. Fannie even had a mortgage program it ran with Countrywide called "Fast and Easy." That's not the name of a pawnshop, but a government-backed mortgage program!

We had a simple FOIA request to FHFA: give us the documents showing "the losses that Fannie Mae and Freddie Mac incurred on private-label mortgage-backed securities (PLS) purchased from the 17 financial institutions." Again, we hit a stone wall. The Obama administration continues to maintain that not one record from Fannie or Freddie will be released under FOIA, though we're hopeful, as we file lawsuits and challenge the secrecy, that the courts will eventually force Freddie/Fannie documents out into the light of day.

The documents the Obama administration is keeping secret may go to the heart of the continuing housing crisis. This Obama administration lawsuit is a red herring designed to avert blame from government social engineering and housing policy that has resulted in massive taxpayer losses.

And now that it has a shakedown disguised as a lawsuit against much of the private banking industry, the Obama administration is doubling down on its obsessive secrecy.

The story of Fannie Mae and Freddie Mac is the story of the entire bailout scheme. The government continues to "invest" trillions of taxpayer dollars to prop up failing private institutions, with no end in sight. And the Obama administration continues to stonewall and obfuscate even as it asserts government control of 90 percent of the housing market.

It seems that we're now in the same sorry spot three years after the bailouts and government takeovers that "rescued" our economy. Our credit has been downgraded, the stock market is on a roller coaster, our government continues its gangster ways in attempting to run the private sector, the government-controlled housing market continues to be a mess, and our banks stand on a precipice. Unless our nation reckons with the government corruption behind the ongoing financial crisis, our economy will continue to flounder.

Bailout Nation

When the markets supposedly nearly collapsed in September 2008, the Bush administration, led by the "expertise" of Secretary of the Treasury Hank Paulson and Federal Reserve chairman Ben Bernanke, sought to "protect" our financial system through the $700 billion Troubled Asset Relief Program (TARP). The financial element of the crisis arguably began in March 2008, when global securities firm and investment bank Bear Stearns failed because of the market's loss of confidence as to whether the firm had sufficient liquidity.[13] The Federal Reserve forced Bear Stearns's sale to JPMorgan Chase at $2 per share—an incredible deal for JPMorgan Chase when you consider that the Fed pledged $30 billion to cover Bear Stearns's losses.

In July 2008, Barney Frank said that the prospects for Fannie and Freddie were "solid," which was an outright lie. The *Boston Globe* reported back in 2010:

> In July 2008, then-Treasury Secretary Henry Paulson called Frank and told him the government would need to spend "billions of tax-payer dollars to backstop the institutions from catastrophic failure," according to Paulson's recent book. Frank, despite that conversation, appeared on national television two days later and said the companies were "fundamentally sound, not in danger of going under." Unlike 2003—when, Frank said, he didn't realize what was going on—this time, he was deliberately trying to reassure the public, he said. "It was part of a conscious strategy to say to people, 'Hey, look, we think we can handle this,' " he said. "It didn't work." Less than two months later, the government seized Fannie and Freddie and the bailout began.[14]

On September 7, 2008, the federal government took over Fannie Mae and Freddie Mac. The fallout was growing worse and worse. On September 14, Merrill Lynch was sold to Bank of America—and again, the American government was involved in the deal. In fact, Bank of America later tried to get out of the deal, but the feds told them that they had better accept it or face severe regulatory scrutiny. Meanwhile, Lehman Brothers, also facing market pressures due to concerns about liquidity, collapsed—this time, unaided by the federal government. AIG's credit was downgraded because they carried so much exposure to the mortgage markets via credit default swaps—the American government, once again, stepped in, this time lending them $85 billion to help them avoid bankruptcy. On September 29, the federal government once again facilitated a sale of one major firm to another—this time, the Federal Deposit Insurance Corporation pushed through a sale of Wachovia Corporation to Citigroup, a recipient of bailout cash. Once again, the taxpayer helped Citigroup offset the liabilities associated with Wachovia—but only after, in a strange twist, Wachovia shunned Citigroup and took up with Wells Fargo. Through the flip-flops, the FDIC went from refusing to provide any assistance to offering all sorts of assistance just a week later.

Finally, in late September, Congress passed the bailout bill, bringing out into the open what had already been tacit: that the federal government was using taxpayer money to help specific firms avoid bankruptcy and certain VIP institutions acquire other firms at bargain-basement prices. But the government's involvement wasn't over yet—wherever the government gets involved, so does bullying. That was certainly the case on October 13, 2008, when the Treasury Department met with the CEOs of nine major banks—Vikram Pandit of Citigroup, Jamie Dimon of J.P. Morgan, Richard Kovacevich of Wells Fargo, John Thain of Merrill Lynch, John Mack of Morgan Stanley, Lloyd Blankfein of Goldman Sachs, Robert Kelly of Bank of New York, and Ronald Logue of State Street Bank—as well as future Obama Treasury secretary Tim Geithner, FDIC chairman Sheila Bair, and Fed chairman Ben Bernanke. In that meeting, the government leveraged the banks into playing ball. Many of the banks didn't need financial assistance at the time, but the government wanted all the major banks to participate so no particular bank would be penalized by the markets for taking government assistance. As President Bush, sounding like the Mad Hatter, said in his last month in office, "I've abandoned free-market principles to save the free-market system." [15]

The magnitude of government intervention and the cost to the taxpayer were unprecedented. Congressman Ron Paul (R-TX) rightly compared the economy in bailout to being "like a drug addict." If the federal government keeps bailing out institutions and passing regulations, Paul said, then it is simply feeding an already bad habit with a quick fix.[16]

In 2008, respected banking policy analyst and attorney Vern McKinley (who would later become a legal client of Judicial Watch) argued that "part of the churning process of capitalism [is letting] institutions fail." He was right. And McKinley would know—he worked at the Board of Governors of the Fed, the U.S. Department of Treasury's Office of Thrift Supervision, Resolution Trust Corporation, the FDIC, and as an expert advisor to central banks around the world. Way back in 1997 he sounded the alarm on Freddie Mac and Fannie Mae and likened their policies to "homeownership on steroids."

For his research and for ensuring better short- and long-term decisions, McKinley asked for meeting minutes from the September 29, 2008, Wachovia meeting and the Fed's and FDIC's documents on Bear Stearns. He wanted records that would show the analysis, legal rationale, and other justification for the government's unprecedented actions.

While people have a general idea of the theory of contagion as justification for government intervention, McKinley noted that there was "no meat on the bones." With blatant disregard for the law, the government refused to grant McKinley's FOIA requests. Upon appeal of his FDIC request, McKinley received a few pages in which there was really "no marginal value between a blanket refusal to disclose and the redacted version." In fact, in one of the lawsuits we filed on behalf of McKinley, U.S. District Court judge Emmet G. Sullivan slapped the FDIC for redacting virtually everything in the documents they turned over—the papers looked as though they had been attacked with a Sharpie. "Although the agency has released portions of certain agency documents, these additional issues remain in dispute, and the Court has jurisdiction to hear these claims," Sullivan wrote. "The agency has not provided a sufficient declaration from which the Court can conclude it conducted an adequate search for all records within its possession and control. The Court further concludes that, based on the current record, the [FDIC] has not fulfilled its obligations under FOIA or the Sunshine Act to justify withholding of documents or parts of documents pursuant to the Act's exemptions." [17]

What McKinley encountered was the same pervasive problem with getting information about financial regulatory actions that we had been fighting on our own. In free-market economics, Adam Smith described an "invisible hand" dictating movement in a market economy. With the Bush-Obama statist economics, the hand is no longer invisible but rather belongs to the Fed, Treasury, and FDIC as part of a "patchwork regulatory system"—and the records of this system should be available to the public. The government liked to argue that it was spread so thin that it couldn't deal with the FOIA requests. Yet McKinley was outnumbered on a conference call to discuss one of his requests by 3 to 1 with an agency's "full army of attorneys." Eventually, we filed four lawsuits on McKinley's behalf as part of our commitment to try to provide independent oversight of the bailouts. We separately sent over twenty-five FOIA requests related to the economy and federal government's role, with particular focus on the financial issues of "too big to fail" and the efficient use of taxpayer money. What we found was shocking.

Eventually, we forced the Obama administration to release documents about that October 13, 2008, Treasury Department meeting during which the Bush administration allegedly bailed out the nation's nine major banks. I recall reading a news article in the days following the meeting quoting those representing the major banks; they said they were forced to take the money. I thought that was worth further investigation. Did our government force private companies to accept government control through taxpayer-financed stock ownership?

Paulson and his colleagues evidently changed their minds on how to use TARP. Congress and the American people were told that TARP was going to be used to buy the "distressed" subprime mortgage assets that could bankrupt the economy. Specifically, the major banks were told that the government was taking $125 billion in equity stakes in their institutions. Of course, there was a catch. Along with the government "investment" came government control of compensation policies and other operations.

We followed up with a Freedom of Information request dated three days after the crucial October 13 meeting. As usual, the Bush administration, then in its end days, stonewalled our request.

So we filed a FOIA lawsuit against the Obama Treasury Department on January 27, 2009. It was one of our first lawsuits against the new administration. Following the Bush secrecy model, on February 4, Obama Treasury responded it had no documents about the historic meeting. Obviously, there had to be documents for a meeting during which $125 billion was spent! Pressure from Judicial Watch forced Treasury to reevaluate its response, which resulted in an important document dump in May 2009.

The documents were blockbuster.

Included in those documents were "CEO Talking Points" used by former Treasury secretary Paulson, confirming that the nine bank CEOs present at the October 13 meeting had no choice but to accede to the government's demands for equity stakes and the resulting government control. The talking points emphasize that "if a capital infusion is not appealing, you should be aware your regulator will require it in any circumstance." And the top regulators were all there at the meeting. Predictably enough, suggested edits of the "talking points" by Tim Geithner, then–New York Fed president, were withheld by the Obama Treasury Department—controlled by none other than the same Tim Geithner.

Another document, titled "Major Financial Institution Participation Commitments," was signed by the nine bankers on October 13. The CEOs not only handwrote their institution's names but also handwrote the prescribed multibillion-dollar amounts of "preferred shares" to be issued to the government. The CEOs were forced to sign a document that looked no more sophisticated than a school permission slip for a child's class trip. The "permission slip" for Citibank is reproduced below:

Major Financial Institution Participation Commitment

In support of the US financial system and the broader US economy, the [name of QFIT] ~~Citigroup~~ *Citigroup*
agrees to:

$25 billion.

- Issue Preferred Shares in the amount of [ ] to the US Treasury under the terms and conditions of the TARP Capital Purchase Program announced today.

- Participate in the FDIC program guaranteeing new issues of eligible senior liabilities by banks and bank holding companies and transaction accounts as announced today under the systemic risk exemption invoked by the FDIC, US Treasury, and the Federal Reserve.

- Expand the flow of credit to US consumers and businesses on competitive terms to promote the sustained growth and vitality of the US economy.

- Continue to work diligently, under existing programs, to modify the terms of residential mortgages as appropriate to strengthen the health of the US housing market.

_____
Signature

October 13 '08
_____
Date

This forced takeover was rammed through by bureaucrats, who despite running Treasury, seemed not to know who the country's major banks were. The emails show that, on the very day of the meeting, the chief of staff to the Treasury secretary and other top Treasury staff did not know the names of the top nine banks that were to be invited to the meeting—but that didn't stop them from cramming down the bailouts on the unwilling banks. In exchange for unwanted bailouts, the Paulson "talking points" detail how the government would say that they were "healthy institutions, participating in order to help the U.S. economy." It turns out that some of the banks, such as Citigroup, were quite unhealthy—but that truth wasn't part of the talking points.[18]

Other emails show that Treasury officials wanted to use the Secret Service to help keep the press away from the CEOs arriving at the meeting, and that there was a planned public relations effort, run at least in part out of the Bush White House, to tamp down public concerns about "nationalizing the banks." According to the documents we uncovered, Paulson immediately briefed then-senator Obama about the bankers meeting—but, for some odd reason, was unable to reach Senator John McCain, Obama's opponent in the presidential race.

The government pressure evident at this meeting would seem more at place in Putin's Russia or Chavez's Venezuela. This government control, which began during the Bush presidency, only metastasized under the Obama administration—as we'll discuss in detail later, Obama expanded his control from the financial industry to large swaths of domestic industry, including the auto and health-care industries.

The Treasury bankers' meeting documents showed our government exercising unrestrained power over the private sector. It started under Bush; it continued under Obama. So did the attendant secrecy. Despite its promises of transparency, the Obama administration tried to cover up the very existence of these smoking-gun documents. And the cover-up continues, as the Obama administration protects its own Timothy Geithner by using FOIA exemptions to withhold Geithner's personal edits to the infamous Paulson "Talking Points" memo.

The "bailout" cover-up started from the very beginning. There was never any doubt the federal government used the financial crisis to interfere in the private sector and expand its power and influence, but we uncovered new documents illustrating just how meddlesome the feds can be. As described by CNBC, "Negotiations to have JP Morgan take over Bear Stearns in March of 2008 produced an avalanche of emails from government officials. Worried that the collapse of Bear would trigger a worldwide domino effect, the Federal Reserve and Treasury urged JP Morgan to take over Bear." [19] Some of the names mentioned in that "avalanche" of emails include former president George W. Bush, former Treasury secretary Paulson, and current Treasury secretary Tim Geithner.

Later on, we discovered yet more evidence showing that the federal government rammed through the Bear Stearns deal on the backs of the taxpayers. The Treasury Department released "confidential" term sheets describing the Bear Stearns deal, as well as emails from Treasury officials stating that J.P. Morgan thought Bear Stearns was "nearly worthless" just hours before its acquisition deal was announced. One email sent by New York Federal Reserve Board official Michael Holscher to then-head of the New York Fed and now Treasury secretary Geithner explained, "JPM [J.P. Morgan] has discovered a large (50bn) structured mortgage position funded by BSC [Bear Stearns Capital], as well as other risk positions that are making them balk on the deal. I have asked for a report on their findings to assess the exposures. They also indicated that BSC's risk positions are exactly what JPM has avoided in recent years. They estimate the book value of the firm to be nearly worthless . . . and that risks on other unknowns are to the downside. They inquired about options that the federal government may have to bail out/purchase BSC, we indicated that options are extremely limited." Ultimately, J.P. Morgan received the taxpayer-backed guarantees it needed from the Treasury Department to consummate the deal to obtain the "worthless" Bear Stearns later that evening.

These FOIA documents were initially withheld from us and were only released after an administrative appeal to the Treasury Department. The documents suggested that J.P. Morgan leveraged the Treasury Department into footing the bill for Bear Stearns—despite the fact that, according to the SEC, Bear Stearns was

> in compliance with the SEC's capital and customer protection rules. The SEC also supervises the Bear Stearns parent company, whose capital also exceeded relevant regulatory standards, and whose liquidity position had been relatively stable, ranging between $15 and

$20 billion in the weeks preceding March 11. As of the morning of Tuesday, March 11, the parent company had over $17 billion in cash and unencumbered liquid assets.

The only problem with Bear, according to the SEC, was that its capital was not liquid, meaning that it couldn't be easily translated into cash.[20] Bottom line: this was a scam. The bailout did little to stave off the economic crisis; since Bear Stearns, the feds have had to commit trillions of taxpayer dollars to prop up other supposedly "worthless" financial institutions that could have been put into bankruptcy and sold off without taxpayers having to subsidize the failures. (The Federal Reserve has had to "invest" $26.3 billion to cover Bear Sterns' losses.)[21]

When we sought documents related to the Federal Reserve System Board of Governors' justification for authorizing the Federal Reserve Bank of New York to provide "temporary emergency financing" to Bear Stearns via J.P. Morgan, the government stonewalled, stating that FOIA law didn't apply. More specifically, they claimed that under the "deliberative process privilege" exemption, they weren't required under law to turn over such documents. This exemption allows the government to withhold certain "pre-decisional" material, supposedly to protect the deliberative processes of government decision-making. Unfortunately, the judicial branch ruled with the Obama administration here, making the incredible statement that any information can be withheld under the "deliberative process privilege," even *without showing proof of harm*. In other words, the government doesn't even need to show that the deliberative process is harmed by release of documents in order to prevent the release of documents. As our lawyers argued in an effort to persuade the Supreme Court, the lower court "created a sweeping exemption that is in direct conflict with decades of decisions holding that material may be withheld under the deliberative process privilege only if a government agency demonstrates that disclosure of the withheld material would harm the agency's decision-making process." The Supreme Court declined to take up our case. Too often, the burden of getting the truth is on the people of the United States in opposition to a secrecy-driven government.

When it came to the broader bailout, we forced the FDIC to turn over documents showing that officials from the Department of the Treasury may have improperly pressured the independent FDIC to accept key bailout deals. We had to pursue these FDIC documents, released in conjunction with a Financial Crisis Inquiry Commission investigation, for more than a year on our client Vern McKinley's behalf. We forced release of a key transcript of the meeting of the FDIC Board of Directors on September 29, 2008. The document shows that Chairman Sheila Bair indicated regarding the bailout of Wachovia that she "acquiesced" to pressure from Treasury, which was "vigorously pushing" the bailout plan. "I'm not completely comfortable with it but we need to move forward with something," Chairman Bair said. In meeting minutes from January 15, 2009, during which the FDIC approved the Bank of America bailout, Bair again showed that she wasn't standing up for the independence of the FDIC. According to those minutes, Bair admitted the agency "was relying on data analysis by the Federal Reserve" and that therefore the FDIC "very much needs to proceed with a systemic risk determination with respect to [Bank of America]." Bair characterized the decision to bail out Bank of America as demonstrating that the FDIC, an independent agency, was a "team player along with the Federal Reserve and the Treasury to prove the systemic risk case." Translation: Treasury and the Fed really want this so we have no choice but to go along. The FDIC is an independent agency of the federal government so that it insulated itself from political pressure brought by other government agencies, including Treasury. The FDIC's independence seemed nowhere to be found in these bailout documents.

Incidentally, these meeting minutes are consistent with a separate report by the Special Inspector General for the Troubled Asset Relief Program (known in Washington by the wonderful bureaucratic SIGTARP) released on January 13, 2011. According to the report, Chairman Bair admitted: "We were told by the New York Fed that problems would occur in the global markets if Citi were to fail. We didn't have our own information to verify this statement, so I didn't want to dispute that with them."

Regarding the consequences of allowing Bank of America to fail, the arguments noted in the meeting minutes were similar to those articulated during the Citigroup meeting and included the general observation that "both financial stability and overall economic conditions would be adversely affected, and that staff believes the consequences could extend to the broader economy." You read that right. The FDIC authorized the radical expansion of its powers because the fallout from the failure of Citigroup and Bank of America "could" extend to the rest of the economy. How's that for definitive?

We also received never-before-seen documents regarding the FDIC's Temporary Liquidity Guarantee Program (TLGP), which guaranteed unsecured debt of private financial institutions and provided them "full coverage of non-interest bearing [sic] deposit transaction accounts, regardless of dollar amount." This was another important part of the programmatic umbrella under which the bailouts were made, and it represented a radical expansion of the FDIC's power, allowing the agency to go well beyond the narrow scope of its lending authority to provide backing for bank-issued corporate bonds and long-term financing for banks.[22] To justify this expansion of power, documents referenced a "recent study" by the FDIC on the effect of a run on uninsured deposits and its impact on economic activity. However, to date, this report has not been released to the American people, despite the fact that it is within the parameters of McKinley's FOIA request. This program, by the way, continues to insure hundreds of billions of dollars in debt.

Some of those documents we *did* uncover concerning the TLGP demonstrate a remarkable lack of forethought and consideration. The FDIC board meeting minutes from November 23, 2008, for example—the meeting during which the FDIC approved the Citigroup bailout—showed that government officials described only in vague terms the consequences of allowing Citigroup to fail, including "the effects on money market liquidity could be expected on a global basis," "term funding markets remain under considerable stress," and the fact that it would "significantly undermine business and household confidence." One FDIC board member who was in attendance, John Reich, cautioned federal bank regulators and the Treasury Department to "avoid 'selective creativity' in determining what constitutes systemic risk and what does not and what is possible for the government to do and what is not." It's comforting to know that at least one FDIC official cautioned against "making stuff up" to justify bailouts. Unfortunately, no decision-maker seems to have paid heed to the advice.

Our analysis of the documents also indicated that, despite apparently lacking any legal authority to do so, Treasury agreed to cover any losses associated with the sale of Wachovia to Citigroup; this bailout was in September 2008, before Congress established Treasury's authority under TARP in October 2008. According to minutes of a meeting of the FDIC Board on September 29, 2008:

> [FDIC board] Chairman Bair then added that the Department of the Treasury has already agreed that, if there are any losses attendant with the transaction, it will separately fund those so that the Corporation's cash balance would not be depleted in any way. She said that this was in contrast to the Department of Treasury's usual rule that the Corporation must spend down its entire cash balance before the Corporation can borrow from the Treasury.

Here's the big problem: Treasury may cover losses in a transaction only when granted the proper legal authority by Congress.

The FDIC documents also indicated that the federal government, while noting some concerns about Wachovia Bank's policies and procedures, granted the Wachovia holding company and bank a passing grade in multiple assessments just prior to the bailout. For example, an August 4, 2008 "Report of Examination" of Wachovia by the comptroller of the currency concluded, "At this time, capital is rated a '2' and the bank is within the 'well capitalized' level for Prompt Corrective Action (PCA) purposes. Wachovia's capital levels are projected to remain adequate through year-end 2008 and into 2009." Overall, Wachovia earned a 3 rating on a scale of 1 to 5 with 1 indicating an "outstanding" rating. Moreover, according to a July 22, 2008, assessment by the Federal Reserve, Wachovia earned a 3 rating, or "fair." According to this assessment the Federal Reserve concluded that "the risk management and financial capacity of the company . . . pose only a remote threat to its continued viability." There's no question that the FDIC documents raised more questions than they answered. It looks like Treasury bullied the FDIC the same way former secretary Paulson forced banks to accept the government "investments." How on earth could government officials give Wachovia a "fair" grade just weeks before it melted down and became in need of an FDIC bailout? Frankly one must ask whether it needed a bailout at all. Under what authority did Treasury act to so obtrusively interfere with the private sector in the first place?

As for the bailout of AIG, it turns out that our government knew full well that we'd never see that $85 billion in bailout cash again. In fact, taxpayers spent far more than $85 billion on AIG— overall, we spent in excess of $150 billion. Via FOIA, we recovered internal Treasury Department emails and a series of outlines, presentation slides, and articles outlining the details and terms of the government's AIG bailout. Included among the items is a slide titled "Investment Considerations." On the slide is this statement: "The prospects of recovery of capital and a return on the equity investment to the taxpayer are highly speculative." The comments are crossed out by hand.

Another document is an outline describing the strict control "imposed" on AIG as a condition of the government's cash infusion, including those related to private executive compensation and corporate expenses. One document notes that with respect to corporate expenses, the government's corporate expense policy "shall remain in effect at least until such time as any of the shares of the Senior Preferred are owned by the UST (United States Treasury). Any material amendments to such policy shall require the prior written consent of the UST until such time as the UST no longer owns any shares of Senior Preferred." In essence, the federal government had now bought control of the world's largest insurer, at least with regard to corporate expenses.

On December 15, 2008, we found out, Jonathan Fletcher, chief interim risk officer for TARP, sent an email. It revealed the existence of an internal government program to track the effectiveness (or lack thereof) of the AIG bailout. Fletcher writes: "As you know, we are obligated by EESA [Emergency Economic Stabilization Act] to determine the effectiveness of TARP investments. . . . We would propose to follow up on the TARP investment by preparing a risk assessment note that spells out the objectives . . . and then create both a benchmark for AIG today and then establish metrics to track AIG's progress (or lack thereof) in coming months." No documents related to this government tracking program have been released to the public—so we may never know whether TARP money given to AIG was money well spent, even though the government knows. This is the height of gall—it is our money that was spent on AIG. Apparently, although some government officials recognized their responsibility to measure the effectiveness of their TARP investments, at the same time the American people are misinformed and remain in the dark about how their money is being spent.

The controversy and corruption surrounding AIG didn't end with the bailout. We filed a lawsuit against the Obama Treasury Department to obtain documents regarding meetings involving Kenneth Feinberg, special master for executive compensation under TARP; AIG chairman Robert Benmosche; and New York Federal Reserve Bank president William Dudley. Feinberg, also known as the Obama administration's "pay czar," is the federal official who was responsible for setting compensation guidelines for the seven largest firms, including AIG, using funds from TARP.

In March 2009, AIG disbursed $165 million in taxpayer-funded TARP funds to its top executives, prompting a massive public backlash. Obama officials reportedly lobbied Congress to insert legislative language allowing the AIG bonus payments and then apparently lied about their knowledge of the payment scheme. (As then–head of the New York Federal Reserve, current Treasury secretary Timothy Geithner helped craft the original AIG deal.)

We made a FOIA request regarding a meeting that took place in November 2009, just weeks after Feinberg publicly announced pay cuts and salary caps for AIG's top paid executives. According to press reports, despite the Obama administration's tough rhetoric on AIG, the insurance giant was set to pay out a fresh round of bonus payments to its executives in the amount of $100 million in 2010. All in all, the bonuses totaled $165 million.

We sent our FOIA request to the Treasury Department. They acknowledged its receipt and granted themselves a ten-day extension for processing. Treasury failed to respond further, however. This kind of obstruction had already become a typical modus operandi for the Treasury Department. So we filed a lawsuit. As we noted in that lawsuit, "This is not the first time in which [Treasury] has acknowledged [Judicial Watch's] FOIA request, granted itself a ten day extension, and failed to take any other action within the statutory time period. [Judicial Watch] currently has eight additional FOIA requests pending with [Treasury] in which [Treasury] has acted in the same or a similar manner." Once again, big government, big corruption, and big secrecy were all rolled into one enormous ball.

At first, Senator Chris Dodd pretended not to know how a provision had gotten into the Obama stimulus bill that was used to authorize and excuse the AIG bonuses.[23] It eventually came out that Senator Dodd had lied about his approval of the AIG bonuses—and was forced to admit that under pressure from the Obama Treasury Department he slipped language into the bailout bill that paved the way for the bonuses. "As many know, the administration was, among others, not happy with the language. They wanted some modifications to it," Dodd explained. "They came to us, our staff, and asked for changes, and the changes at the time did not seem that obnoxious or onerous."[24] One newspaper in Dodd's home state of Connecticut called him a "lying weasel" for his games on AIG.[25]

At least twenty criminal investigations have been launched into the controversial bailout—and according to a scathing report released by the Treasury Department's inspector general, TARP recipients were not reporting on their actual use of TARP funds.

Neil Barofsky, who was SIGTARP (the Special Inspector General for TARP) at the time, complained, "Promoting transparency in the management and operation of TARP is one of [the inspector general]'s primary roles. . . . [T]he American taxpayer has been asked to fund—through programs now involving up to approximately $3 trillion—an unprecedented effort to stabilize the financial system and promote economic recovery. In this context, the public has a right to know how the U.S. Department of the Treasury decides to invest that money, how it manages the assets it obtains, and how TARP recipients use these funds. Transparency is a powerful tool to ensure accountability and that all those managing and receiving TARP funds will act appropriately, consistent with the law, and in the best interests of the country."[26] The program, the SIGTARP said, was "inherently vulnerable to fraud, waste and abuse." SIGTARP currently reports that it has launched investigations into "TARP-related accounting fraud, securities fraud, insider trading, bank fraud, mortgage fraud, mortgage modification fraud, wire fraud, false statements, obstruction of justice, money laundering, and tax crimes. SIGTARP currently has more than 150 ongoing criminal and civil investigations."[27]

Naturally, our politicians don't want us to know exactly where the $2 trillion in other emergency bailout money went—remember, while TARP was supposedly just $700 billion, the government secretly lent $2 trillion in separate rescue programs that didn't require approval by Congress, allowing the agencies responsible to claim that the beneficiaries should remain private. The Federal Reserve made the mystery loans under the terms of eleven relatively obscure programs, eight of them created from mid-2007 to late 2008.

In 2011, the Government Accountability Office released a report on the financial crisis and came to a stunning conclusion—or at least, a conclusion stunning to those who didn't follow the entire chain of events closely. The government, the GAO said, failed to provide a rationale for its unprecedented intrusion into the private sector through the massive bailout scheme initiated in 2008. And more transparency is needed to get to the truth. Judicial Watch and our client Vern McKinley had been saying this very thing for years. Our comprehensive investigation showed that the rule of law was subject to the whims and seat-of-the-pants decision-making by the government financial agencies.

When questioned about their rationale for the bailouts by the GAO, government officials simply repeat their standard line: there were "unusual and exigent circumstances" that warranted extreme measures. But the GAO found that the Fed couldn't explain why it provided bailouts to certain firms and corporations rather than others. When asked for documents about the exigent circumstances findings, the Fed said they had never written down their views. Normally, a financial firm ("broker-dealer subsidiary") that traded stock and other investment instruments that could lose value was not eligible for federal bailouts. But the government found a way to make an exception to the rules—through the exercise of raw fiat. "Without more complete documentation," the GAO noted, "how assistance to these broker-dealer subsidiaries satisfied the statutory requirements for using this authority remains unclear. Moreover, without more complete public disclosure of the basis for these actions," the report continued, "these decisions may not be subject to an appropriate level of transparency and accountability." [28] The most expensive taxpayer expenditures in American history have not been "subject to an appropriate level of transparency and accountability"—that is the legacy of the Bush administration and the continuing legacy of the Obama administration—and the bungling Congresses that went along with out-of-control spending. Lord help this country.

Where does TARP stand today? The TARP authority ended in 2010 but its investments and losses will go on—practically speaking, forever. According to the Treasury website's TARP Tracker, as of mid-June 2011, $245 billion had been disbursed to banks and $263 billion recovered. We made money, you think? Wrong. Banks who had the TARP "investment" forced on them were forced to pay it back on onerous terms. The profit came out of the pockets of bank depositors, lendees, and shareholders. In the meantime, the government still has "investments" in hundreds of banks across the United States.[29]

The Obama administration would have you think that all car industry bailouts were paid back. Wrong! Treasury admits that $80 billion was paid out and $41 billion was paid in—for a net loss of

$39 billion for the taxpayer. The AIG debacle is another monstrous expense. Treasury's TARP Tracker details that $68 billion was paid out for AIG, but only $29 billion has since been taken in. And the "credit market programs" have resulted in a $14 billion loss for the taxpayer. Adding all this up, TARP cost taxpayers $74 billion. This figure does not include the $150 billion in Fannie/Freddie losses and the other federal bailouts through the Federal Reserve and the FDIC. CNN estimates that Bailout Nation has cost taxpayers $3 trillion thus far.[30] Others place the bailouts as costing taxpayers anywhere from $24–$29 trillion.[31]

What is frightening is that only Vern McKinley, Judicial Watch, and one or two news agencies seem interested in how or why all that money was spent. Actually, a few politicians have an interest—for corrupt reasons.

OneUnited: Bailout Corruption

One of the worst examples of bailout corruption once again involves Barney Frank. His co-conspirator was Representative Maxine Waters (D-CA). We obtained documents from the Treasury Department showing that one particular bank, Boston-based OneUnited, was in serious trouble, didn't even do its job under the subprime-loan-creating Community Reinvestment Act, and didn't deserve a bailout. "There are some really good people expressing very strong opinions regarding what they view as a travesty of justice regarding the special treatment this institution is receiving," acting FDIC regional director John M. Lane wrote to Christopher J. Spoth, a senior FDIC consumer protection official in March 2009.[32] He was right on the money.

OneUnited had snagged a $12 million bailout nonetheless, thanks to the intervention of Frank and of Waters, who had a very real stake in the bank. The *Wall Street Journal* reported, "Congressional financial-disclosure forms show Ms. Waters acquired OneUnited stock worth between $250,000 and $500,000 in March 2004, as did [her husband, Sidney Williams]. Mr. Williams joined the board of OneUnited that year. Each sold shares in September 2004—including Ms. Waters's entire stake—but Mr. Williams continued to hold varying amount of the company's stock. In the lawmaker's most recent financial-disclosure form, dated May 2008 and covering the prior year, Ms. Waters reported that her husband held between $250,000 and $500,000 worth of the bank's stock. Mr. Williams also received interest payments from a separate holding at the bank, also worth between $250,000 and $500,000."[33]

Michelle Malkin reported, "Waters (along with Rep. Frank) participated directly in pressuring the feds for OneUnited's piece of the bailout pie. She personally contacted the Treasury Department . . . requesting $50 million for the company—and failed to disclose her ties to the bank to them."[34]

When asked about the scandal, Frank admitted that he spoke to a "federal regulator" but, according to the *Wall Street Journal*, "he didn't remember which federal regulator he spoke with."[35] That Frank "didn't remember" seemed a lie at the time, so Judicial Watch investigated. We extracted smoking-gun Treasury Department emails that show this nameless bureaucrat was none other than then–Treasury secretary Hank Paulson. Here is just a sample email, written on October 17, 2008, from one Treasury official to other top officials:

> Just spoke w/ Jim in BF's [Barney Frank's] office. This is about One United Bank (a minority owned bank in BF's district). is interested in the bank as well, Treas and others met w/ them (minority bankers assoc) last month per the Water's request. They were a big holder in f/f preferred [Fannie/Freddie preferred stock]. BF is interested and may call HMP [Treasury Secretary Hank M. Paulson] again about this. FDIC is their primary federal regulator-

Does anyone really believe that Frank "didn't remember" that he didn't talk to the Treasury secretary of the United States?

Other documents we culled from Treasury included the agency's emails describing the substandard condition of OneUnited prior to the taxpayer-funded bailout.

One September 15, 2008, email from former Treasury senior advisor Michael Scott to Director of the Office of Financial Institutions Mario Ugoletti included a Community Reinvestment Act (CRA) evaluation administered by the Federal Financial Institutions Examination Council (FFIEC). It noted serious issues with OneUnited's lending practices. The 2004 CRA Public Evaluation showed that while OneUnited received a rating of "Low Satisfactory" overall, its Massachusetts rating for the Lending Test and the Investment Test showed a "Needs to Improve." The Lending Test evaluates whether a bank helps to meet the needs of the community it serves. The Investment Test gauges whether a bank has a good record of meeting the credit needs of the area through "qualified investments and grants." In Florida, the institution clocked in at "Substantial Noncompliance" on the Lending Test. The 2007 CRA evaluation showed similar problems in Florida again.

Another email, sent on January 3, 2009, from Brooklyn McLaughlin, Treasury's deputy assistant secretary for public affairs, to former assistant Treasury secretary Neel Kashkari, highlighted Barney Frank's intervention in the OneUnited Bank bailout and called attention to significant concerns about the OneUnited transaction. "According to the WSJ [*Wall Street Journal*]," the email noted, "Barney Frank told them that he specifically put section 103-6 in the bill in order to help this particular bank. Apparently this bank also had an issue with a Porsche that the regulators had made them get rid of. The story will run later this week and will highlight three banks that they think raise questions and are not 'healthy' banks. . . ." Normally, the Treasury Department was supposed to provide bailout funds (or "investments") to otherwise healthy banks to jump-start lending. This discrepancy prompted McLaughlin to write on January 13, 2009, "Further to email below, WSJ [*Wall Street Journal*] tells me: . . . Apparently this bank is the only one that has gotten money through section 103-6 of the EESA law. And Maxine Waters' husband is on the board of the bank. ??????" That's a lot of question marks. And there's a reason for them.

One Treasury memorandum was titled "Regulatory Financial Highlights." It should have been labeled "lowlights." The government document detailed OneUnited financial information as well as a summary of information collected by Treasury during its investigation of the bank. According to these documents, OneUnited sought government assistance in part because the company owned $52 million in Fannie Mae and Freddie Mac stock that was "irrevocably impaired" when the government seized control of the two GSEs. However, as noted by one Treasury email from Michael Scott, OneUnited "purchased their Fannie/Freddie stock in the first quarter of 2008," long after the problems cited in the government's two CRA assessments. The official commented, "Interesting, huh?"

Indeed, an independent analysis by MSNBC.com and the Independent Reporting Workshop found that OneUnited was the weakest bank to receive TARP support. In fact, it had been operating under a "cease and desist order" imposed by the FDIC and its Massachusetts state regulator that said the agencies "had reason to believe that the Bank had engaged in unsafe or unsound banking practices and violations of law." [36]

And the *Washington Post* obtained documents from the FDIC that provide new details on something Judicial Watch already had uncovered—OneUnited Bank was in deplorable financial shape at the time of the TARP grant (partially because of a questionable $50 million investment in the sinking ship that was Fannie Mae and Freddie Mac) and would never have received government assistance without political intervention:

> The chairman of OneUnited Bank, a friend of Rep. Maxine Waters (D-Calif.), had rendered it insolvent through lavish spending and bad investments, according to the examiners' written accounts. But by the end of that year, after Waters arranged a key Treasury Department meeting for the bank, it had won a bailout loan and a unique exemption from the FDIC's accounting rules. "There are some really good people expressing very strong opinions regarding what they view as a travesty of justice regarding the special treatment this institution is receiving," acting regional director John M. Lane warned in a March 2009 e-mail to Christopher J. Spoth, a senior FDIC consumer protection official. [37]

The documentary record shows that but for the corrupt intervention of Barney Frank and Maxine Waters, OneUnited would not have gotten a $12 million taxpayer bailout. The documents also showed that the so-called community bank wasn't actually lending much to the "community" that Frank and Waters were purporting to help. That was just the material the Obama administration turned over—they produced 639 pages, but they withheld a full 203 more. By the way, OneUnited remains in that dubious category of banks that haven't paid back their TARP investments.[38]

So what happened to Maxine Waters? For a while, it appeared that the House Committee on Standards of Official Conduct (the House Ethics Committee) would get off its duff and do something about her. In 2010, the committee announced that there would be a speedy trial to consider the charges against Waters. And, on the heels of the massive investigation and very public trial of Representative Charles Rangel (D-NY), there was reason to be somewhat optimistic that Waters would be held accountable.

Until House Ethics Committee chairman Zoe Lofgren (D-CA) started meddling in the process, that is. Not only did Lofgren fail to issue subpoenas for records related to the scandal, but she also delayed the Ethics Committee hearing after doing everything in her power to undermine the professional committee staff leading the investigation. And, as if that were not enough, Lofgren then improperly tried to fire two attorneys working on the investigation.

Now the Waters investigation is stuck in the mud, as an independent counsel investigates both the committee's handling of the case and Waters's alleged transgressions.

For her part, Waters believes that she has unfairly been singled out. Believe it or not, I have some sympathy for her. The Office of Congressional Ethics report provides damning detail about her co-conspirator Barney Frank's involvement in the scandal. Frank is mentioned repeatedly in the Waters report from the Ethics Committee (he's described as "Representative A"). To quote from the report:

> . . . Representative Waters told Representative A that she was in a predicament because her husband had been involved in the bank,

but "OneUnited people" were coming to her for help. According to Representative A, she knew she should say no, but it bothered her. It was clear to Representative A that this was a "conflict of interest problem."

　. . . Representative A's advice to Representative Waters was to "stay out if it"—OneUnited was a Boston bank and he had a commitment to minority banks. He would address the problem. Representative A then asked his staff to take over the OneUnited issue from Representative Waters.

　Representative A had at least two conversations with Representative Waters in which he told her to not get involved in the OneUnited matter. The conversations likely occurred in September 2008, but he could not recall any specific dates.[39]

Waters shouldn't have focused on race—she should have asked why it would be improper for her to contact Treasury because of a conflict of interest but okay for Frank to do it for her, knowing this same conflict of interest. Frank has gotten a pass from the Ethics Committee. To avoid surely being caught up in a Waters ethics trial, Frank is retiring. The scandals have been too much.

　But guess who's angling to replace Frank as ranking Democrat on the House Financial Services Committee (which would mean the chairmanship if Democrats take back the House)? Maxine Waters! It is quite obvious that Representative Waters has neither the integrity nor the ethics necessary to hold such a position of public trust. If Nancy Pelosi agrees, Waters will lose out. Either way, expect a nasty political fight that, shamefully, will have little to do with upholding the public trust but everything to do with power and racial politics.

PART 2

JUDICIAL WATCH AND
THE OBAMA ADMINISTRATION

4.

INTRODUCING BARACK OBAMA

A s we'll see, if the Clinton and Bush administrations couldn't stand transparency, the Obama administration, in key areas, made it its special mission to prevent governmental transparency at every turn. As we've emphasized again and again, truth fears no inquiry—when you have nothing to hide, you generally care very little about being exposed. The Obama administration cares deeply about being exposed. That is an extension of Obama personally. We knew less about Senator Obama than about any presidential candidate in the history of the United States—and all of that was on purpose. Senator Obama would not release his college records; he would not release his work from Harvard Law School. He was secretive from the start. That secrecy extended throughout his years in Chicago and Illinois politics, his U.S. senatorial term, and his 2008 campaign.

The most egregious early indicator of Obama's attitude toward transparency was his attempts to hide even his record as an Illinois state senator. We investigated his record there, and we found that the maintenance of his files was highly suspect. We sent a state FOIA request to the Illinois State Archive to obtain his records and papers, including any and all "public documents . . . resulting from Illinois State Senator Barack Obama's years in the office (1997–2004) that the ISA [has] in its possession."

During a campaign stop in fall 2007, Obama at first claimed he did not have any records of his eight years in the Illinois legislature.

"I don't have—I don't maintain—a file of eight years of work in the state Senate because I didn't have the resources available to maintain those kinds of records," he said. When questioned about the records by *Meet the Press* host Tim Russert on November 11, 2007, Obama said: "Well, let's be clear. In the state Senate, every single piece of information, every document related to state government was kept by the state of Illinois and has been disclosed and is available and has been gone through with a fine-toothed comb by news outlets in Illinois . . . every document related to my interactions with government is available right now."

This was a lie. According to a February 25, 2008, letter from the Illinois Office of the Secretary of State in response to Judicial Watch's open records request, "The ISA does not maintain Senator Obama's personal records or papers. [Nor] does the ISA maintain records generated by his office. In addition, the ISA has received no requests from Senator Obama to archive any records formerly in his possession." We also contacted Obama's successor, Kwame Raoul, who stated in a March 5 letter to Judicial Watch, "Any documents I would have inherited from Senator Obama would have been con-stituent work files, and those were reviewed and discarded upon me taking office." State senator Raoul also argued that even if he had any Obama records, he would not be required to disclose them.

Obama could have had his records archived so that they were available to the public, but he chose not to do so. Apparently, he did not want a complete paper trail of his time in the Illinois State Senate. That went also for his time in college, law school, as a com-munity organizer, and in the U.S. Senate.

As always, where there was this much secrecy, there was a lot to hide.

The Rezko Scandals

The first indication that Senator Barack Obama was personally cor-rupt was his relationship with dirty real estate magnate and political fund-raiser Tony Rezko. The ties between the two were long and deep, as the *Chicago Tribune* has reported.[1] Shortly after Obama became president (not editor) of the *Harvard Law Review,* Rezko offered to hire Obama at Rezmar Corporation, which was helping to build inner-city homes. The offer was due to Obama's celebrated past as a community organizer. By 1995, when Obama decided to run for Illinois Senate, Rezko had become Obama's biggest campaign financer. In his first three runs, Rezko put together over $250,000 for his man, and according to Obama, at least one-tenth of Obama's total budget for his first Illinois state senate run. Rezko put his checkbook behind every single one of Obama's subsequent campaigns. For Obama's unsuccessful congressional run against Representative Bobby Rush, Rezko bundled between $50,000 and $75,000 for the young state senator. Rezko was an official member of the Obama finance committee for Obama's 2004 run and used his home to hold a fund-raiser for him. Obama would later falsely claim that his relationship with Rezko was de minimis.

In 2004, Obama attended a meeting brokered by Rezko for Middle Eastern bankers, including Iraqi billionaire Nadhmi Auchi. According to the *New York Times,* Rezko called Obama into the meeting in order to demonstrate his political connections. At that time Auchi had already been convicted for financial misconduct as part of a massive corruption investigation in France. (Auchi reportedly denies any wrongdoing.)

Obama, by contrast, claimed that he only remembered talking with Rezko about government business one time. "When the [then-Illinois governor Rod] Blagojevich administration first came in, they contacted us and many other people, asking for recommendations for people who might be interested in filling out state jobs," Obama told the *Chicago Tribune*:

> My recollection is that we sent a list of people but it was not a list of people who I was particularly close to. If I'm not mistaken, it included people who came into our office asking for jobs, or this or that or the other. I did not have any formal discussions with Tony beyond one individual, and that was Dr. Eric Whitaker, who ultimately became the head of the Illinois Department of Public Health and

who had been a longtime friend of mine, whom I had known since
he was getting his master's at Harvard and I was at the law school
there. He had expressed an interest in that post. I think he had applied separately, but I don't recall whether I called Tony or he called
me. And I simply said, I think this guy is outstanding and is certainly
somebody who is worthy of an interview.

When the *Tribune* questioned whether Rezko was the designated
conduit for Whitaker to get a job with the new administration of
Governor Rod Blagojevich, Obama said that he wasn't. Rezko, said
Obama, was just "one of a number of people within the Blagojevich
circle who were, you know, helping to screen or interview potential
candidates for administration posts." This was the beginning of a
pattern of dishonest disavowal that would continue throughout the
Rezko saga.

Rezko, who was only just "one of a number of people" Obama
supposedly knew to help secure political patronage, helped Obama
buy a house in 2005. After being sworn in to the U.S. Senate,
Obama decided to buy a "96-year-old, South Side Georgian re-
vival home with four fireplaces, glass-door bookcases fashioned
from Honduran mahogany and a wine cellar with space for 1,000
bottles," the *Tribune* reported. "The house and the adjoining yard
had been owned as a single property. But now the owners are listing
them separately, asking $1.95 million for the house and $625,000
for the garden lot."

There was only one problem: somebody already owned the option
on the garden lot. What was a poor, troubled U.S. senator to do?
How about call up an old buddy and ask for a hand? Obama denies
that happened, of course. But somehow, Rezko got hold of the option after learning that Obama had bid on the house. Either this was
the greatest coincidence of all time, or something fishy was going
on. And, of course, something fishy *was* going on.

On January 23, 2005, Obama put forward a final bid of $1.65
million. This price was steeply discounted—how could the sellers accept a bid of $1.65 million for a house with a selling price of $1.95

million in a booming real estate market? They could do it only if they also got a great price for the garden lot.

As Obama later admitted, he and Rezko had a conversation about buying that garden lot:

> Tony asked me during the course of one of these conversations why I might not be interested in buying the lot and keep the property intact. And I said that, you know, it wasn't worth it to us to spend an extra $600,000 or so on a lot next door when Michelle and I were really interested in the house. So, he said, "Well, I might be interested in purchasing the lot." And my response was, "That would be fine." And my thinking at the time, and this is just to sort of flag this, this is an area where I can see sort of a lapse in judgment. Where I could have said, "You know, I'm not sure that's a great idea." But my view at the time when he expressed an interest was that he was a developer in this area that owned lots, that he thought it was going to be a good investment. And my interest, or my motivation was here's somebody that I knew who, if this lot was being developed, it'd be better to have somebody who knew, who I knew, who you know would give me schedules, keep me apprised of what was taking place and so forth. So I didn't object.[2]

A *lapse in judgment?* Asking a decade-long major fund-raiser to buy a piece of property adjoining your land so that you can broker a cozy deal is not a lapse in judgment. It was a corrupt gift to Obama plain and simple. It was Obama's Whitewater (which was the name of the Clintons' sweetheart real estate deal in Arkansas), whether or not the liberal media wanted to cover the story.

The rest of Obama's story didn't back up the "lapse of judgment" characterization, either. Before the closing on the property occurred, Obama actually took Rezko out to the property to check it out. According to the Obama campaign, this was just an innocent outing during which Rezko was supposed to tell Obama whether the property was a solid purchase or not, since Rezko was in the real estate business. But it took Obama until 2008 to divulge the visit at all.

In fact, in 2006, Obama explicitly denied any such meeting to the *Tribune*, saying that he and Rezko chatted about the property "either at an event or some conversation we had where they mentioned to me that they either knew the property or knew the developer or something like that. . . . I actually asked him what he thought of the house and he thought it was a good house. And I said, 'I'm looking at putting in a bid on it.' And from that point on I just worked through my real estate broker, purchased the property." When Obama revealed that he and Rezko had had a nice jaunt out to the property before the purchase, he dismissed it as irrelevant, stating, "The fact that he had taken a physical tour was not something that I thought was new information." It was new information because *Obama had hidden it.* (Judicial Watch sent its investigators to Chicago to pull the real estate records for the Rezko-Obama properties.)

By the time the purchase went through in June 2005, Obama knew full well that Rezko was incredibly dirty. In March, Chicago officials accused Rezko of using a minority contractor at O'Hare International Airport as a front group for his own development firm; in May, he was subpoenaed by the Cook County court in an investigation of pay-for-play in the Blagojevich administration. While Obama admitted that he knew that Rezko was under investigation for corruption, he blew off such accusations. After all, this was Chicago. "I started reading the reports that were surfacing and—I'll be honest with you, that, on the couple of occasions that it came up, he gave me assurances that . . . he was not doing anything wrong. And that it wasn't a problem," Obama said. "And there's no doubt that, as things evolved, I became more concerned. But again, this is somebody who, in his interactions with me, had always been above board, and so, my instinct was to believe him."

But when the property finally closed on June 15, it did so for both Rezko and the Obamas. Somehow, Rita Rezko, Tony's wife and a member of the Cook County Employee Appeals Board, obtained a $500,000 loan on a $37,000 per year salary. The corporate attorney for several of Rezko's companies provided a large chunk of the down payment. Obama contradicted himself, saying that he didn't think that Rezko was "doing me a favor," and that there was "no connection between our purchase of the house, the price of the house and the purchase of the lot," but admitting that Rezko "perhaps thought this would strengthen our relationship, that he was doing me a favor."

There were questions about the Obamas' loan, too. In fact, in 2006, we filed ethics complaints with the FEC and the U.S. Senate Ethics Committee against Obama based on his acceptance of a 2005 mortgage loan at a below-market rate that was not available to the general consumer. The Illinois U.S. senator reportedly received a home loan of $1.32 million at a rate of 5.625 percent, although the average going rate on that day according to two different surveys was between 5.93 and 6 percent. Unlike what was reportedly available for the general consumer, this special below-market "super super jumbo" loan was secured without an origination fee or discount points. "It appears that due to his position as a United States Senator, Barack Obama received improper special treatment from Northern Trust resulting in an illicit 'gift' which has a value of almost $125,000 in interest savings," we wrote in our U.S. Senate ethics complaint. "Judicial Watch therefore respectfully requests a full investigation into whether the special Northern Trust mortgage received by Senator Barack Obama constitutes a gift that is prohibited by Senate ethics rules." In our FEC complaint, we also called for a full FEC investigation into whether the special mortgage was a disguised and illegal corporate campaign contribution to Senator Obama.

The lender, Northern Trust, has supported Barack Obama's political campaigns for elected office since 1990. According to the Center for Responsive Politics, cited by the *Washington Post*, Northern Trust employees have donated $71,000 to Obama campaigns. The Northern Trust political action committee gave $1,250 to Obama's 2004 campaign for Senate. Northern Trust vice president John O'Connell essentially admitted the company provided Obama preferential loan terms because of his position in the U.S. Senate. "*A person's occupation* and salary are two factors; I would expect those are two things we would take into consideration," O'Connell told the *Washington Post*. "This was a business proposition for us." That's our emphasis added, but why Obama's occupation should have mattered so much that he was able to get such a wonderful loan remains unexplored.

In the end, the FEC let Obama off the hook. The commission based its decision to exonerate Obama largely on the fact that Northern Trust claims it provided preferential terms to other "similarly situated borrowers" in addition to Obama. Northern Trust's new explanation was that eight of fourteen similarly situated borrowers (including Obama) received a mortgage loan discount. We do know for certain that Obama received a discounted mortgage; just because others received the same sweetheart deal doesn't clear up the matter. Look no further than Countrywide, which doled out corrupt mortgages to numerous public officials (such as Chris Dodd), to see the massive hole in that logic. So then-senator Obama, it can't be denied, received almost half a point off his mortgage simply because he was a United States senator.

There was something even worse lurking beneath the surface of the Obama real estate deal. In order to obtain the money to buy the lot, it seems that Rezko took a loan from the aforementioned Auchi worth approximately $3.5 million. That would be the same Auchi that Obama supposedly toasted at an event at Rezko's house. In 2004, Auchi came under criminal investigation for involvement in corrupt issuance of cell phone licenses in Iraq. Auchi's companies were involved in the Saddam Hussein–United Nations "oil for food" scandal, and his visa to the United States was revoked. (Auchi reportedly denies any participation in the "Oil for Food" scandal or any wrongdoing in the Iraqi cell phone controversy. And of course Auchi's lawyer denies that his client remembers meeting Obama.) As John Fund of the *Wall Street Journal* reported, "According to prosecutors, in November 2005 Rezko was able to get two government officials from Illinois to appeal to the State Department to get the visa restored. Asked if anyone in his office was involved in such an appeal, Mr. Obama told the *Chicago Sun-Times* last March, 'not that I know of.' FOIA requests to the State Department for any documents haven't been responded to for months." As Fund pointed out, "Some inquiries could be cleared up if the Obama campaign were forthcoming with key documents. . . . But the key data are still being withheld."³

Shortly after purchasing the property, the Obamas decided to build a fence between their property and Rezko's. They paid for all the legal work. Who paid for the erection of the fence? You guessed it: Tony Rezko.

Even as all of this shady dealing was going on, the Democratic-led Senate established a new regime of lobbying and ethics reforms. Who did they make into the point man for congressional ethics? You guessed it: Barack Obama.

Now Obama really stepped into it. Looking to buy up some of the land around the fence, Obama approached Rezko and asked to buy it. The parcel of land was worth approximately $40,500. But for some odd reason, Obama paid Rezko $104,500, more than twice what it was worth. Why would he do such a thing? By selling him the parcel of land, Rezko made his lot unbuildable. Said Obama,

> A larger lapse of judgment existed when it came to the strip of property. Because at that time, it became clear that Rezko was getting into bigger problems. And this was now a business transaction with him. And this is what I've referred to as a "boneheaded" move. But it is in the context of, somebody, again, that I had known for a long time, who I was now a neighbor with; who, frankly, I did not think was doing me a favor because I was paying a substantial amount of money, and he continued to have a developable piece of property. In retrospect, this was an error. And I've said so publicly and repeatedly.

If you're counting, that's now three separate boneheaded moves: the original purchase, the fence, and the parcel of land. Inquiring minds wonder: why would a United States senator give all that unnecessary cash to a campaign contributor under criminal investigation? Was Obama buying more than a piece of land?

During this period, Obama paid his landscaper to mow and garden Rezko's lot as well as his own property. Obama says it wasn't a lot of money: "[I] confess that I didn't look at it carefully. . . . I'm assuming a couple of thousand dollars. . . . We were probably paying a hundred to a couple of hundred dollars a month. I mean this is basically mowing a lawn and maybe trimming some brush. And, so, his half of it, I know that we actually got this reimbursed by the subsequent seller, or the subsequent owner. And so I can probably get you that figure. But I can't imagine that it's more than $1,000 or so." Let's take his upper estimate, $2,000 per month. Over the course of two years, we're talking almost $50,000. Finally, in 2006, Rezko was indicted for his corruption. A now-contrite Obama apologized for ever having dealt with Rezko on a business level—after reaping the rewards of the relationship, of course. "The mistake, by the way, was not just engaging in a transaction with Tony because he was having legal problems, the mistake was because he was a contributor and somebody who was involved in politics, and I should not have engaged in a business dealing with him in general," said Obama. "And I've acknowledged that, because it's raised the appearance of impropriety." Of course, it only took him approximately fourteen years to acknowledge that working so closely with Rezko was bad judgment. By contrast, he sat in Jeremiah Wright's pews for twenty years without so much as a second thought. Perhaps his learning curve was getting less steep.

(By the way, it was the shady Rezko real estate deal that first pinged Obama on the Judicial Watch anticorruption radar screen, all the way back in 2006. The Rezko deal earned Obama a "dishonorable mention" that year on our first-ever list of Washington's "Ten Most Wanted Corrupt Politicians." He's appeared on the Top Ten each year since.)

Here's how Obama summed up the Rezko scandal: "I think that the way [voters should view the Rezko relationship] is that I made a mistake in not seeing the potential conflicts of interest or appearances of impropriety. But they should see somebody who was not engaged in any wrongdoing, who did not in any way betray the public trust, who has maintained consistently high ethical standards and who they can trust."[4] The audacity of Obama to suggest that his behavior evidenced "consistently high ethical standards"! But with a cheerleading media and a hapless political opposition, only followers of Judicial Watch and a few other independent investigators would have known the full truth about Obama's burgeoning corruption.

That was the Rezko scandal that some people knew about. What most *don't* know was something even more troubling: Obama's relationship with Rezko also included Obama funneling government cash to his good buddy, campaign contributor, and real estate angel investor. The *Chicago Sun-Times* reported that Rezko, with Obama's help, snagged $43 million in government funding to renovate dozens of low-income housing structures he owned. As the *Sun-Times* reported, "As a state senator, Barack Obama wrote letters to city and state officials supporting his political patron Tony Rezko's successful bid to get more than $14 million from taxpayers to build apartments for senior citizens. The deal included $855,000 in development fees for Rezko and his partner, Allison S. Davis, Obama's former boss, according to records from the project, which was four blocks outside Obama's state Senate district. . . . The letters appear to contradict a statement last December from Obama, who told the *Chicago Tribune* that, in all the years he's known Rezko, 'I've never done any favors for him.' " Naturally, Obama's press secretary, Bill Burton, said that this "wasn't done as a favor for anyone." It was just in the best interest of the "people in the community who have benefited from the project."[5] There's only one problem with that explanation. Whatever Rezko did with the money, he apparently had no interest in fixing the properties, which were decrepit and beset with code violations. In fact, many of the tenants, who live in Obama's former state senate district, were forced to endure a brutal Chicago winter without any heat.

Rezko was destined to plague Obama later, when Obama was embroiled in the Blagojevich controversy. But Rezko was hardly Obama's only "appearance of impropriety." Barack Obama made a habit throughout his political career of working the nasty side of the tracks.

Obama's Pals

Obama's relationship with Tony Rezko was only the beginning. As an aspiring politico, the young Obama was quickly enmeshed in the famously corrupt politics of Chicago, working with machine politicians like the Daley family and Rod Blagojevich—as we'll detail soon. He also began working with allies at places like the Chicago Annenberg Challenge, staffed with radicals like former terrorist Bill Ayers. During the 2008 campaign, Obama attempted to shield as much of this as possible from public view.

It started with his sensitivity about his pastor and spiritual mentor, the radical Marxist Reverend Jeremiah Wright, pastor of Trinity United Church of Christ in Chicago. I like to think of Wright as Obama's "life coach." Wright blamed the United States for causing the 2001 terrorist attacks and damned America for treating blacks as less than human, creating a nightmare for his close friend Obama in March 2008 when the media exposed the inflammatory sermons that he regularly delivers. In fact, in a sermon delivered the Sunday after 9/11, Wright said: "We bombed Hiroshima, we bombed Nagasaki and we nuked far more than the thousands in New York and the Pentagon, and we never batted an eye." He added that the United States has "supported state terrorism against the Palestinians and black South Africans and now we are indignant because the stuff we have done overseas is brought back to our own front yards."

Although Wright and Obama have been close for two decades and Wright officiated the Obamas' marriage ceremony and baptized their children, Obama publicly denounced the veteran Baptist preacher and, after suggesting that he no more disavows Wright than his own poor "typically white" grandmother, distanced himself from his church. Obama also removed Wright as an advisor to his presidential campaign. But then Wright revealed that it was all a sham. He said Obama did not really denounce him and Obama didn't even distance himself from Wright's radical, anti-American views. Rather, the presidential candidate did what politicians do in order to appease the public: lie. Wright implied that his good buddy Obama still agreed with his anti-American, racist views but had to do what politicians do. Then Wright assured the press that if Obama gets elected, Wright would come after Obama to change existing U.S. policies. Wright also confirmed that Obama was still a member of his church and they were still quite close. The good reverend's story was vastly different than the presidential candidate's. Forced to address the controversy during a mid-April 2008 Democratic debate, Obama referred to Wright as "somebody who is associated to me that I have disowned."

Incidentally, Wright is also a huge admirer and ally of Louis Farrakhan, the renowned anti-Christian and anti-Semitic cult leader who endorsed Obama, calling him the "hope of the entire world." Wright actually honored Farrakhan with a prestigious award earlier in 2008, saying that the Nation of Islam leader "truly epitomizes greatness."

Obama, though, was most sensitive about revealing information regarding his relationship with Bill Ayers, the Weather Underground terrorist responsible for several bombings—and the same nice-sounding fellow who stated in the *New York Times* on 9/11 (coincidentally) that he didn't regret setting bombs and said he might do it all over again.

For years, Obama enjoyed a close and mutual relationship with Ayers. Ayers and his wife, a fellow Weather Underground terrorist, long supported and collaborated with Obama, donating money to his presidential campaign and hosting fund-raising events at their home. The Illinois senator and aging radical hung out in the same political and social circles, lived in the same Chicago neighborhood, and for years served on the board of a renowned Chicago nonprofit, the Chicago Annenberg Challenge. In fact, certain reports say that Ayers got Obama his board position at the Challenge. Obama, though, claimed that Ayers was merely "a guy who lives in my neighborhood."

But Obama's allies refused to reveal documents tying the senator to his terrorist pal. In an apparent cover-up, the University of Illinois at Chicago (UIC) refused to make public hundreds of files that document the Democratic presidential candidate's decades-long relationship with Ayers, professor at UIC. The school's library—named after Chicago's former longtime corrupt Democrat mayor Richard J. Daley—houses 132 boxes containing nearly one thousand folders of records relating to Obama's ties to Ayers, various radical organizations, and other questionable political allies. Stanley Kurtz, a senior fellow at the Ethics and Public Policy Center, tried to track down the documents, but was initially stonewalled.

After initially agreeing to make the files public, the school reneged, claiming that the mystery donor who provided the collection refuses to make the information public. The UIC professor in charge of the library's special collections department later provided a rather bizarre explanation for the sudden change of heart by saying that it has come to the school's attention that there is "restricted" material in the collection.

When the documents were finally released, Kurtz got a solid look at the depth and breadth of the Obama-Ayers relationship—and it became more and more clear why Obama wanted to hide the details. Kurtz wrote in the *Wall Street Journal*:

> From 1995 to 1999, [Obama] led an education foundation called the Chicago Annenberg Challenge (CAC), and remained on the board until 2001. The group poured more than $100 million into the hands of community organizers and radical education activists. The CAC was the brainchild of Bill Ayers. . . . CAC translated Mr. Ayers's radicalism into practice. Instead of funding schools directly, it required schools to affiliate with "external partners," which actually got the money. Proposals from groups focused on math/science achievement were turned down. Instead CAC disbursed money through various far-left community organizers, such as the Association of Community Organizations for Reform Now (or ACORN). Mr. Obama once conducted "leadership training" seminars with ACORN, and ACORN members also served as volunteers in Mr. Obama's early campaigns. External partners like the South Shore African Village Collaborative and the Dual Language Exchange focused more on political consciousness, Afrocentricity and bilingualism than traditional education.[6]

ACORN went on to play an enormous role in the Obama election effort. Although Kurtz uncovered the story, Obama's allies in the media downplayed it—as Rich Noyes of NewsBusters noted, out of 1,365 broadcast evening news stories about Obama prior to the close of the primary season, just two mentioned Ayers at all—and not a single network had run an in-depth report on the Ayers connection as of September 23, 2008.[7]

While Obama was serving as chairman of the Annenberg Challenge, the program designed by Ayers, Obama okayed a housing development project known as Cottage View Terrace, yielding $900,000 in developers' fees for Rezko and Obama's employer, Allison Davis. We also uncovered a document listing the number of community institutions involved with the Cottage View Terrace project, including the University of Chicago. At the time, Michelle Obama was working for the University of Chicago as associate dean of student services. She was in charge of developing the university's Community Service Center. The university wrote three letters in which it "enthusiastically" supported the project. We also found documents showing that another Obama associate, Valerie Jarrett—who would play a significant role in the Obama administration—was connected with Rezko. She served on the Board of Directors for the Fund for Community Redevelopment and Revitalization, an organization that worked with Rezko and Davis, and also voiced her support for other Rezko projects.

Ominously, the Obama team attempted to shut down Kurtz's reportage with basic community organizing intimidation tactics. When Kurtz appeared on the Milt Rosenberg radio show on WGN in Chicago, the Obama campaign tried to shut it down. Andy McCarthy of *National Review* reported that Obama had gotten his activists to overwhelm the show's phone lines in an attempt to stop Kurtz from putting his information out over the airwaves. In fact, Obama's official website put out talking points and gave out Rosenberg's studio phone number.[8] The campaign actually emailed Chicago residents and ripped Kurtz by name: "It is absolutely unacceptable that WGN would give a slimy character assassin like Kurtz time for his divisive, destructive ranting on our public airwaves. At the very least, they should offer sane, honest rebuttal to every one of Kurtz's lies," the email said, even though Rosenberg had attempted to get an Obama representative to appear with Kurtz. Even *Politico,* a typically liberal news outfit, said the email "marks a coordinated battle with the conservative media on a scale rarely seen from a political campaign."[9]

Obama's relationship through Annenberg with Ayers was only one indication of just how corrupt this aspiring president was. In his first three years in the U.S. Senate, Barack Obama requested hundreds of millions of dollars in earmarks for pet projects for his state of Illinois. But it was one particular earmark he obtained while serving as a state senator that earned our attention.

That earmark was a $100,000 grant obtained by Obama for a garden project in Englewood, Illinois, spearheaded by Obama's former campaign volunteer Kenny Smith. We uncovered documents that included all relevant correspondence between Smith, who runs the Chicago Better Housing Association, and the state of Illinois, the project application, the contract and a detailed budget.

There's only one problem. The "Englewood Botanical Garden" project never happened. In fact, according to the *Chicago Sun-Times,* which had been covering the story, "today the garden site is a mess of weeds, chunks of concrete and garbage." So if Smith didn't finish the garden project, what happened to all that money? The Illinois state attorney general announced an investigation. The *Sun-Times* continued: "state records obtained by the Sun-Times show $65,000 of the grant money went to the wife of Kenny B. Smith, the Obama 2000 congressional campaign volunteer who heads the Chicago Better Housing Association, which was in charge of the project for the blighted South Side neighborhood. Smith wrote another $20,000 in grant-related checks to K.D. Contractors, a construction company that his wife, Karen D. Smith, created five months after work on the garden was supposed to have begun, records show. K.D. is no longer in business."

When initially asked about the "Englewood Botanical Garden," Smith claimed he was never able to raise all the funds he needed to complete the project, but that the grant obtained by Obama on his behalf was spent properly on "underground site preparation." However, the contractor hired for that job, according to his recollection, was paid no more than $3,000 and claims all he did was clear a few trees. Obama and Smith's relationship goes back about ten years or so. The pair announced the project at a January 2000 press conference during Obama's failed bid to win a seat in the U.S. Congress. One report suggests that, after ten years, the garden was completed in 2011; we can find no information as to the status of the state investigation, which was probably just for show anyway.

The Botanical Garden signified that Obama was willing to use public office in order to direct cash to his friends—but it wasn't the only indicator. Obama helped secure a $25,000 grant in August 2000 for the Blue Gargoyle, an organization that was headed by Capers C. Funnye Jr., Michelle Obama's first cousin once removed. In July 2000, Obama helped secure a $100,000 grant for the Community of St. Sabina, a church headed by Father Michael Pfleger, a controversial and radical Catholic priest and Obama campaign contributor. Pfleger made news in March 2008 for mocking then–presidential candidate Hillary Clinton from the pulpit of Trinity United Church of Christ, formerly run by Obama's personal pastor the Reverend Jeremiah Wright. Similarly, in 2000, Obama gave a $75,000 grant to FORUM, run by Yesse Yehudah. Although Yehudah ran against Obama in a 1998 election, five people from FORUM donated $1,000 each to Obama's campaign after receiving the grant. FORUM also contributed another $5,000 to help pay Obama's debt after he failed to be elected to Congress in 2000. In 2002, the state sued Yehudah for failure to account for hundreds of thousands of dollars he received from Obama's grant. (He ended up settling the suit by paying $10,000 to charity.)

In 2000, after Obama lost his congressional race, he had dire financial problems: campaign debt and a virtually dead law practice. That's when a friend stepped in—a longtime political supporter named Robert Blackwell Jr. arranged an $8,000-per-month retainer for Obama to give legal advice to his firm, Electronic Knowledge Interchange. Blackwell's firm paid Obama over $112,000. Just a few months after Obama finished that lucrative financial arrangement, he sent a letter on his state senate letterhead to Illinois officials, asking them to send a $50,000 grant Blackwell's way, to another one of his companies, Killerspin. Eventually, Killerspin received in excess of $320,000 in state grants between 2002 and 2004. The *Los Angeles Times* reported, "The day after Obama wrote his letter urging the awarding of the state funds, Obama's U.S. Senate campaign received a $1,000 donation from Blackwell." The *Times* reported that the money was to subsidize the company's table tennis tournaments. David Axelrod, Obama's presidential campaign advisor, dismissed any connection out of hand, stating, "Any implication that Sen. Obama would risk an ethical breach in order to secure a small grant for a Ping-Pong tournament is nuts." But it's hardly nuts. It's business as usual in Chicago. And it certainly helps explain why Blackwell raised somewhere between $100,000 and $200,000 for Obama's presidential campaign.[10]

Obama actually built his record in the Illinois Senate on the back of corruption. Actually, Obama's entire record of cosponsored bills in the state senate came during his final year there, when Emil Jones Jr., the new Democratic senate majority leader, worked out an arrangement with Obama to toss him as much credit for bills as humanly possible. According to reporter Todd Spivak, Jones announced, "I'm gonna make me a U.S. Senator," and handpicked Obama. Writes Spivak, "Jones appointed Obama sponsor of virtually every high-profile piece of legislation, angering many rank-and-file state legislators who had more seniority than Obama and had spent years championing the bills." So what did Obama do in return? Once he got to the U.S. Senate, he drove more than $300 million in pet projects back to Illinois, including tens of millions specifically back to Jones's state senate district. As Jones said, "Some call it pork; I call it steak."[11]

Obama was happy to cash in his chips, too. After his election to the U.S. Senate, Obama bought over $50,000 in stock in companies whose investors included some of his biggest donors. As the *New York Times* reported, "One of the companies was a biotech concern that was starting to develop a drug to treat avian flu. In March 2005, two weeks after buying about $5,000 of its shares, Mr. Obama took the lead in a legislative push for more federal spending to battle the disease. The most recent financial disclosure form for Mr. Obama, an Illinois Democrat, also shows that he bought more than $50,000 in stock in a satellite communications business whose principal backers include four friends and donors who had raised more than $150,000 for his political committees." His defense was that Obama's broker bought the stocks without consulting him. If that's the case, why was Obama so eager to unload them for a net loss of $13,000? [12] Keep this stock transaction in mind, as the company will pop up again in these chronicles of the Obama administration.

The Broken Election

President Obama won the 2008 election. But he didn't do it without some help from his friends.

From the very beginning of the election cycle, Obama relied on a playbook that remains the chief threat to election integrity in the United States: find ineligible voters and have them vote. If possible, have them vote repeatedly. As veteran investigative journalist Kenneth Timmerman wrote at Newsmax, "Already in Iowa, the Obama campaign was breaking the rules, busing in supporters from neighboring states to vote illegally in the first contest in the primaries and physically intimidating Hillary supporters, [Hillary Clinton supporters] say." Lynette Long, a Hillary supporter who spent a good deal of time checking out the bizarre caucus and primary results that ended in Obama's nomination, said, "After studying the procedures and results from all 14 caucus states, interviewing dozens of witnesses, and reviewing hundreds of personal stories, my conclusion is that the Obama campaign willfully and intentionally defrauded the American public by systematically undermining the caucus process." Her evidence was publicly available: in Hawaii, Obama allies created fake ballots from Post-it notes and dumped them into the caucus buckets, meaning that when the ballots were tallied, there were more ballots than participants; in Nevada, Obama supporters flushed Hillary ballots down toilets and informed union voters that they could only vote if their names were listed as Obama supporters;

in Texas, over two thousand Clinton and Edwards supporters filed complaints, since the fraud was so blatant and obvious—Hillary won the Texas primary by a margin of four points, but lost the caucus by a margin of 13 points. As Timmerman writes:

> In caucus after caucus, Obama bused in supporters from out of state, intimidated elderly voters and women, and stole election packets so Hillary supporters couldn't vote. Thanks to these and other strong-arm tactics, Obama won victories in all but one of the caucuses, even in states such as Maine where Hillary had been leading by double digits in the polls. Obama's win in the caucuses, which were smaller events than the primaries and were run by the party, not the states, gave him the margin of victory he needed to win a razor-thin majority in the delegate count going into the Democratic National Convention.

One of Obama's chief allies in this effort was the Association of Community Organizations for Reform Now (ACORN). The Obama campaign shelled out over $800,000 to the ACORN network to help with voter turnout in the primaries. ACORN later came under investigation for allegations of severe voter registration fraud and other illegal activities; eventually its various fronts were defunded by Congress. In the 2008 election cycle, the ACORN operation submitted registration forms with false names like "Mickey Mouse," as well as the starting lineup of the Dallas Cowboys not once, but twice. "Fully 30 percent of the 1.3 million new voters ACORN claims to have registered this year are believed to be illegitimate," reported Timmerman. Of course, manipulating the voting process was nothing new to Obama—he won his first state senate seat by having his friends challenge nomination signatures submitted by candidates in order to get on the ballot.[13]

Just how corrupt was ACORN? Essentially, elements of the ACORN network had been on the federal dole for the better part of three decades, and they used all that taxpayer cash to elect their friends to Congress and the presidency. To put those 1.3 million new voters on the rolls, they spent some $16 million. The secretary of state of Michigan said in September 2008 that ACORN had turned in "a sizeable number of duplicate and fraudulent applications"; in Nevada, the secretary of state asked to raid ACORN's office, and the Clark County registrar of voters said there was an insane amount of fraud in the thousands of applications submitted weekly by ACORN; Ohio, Florida, New Mexico, and Missouri were all checking out ACORN's fraudulent activity. In Lake County, Indiana, at least 40 percent of the applications submitted for voter registration were fraudulent.

How close was Obama's relationship with ACORN? When he served on the Woods Fund in Chicago, he directed a steady stream of more than $200,000 to the group; he worked in 1992 with Project Vote, an ally that would soon become an official affiliate of ACORN; he served as a lawyer for ACORN in 1995.[14]

As with the connections involving Ayers, Annenberg, Wright, and Farrakhan, the mainstream media largely ignored Obama's connections with ACORN, which undermined the narrative of the Great Hope Machine emerging from a vast groundswell of spontaneous support. Election fraud lawyer Heather Heidelbaugh, who worked for the Pennsylvania Republican State Committee in a lawsuit against ACORN, said that the *New York Times* spiked stories concerning ACORN out of fear that it would hurt Obama's campaign. Heidelbaugh got her information from former ACORN worker Anita Moncrief, who apparently filled in *Times* reporter Stephanie Strom on the inside scoop with ACORN and Obama. As reported by Warner Todd Huston:

> "Upon learning this information," Heidelbaugh told the House Judiciary [S]ubcommittee [on the Constitution], "Ms. Strom reported to Ms. Moncrief that her editors at the *New York Times* wanted her to kill the story because, and I quote, 'it was a game changer.' " This prompted Representative James Sensenbrenner (R-WI) to blast the *Times*. "If true, the *New York Times* is showing once again that it is not an impartial observer of the political scene," said Sensenbrenner. "If they want to be a mouthpiece for the Democratic Party, they should put 'Barack Obama approves of this' in their newspaper."[15]

When Senator John McCain put the ACORN connection to Obama during one of the debates, Obama played dumb: "The only involvement I've had with ACORN was I represented them alongside the U.S. Justice Department in making Illinois implement a motor voter law that helped people get registered at DMVs. . . . ACORN is a community organization. Apparently what they've done is they were paying people to go out and register folks, and apparently some of the people who were out there didn't really register people, they just filled out a bunch of names. It had nothing to do with us. We were not involved." Just as with Ayers and Rezko, Obama simply told falsehoods to undermine any attempts to link him with his corrupt comrades. He reiterated his comments at the debate in a later interview: "Well, first of all my relationship with ACORN is pretty straightforward. It's probably 13 years ago when I was still practicing law, I represented ACORN and my partner in that investigation was the U.S. Justice Department in having Illinois implement what was called the motor voter law, to make sure people could go to DMV's and driver license facilities to get registered. It wasn't being implemented. That was my relationship and is my relationship to ACORN. There is an ACORN organization in Chicago. They've been active. As an elected official, I've had interactions with them. But, they're not advising my campaign. We've got the best voter registration in politics right now and we don't need ACORN's help." Except for the help for which his campaign paid ACORN $800,000 in his fight against Hillary Clinton for the Democratic presidential nomination.

This denial of his ACORN connection evidently was not in the talking points Obama used when he spoke directly to ACORN. "When I ran Project Vote, the voter registration drive in Illinois, ACORN was smack dab in the middle of it. Once I was elected there wasn't a campaign that ACORN worked on down in Springfield that I wasn't right there with you. Since I have been in the United States Senate I've been always a partner with ACORN as well. I've been fighting with ACORN, alongside ACORN, on issues you care about my entire career." And they would fight for him come 2008. After his election, the Obama administration would turn to ACORN to help with the U.S. Census—only this time, the plan was shut down thanks to our investigative work and the enterprising journalism of James O'Keefe, Hannah Giles, and the late Andrew Breitbart, who later exposed that ACORN activists were willing to help criminals avoid taxes.

Speaking of financial fraud, the Obama campaign was exposed as having been uninterested in following campaign finance laws that prohibited taking campaign donations from most foreign nationals. Obama raised thousands upon thousands of dollars from foreign nationals. For example, he reportedly took $33,000 from three brothers, Osama, Monir, and Hossam Edwan, from the Gaza Strip. Al Jazeera reported that Gazans had put together phone banks on behalf of Obama.[16] Obama also received cash from dozens of foreign countries, including many with significant terrorism problems and/or interests adverse to those of the United States.[17]

According to the *Washington Post*, which, incidentally, endorsed Senator Obama for the White House, the Obama campaign allowed donors to use prepaid credit cards, which are virtually untraceable and can allow for people to give more than campaign finance law allows or can conceal the donor's location:

> Faced with a huge influx of donations over the Internet, the campaign has also chosen not to use basic security measures to prevent potentially illegal or anonymous contributions from flowing into its accounts, aides acknowledged. Instead, the campaign is scrutinizing its books for improper donations after the money has been deposited. . . . In recent weeks, questionable contributions have created headaches for Obama's accounting team as it has tried to explain why campaign finance filings have included itemized donations from individuals using fake names, such as Es Esh or Doodad Pro.

If "basic security measures" exist to prevent fraudulent online donations, why did the Obama campaign choose not to employ them? Why employ a labor-intensive painstaking back-end review of all donations instead?

The answer is simple. The Obama campaign wanted to be able

to use as much money as possible, even if it was illegally obtained, and return only those funds they were forced to return. And they did not want to impose any delays on the processing of donations to the campaign, even if it meant that foreign nationals and other illegal donors were allowed to corrupt our electoral process. Obama's fund-raising system made a mockery of the reporting requirements of our campaign finance laws. The fact is that nearly half of Obama's campaign funds (amounting to hundreds of millions of dollars in donations) was obtained from sources that have yet to be made public. Unlike the McCain campaign, which published the names of all of its donors on its campaign Internet site, no matter how small the donation, the Obama campaign refused to disclose the names of those who donate in increments of $200 or less.

The Obama campaign played fast and loose with campaign finance laws. The FEC, however, did nothing. The Obama campaign never had its books seriously scrutinized.

Obama had help from some of his other friends, too. On election day 2008, a video journalist recorded members of the New Black Panther Party for Self-Defense standing outside a polling place in Philadelphia. One was brandishing a police-style baton weapon. "As I walked up, they closed ranks, next to each other," one witness told Fox News. "So I walked directly in between them, went inside and found the poll watchers. They said they'd been here for about an hour. And they told us not to come outside because a black man is going to win this election no matter what." When the witness came back outside, the Black Panther said, " 'We're tired of white supremacy' and he starts tapping the nightstick in his hand," the witness described. "At which point I said, 'OK, we're not going to get in a fist fight right here,' and I called the police." When one of the poll watchers asked the Panthers why they were there, one of the men responded, "Uh, security." The poll watcher said, "I think it might be a little intimidating that you have a stick in your hand. I am a concerned citizen, and I'm just worried that—" At that point, the Panther with the nightstick interrupted him and said, "So are we, and that's why we're here."

This shouldn't have come as a major surprise to anyone. The

day before the election, the New Black Panthers announced in a letter from Malik Shabazz, leader of the Black Lawyers for Justice and attorney for the party, that they would send people to the polls to intimidate voters. This is the same Shabazz who said two months after September 11, "If 3,000 people perished in the World Trade Center attacks and the Jewish population is 10 percent, you show me records of 300 Jewish people dying in the World Trade Center. . . . We're daring anyone to dispute its truth. They got their people out." The national field marshal for the New Black Panthers, Minister Najee Muhammad, announced on November 3, 2008:

> We will not allow some racists and other angry whites, who are upset over an impending Barack Obama presidential victory, to intimidate blacks at the polls. Most certainly, we cannot allow these racist forces to slaughter our babies or commit other acts of violence against the black population, nor our black president. . . . We must organize to counter and neutralize these threats using all means at our disposal. This is a great time for our people, and we must ensure that peace prevails for our people.

Uhuru Shakur, local chairman of the Atlanta chapter of the New Black Panthers, was even clearer:

> We love Barack Obama—he gives our people great hope and light for advancement. Every president America has had has been a white man. Now the black man must be given his time to rule. Obama is a man of justice and a leader who wants to do right. . . . We will be at the polls in the cities and counties in many states to ensure that the enemy does not sabotage the black vote, which was won through the blood of the martyrs of our people.[18]

Career civil rights attorneys in the Bush Justice Department originally filed a lawsuit against the New Black Panther Party for Self-Defense and several of its members following that Philadelphia incident. According to multiple witnesses, the members didn't just attempt to block access to the polling stations: they also harassed voters and hurled racial epithets. However, the Obama Justice Department ultimately overruled the recommendations of its own staff and dismissed the majority of the pending claims, even though the Panthers had not bothered to show up in court to contest the charges.

That didn't smell right to us, and we weren't the only ones—many major news outlets questioned the dropped charges. How was it possible for this administration to dismiss a clear-cut case of voter intimidation involving the use of weapons? Weren't voting rights important to the Obama Justice Department?

To find out what was really going on, we filed a FOIA request on May 29, 2009. That's when the rigmarole began. The Justice Department acknowledged receiving the request on June 18, 2009, but then referred the request to the Office of Information Policy (OIP) and the Civil Rights Division. On January 15, 2010, the OIP notified Judicial Watch that it would be responding to the request on behalf of the Offices of the Attorney General, the Deputy Attorney General, Associate Attorney General, Public Affairs, Legislative Affairs, Legal Policy, and Intergovernmental and Public Liaison. On January 15, the OIP also indicated that the Office of the Associate Attorney General found 135 pages of records responsive to Judicial Watch's request, but that all records would be withheld in full. On January 26, the OIP advised Judicial Watch that the Office of Public Affairs and Office of Legal Policy had completed their searches and found no responsive documents. On February 10, the Justice Department's Civil Rights Division indicated that after an extensive search it had located "numerous responsive records" but determined that "access to the majority of the records" should be denied. On March 26, the OIP indicated that the Office of Legislative Affairs and the Office of Intergovernmental and Public Liaison completed searches and found no documents.

With this kind of runaround, we were forced to file a lawsuit against the Justice Department. As it turns out, the department's September 15, 2010, index describing the documents and other information they did not want the public to see revealed that the two top political appointees at Justice were involved in the decision to dismiss the case. The documents showed a long email exchange between Assistant Deputy Attorney General Steve Rosenbaum and Deputy Associate Attorney General Sam Hirsch, a man described by *Slate* magazine as a "DC election lawyer who represents a lot of Democrats." In fact, there were eight email exchanges between these two characters, taking place on April 30, 2009, the day before the Justice Department reversed course and declined to pursue anything of substance in the Panther case. The index also showed documents that were being withheld in their entirety, including a series of internal emails between the highest political appointees inside the Justice Department, including former deputy attorney general David Ogden and Associate Attorney General Thomas Perrelli. The department had well over six hundred pages that the most "transparent" administration in history wanted to keep from the public.

This documentary record contradicted sworn testimony by Thomas Perez, assistant attorney general for the Civil Rights Division, who testified before the U.S. Commission on Civil Rights that no political leadership was involved in the Black Panthers decision. During that testimony, Perez denied that there was "any political leadership involved in the decision not to pursue this particular case any further." He said that the internal hubbub surrounding the case was only "a case of career people disagreeing with career people." This was a lie. The documents we uncovered showed that the Obama Justice Department's decision to drop the Black Panther case was certainly political and potentially corrupt, a major scandal for the Obama administration.

Congress and the U.S. Commission on Civil Rights were aghast at what we were able to uncover. The Commission on Civil Rights had been stonewalled in unprecedented (and lawless) fashion by the Justice Department. It was only through Judicial Watch's exemplary legal and investigative work that the independent government agency was able to discover key truths about the Obama gang's Black Panther lies. The commission's interim report acknowledges the unique value to Judicial Watch's transparency efforts:

While the [Justice] Department refused to provide a log or otherwise identify the documents it has withheld documents to the Commission, the FOIA suit by Judicial Watch could not be similarly ignored. Unlike with the demands of the Commission, the Department is not the sole arbiter of what may be withheld from public scrutiny in FOIA cases. Given that the demands of both the Commission and Judicial Watch were similar in nature, the only explanation for the difference in treatment is that the information sought by the Commission could be withheld without judicial scrutiny—especially given the Commission's superior claim to the actual documents and not just an index of withheld materials. It is difficult to attribute the Department's different treatment to anything but a desire to avoid serious scrutiny into its decision making and to prevent disclosure of the extent to which political appointees played a role in the case.[19]

Fights between the executive branch and agencies like the Commission on Civil Rights and Congress are often fundamentally political. Judicial Watch's fights are legal. We sometimes lose, but at least the government must present legal reasons in a court of law for withholding information. That is what our republic is about and that is what we mean by holding the government to account to the rule of law, rather than the rule of politics.

What was really going on behind the scenes in the Black Panther scandal? On October 22, 2010, the *Washington Post* reported, "Interviews and government documents reviewed by the *Washington Post* show that the [New Black Panther Party] case tapped into deep divisions within the Justice Department that persist today over whether the agency should focus on protecting historically oppressed minorities or enforce laws without regard to race."[20] J. Christian Adams, who had been a lawyer with the Civil Rights Division in Washington, said the charges were originally filed because "I thought, 'This is wrong, this is not supposed to happen in this country.' There are armed men in front of a polling place, and I need to find out if they violated the law, because in my mind there's a good chance that they did." When the charges were dismissed, said Adams, it was because the liberal appointees and bureaucrats at the Justice Department were philosophically opposed to pursuing cases against minorities infringing the voting rights of white Americans.

Three other Justice Department lawyers corroborated Adams's story, including longtime civil rights attorney Chris Coates, who told the U.S. Commission on Civil Rights, which conducted a year-long investigation of the Black Panther scandal, that at the department there is "a deep-seated opposition to the equal enforcement of the Voting Rights Act against racial minorities and for the protection of whites who have been discriminated against." Coates testified at some risk to himself, as he was still working for the Justice Department, and had served as chief of the Voting Rights Section. (Adams had resigned in order to be able to tell the truth to the public.) Under the Obama administration, Coates was moved out of his position and replaced by Obama appointees with a race-based view of the law. Unbelievably, we now need a civil rights investigation into the Civil Rights Division of the Justice Department.

Obama's other 2008 campaign allies included groups like the extremist Mexican group the National Council of La Raza, or the "National Council of the Race." Founded in 1968, the National Council of La Raza has somehow managed to carve out an image as a mainstream civil rights organization, but nothing could be further from the truth. It seems to be a public relations arm of the Mexican *reconquista* movement, which seeks to conquer the American Southwest—by force or by ballot box—and return it to Mexico. The organization aggressively lobbies for open borders and supports amnesty for the 12 million illegals currently residing in the United States. In 2007, we found out that La Raza supported the Academia Semillas del Pueblo, a Mexican separatist school in California. Your tax dollars have even been used to support the National Council of La Raza, which has received $30 million in federal grants since 1996.

In a 2007 speech to La Raza, Obama called for a "stop [to] the hateful rhetoric filling our airwaves—rhetoric that poisons our political discourse, degrades our democracy, and has no place in this great nation." He was, of course, attacking opponents of illegal immigration and altogether ignoring the racism of the "La Raza" movement, which is expressed in its very name and in other ideas, like turning the United States into a "bronze nation." La Raza would later cash in, as described below, on its support for Obama.

During the campaign, Obama didn't shy away from vindictively targeting his opponents, either. He had a long history of such vindictiveness, of course. It began early in his career, when he went after Alice Palmer, the communist-sympathizing incumbent in his state senate district. Palmer was actually a supporter of Obama and planned to hand off the baton to him when she decided to run for Congress. Then she lost her congressional race to Jesse Jackson Jr. So she decided to keep her state senate seat. That's when Obama leapt into action. In order to qualify for the ballot, candidates in Illinois have to gather a certain number of signatures. Obama sent his aides to the courthouse to audit Palmer's signatures and try to get her knocked off the ballot. He succeeded, and got his political career jump-started by backstabbing one of his first supporters. One might say that that's just the nature of politics—but it also is a mark of a man who is tempted to do whatever it take to obtain power.

During the 2008 election cycle, America got its first look at the Obama "enemies list." His allies activated almost immediately upon his nomination to attack anyone who did not agree with the Obama agenda. According to the August 8, 2008, edition of the *New York Times*, Accountable America, a liberal group, planned to send a letter "to confront donors to conservative groups, hoping to create a chilling effect that will dry up contributions. . . . The warning letter is intended as a first step, alerting donors who might be considering giving to right-wing groups to a variety of potential dangers, including legal trouble, public exposure and watchdog groups digging through their lives. The group is also hoping to be able to respond if an outside conservative group broadcasts a television advertisement attacking Senator Barack Obama, or another Democratic candidate, by running commercials exposing the donors behind the advertisements."[21]

Attempts to intimidate individuals from participating in the presidential campaign can be a violation of federal law. A key federal civil rights law, popularly known as the Ku Klux Klan Act, may be applicable if "two or more persons conspire to prevent by force, intimidation, or threat, any citizen who is lawfully entitled to vote, from giving his support or advocacy in a legal manner, toward or in favor of the election of any lawfully qualified person as an elector for President or Vice President, or as a Member of Congress of the United States; or to injure any citizen in person or property on account of such support or advocacy" (42 U.S.C. § 1985[3]). The outrageous intimidation tactics would have had Nixon squirming, but Obama's lapdog media seemed uninterested in this assault on fundamental First Amendment rights.

The most obvious entry on the Obama "enemies list" was an unassuming Ohio man named Samuel Joseph Wurzelbacher. On October 12, 2008, Wurzelbacher was in his yard playing football with his son when Barack Obama and his campaign entourage approached, filming Obama's interactions with the public. As a result, Wurzelbacher, an employee of a small plumbing business, was able to ask Obama about the impact of his tax policy on small business owners. Obama's answer became a national hot-button topic: "My attitude is that if the economy's good for folks from the bottom up, it's gonna be good for everybody. If you've got a plumbing business, you're gonna be better off if you've got a whole bunch of customers who can afford to hire you, and right now everybody's so pinched that business is bad for everybody and I think when you spread the wealth around, it's good for everybody." In the next debate, Republican candidate Senator John McCain (R-AZ) cited Wurzelbacher as "Joe the Plumber," and soon Wurzelbacher was a household name.

The Obama campaign obviously would have preferred that Obama's socialist-style philosophy had never been exposed by Wurzelbacher.

As a result of his interaction with Obama, three officials of the state of Ohio instructed state employees to access confidential government databases for information regarding Wurzelbacher. Those employees were Helen Jones-Kelley, Fred Williams, and Doug Thompson, the three highest-ranking employees of the Ohio Department of Job and Family Services at the time of the transgression. All three were Democrats. Jones-Kelley said that she authorized the search because "[g]iven our understanding that Mr. Wurzel-bacher had publicly indicated that he had the means to purchase a substantial business enterprise, ODJFS, consistent with past departmental practice, checked confidential databases to make sure that if Mr. Wurzelbacher did owe child support, or unemployment compensation taxes, or was receiving public assistance, appropriate action was being taken. The result of those checks have never been publicly shared." A subsequent investigation by the office of the state's inspector general concluded that there was "no legitimate agency function or purpose for checking on [Wurzelbacher's] name through the [confidential databases] or for authorizing these searches." Judicial Watch agreed to represent Wurzelbacher in a civil suit claiming that the searches were a violation of his constitutional rights. While Joe ultimately did not prevail in his lawsuit, the search of Joe Wurzelbacher's confidential records is yet another example of Obama allies working to take down his political adversaries, no matter their level of political involvement.

So, for asking a simple question of a political candidate, Joe was then subjected to retaliation by Obama supporters who were officials of the state of Ohio. And what did then–Ohio attorney general Richard Cordray, the state's highest law enforcement officer, do about this criminal act? Absolutely nothing.

But when Judicial Watch sued the state employees on Joe's behalf, Cordray suddenly sprang into action . . . and came to the defense of the lawbreakers! Ohio's Office of the Inspector General said that the Ohio employees committed a "wrongful act" and misused state resources. Not a problem, according to Cordray. Cordray has been rewarded for his cover-up work with an unconstitutional "recess" appointment to run the new federal Consumer Financial Protection Bureau (CFPB).

Throughout his campaign, retaliation was the tactic the Obama team used most frequently for its political opponents. After the *New York Post*, *Dallas Morning News*, and *Washington Times* endorsed McCain for the presidency, Obama booted their reporters from the campaign bus, instead granting access to *Jet* and *Ebony* magazines, two African-American magazines that were bastions of

Obama propaganda throughout the campaign. During the campaign, Obama asked the Justice Department to go after the backers of his critics and then warned station managers that they could face legal liability for running certain ads that criticized Obama. Obama's spokesman said that Obama supporters had sent some 93,000 emails to the stations airing the ads.[22]

A few days after Obama took office, he attacked Rush Limbaugh directly while speaking with congressional Republicans. He assigned Shauna Daly to the White House Counsel's Office—the same Shauna Daly who had virtually no legal experience but who was an opposition researcher for Democratic political campaigns. After a month at the White House, Daly headed back to DNC headquarters. Obama's scorn for his political opponents is no secret, but his misuse of White House resources is. And it started on the day he entered office.

5.

OBAMA'S PICKS

The Obama administration became a morass of corruption and obfuscation. From the time that Senator Obama entered federal office and up until his election to the presidency, we worked ceaselessly to expose his corrupt record when the mainstream media refused to do so. Once he took office, we certainly had no intention of allowing Barack Obama to turn the White House into a Chicago-style political operation.

Unfortunately, that's precisely what Obama intended to do.

Since he is a product of one of the most corrupt political cultures in America, it should come as no surprise that Obama's presidential campaign had some of the ethical trimmings of a Chicago ward election. It was marked with enormous corruption issues, ranging from its alliance with the ACORN "voter registration" and "get out the vote" efforts to its acceptance of untraceable and potentially illegal online contributions. There were Obama's questionable dealings with convicted felon Tony Rezko and unrepentant terrorist Bill Ayers, his sweetheart mortgage loans, his stock dealings and related "earmark" votes in the U.S. Senate, and his missing or nonexistent official papers from his years in the Illinois Senate.

Barack Obama promised to bring "change" to Washington. Most Americans thought he was talking about a new spirit of honesty, integrity, and openness. What he *really* meant is that he was about to change Washington, D.C., into his personal reconstitution of

Chicago, complete with dictatorially appointed czars and corrupt bureaucrats with a history of secret manipulation.

It started with his decision not to follow his own executive order effectively banning lobbyists from serving in his administration. Barely a day later, Obama turned his much ballyhooed antilobbyist initiative into an absolute joke by naming William Lynn III, the former top lobbyist for Raytheon, to the position of deputy secretary of defense, the number-two position at the Defense Department.

The executive order's section titled "Revolving Door Ban" clearly states: "If I was a registered lobbyist within the 2 years before the date of my appointment, in addition to abiding by the limitations of paragraph 2, I will not for a period of 2 years after the date of my appointment . . . seek or accept employment with any executive agency that I lobbied within the 2 years before the date of my appointment." Clearly, Lynn as the top lobbyist for a major defense contractor has lobbied the Defense Department heavily over the last two years. As the *Washington Post* put it: "Lynn . . . lobbied the Pentagon on so many Raytheon projects—acquisitions policy, space, intelligence and command and control, among others—that it might be hard to find an area within the department that was untouched by his previous work."[1]

So how did Obama get around his own executive order? Obama calls it a "waiver." We call it loophole. Sneaked into his ethics pledge—which the Obama administration hailed as the most sweeping ethics rules in American history—is a disclaimer that provides that the administration "may grant to any current or former appointee a written waiver of any restrictions contained in the pledge" if it is in the "public interest." Only in Washington could one come up with an act called an "ethics waiver." How can you "waive" ethics! The Obama White House can tell you. By our count, at least forty "ethics waivers" have been issued by the White House or agencies of the Obama administration.

In other words, the pledge isn't worth the paper it's written on. It can be violated at will by President Obama any time he sees fit. And, in fact, according to *Politico*, the pledge has been violated at least a dozen times. *Politico* includes a list of the "Big 12," which includes Eric Holder, Obama's pick for attorney general, and Cecilia Muñoz, who lobbied for the radical Chicano organization National Council of La Raza. She served as Obama's White House director of intergovernmental affairs, before recently being elevated to run Obama's Domestic Policy Council.[2] That's right, the antilobbyist Obama's chief domestic policy advisor is a former lobbyist!

Muñoz is a perfect example of why Obama put the lobbyist ban in place to begin with. La Raza benefited handsomely from Muñoz's White House position. Government cash to La Raza more than doubled the year Muñoz joined the White House, from $4.1 million to $11 million. Not surprisingly, a big chunk of the money (60 percent) came from the Department of Labor, which is headed by a former California congresswoman (Hilda Solis) with close ties to the La Raza movement.

The "lobbyist ban that isn't a lobbyist ban" shows the silliness of the whole idea. Banning lobbyists does little to change the fundamental problem of big government encouraging rent-seeking and corruption. President Obama could address the problem of the undue special influence in Washington by scaling back the size of the federal government rather than increasing the federal leviathan to a scale barely imaginable. But he had no intention of doing that, so it came as no surprise when he began stacking his administration with compromised officials, many of them with deep roots in the Clinton administration.

Chief of Staff: Rahm Emanuel

Talk about getting off on the wrong foot! Barack Obama's first decision as president-elect was to select a veteran Chicago politician and corrupt Clinton attack dog to serve as his chief of staff. Born in Chicago, Congressman Rahm Emanuel served as President Clinton's chief moneyman in 1992, a campaign that was corrupted by foreign money. Emanuel then became a Clinton White House aide who misused his position to help cover for the Clinton fund-raising and Lewinsky scandals. Emanuel defended the "worst of the worst" Clinton scandals. Indeed, it was his very public role in the Lewinsky scandal that cemented his reputation as Clinton's fiercest defender and apologist. Emanuel denied the Clinton-Lewinsky affair on national television and later, when there was nothing left to deny, he was put in charge of "managing the situation." In short, Emanuel attacked and sought to thwart a federal criminal investigations for the despicable Clinton team.

Nicknamed "Rahmbo" for his ferociously combative style, Emanuel is arrogant, profane, and vindictive. According to one story repeated in the London *Telegraph*, "amid a discussion over a celebratory dinner about which political figures had earned [President Clinton's] enmity, Mr. Emanuel became so enraged that he grabbed a steak knife, stood up and began reciting a list of names, plunging the knife into the table and shouting 'Dead! Dead! Dead!' after each one."[3] We independently confirmed this story.

Emanuel turned for a time to investment banking after the Clinton administration, making a fortune for himself—reportedly $18 million in just three years. During that time he also served on the board of directors for Freddie Mac, just as the company was involved in fraudulent activity.

At first, it seemed that Emanuel served on the board of the mortgage-lending giant for fourteen months without making any noticeable mark, while at the same time reaping huge financial rewards. That was suspicious. Why did the normally obtrusive Emanuel keep his lips zipped when presented with an illegal accounting scheme designed to defraud Freddie Mac investors? The *Chicago Tribune* found out the answer: "Before its portfolio of bad loans helped trigger the current housing crisis, mortgage giant Freddie Mac was the focus of a major accounting scandal that led to a management shake-up, huge fines and scalding condemnation of passive directors by a top federal regulator. One of those allegedly asleep-at-the-switch board members was Chicago's Rahm Emanuel—now chief of staff to President Barack Obama—who made at least $320,000 for a 14-month stint at Freddie Mac that required little effort."[4]

"Little effort" was an understatement. The Freddie Mac board does most of its work in committees. According to the *Tribune*, there is no documented evidence Emanuel even served on a committee.

But it gets worse.

On Emanuel's watch, Freddie Mac hatched an accounting scheme—reviewed by the board—to defraud investors by artificially inflating the value of the company in order to pay out big bonuses to executives. The company was also slapped with a $3.8 million fine by the Federal Election Commission for using corporate funds to bankroll political fund-raisers. In fact, after Emanuel finished his stint at Freddie, the company held one of these tainted fund-raisers on his behalf! In 2002, Emanuel returned to politics, but this time as a candidate. He won election to Congress in Illinois's 5th District.

Essentially, the man Obama tapped to lead his national campaign for bipartisanship, unity, and integrity was a scandal-ridden Clinton apologist and former Freddie Mac board member best known for his violent and vindictive political style. Appropriately, he is now mayor of Chicago.

Special Advisor: Valerie Jarrett

Perhaps the personality with whom Obama is closest is his longtime confidante Valerie Jarrett. Characterized as "the other side of Barack Obama's brain" by CBS News, Jarrett first met the Obamas seventeen years ago when she offered Michelle Obama a job.

We obtained documents linking Jarrett to a series of real estate scandals, including several housing projects operated by Tony Rezko and Allison Davis, Obama's former boss. Jarrett was a member of the Board of Directors for the Woodlawn Preservation and Investment Corporation along with several Davis and Rezko associates, as well as the Fund for Community Redevelopment and Revitalization, an organization that worked with Rezko and Davis. As mentioned previously, according to press reports, housing projects operated by Davis and Rezko have been substandard and beset with code violations. The *Chicago Sun-Times* reported that one Rezko-managed housing project was "riddled with problems—including squalid living conditions . . . lack of heat, squatters and drug dealers."

As chief executive officer of the Habitat Company, Jarrett also managed a controversial housing project located in Obama's former state senate district called Grove Parc Plaza. According to the *Boston Globe* the housing complex was considered "uninhabitable by unfixed problems, such as collapsed roofs and fire damage. . . . In 2006, federal inspectors graded the condition of the complex an 11 on a 100-point scale—a score so bad the buildings now face demolition." Jarrett refused to comment to the *Globe* on the conditions of the complex.

Like Obama, Jarrett was a product of the corrupt Chicago political machine. It's no stretch to say she was a slumlord. We had real concerns about Jarrett's ethics—and those concerns were well justified. Specifically, Jarrett successfully petitioned the president to lift a restriction barring lobbyists from meeting with government officials with regard to economic stimulus projects.[5]

Jarrett served as the administration's leading promoter in the failed attempt to bring the 2016 Olympics to Chicago.[6] Her work on the Olympics bid would have violated Obama's own policy against lobbyists, had fellow czar Norm Eisen (aka the former Ethics Czar) not granted her an "ethics waiver." The waiver exempted her from the restrictions of President Obama's ethics pledge, even though she personally led the bid before entering the White House.[7]

Though Chicago failed in its bid for the 2016 Olympics, the full extent of Valerie Jarrett and the administration's involvement in the bid is still largely unknown. In September 2009, Judicial Watch launched an investigation into the administration's involvement, filing a Freedom of Information Act request with Chicago mayor Richard Daley's office. However, the mayor's office failed to provide a timely response to the request. Due to this noncompliance with the Freedom of Information Act, Judicial Watch was forced to file suit against Daley's office to obtain the requested records.[8]

Presumably at Jarrett's urging, the Obamas took an extraordinary excursion to Copenhagen, Denmark, to visit the International Olympics Committee. Their goal was to persuade the committee to choose Chicago for the next Olympics games. (It was the first time a sitting president was present for an Olympics vote. They usually have better things to do.)

Michelle Obama reportedly made an "impassioned" plea to the International Olympics Committee, but it fell flat. Chicago did not make it past the first round of voting and the Obamas came home empty-handed, and utterly embarrassed.

And after more than two years of Obama administration stonewalling, we finally uncovered that Barack and Michelle Obama's embarrassing junket to Copenhagen cost taxpayers in excess of $467,175. That egregious sum doesn't even include the costs associated with the taxpayer-funded aircrafts for the trips—two Boeing 747s and several air force cargo planes.[9]

White House Counsel: Greg Craig

Obama was clearly stacking his cabinet with Chicago cronies and Clinton political hit men. It was no shock, therefore, that Obama decided to hire Clinton impeachment lawyer and controversial Washington, D.C., attorney Greg Craig as White House counsel. Many thought that Obama had beaten the Clinton political machine. Instead, he embraced it.

Given Craig's defense of Bill Clinton's lies and obstruction of justice, it was pretty obvious that Obama wanted the sort of legal advice that allowed him to distinguish between different meanings of *is*. Not only did Craig defend the worst of the worst of the Clinton scandals, but he also defended the violent government raid that delivered Elian Gonzalez back to Castro's Cuba in 2000. Greg was working with the communist Cuban government during the Elian affair.

Craig defended Ted Kennedy during the trial of Kennedy's nephew William Kennedy Smith in the infamous Palm Beach rape case. He also defended Ronald Reagan's would-be assassin John Hinckley Jr. (Craig helped piece together Hinckley's insanity defense.) He's also represented a war criminal or two. That's quite a record. Unbelievably, the Bush State Department hired Craig to help defend itself against legal claims pursued by Judicial Watch on behalf of a Clinton-era State Department official who blew the whistle on UN corruption. (The litigation ended in settlement.)

If Obama cared about government integrity, he would never have picked Craig in the first place, a lawyer whose key experience seemed to be the defending of government misconduct.

Craig, unsurprisingly, was a failure in the job. He was hung out to dry by fellow leftists in the Obama administration for mishandling the effort to close the Guantanamo Bay terrorist detention facility. He was pushed out of the Obama White House, resigning in January 2010.

Attorney General: Eric Holder

Eric Holder, former Janet Reno deputy, was Obama's pick for attorney general. He could hardy have chosen someone worse for the job. While Obama had promised voters that he would bring change to Washington, he was truly interested only in centralizing power to himself.

Holder derailed investigations of the Clinton fund-raising scandals while at Justice. Holder was also involved in the Elian Gonzalez raid. As deputy attorney general under the craven Reno, he participated in planning the raid that not only traumatized Elian, then six years old, but also led to the violent abuse of peaceful protesters outside the home of Elian's Miami relatives. The protesters, many of them older women, were simply praying the rosary when they were gassed and beaten by heavily armed government agents. We sued Reno and Holder on behalf of the victims.

Remember all of those last-minute, controversial pardons issued by President Clinton in the waning days of his administration? Guess who was in charge of approving the list, which included convicted felons who had paid large sums of cash to the Clintons. That's right: Eric Holder. He was the acting attorney general at the time. That list, by the way, included two Weather Underground terrorists and the infamous fugitive financier Marc Rich, whose ex-wife made substantial contributions to the Clintons. Holder not only personally helped Rich get the pardon, but he also upended the rule of law by undermining Justice Department procedures put in place to protect the pardon process from abuse.

His record is dismal and includes support for commutations for members of FALN, a Puerto Rican terrorist organization. On August 11, 1999, Clinton commuted the sentences of sixteen terrorists from the group, which had ignited 120 bombs in the United States. Those whose sentences were commuted had been involved in sedition and conspiracy. As the *New York Post* reported, a secret FBI report showed that "[m]any of the FALN terrorists offered clemency—including Dylcia Pagan, the wife of FALN master bombmaker William Morales—were linked to bomb factories in the Midwest, New York and New Jersey during the height of the FALN's deadly reign of terror." [10]

Outsiders tied the commutations to the fact that Hillary was running for Senate from New York at the time and desperately wanted more votes from the Puerto Rican community. Former NYPD detectives Rich Pastorella and Anthony Senft, who were injured by FALN bombs, ripped the decision before the Senate. Pastorella said, "President Clinton has sent terrorists a message that the law enforcement community is expendable, and terrorists will not be pursued to the ends of the earth." Added Senft, "Clinton's actions tell would-be terrorists around the world that terrorism against the United States and its people is an acceptable form of demonstrating their political ideology."

Congressional Republicans quickly issued subpoenas for the records surrounding the clemency decision and subpoenaed Janet Reno and deputy White House counsel Cheryl Mills. In typical Clintonian fashion, the Justice Department—helped in no small measure by Eric Holder—barred the FBI from testifying before the Senate on the decision. Acting Assistant Attorney General Jon Jennings sent a letter to Senate Foreign Relations subcommittee chairman Senator Paul Coverdell (R-GA) stating, "We cannot authorize their appearance at tomorrow's hearing. . . . In light of . . . the fact that the hearing may, in significant part, address the exercise of an exclusive presidential prerogative, we are carefully reviewing this matter and consulting with the White House regarding how most appropriately to proceed."[11] The Senate condemned the commutations 95–2 and the House did the same, 311–42. Clinton, naturally, cited executive privilege in refusing to turn over relevant documents to the House Committee on Government Reform.[12]

Just how involved was Holder in the FALN scandal? He was deeply involved. According to the *Los Angeles Times,* "Attorney general nominee Eric H. Holder Jr. repeatedly pushed some of his subordinates at the Clinton Justice Department to drop their opposition to a controversial 1999 grant of clemency to 16 members of two violent Puerto Rican nationalist organizations, according to interviews and documents." Holder ordered his staff at Justice's Office of the Pardon Attorney to dump the first report, which recommended against commutations, in favor of one recommending clemency. When the pardon attorney, Roger Adams, tried to stop Holder from doing that, Holder's chief of staff told Adams to write an "options memo" designed to be agnostic on the question of commutation. "I remember this well, because it was such a big deal to consider clemency for a group of people convicted of such heinous crimes," Adams told the *Times.* Adams told Holder of his "strong opposition to any clemency in several internal memos and a draft report recommending denial" and in a personal meeting. Holder wouldn't accept Adams's opinion, said Adams. Nick Shapiro, a spokesman for Obama's transition team, admitted that Holder was involved: "Eric Holder carefully reviewed the FALN clemency request, weighed the positions of both sides, including law enforcement, and concluded that the sentences of up to 90 years imposed on these prisoners was disproportionate to other federal and state sentences. After reaching that conclusion, he directed his subordinates at the department to draft a memo outlining several options, including how such a commutation could be structured to reflect the seriousness of these crimes and to take account of the lengthy time the prisoners had already served."[13]

As far as Pardongate went, Holder admitted he should have

handled the Rich pardon differently. As I told Politico when I found out that Holder had been appointed, Holder "admits he's on the wrong side of an issue that ruptured Washington at the last day of the Clinton administration, and he gets a promotion?" Now Holder would be the highest law enforcement officer in the land. Holder's appointment suggested that the Obama administration would be like some bad horror movie sequel, *The Clinton Administration, Part III*.

We sent a letter to the members of the Senate Judiciary Committee and published a full-page advertisement in the *Washington Times* raising questions about Holder's corrupt record. "Mr. Holder's record demonstrates a willingness to bend the law in order to protect his political patrons. On his watch at the Clinton Justice Department, the pardon process was upended and corrupted by a 'pay to play' mentality," we wrote in the letter. "This undermined, in the least, the appearance of the fair administration of justice by the Justice Department. Mr. Holder is the wrong person to head the Department of Justice." "Judicial Watch, America's leading government watchdog organization, calls upon the members of the U.S. Senate Committee on the Judiciary to challenge Mr. Holder on . . . questions which relate to his fitness to serve as the nation's chief law enforcement officer," the advertisement stated.

That sort of corruption is frightening. Corrupt pardons for terrorists may not have bothered Obama given his close relationship with Bill Ayers and company. But, as we'll see, it certainly hurt the American people.

Secretary of Health and Human Services: Tom Daschle

Obama wasn't done picking former bad actors for his brand-new administration. For secretary of health and human services, Obama picked out someone with deep potential conflicts of interest: Senator Tom Daschle. "President-elect Barack Obama's selection of former Senator Tom Daschle for secretary of health and human services posed new questions on Wednesday about how broadly the new administration would apply Mr. Obama's campaign promises to limit potential conflicts of interest among his appointees," reported the *New York Times*. "At issue is Mr. Daschle's work since leaving the Senate four years ago as a board member of the Mayo Clinic and a highly paid adviser to health care clients at the law and lobbying firm Alston & Bird. In a detailed list of campaign promises, Mr. Obama pledged that 'no political appointees in an Obama administration will be permitted to work on regulations or contracts directly and substantially related to their prior employer for two years.' "[14] In the years in which Daschle was out of Congress, he earned over $5 million.

Daschle was charged with pushing through Obama's planned health-care system overhaul, which would most certainly have an impact on all of the industries served by Daschle. Daschle wouldn't have recused himself from leading the charge for health-care reform. On the contrary—he would have dealt directly with the very group of folks for whom he had been working.

In addition to Daschle's personal conflicts of interest, there was also the matter of his wife, Linda Daschle, who has been a lobbyist for many years. As one report noted, "One area of [Tom Daschle's] review will include the lobbying connections of his wife, Linda Hall Daschle, who has worked mostly on behalf of airline-related companies over the years." Following the terror attacks of 9/11, by the way, we investigated Tom and Linda Daschle for their role in selecting faulty bomb-detecting equipment for the airline industry. We also raised ethics questions about Mrs. Daschle's lobbying of the Senate while her husband was in office.

Shortly after selecting Daschle, Obama was forced to dump him when it broke that Daschle had failed to pay his taxes. Daschle had to pay over $100,000 in back taxes and interest the same month as his nomination for using a car and driver without paying taxes on it. Daschle's spokeswoman said that he thought the car service was a "generous offer from a friend," and only later figured out that it was reportable income. Despite these revelations, Senate Majority Leader Harry Reid's spokesman was confident that Daschle would survive the nomination process: "Senator Daschle will be confirmed as Secretary of Health and Human Services. He has a long and distinguished career and record in public service and is the best person to help reform health care in this country. Senator Reid looks forward to a swift hearing and is confident Daschle will be confirmed." [15]

Not so much. On February 3, 2009, Daschle withdrew his nomination, saying he wouldn't have had the "full faith of Congress and the American people." File that one under "you can say that again." "This morning, Tom Daschle asked me to withdraw his nomination for Secretary of Health and Human Services," President Obama said in a statement. "I accept his decision with sadness and regret." This came a mere two hours after Nancy Killefer, Obama's pick for the made-up position of "chief performance officer," pulled her name from contention because she had a tax issue in Washington—she didn't pay employment taxes for a house cleaner. "I recognize that your agenda and the duties facing your Chief Performance Officer are urgent," Killefer wrote to Obama. "I have also come to realize in the current environment that my personal tax issue of DC Unemployment tax could be used to create exactly the kind of distraction and delay those duties must avoid." Obama accepted her withdrawal, too. [16]

As Daschle's replacement, Obama settled on Kathleen Sebelius, governor of Kansas. She turned out to be just as craven as the rest of the Obama administration, as America soon found out.

Secretary of State: Hillary Clinton

Hillary was one of the most scandal-ridden politicians in history, and certainly the most scandal-ridden First Lady. Hillary's political operators sought to destroy the lives of women who had the courage to come forward and publicly disclose the abuse they suffered at the hands of Bill Clinton, all part of Hillary Clinton's "slash and burn" campaign used against anyone who dared to cross them; she failed to report a $2 million campaign contribution in the form of a star-studded Hollywood fund-raiser dedicated to her husband, a failure for which her national finance director in the 2000 campaign was indicted and her campaign finance operation was fined by the FEC. That doesn't even mention her attempts to funnel cash to her brothers, the pardoning of terrorists, Whitewater, paid sleepovers in the Lincoln Bedroom, and stealing the White House furniture.

With specific relevance to her new job as secretary of state, there were also the serious conflicts of interest involving Bill Clinton, who has become something of an international sensation since leaving the White House, brokering international business deals and reaping huge fees for foreign speaking engagements. Even the longtime Clinton media ally CNN reported that Bill Clinton's "complicated global business interests could present future conflicts of interest that result in unneeded headaches for the incoming commander-in-chief."

Hillary Clinton is ethically challenged. Her husband is ethically challenged. Has any other secretary of state nominee been the subject of a grand jury criminal investigation? From their days in the White House to the present day, the Clintons have consistently abused their public office for personal and political gain.

We believe that Obama offered Hillary the secretary of state slot at the Democratic National Convention to avoid a floor fight. It may have served him politically, but the public suffered the consequences. In putting forward Hillary, Obama took full ownership of the Clinton scandals. The vetting of Hillary seems to have been run by John Podesta (her husband's former chief of staff) and Cheryl Mills (the ethically challenged lawyer who served as Clinton White House counsel).

Judicial Watch pointed out that Hillary was constitutionally ineligible for the office she held, and we even filed a lawsuit against her on behalf of U.S. Foreign Service officer and State Department employee David C. Rodearmel. Our argument was that Rodearmel could not be compelled to serve under the former U.S. senator, as it would violate the oath he took as a Foreign Service officer in 1991 to "support and defend" and "bear true faith and allegiance" to the Constitution of the United States.

Our case for Hillary's constitutional ineligibility sprang from her position in the Senate. The U.S. Constitution prohibited Clinton from serving as secretary of state until 2013, when her second term in the U.S. Senate expires.

Here's the constitutional issue at play: under the "emoluments" or "ineligibility" clause of the U.S. Constitution, no member of Congress can be appointed to a civilian position within the U.S. government if the "emoluments" of the position, such as the salary or benefits paid to whoever occupies the office, increased during the term for which the senator or representative was elected. Specifically, Article I, section 6 of the U.S. Constitution provides, "No Senator or Representative shall, during the Time for which he was elected, be appointed to any civil Office under the Authority of the United States which shall have been created, or the Emoluments whereof shall have been increased during such time. . . ." The text of the provision is an absolute prohibition and does not allow for any exceptions.

The "emoluments" of the office of U.S. secretary of state increased three times during Mrs. Clinton's most recent U.S. Senate term. That term, which began on January 4, 2007, did not expire until January 2013, regardless of Mrs. Clinton's resignation. Members of Congress, well aware of the "emoluments clause," attempted to evade this clear constitutional prohibition with a so-called Saxbe fix, reducing the secretary of state's salary to the level in effect on January 1, 2007. This maneuver, first used in the Taft administration, has been more frequently used in recent years by both parties, allowing Republican senator William Saxbe to become U.S. attorney general in 1973 and Democratic senator Lloyd Bentsen to become Treasury secretary in 1993. A similar "fix" has been enacted for Senator Ken Salazar to join the Obama cabinet as secretary of the interior.

Our lawsuit, however, pointed out that the legislation "does not and cannot change the historical fact that the 'compensation and other emoluments' of the office of the U.S. Secretary of State increased during Defendant Clinton's tenure in the U.S. Senate. . . ." This was a historic legal challenge. Our goal was to remind politicians of both parties that the U.S. Constitution is not to be trifled with.

Our client, Rodearmel, rightly stated that this was not "a partisan, political or personal issue. I have faithfully served under six prior Secretaries of State of both parties, and under eight Presidents since first taking the oath to uphold the Constitution as a young Army officer cadet. During a prior assignment as State Department representative on the faculty of a U.S. service academy, we taught our cadets: 'Officers serve the Nation for one and only one purpose: to support and defend the Constitution.' As a commissioned State Department Foreign Service Officer, a retired Army Reserve Judge Advocate Officer, and as a lawyer, I consider it my Constitutional duty to bring this case to the courts."

The court dismissed the lawsuit on the grounds that Rodearmel didn't have standing—essentially, it stated that he hadn't been damaged by Clinton's accession to office; it didn't reach the baseline issue of whether she was eligible for the office, which still remains an open question. The Senate never cares about one of their own being appointed in violation of the U.S. Constitution; the limits of the U.S. Constitution on the federal government have long ceased to matter to Washington (as we would see later with Obamacare). Hillary Clinton was confirmed 94–2.

Hillary immediately began surrounding herself with her corrupt cronies. For her assistant, she tapped Cheryl Mills, who had fingerprints near virtually every scandal that plagued the Clinton administration. *Politico* speculated that Mills would "bring order" to the new Hillary State Department.[17]

Here's what *Politico* didn't say: in addition to "bringing order" to Hillary's campaign, Cheryl Mills also negotiated on behalf of Bill Clinton in discussions with the Obama administration related to the former president's enormous conflicts of interest. The Obama team was reportedly concerned about Bill (and Hillary) Clinton's business dealings when it was considering Hillary Clinton for the position of secretary of state.

Presumably, as chief of staff, Cheryl Mills ought to be raising red flags when Bill Clinton's business and foundation interests intersect with official State Department business. This brings up a key question: how could Cheryl Mills be trusted to keep tabs on Bill Clinton at the State Department when she had served as his chief negotiator just a few months earlier? Mills's "double agent" status ought to have made her ineligible to serve in this capacity. But there's more.

Cheryl Mills was a key player in Emailgate, the Clinton scandal in which the administration covered up the existence of nearly two million lost or hidden emails. When White House computer contractor Betty Lambuth discovered the email communications, high-level White House officials instructed her to keep her mouth shut about the hidden email or face dismissal and jail time. They issued the same threat to other White House contractors aware of the hidden email.

This resulted in a six-month federal court hearing into the email scandal, during which Clinton officials were deposed, including Cheryl Mills. Mills was, in fact, aware of the missing White House emails but "assumed" someone else was handling the matter. In his 2008 ruling in the email scandal, Judge Royce C. Lamberth called Cheryl Mills's participation in the matter "loathsome." He further stated Mills was responsible for "the most critical error made in this entire fiasco. . . . Mills' actions were totally inadequate to address the problem." (Unfortunately, Judge Lamberth ruled there was no evidence of a conspiracy or obstruction of justice.)

Mills was also one of three Clinton White House lawyers who recommended Bill Clinton release the private letters of Kathleen Willey. (This release was a naked attempt by government officials to destroy and intimidate her—as she was a potential witness against Bill Clinton.) Mills was one of the lawyers who defended Bill Clinton's perjury and obstruction of justice in the failed Senate trial to remove the impeached president. Clearly, Mills was not fit to serve in any official capacity in the government, but most especially as chief of staff at our Department of State.

Secretary of Commerce: Bill Richardson

Obama also reached out to Clinton secretary of energy Bill Richardson to serve at the Commerce Department. While Richardson didn't have the corruption résumé of, say, a Hillary (but who does?), he had significant ethical skeletons in his own right.

Richardson was secretary of energy at the time nuclear secrets were somehow stolen from the Los Alamos National Laboratory and possibly transferred to the Communist Chinese.[18] One of our clients, Notra Trulock, the Energy Department director of intelligence who uncovered this serious breach of national security, was subjected to a massive smear campaign by Clinton officials in retaliation, led by Bill Richardson. Trulock was demoted and ultimately forced out of the agency. We actually deposed Richardson in litigation on behalf of Trulock. Richardson was roundly criticized for his mishandling of the Los Alamos fiasco, but that didn't stop him from publishing a book titled *Leading by Example: How We Can Inspire an Energy and Security Revolution*. You have to admit, the man had nerve.

While serving as Clinton's ambassador to the United Nations, Richardson also narrowly escaped prosecution for his alleged participation in the attempted Monica Lewinsky cover-up. Richardson met with Lewinsky on several occasions in her Watergate condo and offered her a job at the UN. This was an attempt to keep Lewinsky quiet about the affair. In fact, Richardson apparently lied during his secretary of energy confirmation hearings when he said he offered a job to Lewinsky to fill an "existing opening." Evidence suggests there was no such job.

Still, Richardson was confirmed and, following the Clinton administration, was elected governor of New Mexico. Now Obama wanted to put him in charge of guiding the nation's Commerce Department through the most serious financial crisis in sixty years. During the Clinton years, Commerce was a bazaar where taxpayer-funded seats on trade mission junkets (and waivers for missile technology transfers to Communist China) were "sold" to companies in exchange for political donations. It was fair to ask whether Richardson would follow the corrupt model of the Clinton years at Commerce. But, of course, nobody did.

What actually sank Richardson were his political maneuverings back in New Mexico. Even as Obama nominated him, a grand jury was investigating accusations that Richardson's administration sent contracts a big political donor's way in order to pay him back for all his help. "Since August, federal investigators have been examining how CDR Financial Products Inc., of Beverly Hills, Calif., got two consulting contracts in 2004 worth about $1.4 million to advise the state on a large bond issue for building infrastructure, one of Mr. Richardson's initiatives," the *New York Times* reported. "In 2003 and 2004, CDR's president, David Rubin, a major Democratic contributor, gave about $100,000 to two political action committees controlled by Mr. Richardson, as well as $10,000 to his re-election campaign in 2005, according to published reports." [19]

Like Daschle, Richardson withdrew his nomination before the Senate could make an up-or-down vote. "I have concluded that the ongoing investigation also would have forced an untenable delay in the confirmation process," said Richardson. "Given the gravity of the economic situation the nation is facing, I could not in good conscience ask the president-elect and his administration to delay for one day the important work that needs to be done." [20] Richardson is now evidently the subject of a new grand jury investigation into his campaign finances and allegations of a payoff to cover up an affair. Obama settled on Republican senator Judd Gregg of New Hampshire . . . who promptly withdrew his nomination based on Obama's decision to remove Commerce's jurisdiction over the U.S. Census and centralize control of it in the White House.

The eventual Commerce secretary was Gary Locke, who had questionably close ties to companies that do business with China as well as shady Chinese fund-raisers yet had the power to approve sensitive imports to the country. The *Washington Times* reported that Locke represented major firms doing business with Beijing and that he was forced to refund several political donations from key players in a Chinese influence-buying investigation. The former Washington state governor was an attorney at a major Seattle law firm since completing his second term in 2005. Locke was a key part of the firm's China practice, which has offices in Shanghai and represents several state-run Chinese companies, including banks, airlines, and technology firms.

This certainly presented a conflict of interest if not the potential for corruption, since the nation's commerce secretary oversees all export controls and technology transfers at the agency. One government official who held senior positions at various agencies stressed the urgency in disclosing Locke's past fund-raising and views on high-technology transfers to nations such as China. Because the Commerce Department has total control over all dual-use technology, as the agency's head Locke had the ability to steamroll any military concerns coming from the Pentagon. After viewing the Obama administration's friendliness to China—including funding our debt via China, our president bowing to the prime minister of China, and our vice president mouthing support for China's one-child policy—it is difficult to believe that time will not uncover anything suspicious about the relationship between the Commerce Department and the Chinese government. Locke has since moved on to become the nation's ambassador to Communist China.

Treasury Secretary: Tim Geithner

We didn't find out until later about Tim Geithner's deep involvement in the bailouts and the TARP program while at the New York Federal Reserve Bank. And it wasn't until later that we found out what he would do with Fannie and Freddie and the auto companies and AIG. But we did know when he was nominated that he was a tax cheat. Like Daschle, Geithner had his issues with the law, failing to pay $34,000 in Social Security and Medicare taxes in the early years of the century. He didn't pay payroll taxes from 2001 to 2004 while at the International Monetary Fund. "These were careless mistakes. They were avoidable mistakes. . . . I have paid what I owed," he told Congress. He also said to the Senate Finance Committee that he was sorry that his tax evasion was providing an issue to confirmation, especially during the stormy economy following the economic collapse of September 2008.

As head of the Treasury Department, Geithner would be in charge of the Internal Revenue Service. During Geithner's confirmation hearing, Senator Charles Grassley (R-IA) noted the danger of sweeping the scandal under the rug in the rush to get him confirmed. But that's exactly what happened. In fact, Republican senator Pat

Roberts of Kansas flat-out told Geithner, "You will be confirmed," while at the same time noting that his Senate office phones were "ringing off the hook" with calls from constituents furious about Geithner's tax problems.

That seemed to be par for the course in terms of the Obama appointments. Republicans blustered a bit about this scandal and that, but in the end they rubber-stamped Obama's appointees, few questions asked. Even the Associated Press noted, "Although the tax disclosures provided a bump in Geithner's confirmation process, he appeared to have wide support from both parties."

As government grows, two classes are created in this country: the privileged class, who think they are not bound by the rule of law, and the rest of us. For some people, not paying taxes is a jailable offense. For others, it's a "bump in the road" on the way to being confirmed for a top cabinet position. The Finance Committee approved Geithner by a vote of 18–5, and full Senate by a vote of 60–34.

CIA Director: Leon Panetta

Obama's affinity for former Clinton officials prompted him to pick the leftist Leon Panetta as head of the CIA. This appointment to a critical agency even brought questions from Democrats. The chief complaint—and the most logical—is that Panetta had no previous direct intelligence experience.

We, however, were just as concerned by Panetta's history as Bill Clinton's second White House chief of staff. Others may have thought of it as a résumé enhancement, but after viewing the corruption and obfuscation of the Clinton administration, this was about as black a mark as humanly possible.

Let's start with the Clintons' illegal scheme to "sell" taxpayer-financed trade missions in exchange for contributions to the Clinton-Gore reelection campaign. Take a look at what Nolanda Hill, a personal confidante and business partner of the late Clinton commerce secretary Ron Brown, had to say about Panetta's involvement in the scheme. Hill declared: "I further learned through discussions with Ron [Brown] that the White House, through Leon Panetta and John Podesta, had instructed him to delay the case by withholding the production of documents prior to the 1996 elections, and to devise a way not to comply with the court's orders."

That is obstruction of justice.

Then there were the "White House coffees": illegal fund-raising events the Clintons actually held in the White House to haul in massive amounts of cash for the Democratic National Committee. The idea, of course, was to sell access to President Clinton and Vice President Gore in exchange for campaign contributions. And it worked. The Clintons held at least 107 such events. The *Washington Post* estimates $27 million was illegally raised for the DNC in 1995 and 1996.

The guest list for these coffees included "straw donors" acting at the behest of the Chinese military. The guest list also included then-Clinton chief of staff Leon Panetta, who attended three of these coffees in February, April, and May 1995. He was also in charge at the White House when the Clintons sold sleepovers in the Lincoln Bedroom to campaign contributors. At the time, the *Washington Post* called the scandal "crass." Others called it "criminal."

Under Panetta, the White House was turned into a brazen bazaar of bribes and extortion that would make Rod Blagojevich blush. And lest we forget, Panetta was in charge of the White House staff when Monica Lewinsky served as a White House intern. (In other words, Lewinsky worked for Panetta while she was carrying on an affair with President Clinton.) Under Clinton, Panetta opened the White House to foreign governments that were illegally trying to influence our elections and government decision-making. Panetta has moved from the CIA and now serves as defense secretary. So the next time you have or hear a complaint about Obama's foreign or defense policies, remember Leon Panetta, the compromised figure at Obama's side.

Environmental Protection Agency: Jon Cannon

In February 2009, President Obama admitted that he had "screwed up" on a couple of his presidential appointments. With his selection

of Jon Cannon as second in command at the EPA, he screwed up
again. Cannon had to resign when it became known that in 2007 the
EPA inspector general published a report regarding the mismanage-
ment of $25 million in grants awarded to the now-defunct America's
Clean Water Foundation. Cannon was a member of the foundation's
board of directors. The EPA report concluded that the foundation
violated conflict of interest provisions by awarding a large contract
to a member of its board of directors. The report also found that the
organization cheated in its accounting, could not support costs, and
submitted incorrect proposals to the government. Cannon said he
withdrew because he didn't want to become a "distraction." [21]

Supreme Court: Sonia Sotomayor

Obama's decision to nominate Judge Sonia Sotomayor to the United
States Supreme Court represented yet another damning indictment
of his unconcern for the rule of law. Obama went on record saying he favors judges who will let their "empathy" or bias for certain
individuals color their decision-making. Judge Sotomayor shared
Obama's activist judicial philosophy.

She also shared his radical point of view on racial matters. During
an October 2001 speech at the University of California, Berkeley,
for example, Sotomayor said the following: "I would hope that a
wise Latina woman with the richness of her experiences would more
often than not reach a better conclusion than a white male who
hasn't lived that life." Judge Sotomayor has also promoted the idea
that the "gender and national origins" of judges "may and will make
a difference in our judging."

Just before her nomination, Sotomayor resigned her membership
from the Belizean Grove, a private organization consisting entirely
of professional women that claims to represent the counterweight to
the "elite old boys' network." In her Senate questionnaire Judge Sotomayor wrote the following with respect to her organizational af-
filiations: "None of the above organizations, other than the Belizean
Grove, discriminates on the basis of race, sex, religion, or national

origin." Judge Sotomayor stated that the group does not "invidiously" discriminate, a singularly unimpressive defense of her club.

On April 17, 2009, Judge Sotomayor made a political speech to the Black, Latino, Asian-Pacific American Law Alumni Association. Among the statements made by Judge Sotomayor during that speech: "The wide coalition of groups that joined forces to elect America's first Afro-American President was awe inspiring in both the passion the members of the coalition exhibited in their efforts and the discipline they showed in the execution of their goals. . . . Our challenge as lawyers and court related professionals and staff, as citizens of the world is to keep the spirit of the common joy we shared on November 4 alive in our everyday existence."

We also uncovered Sotomayor's twelve-year relationship with the radical race-baiting Puerto Rican Legal Defense and Education Fund (PRLDEF). Sotomayor was the "top policy maker" on the PRLDEF's Board of Directors. And during her tenure the organization aggressively pursued a number of controversial lawsuits and took objectionable public positions. To give just two examples of many, in 1998, the PRLDEF filed a lawsuit against the New York City Police Department over a promotion exam they deemed "racist," which forced the NYPD to change to a more "race sensitive" and less difficult version. In 1990, meanwhile, a spokesman for Sotomayor's group also said that the FALN terrorists who shot five members of Congress in 1954 were merely "fighters for freedom" like Nelson Mandela. In 1981, the PRLDEF filed a complaint against Elizabeth, New Jersey, mayor Thomas Dunn following a City Hall directive requiring staff to speak English while on the job. In 1990, the organization also opposed a law to require merchants to post an English sign in the storefront explaining the nature of business.

In a March 1981 memo to the directors of the PRLDEF, Sotomayor and two colleagues argued against the death penalty because it is "associated with evident racism in our society" and because it "creates inhuman psychological burdens for the offender." The memo, which Sotomayor initially failed to turn over to the Senate Judiciary Committee, which was considering her nomination, argued that the PRLDEF should oppose the restoration of the death penalty in New York state. In 1981, the PRLDEF applauded a decision by a federal judge that forced teachers at an Ann Arbor, Michigan, elementary school to undergo "consciousness raising" about a dialect spoken by young black children called "Black English." The training program cost taxpayers $44,000.

Sotomayor was also a member of the National Council of La Raza—an extreme racial group you'll remember from our earlier discussion of Celia Muñoz. La Raza was quick to issue a press release lauding the president's "historic appointment" of Sotomayor to the nation's highest court, calling it a "monumental day for Latinos." There was no mention of the judge's membership in the group, however.

When the media made several FOIA requests to the Clinton Presidential Library for records on Sotomayor's 1997 nomination to the U.S. Court of Appeals for the Second Circuit, the Clinton Library purposely excluded crucial files. The omitted documents were rumored to include revealing memos between Clinton White House officials about Sotomayor as well as early drafts and answers to questions posed by the Senate Judiciary Committee. There were also files related to Sotomayor's FBI background check.

The excluded information certainly seemed more relevant and important than the mundane stuff that was promptly made public. Those documents mainly featured previously public information such as Sotomayor's judicial opinions as a district court judge, press releases, past speeches and reports, as well as a plethora of letters sent to the White House by supporters. Basically, lots of puff.

Clinton got to keep the juicy stuff private by invoking a measure that allows a president to essentially hide from the public information about his administration for the first twelve years after leaving office. The former president could, however, issue a waiver or direct a representative to allow the National Archives to release the material sooner. When Hillary was still going strong in the last presidential primary, Obama called on Bill to issue such a waiver relating to the cabinet-level Task Force on National Health Care Reform, chaired by the former First Lady. We filed a FOIA lawsuit to obtain the documents, which are archived at the Clinton Presidential Library in Little Rock, Arkansas. Bill opted to keep the files from the public, however, and Camp Obama went to town speculating what the famous First Couple could be hiding. But Obama had no such complaints about Bill Clinton secreting documents about this controversial judicial pick.

Since joining the court, Justice Sotomayor has been a reliable vote in support of liberal judicial activist opinions.

Supreme Court: Elena Kagan

Liberal presidents have an excellent record of choosing Supreme Court justices who go on to completely reshape the law by ignoring the plain language of the U.S. Constitution. Obama's first activist pick for the High Court was Sonia Sotomayor; his next was his then–solicitor general, Elena Kagan.

The nomination was deeply irresponsible. Kagan was a liberal activist and political operative with no experience as judge. A judicial nominee ought to have significant practical experience as a lawyer or a judge—especially a nominee for the nation's highest court. Kagan's political biography includes work for the campaigns of ardent liberals Elizabeth Holtzman (a radical feminist in New York) and Michael Dukakis. She practiced law for a total of three years, one of them for the Clinton White House. She also clerked for the late Thurgood Marshall, one of the most liberal Supreme Court members in recent history. The rest of her career was spent working as a domestic policy aide in the Clinton White House and in academia, where she became the first female dean of Harvard Law School. So three years of practical legal experience and a few years clerking in the federal courts . . . that's suddenly enough to sit on the nation's highest court?

She continued to work in the Clinton White House even after it became clear that President Clinton lied under oath, which raised questions about her ethical judgment. Her record was radical, too. She made the decision to throw military recruiters off the campus of Harvard Law School during a time of war, demonstrating her far-left credentials. In kicking out the military, Kagan was arguably in violation of the law known as the Solomon Amendment. And she only let recruiters back on her campus when the Department of Defense told her school it would withhold federal funds otherwise. Kagan sought to have the Solomon Amendment overturned, but the Supreme Court knocked her effort down, 8–0 in 2006. Not even leftists on the Court, including Justice John Paul Stevens (whom Kagan ultimately replaced), agreed with her radical effort to force the federal government to fund colleges that ban military recruiters from campus.

And her record, as spotty as it was, showed that Kagan is a committed liberal judicial activist. Even President Obama, in his statement introducing her nomination, extolled her personal interest in supporting government regulation (and outright banning) of political speech. (See the Supreme Court decision in *Citizens United*, where Solicitor General Kagan was on the losing end.)

The White House did its best—as always—to prevent the media from checking Kagan out in full. Nonetheless, we obtained documents from Hunter College High School regarding a White House effort to deny *New York Times* education reporter Sharon Otterman access to Kagan's brother Irving, who currently teaches at the New York school. Otterman requested and received permission from both the school and Irving Kagan to attend one of Kagan's constitutional law classes, but then White House Deputy Press Secretary Joshua Earnest intervened. "I'm definitely not comfortable with that at this point," Earnest wrote to Otterman on May 11, 2010. Earnest instructed Irving Kagan in an email on May 11 to direct press inquiries directly to the White House: "This reporter says she has permission from you and from the school to sit in on your class. I've articulated my concerns to the [Hunter College public relations representative] Meredith [Halpern]—who now says she agrees with me. I've articulated my concerns to the reporter, who's feeling misled that we're telling her no and she says she was told yes. In the future, it's important to direct all reporter inquiries to the White House. It'll be easier for you to stay out of the middle of these conversations if you send them directly to us without responding."

Irving Kagan appeared to have no issues with Otterman's presence in his classroom. "I told my folks at school I was willing to participate, but only with your agreement. Was that a mistake? If I hadn't [been] willing to do it, I would have just said no, and not wasted your time."

There was no indication in any of the documents regarding the White House's specific objections to Otterman's request. The documents showed that the Obama White House couldn't care less about transparency on the Kagan nomination and is no friend of an independent media.

With looming constitutional battles ranging from Obamacare to illegal immigration, Obama knew that he had to leverage one of his allies into power on the court.

We FOIA'd the Department of Justice, Elena Kagan's former workplace, for records regarding her role in defending Obamacare. While Kagan said she wasn't actively involved in the department's discussions regarding Obamacare, the documents we uncovered showed that Kagan's office had more involvement than had been previously understood and that Kagan personally supported the passage of Obamacare.

For example, in an October 13, 2009, exchange between Kagan and then–deputy solicitor general Neal Katyal, Katyal told Kagan, "We just got Snowe on health care," referring to Senator Olympia Snowe (R-ME). A March 21, 2010, email from Kagan to then–senior counselor for access to justice Laurence Tribe cheered, "I hear they have the votes Larry!! Simply amazing . . ." Tribe responded, "So healthcare is basically done! Remarkable." The excerpt is reproduced below:

From: Elena Kagan ███████████████████
Sent: Sunday, March 21, 2010 11:39 AM
To: Larry Tribe
Subject: Re: fingers and toes crossed today!

I hear they have the votes, Larry!! Simply amazing. Let's go wherever you want; I think you mentioned a place in the Mandarin, which would be great. Give me any dates you want after March 31. ██████ ████ expressed an interest in joining as well.

From: Larry Tribe ████████████████

A March 16, 2010, email from Kagan to David Barron, then–acting head of the Justice Department's Office of Legal Counsel, asked if Barron had seen an article by Michael McConnell published in the *Wall Street Journal* that discussed a strategy by Democrats to " 'deem' ObamaCare into Law without voting." "Did you seee [*sic*] Michael McConnell's piece in the wsj?" Kagan writes in an email with the subject line "Health care q." "YES, HE IS GETTING THIS GOING," replied Barron.

These and other emails uncovered by Judicial Watch have created a furor, raising questions about whether Kagan ought to participate in High Court deliberations on Obamacare. Certainly, if these documents were known at the time of her confirmation, there may have been quite a different Senate debate. We had to fight tooth and nail for these documents; the slow-walking of documents out of the Obama Justice Department was scandalous—and makes us wonder what other information they are sitting on. We discuss the Kagan controversy in further detail below in the Obamacare section, but the controversy is sure to be an unfortunate part of Justice Kagan's legacy, no matter how Obamacare is decided by the Supreme Court.

The Czars

President Obama's disregard for the rule of law was nowhere more pronounced than in his repeated attempts to create a mini-government inside the executive branch, subject to no legislative oversight or control. Instead of creating officers who required congressional approval, Obama created "czars"—at least the tyrannical language was appropriate—many of whom were far too radical for Congress. Judicial Watch sought, through FOIA and other requests, information on the staffing, budget, and mission on most every Obama czar.

Only Judicial Watch has tried to get a handle on all of Obama's czars and our resulting lists of czars is authoritative. Many of these Obama "policy advisors" enjoy positions of power and authority in the administration and yet have not been subjected to vetting and confirmation by the U.S. Senate. Our investigators have documented that the number of czars that have been appointed by the president, or by others in his administration, appears to total forty-five. In addition, there are as many as eighteen other unfilled or planned czar positions. Many of these "czars" are unconfirmed by the Senate and are largely unaccountable to Congress. Further, their activities are often outside the reach of the Freedom of Information Act, creating a veil of secrecy about their precise role in the administration.

Barack Obama's unconstitutional use of czars to help run his administration is at odds with republican, limited, and accountable government. Obama has simply installed his radical leftist allies in various positions of power while thumbing his nose at Congress and the American people. Too many of these czars have proven to be corrupt or radicals (or sometimes both). No wonder the Obama administration is so keen to allow these czars to operate in secret.

One of the most radical czars was Van Jones, the White House "green jobs" czar. He was forced to resign after some of his past remarks came to light. He called Republicans "assholes" during a videotaped address in 2009. He also signed a petition in 2004 supporting the 9/11 truthers, who think that the Bush administration was somehow involved in the 9/11 attacks.

Obviously, anyone who would associate himself with the insane notion that the Bush administration played a role in 9/11 had no business serving in the White House, any White House. Judicial Watch took on the truthers early on when we obtained and released historic video documenting that American Airlines Flight #77 hit the Pentagon on 9/11, not a missile or a drone as Van Jones and the truthers had alleged.

Obama has a czar to help implement virtually every aspect of the liberal agenda: the environment, Middle East peace, health care. We even have a "manufacturing czar." Obama appointed former United Auto Workers executive and current Treasury official Ron Bloom to preside over the automobile manufacturing industry—an incredible concession to the unions, considering that they brought down the

American auto industry in the first place. In fact, Bloom is more controversial than just his union card: in a 2008 speech, Bloom asserted that the free market is "nonsense," and said, "Generally speaking, we get the joke. We know that the free market is nonsense. We know that the whole point is to game the system, to beat the market or at least find someone who will pay you a lot of money, 'cause they're convinced that there is a free lunch. We know this is largely about power, that it's an adults only no limit game. We kind of agree with Mao that political power comes largely from the barrel of a gun."[22] Eventually, Bloom was kicked upstairs—but to have a manufacturing czar with such contempt for the marketplace is certainly change of a different sort.

Many of these advisors can wield a tremendous amount of power and influence with zero congressional oversight. And, as with Bloom, many of them hold leftist views well outside the mainstream. So for every Van Jones who resigns after the conservative media and Internet raise the alarm, others—such as science czar John Holdren and media diversity czar Mark Lloyd—remain. Holdren once suggested "compulsory sterilization" to keep overpopulation under control; Lloyd has ripped private ownership of the media, blaming such ownership for conservative talk radio.

We actually FOIA'd the Federal Communications Commission regarding Lloyd's responsibilities. According to the documents, Lloyd's mission is "to open up opportunities for all Americans, in particular women, minorities, small business owners, to participate in and benefit from a robust communications marketplace." Among Lloyd's duties and responsibilities: "To work with the Consumer Bureau (and other bureaus as appropriate) to collect relevant data and assess the interaction between communications service providers and consumers in minority communities" and "to consult with other federal agencies to determine best practices for advancing the goal of greater inclusion and diversity in government programs." If this agenda doesn't sound suspicious to you, you're not watching carefully enough—whenever government takes more power, it uses it to quash its opponents. Many suspect that the focus on minority broadcasting threatens traditional radio in particular, since the Obama administration has shown that it despises conservative talk radio.

Lloyd, meanwhile, has been criticized heavily for making a number of controversial statements on race. For example, during a conference in 2005, Lloyd said, "There's nothing more difficult than this. Because we have really, truly good white people in important positions. And the fact of the matter is that there are a limited number of those positions. And unless we are conscious of the need to have more people of color, gays, other people in those positions we will not change the problem. We're in a position where you have to say who is going to step down so someone else can have power." During a 2008 National Conference for Media Reform, Lloyd also said Venezuelan dictator Hugo Chavez's rise to power was "really an incredible revolution—a democratic revolution."

"The property owners and the folks who then controlled the media in Venezuela rebelled—worked, frankly, with folks here in the U.S. government—worked to oust him," Lloyd gushed. "But he came back with another revolution, and then Chavez began to take very seriously the media in his country." The *Washington Times* reported that Lloyd has appeared at meetings held by the FCC's advisory committee that discuss licensing to minority-owned media outlets.[23] This helps to stoke fears that Lloyd is exerting his influence to bring about changes in FCC policy—while still remaining largely unaccountable. In keeping with the Obama administration's habit of masking the duties and budgets of the czars, as opposed to Obama's earlier commitments to "transparency," Lloyd reportedly shares staff with the FCC's Office of General Counsel. Supposedly, no one was hired or assigned specifically to support him in his work. His position is funded out of the agency's fiscal year budget, and as such, he has no separate identifiable budget for operation and administration.

Then there was "Climate Czar" Carol Browner. We filed a FOIA request against the Department of Energy and the Environmental Protection Agency (EPA) to obtain documents related to President Obama's Special Assistant on Energy and Climate Browner and her role in crafting official U.S. climate policy. Browner, who was never subjected to Senate confirmation, reportedly served as the Obama administration's point person in secret negotiations to establish automobile emission standards and also participated in negotiations involving cap-and-trade legislation. According to press reports, Browner instructed individuals involved in auto emissions negotiations to "put nothing in writing, ever." The *New York Times* reported that Browner made every effort to "keep their discussions as quiet as possible." This was the perfect storm for corruption: concentrated executive power with no congressional oversight and conscious attempts to avoid transparency.[24]

Then there's "safe schools" czar Kevin Jennings. Because Jennings was appointed without Senate vetting, it was only after he was already in a position of authority that controversy surfaced. Many were taken aback to learn of Jennings's past efforts to overtly promote homosexuality in public schools. During the 1990s, Jennings established the Gay Straight Alliance (GSA), along with the Gay, Lesbian and Straight Education Network (GLSEN). The GLSEN caused a controversy in 2000 for holding an educational seminar that described to children various unorthodox sexual practices.[25] Further, Jennings has publicly praised the late Harry Hay, who was associated with the North American Man/Boy Love Association (NAMBLA). Jennings also wrote the foreword to a book titled *Queering Elementary Education*.[26]

The public was most shocked, however, to hear his own account of the advice he, the "Safe Schools Czar," had given as a teacher to a sixteen-year-old gay student in 1988. Jennings recounted an incident in which a male student he believed to be fifteen (later revealed to have been sixteen at the time) told him that he was meeting older men for sex at Boston bus stops. A teacher back then, Jennings reported that his response to the boy was "You know, I hope you knew to use a condom." Jennings reportedly talked about this incident during a speech to a GLSEN rally in Iowa in 2000. The surfacing of this speech created a big enough stir to have fifty-three House Republicans call for Jennings's removal from his position at the Department of Education.[27] The pressure worked and Jennings left the administration in the middle of 2011.

Obama's regulatory czar is Cass Sunstein—and at least he was confirmed by the Senate. Sunstein is President Obama's friend from their days at the University of Chicago Law School. Sunstein had a penchant for controversial statements and unconventional thinking since well before his nomination, including back in 2002 when he wrote a book titled *Republic.com*. In the book, Sunstein discussed the drawbacks of limitless choices on the Internet that allow people to seek out only like-minded people and opinions that merely fortify their views. He presented the idea of the government requiring sites to link to opposing views, before he came to realize it was a bad idea and almost certainly unconstitutional.[28]

In his 2004 book, *Animal Rights*, Sunstein suggested that animals ought to be able to bring suit, with private citizens acting as their representatives, to ensure that animals are not treated in a way that violates current law.[29] In 2007, in a speech at Harvard that must have raised the hackles of the National Rifle Association and millions of gun-owning Americans, Sunstein proposed that the government ban hunting.

Obama's urban affairs/housing czar—why did he need a czar when there's already an entire department?—was Adolfo Carrion. Carrion's qualification for the role stemmed from his work in urban development as the Bronx borough president. However, in March 2009, the *New York Daily News* ran several stories revealing numerous conflicts of interest concerning donors to Carrion's campaign. These were contributions from New York developers who were receiving, or subsequently received, approval and taxpayer funding for major development projects under Carrion's jurisdiction.

One questionable donor was the Jackson Development Group. In 2007, the group was sitting on a stalled project for the development of affordable housing. In 2007, employees from Jackson donated $35,650 to Carrion's campaign, and a year later in 2008, Carrion announced $3 million in taxpayer funds for the project. Another questionable Carrion donor was Jose Velazquez, owner of Tri-Line Contracting. As a fund-raiser, Velazquez raised $83,700 for Carrion's campaign. During this period, Tri-Line was one of the contractors working on the Bronx's new Yankee Stadium, on which Carrion signed off.[30]

Among Carrion's dubious donations, the most suspicious are those involved in the Bronx's Boricua Village project—which included 679 housing units and a fourteen-story tower—and provided $7.5 million in taxpayer funding by Carrion.[31] The project's developer was the Atlantic Development Group, whose owner (Peter Fine) and employees donated $52,400 to Carrion's campaign. This was Carrion's largest single source of donations. Further, the project's architect, Hugo Subotovsky, was hired by Carrion to design a new front porch for his Victorian house. The porch was originally estimated at $50,000, but according to the *New York Daily News*, the final price for the project ended up being only $24,000. Carrion eventually stepped down.

That's big-time theft. But Obama also had a czar of petty theft. Only this czar was the information technology czar, Vivek Kundra. As a twenty-one-year-old in 1996, Kundra was convicted of misdemeanor theft, having stolen a handful of men's shirts from a JCPenney department store (plus running away in a failed attempt to avoid arrest).[32] The White House has downplayed the incident as "youthful indiscretion," and Obama has enthusiastically promoted Kundra as playing "a key role in making sure our government is running in the most secure, open, and efficient way possible." Try to stifle your laughter.

Kundra is also under an umbrella of suspicion for other concerns and relationships. For instance, before moving over to the White House, he was serving as the chief technology officer for the District of Columbia. During the transition, two of his underlings, Yusuf Acar (who had received several promotions from Kundra) and Sushil Bansal, were charged in an alleged scheme of bribery, kickbacks, ghost employees, and forged timesheets.[33] Kundra was put on leave for five days and reinstated after the government informed him that he was neither a subject nor a target of the investigation. The Obama White House then defended Kundra by suggesting he was ignorant of the goings-on in his workplace of some three hundred employees. This seems reasonable, except that now, his job was to help police the entire federal government. (Kundra left the Obama administration late last year.)

Kundra wasn't the only Obama czar whose prior work raises ethical concerns. Car czar Steve Rattner headed up Obama's auto task force, overseeing the restructuring of General Motors and Chrysler. In April 2009, details emerged concerning Quadrangle Group, the private equity firm that Rattner founded and ran until February 2009. Quadrangle was in the middle of a joint investigation by the Securities and Exchange Commission and New York State Office of the Attorney General into pay-for-play schemes (kickbacks).

According to the *Washington Post*, sources identified Rattner as being directly involved in paying over $1 million to middlemen in order to win investments from the New York state pension funds. As a result, he was accused by the SEC and the state attorney general of improper payments. While the SEC charges were settled (a two-year ban from certain Wall Street businesses and a $6.2 million fine), further action against Rattner was pursued by the state attorney general.[34] On November 18, 2010, Rattner was formally accused by Andrew Cuomo, New York's attorney general at that time, of engaging in a kickback scheme involving the state's pension system. (Cuomo subsequently won the race for New York governor in the November election and assumed office on January 2, 2011.) Despite being a Democrat, Cuomo was seeking a $26 million fine and to ban Rattner for life from the securities business in New York. A settlement was announced on December 30, 2010. Rattner "agreed to pay $10 million to settle influence-peddling allegations in New York," but as part of the deal, "he admitted no wrongdoing."[35]

Another worrisome matter of Rattner's term as auto czar is his personal connections to a firm directly involved in the bailout that he oversaw. Rattner's brother-in-law is a partner at Cadwalader, Wickersham & Taft, the law firm hired by the government to develop the bankruptcy framework eventually used for GM and Chrysler.[36] The plans for bankruptcy that Cadwalader helped develop (involving the sale of Chrysler to Fiat and the reemergence of GM) were approved only upon Rattner's denial of the restructuring plans submitted by GM and Chrysler on February 17, 2009.

Though there is no evidence as yet that Rattner was directly influenced by his family ties, the mere appearance of a possible conflict of interest is, nevertheless, unsettling.[37]

Perhaps the most egregious example of the "czar" system was Obama's "pay czar," Kenneth Feinberg. The fact that the federal government now had a person specifically designated to overlook pay in the private sector was bad enough. But then we found out that we were actually *paying* the pay czar despite assurances to the contrary. According to documents we unearthed, Feinberg received a $120,830 annual salary to establish executive compensation levels at companies bailed out by the federal government. These documents contradict multiple press reports that Feinberg would not be compensated for this work for the Treasury Department. Judicial Watch received the documents pursuant to its Freedom of Information Act request filed July 20, 2010.

When President Obama appointed Washington lawyer Feinberg as "pay czar" in 2009, the press reported that he would perform his duties pro bono. Dozens of mainstream media stories confirmed that Feinberg, founder and managing partner of the Washington, D.C., firm Feinberg Rozen LLP, would not receive a salary to set pay limits for more than two dozen executives at companies receiving government bailouts.

However, Judicial Watch obtained the Treasury Department's June 8, 2009, welcome letter to Feinberg, congratulating him for being selected "Special Master of Executive Compensation" and listing his annual salary at $120,830. Judicial Watch has also uncovered a "Notification of Personnel Action," from the U.S. Office of Personnel Management dated June 8, 2009, also establishing Feinberg's salary level at $120,830.

We repeatedly contacted Kenneth Feinberg at both his Washington, D.C., law firm and the U.S. Department of the Treasury. We also contacted Treasury press secretary Mark Paustenbach. Neither Feinberg nor the Treasury Department provided an explanation for the discrepancy until after we went public. A representative of Feinberg finally called Judicial Watch and stated that Feinberg pays his government salary back "every two weeks." That way of doing things doesn't make much sense—but in this Bizzaroworld of unaccountable czars, what does? (Feinberg is no longer the nation's pay czar.) You can see below part of the letter giving the pay czar his job:

June 8, 2009

Dear Mr. Feinberg:

Welcome to the Department of the Treasury, Office of Financial Stability. Congratulations on your selection for the position of Special Master of Executive Compensation, GS-0301-15, Step 01, effective June 9, 2009. Your salary will be $120,830 per year. You are being hired under a Schedule A Appointment.

This was yet another reason why more of these Obama czars should have gone through the Senate confirmation process, rather than being simply installed into power by Obama. We shouldn't have had to pepper the Obama administration with FOIA requests to know what these czars are doing and how much they're getting paid to do it.

We also heard about a "consumer czar," slated to set up a brand-new big-government agency called the Bureau of Consumer Financial Protection, a brainchild of the corrupt Fannie and Freddie twins, Barney Frank and Chris Dodd. Obama's first consumer czar was Elizabeth Warren, the left-wing patron saint of so-called consumer protection.

There was only one problem. In the dubious tradition of Obama czars, Warren was a leftist radical and had very little chance of being confirmed by even a Democratic Senate. How antibusiness? Well, in a blog post she crafted for TPMCafe.com in 2005, Warren said that "big corporate interests, led by the consumer finance industry, are devouring families and spitting out the bones."

And that's just one example.

Even Democrat senator Chris Dodd, then-chairman of the Senate Banking Committee, saw the writing on the wall on a Warren appointment. Dodd publicly stated that he doubts Warren could muster the votes for confirmation.

So, how do you think the president planned to "move forward"

182 CORRUPTION CHRONICLES

with this appointment in light of a looming confirmation war? By ignoring the Senate confirmation process! The Obama White House had Warren post a propaganda item announcing her appointment: "The President asked me, and I enthusiastically agreed, to serve as an Assistant to the President and Special Advisor to the Secretary of the Treasury on the Consumer Financial Protection Bureau. He has also asked me to take on the job to get the new CFPB started—right now." Warren went on in her statement to push the socialist trope of "leveling the playing field" in the consumer credit market. Obama White House officials are spinning this as an "interim appointment."

But we all knew the strategy: get Warren in the back door, and have her put her stamp on the "creation" of this powerful new agency, while really running it. (Obama calls this an "interim appointment." We call it a "czar.") Indeed, Obama's statement about the Warren appointment showed that he essentially gave her the keys to the kingdom of the new government agency.

Even the left raised questions about this lawlessness. The notoriously radical Internet site Daily Kos posted an article that highlights the legally dubious nature of Obama's new Warren appointment. The piece, by a *supporter* of Warren's, suggests that Obama has no authority to install her. Warren is now running for Senate as a Democrat from Massachusetts.

But Warren is not really a "Consumer Czar."

In 2011, we uncovered documents showing that Warren's CFPB has been intensely involved in a fifty-state settlement discussion under way with the nation's largest mortgage lenders regarding alleged improper foreclosure procedures. Antibusiness zealots in the Obama administration and state attorneys general offices are trying to extract a $20 billion "settlement" from banks to settle paperwork issues related to foreclosures.

The documents, obtained in response to open records requests with CFPB and the offices of attorneys general from all fifty states, seem to contradict Warren's statements before Congress that suggested her office merely responded to requests for advice and did not seek to push its views. During a March 16, 2011, hearing of the House Financial Services Subcommittee on Financial Institutions and Consumer Credit, for example, Warren downplayed her agency's involvement in the state settlement negotiations: "We have been asked for advice by the Department of Justice, by the Secretary of the Treasury, and by other federal agencies. And when asked for advice, we have given our advice."

But this does not come close to telling the full story. Emails obtained by Judicial Watch from several states suggest her agency's participation was far more intense and aggressive. Warren called emergency meetings by phone and in person with attorneys general nationwide to contribute unsolicited input on the matter. The documents also indicate that Warren's office insisted on keeping its contact with the state attorneys general secret (which, as I've pointed out, is never a good sign).

For example, in a February 25, 2011, email to the Executive Committee of the National Association of Attorneys General (NAAG), Iowa assistant attorney general Patrick Madigan wrote: "Elizabeth Warren would like to present the CFPB's view on loan modifications." And two weeks earlier, a similar email was distributed to NAAG's Loss Mitigation Subgroup on Warren's behalf. In an email on February 15 regarding that meeting, Madigan points out that "[t]he CFPB wanted me to stress the confidential nature of this briefing."

A March 22, 2011, Freedom of Information Act request to the CFPB for all records of Warren's communications with each state's attorney general produced a single heavily redacted document respecting a February 24 meeting with Illinois attorney general Lisa Madigan.

Now, this is particularly curious given the fact that state attorneys general nationwide have supplied dozens of documents to Judicial Watch showing contact between their offices and Warren's, including emails establishing closed-door meetings between Warren and New York attorney general Eric Schneiderman on February 14 and March 7.

Several states refused to turn over responsive documents in their possession based on confidentiality concerns arising from, as the state of Colorado put it, "the Consumer Financial Protection

Bureau's participation in the ongoing investigation into bank and loan servicers mortgage processes."

Again, the CFPB is the new federal agency arising out of the laughably named Dodd-Frank Wall Street Reform and Consumer Act. The "Bureau" officially gained its authority under the law on July 21, 2011 (after Warren was already abusing its authority to intimidate banks). Many conservatives, including Judicial Watch, are concerned this agency will wield a tremendous amount of power with little oversight. Through this new massive agency, which is funded not by congressional appropriations (and hence not subject to effective oversight) but by the Federal Reserve, the Obama administration has gained federal regulatory control of every consumer financial product in America: mortgages, car loans, credit cards, etc. The agency is a constitutional monstrosity.

On April 16, 2011, Judicial Watch and other open government advocates were invited to meet with Warren to discuss transparency and other policy issues. *That* was an interesting meeting! Because my colleague and I confronted Warren quite directly on her agency's stonewalling and dubious powers, we caused a bit of a stir. After the meeting, another attendee said (referring to us), "That's the last time we invite the black hats." Only in corrupt Washington are you a "black hat" for confronting government officials.

Following up on Judicial Watch's blockbuster disclosures, Congressman Darrell Issa (R-CA), chairman of the powerful House Oversight and Government Reform Committee, asked Warren during a committee hearing on July 14, 2011 about the CFPB's attempts to block Judicial Watch's FOIA requests.

After quoting from Judicial Watch's FOIA appeal that the CFPB's response was "an abuse of disclosure," Issa held up a completely blacked-out piece of paper received by Judicial Watch from the CFPB in "response" to our FOIA request. "They received documents that look like this," Congressman Issa said, noting that the documents were redacted, "so much so that you violated the law." [38]

Congressman Issa made his point. And now Warren is out as "Consumer Czar."

Article II, section 2 of the Constitution states that "[the President] shall nominate, and by and with the Advice and Consent of the Senate, shall appoint Ambassadors, other public Ministers and Consuls, Judges of the Supreme Court, and all other Officers of the United States, whose Appointments are not herein otherwise provided for, and which shall be established by Law."

Unlike the heads of other executive departments (such as the secretaries of energy, transportation, etc.), many of Obama's czars were not confirmed by the U.S. Senate. Some of them might not have even been subjected to a basic FBI background check. Importantly, as advisors to the president, these individuals rarely testify before Congress. And they are not directly subject to transparency laws. They answer to no one but President Obama.

We launched a full investigation of Obama's czars. We filed a FOIA request with the Office of Management and Budget as well as requests with each separate czar office. (Of course we included Van Jones on our list. The White House, in a snarky reply, said it had no documents responsive to our request because Jones "was not appointed as a 'czar.' Mr. Jones was appointed as Special Advisor for Green Jobs.") On all of these requests, we were after any and all documents pertaining to the mission statements, staffing, and budgets for these offices.

The story of the new dominance of czars in the Obama administration continues. Just to give a basic idea of the scope of the czar power within the Obama administration, here's a reference list of czars Obama has appointed or is thinking of appointing during his first term. Some of them have been confirmed by the Senate; many have not:

- Afghanistan and Pakistan Czar (Richard Holbrooke, 2009–2010)

- AIDS Czar (Jeffrey Crowley, 2009–)

- Asian Carp Czar (John Goss, 2010–)

- Auto Czar (Steve Rattner, 2009, Ron Bloom, 2009–)

- Auto Recovery Czar (Ed Montgomery, 2009–)

- Bank Bailout Czar (Allison Herbert, 2009–)

- Border Czar (Alan Bersin, 2009–)

- Climate Czar (Todd Stern, 2009)

- Copyright Czar (Victoria Espinel, 2009–)

- Consumer Czar (Elizabeth Warren, 2010–2011)

- Cyber Security Czar (Melissa Hathaway, 2009, Howard Schmidt, 2009–)

- Domestic Violence Czar (Lynn Rosenthal, 2009)

- Drug Czar (Gil Kerlikowske, 2009–)

- Economic Czar (Paul Volcker, 2009)

- Ethics Czar (Norm Eisen, 2009–2010, Robert Bauer, 2010–)

- Faith-Based Czar (Joshua DuBois, 2009–)

- Global Warming Czar (Carol Browner, 2009–2011)

- Great Lakes Czar (Cameron Davis, 2009–)

- Green Jobs Czar (Van Jones, 2009)

- Guantanamo Bay Closure Czar (Daniel Fried, 2009–)

- Health Czar (Nancy-Ann DeParle, 2009–)

- Health IT Czar (Dr. David Blumenthal, 2009–)

- Information Czar (Vivek Kundra, 2009–)

- Intelligence Czar (John McConnell, 2007–2009, Dennis Blair, 2009–)

- Manufacturing Czar (Ron Bloom, 2009–)

- Middle East Czar (George Mitchell, 2009–)

- Pay Czar (Kenneth Feinberg, 2009–)

- Performance Czar (Jeffrey Zients, 2009–)

- Regulatory Czar (Cass Sunstein, 2009–)

- Science Czar (John Holdren, 2009–)

- Stimulus Accountability (Earl Devaney, 2009–)

- Technology Czar (Aneesh Chopra, 2009–)

- Terrorism Czar (John Brennan, 2009–)

- Urban Affairs Czar (Adolfo Carrion, 2009–)

- War Czar (Lute Douglas, 2007–, holdover)

- Weapons Czar (Ashton Carter, 2009–)

- Weapons of Mass Destruction Czar (Gary Samore, 2009–)

- Weatherization Czar (Gil Sperling, 2008–, holdover)

Obama managed to make matters worse by replacing the unconfirmable Warren (who may be the next United States senator from Massachusetts) with Richard Cordray, the Ohio attorney general whose defense of the "Joe the Plumber" I highlighted above.

In January 2012, Obama made a "recess" appointment of Cordray to head the Consumer Financial Protection Bureau. Just a few hours later, Obama made three additional appointments to the National Labor Relations Board (NLRB), which has become little more than a Big Labor battering ram under this president.

Obama is terming his appointments "recess" appointments. They are nothing of the sort, because Congress was not in recess. Article I, section 5, clause 4 of the U.S. Constitution provides that "Neither House, during the Session of Congress, shall, without the Consent of the other, adjourn for more than three days. . . ." To prevent any recess appointment, the Republican-controlled House has refused to consent to Senate adjournment, resulting in the Senate coming into pro forma session every three days. But as Ed Meese, who served as attorney general under Ronald Reagan, points out, these pro forma sessions aren't gimmicks. The two-month extension of the payroll tax holiday was approved during a pro forma Senate session.

In an unprecedented power grab, Obama has decided that he can decide when Congress is or is not in session. Meese rightly calls it a "constitutional abuse of a high order." If this abuse stands, the U.S. Senate's constitutional role to advise and consent in the confirmation of key executive appointees, already undermined by Obama's many czar appointments, could become moot.

The response to these outrageous and unconstitutional appointments was swift and severe. The editors at Bloomberg immediately splashed an editorial on its website warning that the "president is playing with fire" and choosing "politics over principle" with these appointments. "He risks an election-year legal challenge that could hamstring the consumer bureau and several other financial regulators whose pending confirmations will probably now stall," they warned.

Any substantial actions by Obama's pretender appointees at the CFPB or the NLRB would be, it can seriously be argued, "null and void."

Nonetheless, Barack Obama appears undeterred by such considerations.

If Cordray is the "right man for the job," as Obama alleges, then why would the president need to resort to such extreme measures to get "his guy" in position at the CFPB? Because given Cordray's controversial background and penchant for inflammatory and irresponsible rhetoric, there is no chance he could survive the confirmation process—especially when you consider that Congress does not control the agency's purse strings. The CFPB gets its funding from the Federal Reserve.

Here's what I mean by "inflammatory and irresponsible."

In a scathing editorial when Cordray was first nominated, the *Wall Street Journal* said that throughout his career, Cordray has demonstrated a "hostility toward business." The *Journal* explains:

[Cordray] sued Ally Financial's GMAC Mortgage over its foreclosure practices—a lawsuit that helped spawn the national robo-signing uproar, which has mushroomed into an effort to force big banks to cough up billions for Democrats to redistribute. He sued rating agencies for grading mortgage-backed securities as safe investments. He sued Bank of America for purportedly hiding losses and bonuses prior to the Merrill Lynch merger. The list of cases is long.

In an interview with the *Journal*, Cordray also compared employees of a financial services company to the "Nazis at Nuremberg" who said they were just following orders. And, as John Berlau pointed out in the *American Spectator*, "Cordray has long supported ESOP, formerly known as the East Side Organizing Project, an Ohio housing advocacy group that has distinguished itself by storming into banks and launching plastic 'shark attacks' on the lawns of private homes." These are tactics that would make any Wall Street Occupier proud. And one can imagine how they would appeal to Obama, "the president from ACORN."

Commenting on his decision to bypass Senate confirmation, the president explained, "I'm not going to stand by while a minority in the Senate puts party ideology ahead of the people they were elected to serve." The president said it was his "obligation" to ignore the Senate and simply install Cordray.

The other three NLRB appointments were just as bad. I understand this president fantasizes about being dictator—as he said in 2011, "I wish I had a magic wand and could make this all happen on my own. There are times where—until Nancy Pelosi is speaker again—I'd like to work my way around Congress"[39]—but this brazen act shows that he is acting out his fantasy.

According to *Washington Post* blogger Greg Sargent, "The move, which is arguably as important as the Cordray appointment, will ratchet up opposition from Republicans and make this an even bigger fight, since they have been attacking the NLRB. . . ." Sargent accurately points out that the president's appointments will "help energize unions in advance of the 2012 election."

So, who is it exactly that is putting politics ahead of what's best for the country? Barack Obama cannot toss enough bones to his friends in Big Labor. From Obamacare waivers to recess appointments to the NLRB's controversial Boeing lawsuit to help Boeing's unions (with the threat of keeping Boeing from opening a production line in South Carolina), the president seems intent on paying Big Labor in advance for union votes coming his way in November.

What is there to be done about Obama's power grab? Short of impeachment, Congress can make its displeasure known through the appropriations process and by holding up more nominees—and even that may not suffice, thanks to the president's usurpations.

Our lawyers and investigators will endeavor to consider a variety of approaches to challenge and investigate this lawlessness. Who knows, maybe we'll have a lawsuit or two pending as you read this book.

6.

LET THE STONEWALLING BEGIN

President Obama's antipathy for transparency began from the start. While he was still telling the American people that the White House was the "people's house" and that he wanted us all to know what went on behind closed doors, he was planning to prevent us from ever finding out what happened in the smoky rooms in which America's future is decided.

When it came to FOIA, Obama started off on the right foot. He distributed a memo pledging that agencies would "adopt a presumption in favor of disclosure, in order to renew their commitment to the principles embodied in [the Freedom of Information Act], and to usher in a new era of open government. The presumption of disclosure should be applied to all decisions involving FOIA." President Obama said that "[a] democracy requires accountability, and accountability requires transparency. . . . [The FOIA] encourages accountability through transparency."[1] Amen to that.

But *that* didn't hold up for five minutes. Obama's administration turned down more FOIA requests than any president in history in his first year. Administratively, agencies built additional hurdles and stonewalled even the most basic FOIA requests. The Bush administration was tough and tricky, but the Obama administration is tougher and trickier. In the fall of 2009, Judicial Watch staff visited with senior White House official Norm Eisen, then–special counsel to the president for ethics and government, to discuss Judicial Watch's pursuit of the White House visitor logs. The White House encouraged us to publicly praise the Obama administration's commitment to transparency, saying it would be good for them and good for us. However, the Obama team refused to abandon their legally indefensible contention that Secret Service White House visitor logs are not subject to disclosure under FOIA law. Overall, on major transparency issues, the Obama administration has come down on the side of secrecy. The Obama administration's releasing "high value data sets" from government bureaucracies is meaningless in the face of key decisions to keep politically explosive material out of the public domain. As far as Judicial Watch is concerned, the Obama administration gets a failing grade on transparency.

As the years passed, Obama's appointees became more and more brazen about ignoring the FOIA law by instead embracing full-scale obstruction. The Associated Press reported in 2011, "Two years into its pledge to improve government transparency, the Obama administration took action on fewer requests for federal records from citizens, journalists, companies and others last year even as significantly more people asked for information. . . . People requested information 544,360 times last year under the U.S. Freedom of Information Act from the 35 largest agencies, up nearly 41,000 more than the previous year, according to an analysis by the Associated Press of new federal data. But the government responded to nearly 12,400 fewer requests."[2]

On December 7, 2009, as we later uncovered thanks to those darn pesky FOIA requests the Obama administration dislikes so much, President Obama sponsored a government workshop on transparency while simultaneously taking steps to keep the American people in the dark about their government. The Obama White House actually closed a FOIA training workshop, conducted by the Office of Information Policy in the Justice Department, to reporters. We obtained the documents from the OIP in response to a FOIA request filed on the same day the workshop was held. They consist of a series of emails between White House staff and the director of the OIP.

A few key excerpts from these emails suffice to demonstrate what disrespect this White House has for transparency. "I am going to touch base with my public affairs office re your suggestion to get their reaction. I, personally don't object as my message is the same whether the event is open or not. Our concern had been solely with the inhibiting effect it would have on the gov't 'ees [employees] who might not speak freely if press are there," wrote OIP director Melanie Pustay to Deputy Associate White House Counsel Blake Roberts on December 6. "Ok—please don't have them reach out to any reporters before I clear w/ wh [White House] press [office]," Roberts replied. The chain then went over to Gina Talamona, deputy director for the Justice Department, who wrote to Pustay and Counsel to the Associate Attorney General Brian Hauck, "After talking with . . . ben labolt [then–assistant White House press secretary], the decision is that the training will be closed to the press." Hauck replied, "I think you have the right to give closed training when you want it." Notice something here? Not once is the importance of transparency mentioned—with regard to a *workshop on transparency*. Here's the email documenting the White House directions on controlling access:

From: Roberts, Blake C. ▮▮▮▮▮▮▮▮▮▮▮▮▮▮ Exemption (b)(6)
To: Pustay, Melanie A
Cc: miriam.nisbet@nara.gov <miriam.nisbet@nara.gov>
Sent: Sun Dec 06 18:43:09 2009
Subject: Re: FOIA workshop tomorrow

Ok - please don't have them reach out to any reporters before I clear w/ wh press.

Even more suspicious, the documents included a statement by Pustay regarding previous FOIA workshops: "So far I have always held parallel sessions, one for agency 'ees [employees] and then one that is open." Now that's interesting. A different workshop for "public view" than the one the employees are getting behind closed doors.

When the FOIA training conference was held on December 7, 2009, it was jointly hosted by the OIP and the Office of

Government Information Services as a private workshop ostensibly to provide tips to FOIA public liaison bureaucrats on communicating, negotiating, and resolving disputes with individuals and organizations submitting FOIA requests. But, as we know, the devil is often in the details. And what was actually said and done in this private workshop we may never know.

Now, it is unlikely you've ever heard of the Justice Department's Office of Information Policy—which is just another obscure government agency. Except this office provides policy guidance and oversight for the entire federal government on freedom of information. Specifically, according to its own website, the OIP is responsible "for ensuring that the President's FOIA Memorandum and the Attorney General's FOIA Guidelines are fully implemented across the government." The fact that the lead federal office on transparency kept secret a transparency workshop is beyond ironic.

Even more ironic, the Obama administration, which criticized the Bush administration for not being responsive enough on information requests, has actually tried to impose new regulatory changes that would allow the administration to lie outright when asked for documents. Before, if bureaucrats thought that a document fell under a FOIA exemption, they informed requesters that the documents existed but fell under the exemption. Under the new proposed rule, the administration would have been able to falsely tell the requester that the document doesn't even exist, so long as it relates to an ongoing criminal investigation, a terrorist organization, or a counterintelligence operation.

The *Washington Examiner,* a leading media voice for transparency in government, got it right: "First, by not citing a specific exemption allowed under the FOIA as grounds for denying a request, the proposal would cut off a requestor from appealing to the courts. By thus creating an area of federal activity that is completely exempt from judicial review, the proposal undercuts due process and other constitutional protections. Second, by creating a justification for government lying to FOIA requestors in one area, a legal precedent is created that sooner or later will be asserted by the government in other areas as well." The blowback earned transparency advocates a victory as the Obama administration pulled back the proposed regulation that would have enshrined lying as lawful government policy. (The law already protects the government's reasonable secrecy interests. Government agencies can deny a FOIA request while refusing to confirm or deny the existence of any records. It is called the Glomar response, which is interestingly named after the *Glomar Explorer*, a ship that the CIA allegedly used but didn't want linked to the agency.)

The Obama administration has also made it more difficult for FOIA requesters to recover their costs when the government improperly withholds records. On April 19, 2010, Judicial Watch lawyers presented oral arguments to the U.S. Court of Appeals for the District of Columbia Circuit against the Obama administration's subversion of the FOIA. Here's the bottom line. According to changes in FOIA law signed by President Bush in 2007 under the Open Government Act, the federal government owed Judicial Watch attorneys' fees for dragging its feet in releasing documents related to a suspicious real estate deal involving Senator Harry Reid. Lawyers for the Obama administration didn't want to pay up and they have taken their battle to the appellate court. The total amount owed to Judicial Watch was only $3,605.57. But it wasn't the money that was important here. It was the principle.

The administration seemed to hope that the prospect of expending resources fighting the government would dissuade Americans from pursuing open records requests. And the administration can therefore continue to operate in secret. Prior to the changes in FOIA law signed by President Bush, attorneys' fees could only be recouped if the court ordered the agency to release the documents. However, the new law allows for the collection of attorneys' fees if there is a "a voluntary or unilateral change in position by the agency." In this case, the agency in question changed its tune after Judicial Watch filed a lawsuit.

The Obama administration was asking for the strictest interpretation possible here, claiming that Judicial Watch had to *prove* that the lawsuit caused the documents to be released. (Obama administration lawyers assigned the fancy term "catalyst theory" to this line of reasoning.) In our view, the mere fact that we filed the lawsuit and then the documents were released entitled Judicial Watch to the fees.

As noted by the lower court in its ruling in favor of Judicial Watch: "[Judicial Watch] may not have received an appropriate response to its FOIA request absent the filing of the lawsuit." This was a clear-cut case of cause (lawsuit) and effect (documents released). Unfortunately, the appellate court ruled in the administration's favor by ruling that the analysis of whether fees would be awarded had to be done under the terms of the previous, more restrictive FOIA law. This costly court battle was just more evidence of Obama's "big lie" about his supposed commitment to transparency. The Obama crowd, it seemed to us, actually rolled back an expansion of FOIA by President Bush!

My colleague Judicial Watch director of investigations Chris Farrell told the *Examiner*, "Every day, the Obama administration misrepresents and conceals [relevant documentation]—all the while proclaiming themselves champions of transparency. It's truly Orwellian."[3]

Orwellian is right. Despite his abysmal record on transparency, Obama spent a good deal of time during his 2010 State of the Union address focusing on transparency and ethics. "[W]e have to recognize that we face more than a deficit of dollars right now," he said. "We face a deficit of trust—deep and corrosive doubts about how Washington works that have been growing for years. To close that credibility gap we have to take action on both ends of Pennsylvania Avenue—to end the outsized influence of lobbyists; to do our work openly; to give our people the government they deserve. That's what I came to Washington to do. That's why—for the first time in history—my administration posts our White House visitors online. That's why we've excluded lobbyists from policymaking jobs, or seats on federal boards and commissions."

That was the continuing rhetoric. The truth is more disturbing: lobbyists do work in his administration and do make policy. In reality, Obama is against hiring lobbyists except when he wants to hire lobbyists—hence his infamous "ethics waivers." Even the liberal website PolitiFact rated this line in Obama's speech as "false."[4]

As we'll discuss shortly, Obama was also misleading about the White House visitor logs. Only certain records were released; hundreds of thousands of others were withheld for arbitrary and unlawful reasons. In fact, the Obama administration continues to advance the ridiculous claim that the visitor logs are not agency records and are therefore not subject to the Freedom of Information Act. After Judicial Watch issued a press release critical of Obama's intolerable position on the release of White House visitor logs, his White House invited us over to "make a deal" on the logs, but still refused to change its position. That's why we're in federal court over this issue.

This sort of mendacity is why American people don't trust the government. Judicial Watch conducted a poll with SurveyUSA in December 2009 that made this point very clear. A majority of likely voters (56 percent) said they believe the Obama administration is too secretive. It doesn't take a genius Obama pollster to craft a line about openness in order to appeal to public sentiment. As the *Washington Post* pointed out, over three hundred individuals and groups sued the government under FOIA between January 2009 and January 2010. "In case after case," the *Post* reported, "the plaintiffs say little has changed since the Bush administration years, when most began their quests for records. Agencies still often fight requests for disclosure, contending that national security and internal decision-making need to be protected." The article also noted that the total number of FOIA lawsuits filed against the Obama administration in the first year of Obama's tenure—319—actually represented an increase over the Bush administration. By comparison, in President Bush's last year in office, his administration was slapped with 298 FOIA lawsuits.[5] We were responsible for about twenty of the aforementioned FOIA lawsuits filed against the Obama administration.

To bring you up to date, since the beginning of the Obama administration, we have filed well over eight hundred requests for information and over seventy-five lawsuits seeking enforcement of the Freedom of Information Act. We'd file more but we have only so many lawyers.

Targeting Enemies

It was supposed to be a scandal beyond all scandals when the Bush White House expressed opinions on the hiring and firing of U.S. attorneys appointed by the president. This so-called politicization of the Justice Department was supposed to end with the installation of Attorney General Eric Holder. Well, Judicial Watch understood that it would actually get worse, as Holder is a notorious political hack. And get worse it did with the firing of Gerald Walpin, the inspector general of the Corporation for National and Community Service. As we've seen already, both the Clinton administration and the Bush administration violated the safeguards surrounding the independence of government agency watchdogs. Obama followed in their footsteps in order to protect one of his political allies, Kevin Johnson, the former point guard for the Phoenix Suns and now Sacramento mayor.

Walpin uncovered corruption in AmeriCorps, one of the government's so-called national service programs, which receives millions of federal dollars annually to conquer everything from illiteracy to affordable housing and the environment. Walpin uncovered a multimillion-dollar fraud scheme in AmeriCorps' most expensive program, a teaching fellow project at the City University of New York. Walpin found that AmeriCorps' funding duplicated existing programs and that the government should recover up to $75 million that it had spent on the project in the past six years. Clearly, Walpin was doing his job—rooting out government fraud, waste, and abuse—quite efficiently.

That wasn't the end of the story, however. Much of the AmeriCorps work is done through local nonprofits that receive hundreds of thousands of dollars in federal grants from the agency. One of the local charities (St. HOPE Academy) that has benefited tremendously from the arrangement is based in Sacramento and was operated by Johnson. Walpin found that Johnson's nonprofit education group misused nearly $1 million in federal grants. The inspector general determined that Johnson illegally used the money to pay volunteers for political activities, run personal errands, and even wash his car. Walpin's office declared that Johnson and St. HOPE be "suspended" from receiving any federal funds, including stimulus cash.

Despite the strong allegations, the local U.S. attorney's office, led by Lawrence Brown, a career prosecutor who took over from a Bush appointee, decided not to file criminal charges. When Walpin insisted that a financial settlement would be okay, but that the suspension would remain, Brown simply cut him out of the loop. Brown instead began negotiating with the AmeriCorps directly— a move that made more sense in light of the fact that it was now headed up by Alan Solomont, a major Obama fund-raiser. As the *Wall Street Journal* reported, "A few days later, Mr. Brown's office produced a settlement draft that significantly watered down any financial repayment and cleared Mr. Johnson. Mr. Walpin told us that in all his time working with U.S. Attorneys on cases he'd referred, he'd never been cut out in such fashion. Mr. Walpin brought his concerns to the Corporation for National and Community Service's board, but some board members were angry over a separate Walpin investigation into the wrongful disbursement of $80 million to the City University of New York. Concerned about the St. HOPE mess, Mr. Walpin wrote a 29-page report, signed by two other senior members of his office, and submitted it in April to Congress. [A few days later] he got a phone call from a White House lawyer telling him to resign within an hour or be fired."[6] The mayor, who later acknowledged that there "may have been administrative errors," reached a settlement with federal prosecutors to repay half of the money.

These events led Senator Charles Grassley (R-IA) to write a letter to Obama excoriating the firing, especially since Obama had cosponsored the bill requiring "cause" to be shown for removing an inspector general. The letter and spirit of the law, intended to safeguard the independence of inspectors general from the heavy hand of the executive branch, may have been circumvented, according to the veteran Republican.

The criticism of Obama's decision was bipartisan. The Democratic senator who authored the law relating to the termination of government agency watchdogs blasted Obama, too, for abruptly removing an inspector general who has exposed widespread waste in taxpayer-financed community service groups. In a statement posted on her U.S. Senate website, Missouri senator Claire McCaskill said Obama "failed to follow the proper procedure" in notifying Congress about the inspector general removal and for failing to give a valid reason for the termination. Obama's only excuse for firing Walpin was that the president had somehow lost confidence in him. He then amended his story, blaming Walpin's removal on the fact that Walpin was "confused" and "disoriented" at a meeting. Walpin certainly seemed lucid during his tenure as inspector general of the country's national service programs, however. "This," pronounced the *Wall Street Journal*, "is a case that smells of political favoritism and Chicago rules."

Then the Obama administration decided to cover it up. First Lady Michelle Obama was reportedly behind the contentious dismissal, and congressional investigators wanted to interview the aide (Jackie Norris) who may have given the order. At the time Norris was the First Lady's chief of staff, but the White House counsel's office blocked investigators from interviewing her, according to a national news report. Norris later became a senior advisor at the Corporation for National and Community Service.

Solomont, when interviewed by the House Committee on Oversight and Government Reform, said that he hadn't discussed any corporation business specifically with Norris. As it turns out, however, when the White House released visitor records, it showed that Solomont had visited Norris three times, including the day before Walpin was fired. When the committee attempted to probe Solomont more deeply, the White House cut off the questioning. Darrell Issa, the ranking member of the committee, observed to Solomont, "Because the records contained in the White House visitor logs are inconsistent with your statements to the Committee investigators on July 15, 2009, and because you did not satisfactorily reconcile your testimony with the visitor logs, there remain unanswered questions.

Most importantly, on July 15, 2009, why did you fail to include Jackie Norris among those people whom you acknowledged having discussed CNCS business. . . . [I]n light of these records and the fact that Ms. Norris was transitioning from the White House to CNCS, it seems implausible that you would not remember your meetings with her."[7] Sadly, justice was never attained for Walpin; a court ruled that he didn't have a right to his old job. As Grassley put it, "That's bad news for accountability in government."[8]

Sure enough, the Obama administration hasn't bothered to fill Walpin's position and the inspector general's office at the Ameri-Corps organization is set to be downsized. Obama's buddy, the corrupt Kevin Johnson, must be thrilled—but taxpayers have no advocate in this notorious agency.[9] This evidently suits Obama just fine since a number of key agencies have no permanent inspector general. According to the Council of the Inspectors General on Integrity and Efficiency, twelve of seventy-three agencies do not have permanent inspectors general. Obama administration agencies without permanent inspectors general include some of the most important in the federal government: the Department of Justice, the Department of State, the Department of Labor, the Department of Homeland Security, and the Department of Defense.

As the Project on Government Oversight explains, if you want credible oversight in federal agencies, it is crucial that permanent investigators be appointed:

> [Offices of Inspectors General] are best positioned to be effective when led by a highly qualified permanent IG, rather than an acting official or no IG at all. Permanent IGs undergo significant vetting—especially the IGs that require Senate confirmation—before taking their position. That vetting process helps to instill confidence among OIG stakeholders—Congress, agency officials, whistleblowers, and the public—that the OIG is truly independent and that its investigations and audits are accurate and credible.
>
> In addition, a permanent IG has the ability to set a long-term strategic plan for the office, including setting investigative and audit priorities. An acting official, on the other hand, is known by all OIG

staff to be temporary, which one former IG has argued "can have a debilitating effect on [an] OIG, particularly over a lengthy period." Senator Charles Grassley (R-IA) has echoed that sentiment, saying "Even the best acting inspector general lacks the standing to make lasting changes needed to improve his or her office."[10]

In the meantime, Judicial Watch is happy to do its part as the American people's private inspector general. In the age of Obama, his government has grown but his administration has literally decimated the government's own oversight mechanisms. Once again, the job of serious government oversight in Washington falls in no small measure to our independent group.

Obama's Nixonian Approach to Fox News

Speaking of enemies, the Obama administration's distaste for Fox News has been on display from the outset. But it reached a whole new level when reports appeared in the press that the White House attempted to boycott the network from a round of interviews organized by the Treasury Department with "Executive Pay Czar" Kenneth Feinberg on October 22, 2009.

The scandal ultimately led to a backlash from the other networks and a reversal by the Obama White House. Of course, the White House denied the charge that Fox was singled out for exclusion repeatedly; they blamed the issue on a miscommunication. We didn't believe that for one minute, so we filed a Freedom of Information Act request with the Treasury Department.

Well, it took nearly two years, but we managed to obtain some documents in response to our request. And we once again caught the Obama gang in big fat lie. Contrary to the administration's repeated denials, these documents did, in fact, demonstrate that the Obama White House attempted to exclude Fox News Channel. But it gets worse than that. The documents, which include email exchanges within the Department of the Treasury and between Treasury and

White House staff, also provided colorful evidence of a pervasive anti–Fox News bias within the Obama White House.

And when I say colorful, I mean colorful.

Now, when this scandal first erupted in the press back in 2009, it seemed everyone had an issue with the Obama administration's handling of the interviews (except the Obama administration). Even the ultraliberal *New York Times*: "Fox's television news competitors refused to go along with a Treasury Department effort on Thursday [October 22, 2009] to exclude Fox from a round of interviews with the executive-pay czar Kenneth R. Feinberg that was to be conducted with a 'pool' camera crew."

Fox News Channel's James Rosen reported at the time that this backlash forced the Obama administration to reconsider its position on the matter: "The Washington bureau chiefs of the five TV news networks . . . consulted and decided that none of them would interview Feinberg unless Fox was included, and the administration relented," reported Rosen. Ultimately, after other media representatives objected, Fox News Channel was allowed to participate in the interviews.

The Treasury Department's official response, as detailed in back-and-forth emails uncovered by Judicial Watch, included a clear denial of any such plot to exclude Fox News from the interviews: "There was no plan to exclude Fox News, and they had the same interview that their competitors did. Much ado about absolutely nothing."

Moreover, in an email to the *Times'* Jim Rutenberg on October 23, 2009, Jake Siewert, counselor to Treasury secretary Timothy Geithner, repeated the denial that there was an effort to exclude Fox News Channel: "Call me today on your Fox Treasury report," Siewert wrote. "Not true that there was an 'effort to exclude' Fox." Then how did the White House explain this October 22, 2009, email exchange between Dag Vega, director of broadcast media on the White House staff, and Jenni LeCompte, then–assistant secretary for public affairs in the Treasury Department? When LeCompte asked Vega whether Fox should be included in the list of invited cable networks,

Vega informed LeCompte that "we'd prefer if you skip Fox please."
You can see that email below:

LeCompte, Jenni

From: Vega, Dag (b) (6) ███████████████
Sent: Thursday, October 22, 2009 11:10 AM
To: LeCompte, Jenni
Subject: RE: Change of Plans

Great, let me know which cables you add... and, we'd prefer if you skip Fox please.

Regarding general anti–Fox News bias within the Obama
White House in an October 23, 2009, email exchange between
deputy White House communications director Jennifer Psaki and
LeCompte, Psaki wrote, "I am putting some dead fish in the fox
cubby—just cause." In an email on the night of October 22, 2009,
commenting on a report by Fox News Channel anchor Bret Baier
that noted the exclusion of the network from the pool, Psaki wrote
to LeCompte and fellow White House colleagues that "brett [*sic*]
baier just did a stupid piece on it—but he is a lunatic." Below is the
"lunatic" email:

Williams, Andrew

From: Psaki, Jennifer R. (b) (6) ███████████████
Sent: Thursday, October 22, 2009 6:59 PM
To: Siewert, Jake; Williams, Andrew; LeCompte, Jenni
Subject: RE: you know about fox telling rutenberg about feinberg not initially doing fox?

Sounds good--brett baier just did a stupid piece on it---but he is a lunatic

---

Deputy White House press secretary Josh Earnest bluntly described the White House's position on Fox News Channel in an
October 23, 2009, email to LeCompte: "We've demonstrated our
willingness and ability to exclude Fox News from significant interviews. . . ."

The Obama administration lied about its attempt to exclude Fox
News Channel from access to an interview with the "pay czar." And
these documents showed there was a pervasive anti-Fox bias in the

Obama White House. Certainly the juvenile mafioso-like talk in these emails has no place in any White House.

Even more important, the Obama administration's attempt to purposely exclude a major news organization from access to information had troubling First Amendment implications—a point everyone seemed to get except the Obama White House.

The White House was asked at one of its daily press briefings about Judicial Watch's work:

> Q: Jay [Carney], I need to switch gears for a second. Judicial Watch, the watchdog group, has obtained some emails from the administration about an October 2009 incident about whether or not FOX News would get an interview with Ken Feinberg, then the executive pay czar. And publicly, the administration was saying that FOX was not excluded. The emails seemed to suggest that FOX was perhaps punished and was excluded. Has the administration concluded there was any inappropriate activity there?
>
> MR. (JAY) CARNEY: Well, Mike, first of all, let me address a serious matter here, that I can say, having looked into this matter, that no one at the White House, either a current or former employee, ever placed a dead fish in the FOX News cubbyhole, which I know is a suggestion. (Laughter.) I can also say that it is well known that at the time there was a dispute between FOX News and its coverage and the White House and its feelings about the coverage. I mean, that was then, and we obviously deal with FOX News regularly. I call on you regularly. We give interviews to FOX News, including to Bill O'Reilly. But beyond that, I don't really know much about it.

It is good that we forced the Obama White House to run away from its inappropriate behavior. For its part, Fox News was in no mood to start a fight again. A top Fox official was quoted as saying, "On and off-the-air relations with this administration have come a long way since then, and if that unfortunate incident helped get things on a better track, then it served its purpose."

I don't believe that all is sweetness and light between the Obama gang and Fox. And the fact remains: we caught the Obama White House in a big lie and gained a glimpse of this administration's Nixonian approach to the media. David Zurawik, the *Baltimore Sun* media critic, who is no fan of Fox News, summed it up: "Not since Richard Nixon and Spiro Agnew, have I seen a White House with such contempt for the press—and disregard for the historic role a free press plays in this society."

The Fairness Doctrine and Campaign Finance Reform

If the hallmark of rule of law and rule of the people is transparency in government, the press is a vital component of that equation. "[T]he freedom of the press is one of the greatest bulwarks of liberty and can never be restrained but by despotic governments," George Mason wrote in the Virginia Declaration of Rights in 1776. "The liberty of the press is essential to the security of freedom in a state: it ought not, therefore, to be restrained in this commonwealth," John Adams wrote in the Massachusetts Constitution in 1780. "The only security of all is in a free press," Thomas Jefferson wrote. "The force of public opinion cannot be resisted when permitted freely to be expressed. The agitation it produces must be submitted to. It is necessary, to keep the waters pure."

Government, however, has a long and nasty history of attempting to quash the freedom of the press to suppress criticism. Since the rise of conservative talk radio in particular over the last two decades, the left has seen fit to try to reanimate the long-dead, misnamed "Fairness Doctrine," an FCC rule that forced broadcast licensees to present all sides of a political issue. Of course, this rule is inherently biased in favor of bigger government, since it is the government itself that gets to decide if an issue has been treated fairly under this doctrine. Since 1987, it has been defunct.

President Obama maintained that he had no interest in re-creating the Fairness Doctrine. If the Fairness Doctrine was truly dead, however, you wouldn't have known it from the batch of documents we got from the FCC in May 2009. We filed our original

FOIA back in December 2008 to find out what internal government discussions have taken place surrounding the reimplementation of the Fairness Doctrine. And there was much discussion for sure.

Not only did the documents show that controversy continued concerning the Fairness Doctrine; the FCC was considering alternative proposals that may regulate free speech in the media just as much as the Fairness Doctrine, but under the professed goal of "diversity."

In December 2007, for example, the FCC proposed new "localism" measures to force broadcast stations to offer programming more "responsive to the needs and interests of the communities that they are licensed to serve." These proposed measures, highlighted in a document titled "The Report on Broadcast Localism and Notice of Approved Rulemaking," included a requirement that broadcasters "provide 3 hours per week of locally-produced program" and that licensees establish "permanent advisory boards (including representatives of underserved community segments)." The FCC noted that these measures would become part of the application renewal process to make sure broadcasters "meet their responsibilities" (a nice way for the government to say, "Do it or else").

Problems with this "localism" proposal are highlighted in a legal memo written by Kathleen Kirby of the law firm Wiley Rein and submitted to Rosemary Harold, serving as legal counsel to FCC commissioner Robert McDowell. In the document, which was distributed internally at the FCC, Kirby advises that the Fairness Doctrine "would do well to stay dead." Kirby then turns her attention to "localism," advising that such a policy could represent a "stealth enactment" of the Fairness Doctrine. Kirby states: "Convene permanent advisory boards? Give aggrieved listeners 'more straightforward guidance' on 'how individuals can directly participate in the license renewal process'? That sounds mild. But then again, so did the Fairness Doctrine."

It took the landmark election of 2010 to end the speculation about the Fairness Doctrine. In August 2011, the FCC finally voted to remove from the Federal Register the language implementing the Fairness Doctrine.

That wasn't the last time the Obama administration would attempt to play secret politics with the FCC. On February 13, 2009, Judicial Watch filed a FOIA request with the FCC seeking access to the following records: "Any records concerning the decision to delay the transition to digital television until June 12, 2009 . . . Any and all records of communication between the Federal Communications [Commission] and the White House concerning the delays in the transition to digital television." We sent this FOIA request because at the time, press reports said that a donor and advisor to President Obama on digital television issues, R. Gerard Salemme, was an executive with Clearwire, a telecommunications company that stood to benefit from the delay. The digital transition delay allegedly allowed Clearwire (and its partner, Sprint) to maintain an edge over competitor Verizon. The delay in the digital transition also would have had the effect of delaying Verizon's launch of a new broadband wireless network that would compete with a network currently operated by Clearwire/Sprint.

On May 8, 2009, the FCC told us that it had uncovered documents related to the first part of Judicial Watch's request and that the FCC would soon release some documents while withholding others. With respect to the second part of Judicial Watch's request, involving communications with the Obama administration, Joel Kaufman, associate general counsel for the FCC, indicated that the agency was required to "consult with the White House." The FCC "is unable to respond to this part of your FOIA request until we receive instructions from the White House," Kaufman wrote in his response letter.

This response was not only highly unusual; it was also extremely troubling given that our FOIA request actually involved alleged corruption inside the Obama White House. So why was the Obama White House meddling in a routine FOIA request?

There is no provision of FOIA law that allows the White House to screen requests for potentially damaging information. The FCC, however, does have an obligation to abide by the law and either release the documents or provide a justification for withholding them. The answer: Obama White House sensitivities trump the FCC's legal obligations. Just another day at the office for the least-transparent administration in American history.

Even as the Obama administration tried to shut down free speech that didn't buy into the Obama point of view, they ripped the Supreme Court for opening up the political process to corporations who sought to give money to candidates. Now, Obama had been the beneficiary of enormous union spending during the 2008 campaign. So what was his objection to other organized groups getting involved? Simply this: they weren't on his side. Therefore, according to Obama's logic, they could be legally banned from participation in elections.

In a January 2010 landmark decision, the Supreme Court decimated the McCain-Feingold campaign finance law, ruling that the First Amendment allowed corporations and labor unions to engage in independent expenditures (or electioneering communications) in support of political candidates. In other words, corporations and labor unions could independently run ads directly attacking or opposing candidates.

At issue in this lawsuit was a ninety-minute documentary about Hillary Clinton produced by the conservative organization Citizens United. In 2008, the Federal Election Commission, citing McCain-Feingold, prohibited the program from airing on television stations during election season. This prompted Citizens United to file a lawsuit to vindicate its First Amendment rights (*Citizens United v. Federal Election Commission*).

As Judicial Watch does often in legal matters of great importance, we filed an amicus curiae (friend of the court) brief with the Supreme Court in July 2009 on the side of Citizens United. Here's an excerpt from our brief: "The [Supreme] Court . . . was solicitous to protect political speech not only as a matter of individual liberty, and not only because it was the intention of the Framers, but because political speech is crucial to the survival of our representative government and its system of ordered liberty. This principle, in turn, presupposes that First Amendment protection of political speech is the precondition of all other freedoms protected by the Constitution."

In other words, we believe protecting political speech is especially important. Groups like Judicial Watch (which are organized as not-for-profit corporations) should be able to tell the truth about a candidate at any time. The First Amendment shouldn't shut down around election season. In fact, election season is one of the most important times to engage in the open exchange of ideas and opinions.

Thankfully, the Supreme Court agreed with Judicial Watch on almost every point. And President Obama, unhappy with the First Amendment affirmation of free speech, attacked the Supreme Court directly, in his own inimitable fashion, in his State of the Union address in 2010: "Last week, the Supreme Court reversed a century of law to open the floodgates for special interests—including foreign corporations—to spend without limit in our elections. Well I don't think American elections should be bankrolled by America's most powerful interests, or worse, by foreign entities. They should be decided by the American people, and that's why I'm urging Democrats and Republicans to pass a bill that helps to right this wrong."

No president has ever attacked the Supreme Court so directly at a State of the Union address. Obama's attack was a disgrace that undermined the rule of law. It meant that a Supreme Court justice might think twice about any ruling that could rankle President Obama—for fear of being attacked in person in front of a national audience.

And President Obama was wrong about the "century of law": the Supreme Court overturned a precedent that was twenty years old, not one hundred years old. So Obama's statement was "not true," as Justice Samuel Alito mouthed during Obama's attack. The Supreme Court ruling also did not address foreign involvement in our elections, which is still illegal. (Obama may want to ask the Clintons and check with his own campaigns about the foreign money issue.)

Intimidation, attacks, and end runs around the Constitution are nothing new to this president or, frankly, virtually any Congress. Better enforcement of bribery and extortion laws is the key to fighting government corruption—not self-serving restrictions on free speech by politicians. Big-government politicians like Obama will never understand that. Or perhaps they understand it all too well, which is why they are so desperate to shut down their opponents by banning their speech.

Selling Senate Seats

In December 2008, Illinois governor Rod Blagojevich was arrested along with his chief of staff, John Harris, for engaging in a "political corruption crime spree," according to prosecuting U.S. attorney Patrick Fitzgerald, that "would make Lincoln roll over in his grave." That spree included Blagojevich's attempt to sell President Obama's U.S. Senate seat, which was vacant due to Obama's ascension to the presidency. Like Obama himself, the Illinois governor had campaigned on a platform of cleaning up government in the wake of a Republican predecessor, in this case former Illinois governor George Ryan, who was also involved in shady dealings, which resulted in his resignation and later prosecution and conviction. Blagojevich had been recorded in conversation with his staff regarding potential picks to fill the Obama seat—and their qualifications were largely determined by their ability to put money in Blagojevich's pockets. As Blagojevich said in one of the recorded conversations, the seat was "a [bleeping] valuable thing. You just don't give it away. . . . I've got this thing, and it's [bleeping] golden." Blagojevich also thought about appointing himself to the Senate so that he could run for president in 2016; he lobbied too for appointment as secretary of health and human services or to an ambassadorship (he certainly had the credentials for it in the Obama administration, which sought out the most corrupt people it could find for virtually every position imaginable). He tried to broker a deal so that he could get a union-affiliated cash cow job, in exchange for appointing Valerie Jarrett to the Senate seat. Fitzgerald carefully stated "we make no allegation" that Obama knew what Blagojevich was doing. Obama himself played the doe-eyed innocent, stating, "Like the rest of the people of

Illinois, I am saddened and sobered by the news that came out of the U.S. attorney's office today. But as this is an ongoing investigation involving the governor, I don't think it would be appropriate for me to comment on the issue at this time. . . . I had no contact with the governor or his office and so I was not aware of what was happening." Said Robert Grant, the FBI special agent heading up the Chicago office, "If [Illinois] isn't the most corrupt state in the United States, it's certainly one hell of a competitor."[11]

The arrest of Governor Blagojevich came as no surprise. There had been an air of lawlessness around him for some time. We had investigated Blagojevich for over two years and had an ongoing open records lawsuit against him concerning the sale of government jobs. Like other corrupt politicians, he stonewalled and refused to turn over the documents that could have implicated him. We filed an open records lawsuit against the office of the governor on January 16, 2007, in the Cook County, Illinois, circuit court seeking, among other documents, any and all grand jury subpoenas received by the governor's office or any state agencies under the governor's control. The subpoenas reportedly were issued by U.S. attorney Patrick Fitzgerald's office. Blagojevich's office refused to release the subpoenas, claiming falsely that they were exempt from public disclosure. The state's top legal officer, Illinois attorney general Lisa Madigan, said that the grand jury subpoenas were documents subject to public disclosure: "Based upon the information with which we have been furnished, the exceptions to the disclosure requirements of the [Freedom of Information] Act cited by the Governor's office does not authorize the withholding of subpoenas. Without legal support, the Office of the Governor and the agencies under his control cannot withhold Federal grand jury subpoenas in their possession and must release these documents pursuant to a FOIA request." In reaction to Madigan's opinion, Blagojevich fought to have his office represented by his personal attorney, rather than the state attorney general. To have a governor at war with his state's attorney general over a basic interpretation of freedom of information law was an unusual turn of events. So it is safe to say that we were quite familiar with Blagojevich's strategies and diversionary tactics, and we knew that something deeply wrong was going on out of the office he held in trust for the people of Illinois.

In fact, Blagojevich's outrageous stonewalling of our request was one of the reasons he was impeached and removed from office.[12] Our lead litigator, Paul Orfanedes, traveled to Springfield to testify at Blagojevich's impeachment hearing in the Illinois House of Representatives.

However damaging to the already terrible reputation of Illinois's political culture, the most disturbing part of the Blago scandal was the questions it raised about President Obama and his close associates. The criminal complaint filed indicated that Obama and his team knew about Blagojevich's efforts to sell Obama's Senate seat, with Tony Rezko once again implicated in the corrupt activities. But Obama never reported to investigators about any efforts to sell his Senate seat.

The documents that we obtained through our Illinois FOIA requests that were related to Blagojevich's contacts with Obama and his staff, however, bore fruit. On December 3, 2008, less than a week before authorities arrested Blagojevich, Obama sent a letter to Blagojevich stating, "Thank you for meeting with me on Tuesday in Philadelphia. Vice President–elect Joe Biden and I were pleased with the open discussion. As we discussed, I would appreciate any advice you can provide to me and my team on the biggest roadblocks to states in moving forward in 'getting ready to go' projects started quickly. In addition, I welcome any advice you can provide me and my team on revitalizing and reinvigorating the state-federal partnership. I want to make it a priority of my administration to work closely with you. I look forward to working with you and hitting the ground running on January 20th." The two sides were definitely talking.

On November 17, 2008, a letter signed by Valerie Jarrett and John Podesta to Blagojevich said, "On behalf of President-elect Barack Obama and Vice President–elect Joe Biden we want you to know of our strong interest in working with you in the months to come. As you may know we have formed a Presidential Transition Team so that the new administration will be prepared to confront the extraordinary challenges facing our country. Your leadership and experience will be invaluable in this effort and we hope you will not hesitate to share your insights during this process." There's certainly no doubt that the documents undermined Obama's claims that he had no contact with Blagojevich, and they suggested that his transition team was hiding documents about such contacts. Why didn't Obama release the letter himself?

As a reaction to the scandal, and in an attempt to disassociate completely from Blagojevich, the Obama administration attempted to block the seating of Blagojevich's legally appointed successor to Obama, Roland Burris. We insisted that Burris, a Democrat, be seated in accordance with the law. The Seventeenth Amendment allows a state's governor to appoint a U.S. senator in the event of a vacancy, so long as the governor has the support of the state legislature. Illinois law specifically mandates that the "Governor shall make temporary appointment" to fill any vacancy. The U.S. Constitution also guarantees Illinois taxpayers the right to representation by two U.S. senators in the U.S. Senate. Given these facts, the Senate's refusal to allow Burris to be sworn in and to assume his rightful position as member of the U.S. Senate violated the U.S. Constitution. However suspicious we were of Blago and Burris, the law was the law—and it couldn't be avoided because it might embarrass President Obama. Burris was eventually sworn in and seated.

About a month later, we called for him to resign. What happened? Again, the law is the law. Burris apparently lied about his contacts with disgraced and impeached Illinois governor Rod Blagojevich. A wiretap on Blagojevich's line revealed that Burris told Rob Blagojevich, Rod's brother and chairman of his reelection campaign, that he would "personally do something" to help Blagojevich and then said he would "give him a check." Burris knew exactly what he was doing. "It has so many negative connotations that Burris is trying to buy an appointment . . . from the governor . . . for the Senate seat," Burris told Rob. "I'm trying to figure out how to deal with this and still be in the consideration for the appointment."[13] Eventually Burris admitted to trying to raise money for Blagojevich in return for the appointment to the Senate seat. He was apparently going to launch a fund-raiser for Blagojevich even as he made his pitch to Blagojevich to be selected to the Senate. By the *Washington Post's* count, Burris changed his story five times regarding his contacts with Blagojevich prior to the Illinois governor appointing him to the U.S. Senate. Three of those changing explanations came under oath. Of course, when the question was first raised, Burris said there had been no contact with Blagojevich prior to the appointment.

The Senate Ethics Committee investigated; unlike President Obama, Burris didn't have many friends in the Senate. They were looking for a reason from the beginning to keep him out of the Senate. Incredibly, though, Burris didn't resign—and he turned out to be right, since the Ethics Committee dropped all charges against him in June 2009 despite the tapes. He served out the remainder of his term, which ended in 2010, and then didn't run for reelection.

At the conclusion of his first trial, Blagojevich was found guilty of just a single criminal count—lying to the FBI. That was it. Public reaction to the verdict was nearly universal: "One count? That's it!? Is this a joke?" No, it was no joke. And, truthfully, this is the result we expected after the government wrapped up its case. It looked like the prosecution's case was distorted in order to protect President Obama, Rahm Emanuel, and Valerie Jarrett. It's that simple.

We sent our *Corruption Chronicles* (our Internet blog after which this book is named) reporter Irene Garcia to Chicago to report on the 2010 Blagojevich trial firsthand. Irene had been a longtime reporter for the *Los Angeles Times*, so we had a reliable account of the trial. She reported that Blagojevich's former chief of staff John Harris testified that President Obama had personal knowledge of Blagojevich's scheme to get his hands on a presidential cabinet position by appointing a candidate handpicked by the president to take over Obama's former Senate seat. Obama's preferred candidate, at least initially, according to testimony, was Valerie Jarrett, currently the senior advisor and assistant to the president for intergovernmental affairs and public engagement. Explosive federal wiretaps played at trial captured Blagojevich offering Obama's Senate seat for a cabinet position. In one conversation, Blagojevich told Harris he wanted to be named secretary of health and human services if Valerie Jarrett got Obama's seat. If health secretary "was available to me I could do Valerie Jarrett in a heartbeat," Blagojevich said.

The president also sent Blagojevich a list of other "acceptable" Senate candidates to fill his old seat. The list included Tammy Duckworth, Illinois state comptroller Dan Hynes, Congressman Jesse Jackson Jr., and Congresswoman Jan Schakowsky, according to Harris. Harris also testified that three days after the 2008 presidential election Blagojevich told him he felt confident Obama wanted to swap perks.

Blagojevich repeatedly ferried messages to President Obama through White House chief of staff Rahm Emanuel. For example, John Harris testified that Blagojevich asked him to call Emanuel to see if the president was "still in agreement" that the Senate seat should go to Representative Jesse Jackson Jr. (The evidence suggests that Jackson separately sought the Senate seat in exchange for a $1 million payoff.)

The trial was turning into a political nightmare for the Obama White House. And that may explain why the prosecution shut their case down a month early.

Immediately following the first Blagojevich trial verdict, federal prosecutors promised to quickly retry the case, leading the *Washington Post* to speculate whether the Obama White House would be dragged into the mess this time around: "[I]f U.S. Attorney Patrick J. Fitzgerald has his way, there will be a new trial. New attempts by the prosecution to build a case against Blagojevich. New efforts by the defense to subpoena Chief of Staff Rahm Emanuel and senior adviser Valerie Jarrett to the stand."[14]

The first trial and our independent investigation showed that Obama lied about his communications with Blago. Blago's second trial occurred last year. This time around, Blagojevich was not so fortunate. After deliberating for ten days a federal jury convicted Blagojevich of seventeen corruption charges. Emanuel, now mayor of Chicago, did finally testify—for less than five minutes. Emanuel testified he was never asked for anything in exchange for appointing Jarrett to Obama's vacant Senate seat.

Blago was finally sentenced to fourteen years in December 2011. Rahm Emanuel, who knew or should have known about Blago's crooked scheme, was unfortunately allowed to skate, even though he was intimately involved in Blago's crooked scheme. "Rahmbo" served as the liaison between Blago and Barack Obama. Obama was interviewed by the FBI even before he took office but was never asked to testify. And we still don't know the full truth about Obama's role in all this. That's why we're pressuring the FBI to release to us the notes of their historic interview with him.

Make no mistake: Blago is now in jail (he began his sentence on March 14, 2012), but Chicago-style corruption still dogs Illinois— and the White House.

The Blagojevich scheme to abuse federal office for personal gain evidently had some admirers in the Obama White House. In 2009, the White House attempted to bring U.S. Senate candidate Andrew Romanoff (D-CO) into the administration to keep him from mounting a primary challenge against Democratic senator Michael Bennett. As *Politico* reported, "Romanoff revealed that White House Deputy Chief of Staff Jim Messina offered to consider Romanoff for three posts as an alternative to his Senate campaign." [15]

Romanoff actually released an email from Messina to the press— dated September 11, 2009—listing the three jobs that "would be available" if Romanoff were not running for the Senate against Obama's handpicked candidate. Two of them were with United States Agency for International Development and the other was the position of director of the U.S. Trade and Development Agency. So we had the name of a top White House official (Jim Messina, who was Rahm Emanuel's deputy), three specific "paid" jobs offered, and clear evidence of the offer. Eric Holder did nothing to investigate. So we filed a complaint with the Office of Special Counsel requesting an investigation into violations of the Hatch Act by Emanuel and Messina. We're still waiting for OSC to get back to us. Both men are back in Chicago, Emanuel in the mayor's office and Messina as manager for Obama's 2012 reelection campaign.

In the summer of 2009, the White House also offered a job to Representative Joe Sestak (D-PA) so that Sestak would not mount a primary challenge against the newly turned Democrat senator Arlen Specter. Sestak claimed repeatedly that the Obama White House tried to persuade him to abandon his Democratic primary challenge to Specter by offering him a high-level position in the Obama administration.

Sestak's allegations were extremely serious and yet we heard nothing from the Obama White House besides vague denials of wrongdoing and outright stonewalling. There was simply no wiggle room to this story. Either Sestak lied about the federal job offer or someone at the White House likely committed a felony. It's that simple. Attorney General Eric Holder, though, refused to appoint a special counsel to look into the problem.

This bribery allegation reflected a disturbing pattern by the Obama White House. The following laws (among others) may have been violated in the Sestak matter: 18 U.S.C. § 210: Offer to procure appointive public office; 18 U.S.C. § 211: Acceptance of solicitation to obtain appointive public office; 18 U.S.C. § 595: Interference by administrative employees by Federal, State, or Territorial Governments; and 18 U.S.C. § 600: Promise of employment or other benefit for political activity.

Based on Sestak's statements, we filed a congressional ethics complaint against Sestak for allegedly conspiring with the Obama White House to "cover up criminal conduct regarding job offers made to Congressman Sestak in exchange for leaving a political campaign." As we noted in our complaint, Representative Sestak changed his story regarding the details of the job offer "after consulting with the White House."

In his initial statement to the press in February 2010, Sestak said he had been offered a "federal job" in a failed effort to dissuade him from challenging Specter in Pennsylvania's Democratic primary. He remained consistent to this initial statement through the end of May. On May 28 the White House released its official statement on the job offer and unsurprisingly found "no improper conduct regarding

Congressman Sestak." Moreover, the White House claimed Sestak had not been offered a job, but rather "unpaid service on a presidential advisory board" by former President Bill Clinton at the behest of White House chief of staff Rahm Emanuel.

After the White House issued its public statement, Sestak then changed his account by suggesting he was not offered "a federal job," but rather that the White House had made an "advisory board offer." One day before the White House released its statement, Sestak admitted in a press interview that the Obama White House contacted his brother to tell him "what's going to occur." (Sestak beat Specter, but lost his corrupted bid for the U.S. Senate to Pat Toomey in the general election. There's something to be said there about Sestak's selling his soul to the Obama gang for a mess of pottage.)

Under 18 U.S.C. § 371, "If two or more persons conspire either to commit any offense against the United States or to defraud the United States, or any agency thereof in any manner or for any purpose, and one or more of such persons do any act to effect the object of the conspiracy, each shall be fined under this title or imprisoned not more than five years, or both."

It sure looks as though Congressman Sestak and the Obama White House conspired to get their stories straight. They knew they were on the wrong side of the law and seem to have engaged in a cover-up. Why else would Sestak change his story so drastically? The House Ethics Committee never got back to us and Holder's Justice Department is busy suing states for defending the rule of law on immigration.

Hijacking the NEA

When the Obama team wasn't busy playing footsie with corrupt politicians across the nation, they were working to hijack government agencies for illegal purposes. We FOIA'd and received documents related to the controversial conference call by the National Endowment for the Arts on August 10, 2009, encouraging artists to create work that promotes the Obama agenda. This is illegal; the NEA is supposed to be nonpartisan. On August 25, 2009, artist Patrick Courrielche detailed in an email the purpose of the conference call, which was hosted by the NEA, the White House Office of Public Engagement, and United We Serve (AmeriCorps). The goal of the conference call, according to the email, was to encourage "a group of artists, producers, promoters, organizers, influencers, marketers, taste-makers, leaders or just plain cool people to join together and work together to promote a more civically engaged America and celebrate how the arts can be used for a positive change!" The email also included a notice from United We Serve, the taxpayer-funded propaganda arm for Obama-ism: "A call has come in to our generation. A call from the top. A call from a house that is White. . . . President Obama is asking us to come together. . . . Now is the time for us to answer this call."

The documents included internal NEA correspondence, such emails involving disgraced former NEA communications director Yosi Sergant, the fall guy who resigned over the scandal, and actor and then–associate director of the White House Office of Public Engagement, Kalpen Modi. The emails provided stark documentation of the Obama White House's enthusiastic involvement in the controversial conference call. (The Corporation for National and Community Service, which runs the AmeriCorps program, also was represented during the call.)

On August 10, 2009, Sergant sent Modi an email, reading, "[The call is] organized by me. . . . I'd ask you to come on and give the exact spiel you gave on Saturday. Walk them through the WH Arts Policy. They won't know it. Then I will take them into United We Serve and the NEA." Modi replied, "Oy. This would be awesome to be a part of. Let me know if you think it's going long, or maybe I can get someone from here to do it if I can't because of the Social Security mtg." A few minutes later, Modi wrote, "Let me see if we can move Social Sec by a few mins. Agreed, it would be great to be on the call and helpful for us also." Sargent then wrote Buffy Wicks, deputy director of the White House Office of Public Engagement, stating, "We have an important call at 2pm for UWS (United We Serve) and the Arts with my peeps. Indie producers around the country. Kal can't join the call. Any chance you can hop on for 5 minutes and intro with Nellie and I?"

While the names of the individuals on the conference call were redacted due to "privacy concerns," some of their titles were disclosed, including: Green Blogger, Publisher, Musician, Music Writer, Film/Marketing, Actress/Director, Marketing, Magazine, Marketing/Magazine, Event Producer, and Actress. These individuals were described by Sergant in an email as a "rad group, who can really get stuff done."

The NEA is supposed to foster the arts, not serve as a propaganda machine for the White House.

A subsequent batch of documents dribbled out from the NEA included some more interesting emails. One was from an unknown Obama campaign activist to Sergant: "It was good to see you a few weeks ago in Washington," the email read. "After our conversation, I thought it would be a really good idea to convene via a conference call some significant tastemakers/producers who can support United We Serve. As many of us contributed our services to the campaign, I would love to gather some of those folks to use their enthusiasm to get behind the President's very important service initiative. Here are some people who I think should be part of the call. [Names redacted.]" This was a clear offer to use the NEA as a campaign hot spot for Obama.

There were more artists who made the same proposal. One artist wrote Sergant, "How can I get down Yosi? I'm working with [redacted] doing brand consulting and event production for [redacted]. Love to see how we could collaborate our corporate funds with what you're working on." Another artist wrote, "As per a suggestion on the call, below is a list of action items that might be helpful to inspire an idea on how you can participate in the campaign. . . . Ex) If you are a graphic designer tap into your professional network and organize other designers to create a series of United We Serve posters that can be featured in print, through social media and on serve.gov. Ex) If you are a DJ, tap into your professional network and organize other DJs to promote Serve.gov or a specific local opportunity on the radio or at a club." The documents also detailed the use of the 9/11 anniversary as a vehicle for this political effort.

The NEA documents left little doubt that the NEA conference call and the ongoing United We Serve effort were direct extensions of the Obama presidential campaign.

"Come Fly with Me!"

President Obama and Speaker of the House Nancy Pelosi were perhaps the two most vocal politicians in the last decade on the issue of government ethics and reform. So Washington noticed when Speaker Pelosi came briefly under fire in 2007 for supposedly requesting a forty-two-seat air force plane to ferry the Speaker and her staff back and forth between San Francisco and Washington, D.C. (Former House Speaker Dennis Hastert was allowed access to a twelve-seat commuter jet for security reasons after the events of 9/11.) The liberal media establishment never followed up on Pelosi's use of military luxury travel. Once again, the job of oversight of government fell to us.

After years of digging, in 2009 we uncovered documents showing that Nancy Pelosi relied on the Department of Defense to provide her special military escorts and military aircraft, and made last-minute cancellations and changes. In response to a series of Pelosi's requests for military aircraft, one Defense Department official wrote, "Any chance of politely querying [Pelosi's team] if they really intend to do all of these or are they just picking every weekend? . . . [T]here's no need to block every weekend 'just in case.' . . ." The email also notes that Pelosi's office had "a history of canceling many of their past requests." One Defense Department official complained about the "hidden costs" associated with the Speaker's last-minute changes and cancellations. "We have . . . folks prepping the jets and crews driving in (not a short drive for some), cooking meals and preflighting the jets etc." The documents included a discussion of

House ethics rules and Defense Department policies as they apply to the Speaker's requests for staff, spouses, and extended family to accompany her on military aircraft. In May 2008, for example, Pelosi requested that her husband join her on a congressional delegation into Iraq. The Defense Department explained to Pelosi that the agency has a written policy prohibiting spouses from joining CODELs into combat zones. (A CODEL is Washington-speak for a congressional delegation trip using military luxury aircraft. Translated to taxpayer-speak: it is an acronym for "junket.")

Documents obtained from the U.S. Army include correspondence from Speaker Pelosi's office requesting an army escort and three military planes to transport Pelosi and other members of Congress to Cleveland for the funeral services of the late representative Stephanie Tubbs Jones. Pelosi noted in her letter of August 22, 2008, that such a request, labeled "Operation Tribute," was an "exception to standard policy." The documents also detail correspondence from intermediaries for Speaker Pelosi issuing demands for certain aircraft and expressing outrage when requested military planes were not available. "It is my understanding there are no G5s available for the House during the Memorial Day recess. This is totally unacceptable. . . . The speaker will want to know where the planes are. . . . ," wrote Kay King, director of the House Office of Interparliamentary Affairs. In a separate email, when told a certain type of aircraft would not be available, King wrote, "This is not good news, and we will have some very disappointed folks, as well as a very upset [s]peaker." Nice to see our military be treated so derisively by the Office of the Speaker, isn't it? I found it infuriating.

During another email exchange, Defense Department staff advised Kay King that one Pelosi military aircraft request could not be met because of "crew rest requirements" and offered to help secure commercial travel. Kay King responded: "We appreciate the efforts to help the codel [*sic*] fly commercially but you know the problem that creates with spouses. If we can find another way to assist with military assets, we would like to do that." The dirty little Hill secret was that a spouse flew for free if the military was providing the travel. But if the less expensive commercial airlines were used by congresspersons, spouses had to pay their own way. So the "problem" for the spouses was they'd have to pay their own way—which of course would have been no problem for put-upon taxpayers.

We conclusively documented how Speaker Pelosi treated the air force like her personal airline. Not only did Speaker Pelosi issue unreasonable requests for military travel, but her office seemed unconcerned about wasting taxpayer money with last-minute cancellations and other demands.

Speaker Pelosi had the Obama administration to count on when it came to taking us down a peg for uncovering these documents—although the takedown was rather weak tea. When we filed a follow-up request with a unit in the air force for more information, the Obama administration told us we'd have to pay $760 to obtain the documents. It was silly retaliation by the administration. We're the nation's leading organization when it comes to filing Freedom of Information Act requests. We know the law inside and out. Over the years we have filed literally thousands of open records requests. And we are almost never charged a fee like this by the federal government. This was petty payback for holding Nancy Pelosi to account over the Air Pelosi scandal.

Nonetheless, we kept fighting for information. And the more information we got, the worse this story got. The documents from the air force showed that the Speaker's military travel cost the air force $2,100,744.59 over a two-year period—$101,429.14 for in-flight expenses, including food and alcohol. Lots and lots of alcohol. Speaker Pelosi used Air Force aircraft to travel back to her district at an average cost of $28,210.51 per flight. The average cost of an international CODEL is $228,563.33. Of the 103 Pelosi-led CODELs, thirty-one trips included members of the House Speaker's family.

A CODEL traveling from Washington, D.C., through Tel Aviv, Israel, to Baghdad from May 15 to 20, 2008, "to discuss matters of mutual concern with government leaders" included members of Congress and their spouses and cost $17,931 per hour in aircraft alone. Purchases for the CODEL included: Johnnie Walker

Red scotch, Grey Goose vodka, E&J brandy, Bailey's Irish Crème, Maker's Mark whiskey, Courvoisier cognac, Bacardi Light rum, Jim Beam whiskey, Beefeater gin, Dewar's scotch, Bombay Sapphire gin, Jack Daniel's whiskey, Corona beer, and several bottles of wine.

According to a "Memo for Record" from a CODEL from March 29 to April 7, 2007, that involved a stop in Israel, "CODEL could only bring Kosher items into the Hotel. Kosher alcohol for mixing beverages in the Delegation room was purchased on the local economy i.e. Bourbon, Whiskey, Scotch, Vodka, Gin, Triple Sec, Tequila, etc." The Department of Defense advanced a CODEL of fifty-six members of Congress and staff $60,000 to travel to Louisiana and Mississippi from July 19 to 22, 2008, to "view flood relief advances from Hurricane Katrina." The three-day trip cost the U.S. Air Force $65,505.46, exceeding authorized funding by $5,505.46.

As a result of our work on the Pelosi air travel scandal, the media was sensitized to the issue of media travel and a firestorm erupted when it was reported by *Roll Call* that House appropriators sought to force the Pentagon to spend $500 million on luxury jets—which are used, in part, for the congressional junkets that we highlighted with Nancy Pelosi. Thanks to our disclosures, that went nowhere. The *Wall Street Journal* did excellent reporting on increasing use of military airplanes for congressional junkets, including a trip during which a congressman went *scuba-diving* to investigate the alleged global-warming scare.[16]

In the midst of all the controversy, we turned up the heat with the results of our investigation of waste and abuse related to congressional military travel. We released a fresh batch of documents from the Defense Department and the air force related to repeated requests for military aircraft by members of the U.S. Senate. Here are just a few of the highlights. One January 2, 2009, internal Defense Department email discussed a military travel request from Senate Majority Leader Harry Reid's office. A Pentagon official responding to the request wrote: "I was under the impression that they really only had small a/c [aircraft]. Regardless, with Sen Reid being the lead, they would definitely want a vip configured bird. Right now approval is only for one a/c. It's amazing how fast these things grow." Below is a sample of just what our military had to go through to cater to Speaker Pelosi:

```
-----Original Message-----
From: (b)(6)          Lt Col SAF/LLW
Sent: Thursday, March 25, 2010 11:28 AM
To: (b)(6)          Maj USAF 89 AW/CCE
Cc: (b)(6)              SSgt USAF 99 AS/CSO; (b)(6)        TSgt USAF 99 AS/DOV;
(b)(6)                  SSgt USAF 99 AS DOR/SM; (b)(6)        Lt Col USAF 99 AS/DOV; (b)(6)
(b)(6)      TSgt USAF 99 AS/FE
Subject: Re: MSN 16888

(b)(6)

The speakers office is requesting egg salad sandwiches on wheat toast with fruit (watermelon,
etc) for desert. It's the speaker's B-Day tomorrow so we're also asking for something like
chocolate cover strawberries (dark chocolate preferred). We'll have 7 pax including me.
My bb is (b)(5)
I'll plan on being there at 2PM tomorrow, unless time change.
Give me a call with questions.
Thanks
(b)(6)
```

A March 12, 2009, internal Defense Department email related to a military travel request involving a seven-country tour from Senate Minority Leader Mitch McConnell. The defense official responding to the request wrote: "As I expected, the McConnell group wants their C-40 not a C-9. . . . This is the only group that would not shift their dates to be in one half of the month and thus are taking up an asset that could have been used twice but now is being used once. That drove the aircraft decision."

Military assets were used to transport dozens of senators, their spouses, and others to the funerals of retired senators Claiborne Pell and Jesse Helms. John Fund has done important reporting on the size and scope of the congressional travel scandal, which is truly shocking. As he wrote in the *Wall Street Journal* in August 2009, "Frequent flying by Congress is a growth industry. . . . House members last year spent some 3,000 days overseas on taxpayer-funded trips, up from about 550 in 1995. This month, 11 separate congressional delegations will visit Germany. The total cost for congressional overseas travel is never made public because the price tag for State Department advance teams and military planes used by lawmakers are folded into much larger budgets. Members of Congress must only report the total per diem reimbursements they receive in cash for hotels, meals and local transport." [17]

House Speaker John Boehner, trying to distinguish himself from his predecessor, pledged to fly commercial back and forth to his district. We verified that he wasn't abusing the system through repeated inquires with Pentagon. A spokesman for the Speaker emailed me:

> Boehner has used military aircraft once this year for an overseas trip to visit our troops, military commanders, and diplomatic officials in Iraq, Afghanistan, and Pakistan. He has not used military aircraft to fly back and forth to his district as then-Speaker Pelosi customarily did. After Republicans won the election last year Boehner said: "Over the last 20 years, I have flown back and forth to my district on a commercial aircraft and I'm going to continue to do that." He has kept his word.

We checked and double-checked, and the Speaker is telling the truth. Now the Speaker needs to extend his personal austerity to the rest of the House, which still uses military luxury jets for junkets.

Not to be outdone by the amateurs on the Hill, the president and First Lady famously took advantage of the travel perks of high office for a "date night" on May 30, 2009. In a statement to the press, the president said: "I am taking my wife to New York City because I promised her during the campaign that I would take her to a Broadway show after it was all finished." The Obamas dined for two hours at Blue Hill, a West Village restaurant, before heading to the Belasco Theatre for *Joe Turner's Come and Gone*. The Obama White House has refused to detail costs for the trip.

Through an impudent FOIA request, we found out that the Secret Service had to bear nearly $12,000 in security costs just to make "date night" happen. We also sent FOIA requests to the Department of Defense and the U.S. Air Force concerning the costs they had to undertake in order to make this magical evening occur. Press reports suggest the president and his entourage, which included White House staff and the press corps, used three military aircraft.

The Obama administration saddled the country with crushing

debt in the worst economy since the Great Depression and yet President Obama stuck the American people with a massive bill for a "date night" with the First Lady. Some estimates put the total cost upwards of $250,000.[18] No wonder the Obama White House tried to keep secret the costs of this excursion.

ACORN Doesn't Fall Far from the Tree

The Obama administration continued its alliance with the ACORN network. We filed a FOIA request with the U.S. Bureau of the Census on March 23, 2009. As usual, the Obama Commerce Department stonewalled, and we were forced to file a lawsuit on May 14, 2009.

Five days later we finally obtained documents from the Census Bureau detailing the substantial involvement of ACORN in the 2010 Census. Included among the 126 pages of documents is ACORN's original census partnership application. The document describes eighteen different areas of responsibility requested by the community organization, which is under investigation in multiple states for illegal activity during the 2008 election, including voter registration fraud. The documents also list the types of organizations ineligible for partnering with the census. They include: ". . . Hate groups, Law enforcement, anti-immigrant groups, any groups that might make people fearful of participating in the Census . . ." The release of these Commerce Department documents came in the wake of a Department of Homeland Security report released in April 2009 that linked opposition to illegal immigration to "rightwing extremist radicalization."

In its official statement responding to the ACORN controversy, the Commerce Department downplayed ACORN's participation in the census and labeled "baseless" the notion that ACORN would be involved in any census count. However, the Census Bureau offered ACORN the opportunity to "recruit Census workers" who would participate in the count. Moreover, as an "executive level" partner, ACORN had the ability to "organize and/or serve as a member on

a Complete Count Committee," which, according to census documents, helps "develop and implement locally based outreach and
recruitment campaigns."

According to its application, ACORN also signed up to: "Encourage employees and constituents to complete and mail their
questionnaire; identify job candidates and/or distribute and display
recruiting materials; appoint a liaison to work with the Census Bureau; provide space for Be Counted sites and/or Questionnaire Assistance Centers; sponsor community events to promote participation
in the 2010 Census," among eighteen requested areas of responsibility. The documents also showed the decision to add ACORN as a
partner occurred in February 2010, long after the January 15 census
partnership application deadline.

The Census Bureau requested that ACORN "help us highlight
[ACORN's] innovation and hard work and share best practices so
other organizations can learn from your experiences." Members of
the Census Bureau and Department of Commerce staff assigned
to organize the 2010 Census were unaware when the decision to
involve ACORN was made, how the Census Bureau chose and defined partners, or whether partners received payment.

The Census Bureau's carelessness with regard to its help was
nothing new. The bureau didn't conduct background checks on
the 3.7 million people hired to conduct the 2000 Census, unless a
preliminary name check provided a match. In fact, 8 percent of the
applicants, or over 300,000 people, were considered risks for hire.

According to the U.S. Census documents, among other things,
census data is used to allocate $300 billion in federal funds. Census
data also "determines how many seats each state will have in the
House of Representatives as well as the redistricting of state legisla-
tures, county and city councils, and voting districts." Given its history of illegal activity and voter registration fraud, ACORN should
not have been anywhere near the 2010 Census. And yet the chief
concern of the Obama Commerce Department was to continue to
demonize conservatives by lumping together law enforcement and
anti-immigration groups with "hate groups."

ACORN finally came apart at the seams in late 2009, after

Andrew Breitbart, who died in early 2012, and his BigGovernment
.com Internet site released videos showing young conservative journalists masquerading as a pimp and a prostitute, receiving advice
from ACORN workers about how to evade tax, immigration, and
child prostitution laws. The Census Bureau, already in damage control due to our disclosures, severed its ties with ACORN; the U.S.
Senate denied the organization access to housing funds; and—to top
it all off—the House of Representatives voted overwhelmingly to
deny ACORN all federal funds.

Even the "ACORN President" in the White House couldn't
ignore this one. "The conduct that you see on those tapes is completely unacceptable," said Obama White House spokesman Robert
Gibbs after the videos surfaced. Apparently, voter registration fraud
was of no concern to the Obama administration. But fraudulent
loans to fake pimps—now that crossed the line!

Regardless of the defunding, we pushed ahead with our aggressive
investigation of ACORN, filling two new FOIA lawsuits. We filed
the first against the Department of Labor's Employee Benefits Security Administration. It involved monies allegedly embezzled by Dale
Rathke, the brother of ACORN founder Wade Rathke. The *New
York Times* reported that Dale Rathke allegedly embezzled $948,607
in 1999 and 2000.[19] According to a report by the House Committee on Oversight and Government Reform, a portion of these
funds, $215,000, allegedly came in the form of a "loan." Apparently,
the manner in which this "loan" was handled and concealed by
ACORN internally may have violated the Employee Income Retirement Security Act (ERISA).

We filed our FOIA request seeking all records concerning misconduct and violation of law by ACORN, among other groups, with
regard to ERISA. No documents were produced. The second lawsuit
was filed against the Corporation for National and Community
Service (CNCS), which handles the programs and paperwork for
national government grants, including funds distributed under the
AmeriCorps umbrella.

We'd previously uncovered documents indicating that ACORN's
sister organization (ACORN Housing) was no longer eligible for

federal funds due to previous abuses involving an AmeriCorps grant. According to internal CNCS correspondence, "ACORN Housing, an affiliate of ACORN was funded by CNCS in 1994/1995. ACORN Housing was accused of using the funds for protests. . . . Following an issuance of subpoenas by CNS's Inspector General, CNS and ACORN Housing agreed to stop the AmeriCorps grant. CNCS later recovered more than $16,000 of funds that were improperly spent."

We wanted to find out more about these abuses and any related investigations so we filed a FOIA request. Again, no documents were produced. (As we've discussed above, AmeriCorps no longer has an internal watchdog, so who knows what other ACORN-type frauds are being funded through that government agency.)

As we'll see, the Obama administration's lack of interest in ACORN has a deeper rationale. ACORN is not dead. It is not even dying. It's alive and well, thriving in the shadows. And it will play a role in the election of 2012.

The Visitor Logs—Judicial Watch Visits the Obama White House

In September 2009, in an attempt to fool the public into believing that it was being fully transparent and aboveboard, the Obama administration announced that it would post some White House visitors log information on the White House website beginning on December 31, 2009. The "voluntary" disclosures came in a deal with the liberal watchdog CREW, which dropped its lawsuit to force compliance with FOIA in exchange for voluntary disclosures by the White House.

However, records from January 20, 2009, through September 15, 2009, were to be kept secret, except in narrow, specific circumstances. This constituted tens of thousands of records the administration was keeping secret in defiance of FOIA. The Obama White House didn't explain why visitors logs from its first eight months were afforded special protection nor why voluntary disclosure was any substitute for release of the records under FOIA. And there were important categories of records that would not be subject to release under this fraudulent voluntary disclosure policy. The Obama White House helpfully detailed their arbitrary exceptions on its website:

The White House voluntary disclosure policy will be subject to the following exceptions:

1. The White House will not release fields within the access records that implicate personal privacy or law enforcement concerns (e.g., dates of birth, social security numbers, and contact phone numbers); records that implicate the personal safety of EOP staff (their daily arrival and departure); or records whose release would threaten national security interests.

2. The White House will not release access records related to purely personal guests of the first and second families (i.e., visits that do not involve any official or political business).

3. The White House will not release access records related to a small group of particularly sensitive meetings (e.g., visits of potential Supreme Court nominees). The White House will disclose each month the number of records withheld on this basis, and it will release such records once they are no longer sensitive.[20]

So a huge national security exception. A huge personal guests exception. And a sensitive meetings exception. The Obama White House policy, which had absolutely no basis in FOIA, was to release White House visitors records unless it did not want to. As explained earlier, the Obama White House had continued to defend the Bush administration antitransparency legal position that White House visitors logs were not subject to the open records law.

We thought the CREW settlement was nonsense and that CREW

had let the Obama gang off the hook. With President Obama's cozy relationships with everyone from the unions (as we'll explore) to the various industries he seeks to regulate (see, for example, the financial industry), we were very curious to see the White House visitors logs. We therefore FOIA'd the Secret Service for those logs from January 20, 2009, to October 2009—the ones that had been specifically exempted from release under the CREW settlement. Naturally, the Secret Service refused that request. We issued a press release highlighting the denial and warned of a lawsuit.

That's when things got interesting. One of our investigators received a call from a White House lawyer who wanted to express some concern about the accuracy of our press statement. He invited us in to a meeting at the White House to meet with some unnamed officials.

Talk about an offer we couldn't refuse. I'm sure the White House thought we'd be intimidated by getting such a phone call from the White House telling us we were wrong, though we saw through the tactic and happily accepted the invitation.

So on October 21, 2009, my Judicial Watch colleagues and I visited with senior White House officials led by Norm Eisen, then–special counsel to the president for ethics and government. During the meeting, Eisen offered to make some superficial accommodations to us on the visitors logs issue and encouraged us to publicly praise the Obama administration's commitment to transparency. We were told that the White House would praise us in return. "It would be good for us and good for Judicial Watch," Eisen suggested. I couldn't believe what I was hearing. By the way, Eisen founded CREW. To this day, I can't figure out why he thought it appropriate to take a lead on a legal issue that had been fought by his former colleagues!

We shook hands at the end of the meeting but the Obama White House refused to abandon its legally indefensible contention that the visitors logs are not subject to FOIA. In a November 30, 2009, follow-up letter, Eisen reiterated the Obama administration's position and requested that Judicial Watch "focus and narrow your request." We filed suit. As you might guess, we haven't been invited back to the Obama White House. (And Eisen, whose chief job was to issue dozens of dubious "ethics waivers" for Obama appointees, is now our nation's ambassador to the Czech Republic.)

In refusing to abide by FOIA, the Secret Service advanced the erroneous claim that the records belong to the Obama White House, not the Secret Service agency, and therefore may be kept secret under the Presidential Records Act. The courts had repeatedly ruled that White House visitors records belong to the Secret Service and therefore should be available under FOIA.

The Obama administration was giving no ground. It told us: "It is the government's position that the categories of records that you requested are not agency records subject to FOIA. Rather, these records are governed by the Presidential Records Act . . . and remain under the exclusive legal custody and control of the White House Office and the Office of the Vice President." And, as if it mattered legally, we were told the White House might release these records at its discretion.

This was a battle we'd already fought and won—as you'll recall, we successfully forced the release of White House visitors logs related to visits by former lobbyist and convicted felon Jack Abramoff to the Bush White House. As our lawyers argued previously in court filings, the U.S. Secret Service is an agency within the meaning of FOIA and its records are therefore subject to FOIA. The law provides no exceptions for certain types of Secret Service records and does not excuse the Secret Service from complying with FOIA. Moreover, the Presidential Records Act specifically states that presidential records do "not include any documentary materials that are (i) official records of an agency."

The Obama White House would not retreat from its bogus claim that the Secret Service's logs of White House visitors were not subject to FOIA and therefore may be kept secret from the American people. In other words, the Obama administration believes you have no right under law to know who visits the White House or under what circumstances. The Obama Justice Department didn't dispute the fact that the courts are not on their side in this issue. They simply said that "the district court cases on which [Judicial Watch] relies for a contrary conclusion were incorrectly decided." In other words, every judge who had looked at the issue had been wrong, but the Constitutional Law Professor-in-Chief was right.

Just in case the court didn't buy this line of reasoning, Justice Department lawyers also threw out the national security card to see if that would stick. They speculated that there would be "dire national security consequences" if certain White House visitors were disclosed. To guard against these "consequences," the Obama White House wants to be able to withhold visitors logs until as long as twelve years after President Obama leaves office. The Justice Department admitted that the Obama White House is taking records out of the Secret Service in order to ensure that they are not disclosed under FOIA. This illegal paper shuffle to keep the public in the dark is the real truth of the Obama White House's so-called commitment to transparency. In a bit of political grandstanding, the Justice Department also praised the Obama administration's efforts to "voluntarily" release some White House visitors logs to the public, implying that this policy should be sufficient for Judicial Watch and the public at large.

Well, it isn't lawful or sufficient. The White House log information that has been voluntarily disclosed is "riddled with holes," according to an independent report from the Center for Public Integrity:

> The [White House visitors] logs are . . . incomplete for thousands of . . . visitors to the White House, including lobbyists, government employees, campaign donors, policy experts, and friends of the first family, according to an investigation by the Center for Public Integrity.
>
> The White House website proudly boasts of making available "over 1,000,000 records of everyone who's come through the doors of the White House" via a searchable database.
>
> Yet the Center's analysis shows that the logs routinely omit or cloud key details about the identity of visitors, who they met with, the nature of the visit, and even includes the names of people who never showed up. These are critical gaps that raise doubts about their historical accuracy and utility in helping the public understand White House operations from social events to meetings on key policy debates.[21]

Instead of wasting taxpayer resources stonewalling, the Obama administration should have respected the rule of law, as well as court precedent, and released all logs of White House visitors immediately. These hidden and incomplete visitor logs again show the "Big Lie" of Obama's supposed commitment to transparency. Thankfully, the federal court rejected the Obama secrecy gambit. After an unusually long wait, a federal court judge knocked back the administration's arguments for visitors log secrecy. The decision was issued by U.S. district court judge Beryl Howell. (I should note that Judge Howell is an appointee of President Obama.) Here's a quick summary of the court's conclusions:

- Judicial Watch noted in its complaint filed on December 7, 2009, the Obama administration's claim "has been litigated and rejected repeatedly." The Court noted precedent in its ruling: "This Court agrees with the conclusions of the other judges in this District that have considered this question and finds that the records are subject to FOIA."

- The Obama administration argued that Judicial Watch's request is too massive and broad and cannot be processed. Judge Howell was unconvinced. "While the Court is sensitive to the burdens raised by the plaintiff's broad brush request for 'all' records of a certain type over a nine-month period, including the need to review such records for applicable exemptions, the Court is not persuaded that the plaintiff's request requires a blanket rejection."

- The Obama administration argued that Judicial Watch's request would raise Constitutional, "separation of power" issues. Judge Howell ruled, ". . . The Court is skeptical of the underlying premise that the inclusion of [visitors logs] under FOIA raises any serious Constitutional problems . . . since the statutory language is unambiguous in relation to this issue, and the FOIA has built-in exemptions that mitigate the risk of the precise separation of powers concerns the defendant raises, the Court rejects defendant's interpretive argument."

- The Obama administration argued that Judicial Watch's request raises national security concerns. The Court noted, "At no point does the Secret Service assert, however, that there are not at least some records implicated by plaintiff's FOIA request that could be easily searched for, separated out, and disclosed without raising national security concerns."

Ultimately, Judge Howell concluded that "the proper course of action by the Secret Service is duly to process [Judicial Watch's] FOIA request, disclose all segregable, nonexempt records, and then assert specific FOIA exemptions for all records it seeks to withhold."

In other words, release or explain.

What was the Obama administration's response? Appeal.

Yes, to delay the inevitable, the "most transparent administration in history" has appealed the White House visitors logs ruling. There is no way that the Obama White House will want transparency in an election year. Indeed, the appeal of the visitors logs ruling will likely delay any release of records until after the election.

A president who doesn't want you to know who is visiting him in the White House is a president who doesn't want to be accountable to the American people.

7.

REMAKING AMERICA

President Obama campaigned on a platform of remolding America. America, he said, had become a bastion of the two Big C's, corruption and cronyism, plagued by manipulation by the "haves" and disenfranchisement for the "have-nots." And all of that rang true—as we've explored, corruption and cronyism were hallmarks of Obama's predecessors and of Congress. What was so cynical about Obama, however, was that even as he ran against the two C's, he was planning to use them himself to enshrine a third Big C: fundamental change. Unfortunately, this change is potentially deadly to our republican form of government.

The American people are a unique people. We want to live our own lives, and we want the government to enforce and follow the rules and get out of our way. That's what separates us from Europe. As Mark Steyn writes in his book *After America*, "The United States is still different. In the wake of the economic meltdown, the decadent youth of France rioted over the most modern of proposals to increase the retirement age. Elderly 'students' in Britain attacked the heir to the throne's car over footling attempts to constrain bloated, wasteful, and pointless 'university' costs. Everywhere from Iceland to Bulgaria angry mobs besieged their parliaments demanding the same thing: Why didn't you the government do more for me? America was the only nation in the developed world where millions of people took to the streets to tell the state: I can do just fine if you control-freak statists would shove your non-stimulating stimulus, your jobless jobs bill, and your multitrillion-dollar porkathons, and just stay the hell out of my life and my pocket." [1]

Right now, America stands on the brink of a complete government takeover in virtually every major sector of the economy, and most people don't even know that it's happening. *We* at Judicial Watch know, but only because we dedicate the bulk of our waking minutes to pushing the Obama administration to release as much information as possible related to Obama's socialist remaking of America. Restoration of what makes our republic great starts with a vital step: getting informed. Once you realize what the Obama administration is up to in those secret back rooms, you recognize and address any threats to our republic. It's into those back rooms that we travel next. To quote George Will: "The administration's central activity—the political allocation of wealth and opportunity—is not merely susceptible to corruption, it is corruption."

The VIPs

In October 2009, the *Washington Times* reported that during the first nine months of his administration, "President Obama has quietly rewarded scores of top Democratic donors with VIP access to the White House, private briefings with administration advisers and invitations to important speeches and town-hall meetings." [2] This was influence-peddling, and it went right to the heart of what the Obama administration is all about—political payoffs with government goodies to liberal allies. Obama, of course, wasn't the first person to so openly do this sort of thing.

It was perfected by the Clinton White House, which rented out the Lincoln Bedroom to top Democratic donors in the 1990s. In this case, however, it appears the entire White House complex is for sale in the Obama administration. A number of federal laws could have been broken by this White House fund-raising program. For instance, 18 U.S.C. § 1607 states, "It shall be unlawful for an individual who is an officer or employee of the Federal Government, including the President, Vice President, and Members of Congress, to solicit or receive a donation of money or other thing of value in connection with a Federal, State, or local election, while in any room or building occupied in the discharge of official duties by an officer or employee of the United States, from any person."[3] Attorney General Holder could have demonstrated his independence by appointing a special counsel to conduct an independent investigation of these serious allegations—but, of course, he didn't.

Obamacare, Part 1:
Socialism, Secrecy, and Corruption

They often say that when you eat a sausage, the last thing you want to find out is how it's made. When it comes to legislation, precisely the opposite is true: we *need* to know exactly how it's made. That's the critical component to telling who wins, who loses, and who cheated. Despite Obamacare's effective nationalization of one-sixth of the U.S. economy, we never found out what happened behind closed doors. That was by design. Even as the Obamacare bill was sped through Congress, at one of the key moments in American legislative history the American people were largely in the dark about what government takeover of health care meant to them and to the country and how this horrible deal was being forced through. As Nancy Pelosi said, the plan was to pass the bill and then find out what was in it.

That's why the Obama gang fought us so hard in court to prevent turning over documents related to secret, closed-door meetings that President Obama held with high-ranking members of the administration, Democrats, and union leaders. What happened in these secret negotiations? What promises were made? That's what we intended to find out. And that's what the Obama administration was stonewalling about.

Of course health-care reform wasn't supposed to happen this way. Obama promised during the campaign that there would be no backroom deals, no partisan power plays, and no secrecy.

Remember?

During a Democratic primary debate on January 31, 2008, presidential candidate Obama said the following on the issue of health-care reform: "That's what I will do in bringing all parties together, not negotiating behind closed doors, but bringing all parties together, and broadcasting those negotiations on C-SPAN so that the American people can see what the choices are."

In a startling breach of his campaign promise, President Obama, Vice President Biden, Secretary of Health and Human Services Sebelius, and White House Office of Health Reform director Nancy-Ann DeParle met behind closed doors with various groups to reach accord on health-care reform before a final vote occurred in the U.S. House of Representatives. One group of individuals was senior officials of major unions. A second group consisted of Senate Majority Leader Reid and House Speaker Pelosi and other members of Congress.

Because President Obama and Secretary Sebelius held closed-door negotiations at the White House, the public was denied the transparency Obama had promised as a candidate. We filed a FOIA request on January 15, 2010. Health and Human Services acknowledged receipt of the request on January 19, 2010. On January 21, 2010, and March 12, 2010, HHS indicated that two offices within the agency found no responsive requests. However, the Immediate Office of the Secretary and the Office of the Secretary Scheduling Office failed to respond. Of course, these just happen to be the two offices within HHS most likely to keep the requested records.

When they did respond, they did it in ridiculously incomplete fashion. But we forced the Obama administration to provide some information—information that supported the notion that some pretty important happenings were going on behind America's back. We received a copy of Sebelius's schedule for the weeks of January 11–17, 2010, and January 4–10, 2010. Among other things, the schedule showed the attendees of several White House meetings that Sebelius attended, with a January 15 meeting specifically designated for a "POTUS MEETING ON HEALTH REFORM." The meeting was scheduled from 1:30 P.M. to 4:00 P.M. in the White House Cabinet Room.

There was a list of all of the labor union leaders who attended the meetings, along with brief biographical information on each participant. The list included: Richard Trumka, president of the AFL-CIO; Andy Stern, president of the Service Employees International Union; and Jim Hoffa, president of the International Brotherhood of Teamsters, among other Big Labor leaders.

An agenda for a January 13 meeting between Big Labor and White House staff, including Vice President Biden, showed that the meeting wasn't about the public interest in health care, but about Big Labor's concerns. The January 13 meeting with Big Labor was reported on at the time. "Key labor leaders are back at the White House this afternoon for negotiations on health care, according to two sources," *Politico* reported. "Their return suggests potential progress, or maybe a counteroffer, on resolving the standoff over taxing expensive insurance plans—one of the biggest remaining threats to the bill." [4]

In a sign of White House deference to Big Labor, the documents show that this January 13, 2010, meeting was paused so that Richard Trumka could go up to Capitol Hill to meet with "progressive" House members. (Trumka, by the way, is notorious. Back in the 1990s, he invoked the Fifth Amendment in a corruption investigation involving the Teamsters and the Clinton gang. [5])

The day after the meeting took place, the *Washington Post* reported that "[t]he White House has reached a tentative agreement with labor leaders to tax high-cost health insurance policies. . . . The agreement clears one of the last major obstacles on the path to final passage of comprehensive health care legislation." [6]

So there is no question this was a significant meeting, as a deal was struck. And it helped pave the way for the Obamacare monstrosity.

It is shameful that the Obama administration would violate its own supposed commitment to transparency to help ensure passage of Obamacare. But that's precisely what it did. Here's a list of attendees for one of these secret Obamacare meetings:

Meeting with Labor Leaders
EEOB, 230A
Wednesday, January 13, 2010
9:30-10:00am

PURPOSE/TOPIC:

This meeting will be a follow-up on yesterday's POTUS meeting. You will be meeting with White House Staff and labor leaders who have been designated by the other labor leaders to discuss the excise tax with the White House.

PARTICIPANTS:

Vice President Joe Biden
Jim Messina, Deputy Chief of Staff
Nate Tamarin, Associate White House Political Director for Labor
Patrick Gaspard, Director of the Office of Political Affairs
Jason Furman, Deputy Director of the National Economic Council
Anna Burger, Chair, Change to Win
Rich Trumka, President, ALF-CIO
Dennis Van Roekel, President, National Education Association
Andy Stern, President, Service Employees International Union
Randi Weingarten, President, American Federation of Teachers
Gerald McEntee, President, American Federation of State, County and Municipal Employees
Ed Hill, President, International Brotherhood of Electrical Workers
Larry Cohen, President, Communication Workers of America

As you might predict, the Obama administration paid off its political allies. After Obamacare's passage, we discovered that a disproportionately high number of Obamacare waivers were being granted to the president's allies in a secretive process. Essentially, the administration was exempting its financial supporters from some of the more burdensome provisions of the health-care reform law, which President Obama touts as a "new set of rules that treats everybody honestly and treats everybody fairly."[7] Political appointees at the Department of Health and Human Services decided which companies (and powerful unions) were off the hook—and Americans were being kept in the dark.

In early October 2010, Judicial Watch filed a public records request to obtain information on the waiver deals, but the Obama

Health and Human Services Department gave us the stiff arm and Judicial Watch was forced to sue. The agency blew off its legally required deadline to produce the records, without providing any sort of justification for withholding them, a common occurrence when the government wants to keep damaging information from the public.

In a story published in January 2011 by the *Wall Street Journal*, Karl Rove revealed that most of the 222 waivers to that date had gone to administration allies. Over a third of the more than 1.5 million employees covered by the original waivers were union members even though unionized workers make up only 7 percent of the private workforce, Rove points out. Forty-three union organizations were granted Obamacare waivers. That number only grew as time went on.[8] We independently obtained over 3,400 pages of documents from HHS about Obamacare. Many of the documents referenced the waivers exempting companies and unions from the minimum annual cap on the amount payable to an individual in benefits. Such waivers enable companies and unions to keep their existing plans in place until January 1, 2014.

As of July 2011, 1,472 one-year waivers and 106 three-year waivers were granted, covering some 3.4 million enrollees, more than half of whom belong to unions. Yet, according to the U.S. Bureau of Labor Statistics, union members account for only about 12 percent of the total workforce (which includes private and government employees).

Waiving the law for 3.4 million Americans is unfair and an affront to the rule of law. Unions helped write the Obamacare law, and then they got exempted from it. Now Big Labor is paying back these waiver favors with campaign support for Barack Obama.

As of January 6, 2012, the final waiver list totaled over 1,700.[9]

Obama also shamelessly helped those who supported his hostile takeover of the nation's health-care system. For instance, AARP, a key player in passing the Patient Protection and Affordable Care Act, was exempt from many of the law's most costly provisions. Among them are mandates and rate reviews on its lucrative health plans and hefty new taxes on insurance companies. AARP will also be exempt from a $500,000 cap on executive compensation for insurance executives. It's the president's way of thanking the influential and politically connected national group for spending tens of millions of dollars on ads and lobbying on behalf of his health-care takeover.

Obamacare Part 2: The Kagan Controversy, or "Let's Crush Them"

But what about the possibility that the Supreme Court would strike down Obamacare? Good thing for him, Obama may have already rigged the game. By placing Solicitor General Elena Kagan on the Supreme Court—the same Elena Kagan who we know now was practically jumping for joy at the passage of Obamacare—Obama ensured that he'd have at least four votes for Obamacare: Kagan, Sotomayor, Breyer, and Ginsburg.

The big question was whether Kagan would be required to recuse herself. That question took on new heat with the successful FOIA litigation by Judicial Watch and, separately, our friends at the Media Research Center.

Documents obtained through our hard-fought legal pursuits raise new questions about whether Kagan and her employees helped coordinate the Obama administration's legal strategy to defend Obamacare. (Our lawsuit was consolidated with a similar FOIA lawsuit that had been first filed against the Justice Department by the Media Research Center. Many of the documents referenced here were first produced in the Media Research litigation.)

According to a January 8, 2010, email from Neal Katyal, former deputy solicitor general, to Brian Hauck, senior counsel to Associate Attorney General Thomas Perrelli, and headed "Re: Health Care Defense," Kagan was involved in the strategy to defend Obamacare from the very beginning. "Brian," Katyal wrote, "Elena would definitely like OSG [Office of Solicitor General] to be involved in this set of issues . . . [W]e will bring in Elena as needed." (The "set of issues" refers to another email calling for assembling a group to figure out "how to defend against the . . . health care proposals that are pending.")

On March 21, 2010, Katyal urged Kagan to attend a health-care litigation meeting that was evidently organized by the Obama White House: "This is the first I've heard of this. I think you should go, no? I will, regardless, but feel like this is litigation of singular importance." In another email exchange that took place on January 8, 2010, Katyal's colleague Hauck asked Katyal about putting together a group to discuss challenges to Obamacare. "Could you figure out the right person or people for that?" Hauck asked. "Absolutely right on. Let's crush them," Katyal responded. "I'll speak with Elena and designate someone." The "crush them" email is below and is a dramatic illustration of the Justice Kagan recusal debate:

Katyal, Neal (SMO)

From:	Katyal, Neal
Sent:	Friday, January 08, 2010 10:57 AM
To:	Hauck, Brian
Subject:	RE: Health Care Defense

Absolutely right on. Let's crush them. I'll speak with Elena and designate someone.

From:	Hauck, Brian
Sent:	Friday, January 08, 2010 10:54 AM
To:	Katyal, Neal
Subject:	Health Care Defense

Hi Neal -- Tom wants to put together a group to get thinking about how to defend against inevitable challenges to the health care proposals that are pending, and hoped that OSG could participate. Could you figure out the right person or people for that? More the merrier. He is hoping to meet next week if we can.

Thanks,
Brian

However, following the May 10, 2010, announcement that President Obama would nominate Kagan to the U.S. Supreme Court, Katyal's position changed significantly as he began to suggest that Kagan had been "walled off" from Obamacare discussions. Check out this suspect exchange between Kagan, Katyal, and Tracy Schmaler, a Justice Department spokesperson, on May 17:

Schmaler to Katyal: Has Elena been involved in any of that to the extent SG [Solicitor General's] office was consulted? . . .

Katyal to Schmaler: No she has never been involved in any of it. I've run it for the office, and have never discussed the issues with her one bit.

Katyal (forwarded to Kagan): This is what I told Tracy about Health Care.

Kagan to Schmaler: This needs to be coordinated. Tracy you should not say anything about this before talking to me.

Kagan seems to be telling Schmaler to call her rather than put anything in writing, so that they could discuss the best way to finesse the issue. Oral communications are always subject to varying memories and are unproven by nature. Written communications can be certain and clear. It is fair to conclude that Kagan wanted to speak about her health-care involvement with Schmaler because she understood that the answer that "she was not involved in any of it" is demonstrably false.

In the course of our litigation to get at the truth, the Justice Department provided us a "Vaughn index," a privilege log that describes records that are being withheld in whole or in part.

The index raised more questions about Kagan's involvement in Obamacare-related discussions. For example, Kagan was included in an email chain (March 17–18, 2010) in which the following subject was discussed: "on what categories of legal arguments may arise and should be prepared in the anticipated lawsuit." The subject of the email was "Health Care." Another email chain on March 21, 2010, titled "Health care litigation meeting," references an "internal government meeting regarding the expected litigation." Kagan was both an author and a recipient in the chain.

The index also referenced a series of email exchanges on May 17, 2010, between Kagan and Obama White House lawyers and staff regarding Kagan's "draft answer" to potential questions about recusal during the Supreme Court confirmation process. The White House officials involved include: Susan Davies, associate White House counsel; Daniel Meltzer, then–principal deputy White House counsel; Cynthia Hogan, counsel to the vice president; and Ronald Klain, then–chief of staff for Vice President Biden. The Justice Department refused to produce this draft answer.

The Vaughn index also described a March 24, 2010, email exchange between Associate Attorney General Beth Brinkmann and Michael Dreeben, Kagan's deputy solicitor general, with the subject header "Health Care Challenges." The email read, in part, ". . . I had a national conference call with the Civil Chiefs. A memo also went out the day before. I am forwarding right after this. Let's discuss if you have more ideas about what to do."

So what does the law say about these kinds of judicial conflicts of interest? What is the standard for recusal? As reported by CNS News: "In the questionnaire she filled out for the Senate Judiciary Committee during her confirmation process, Kagan said she would abide by the 'letter and spirit' of 28 U.S.C. § 455 in deciding whether she felt compelled to recuse herself as a Supreme Court Justice from any case that came before the High Court. According to the law, a 'justice . . . shall disqualify himself in any proceeding in which his impartiality might be reasonably questioned.' It further says any justice 'shall also disqualify himself . . . [w]here he has served in governmental employment and in such capacity participated as counsel, adviser or material witness concerning the proceedings or expressed an opinion concerning the merits of the particular case in controversy.' "[10]

As long as the Justice Department continues to withhold key documents, the American people won't know for sure whether Kagan's involvement warranted her recusal from any Obamacare litigation that came before the High Court. But there is little doubt that the department will not turn over such documents. Sure enough, we had to sue again for more documents (including Kagan's calendars from her days as Obama's solicitor general). The Department of Justice seems willing to violate FOIA to help its case defending Obamacare.

Just before the Supreme Court oral arguments on Obamacare this past March, we sent a letter directly to Justice Kagan asking her to set the record straight. Our letter noted that it "would be extraordinarily unfortunate if the [Supreme] Court's decision were overshadowed by controversy over [Justice Kagan's] participation in the matter. It would leave a cloud hanging over the Court's decision and could undermine public confidence in the impartiality and integrity of the Court as an institution."

Obamacare Part 3: The Propaganda Campaign

How did the Obama White House make the case for Obamacare? Why, by using your money, of course! In September 2011, we obtained documentation from the Department of Health and Human Services showing that HHS wanted to spend as much as $200 million on a propaganda campaign to convince the American people that they're wrong to doubt the president's socialist health care overhaul. The documents contained new details on a massive, taxpayer-funded multimedia campaign designed to promote the Patient Protection and Affordable Health Care Act (also known as Obamacare) and other HHS policy initiatives (such as the anti-obesity—or food control—campaign that is a vanity project of Michelle Obama).

The documents were stunning. Once again, our taxpayer dollars were being used to promote Obamacare propaganda. An April 27, 2010, HHS released an "Acquisition Plan" titled "National Multimedia & Education Campaign & Grassroots Outreach." That plan detailed a comprehensive *five-year* communications program covering a variety of HHS policy initiatives, including "health care reform." According to a section of the Acquisition Plan titled "Independent Government Health Estimate," the HHS assistant secretary for public affairs (ASPA) stated: "ASPA is unable to provide a definitive government cost estimate. Campaigns vary is [*sic*] size and scope. Some campaigns involve radio, some TV, and some print. Other campaigns may involve all of those avenues plus on ground events, website, bus tours, etc." However, "ASPA is letting this contract in order [to] produce three to four campaigns per year through the life-cycle of the contract. We are requesting a contract with a $200,000,000 maximum." So much for the notion that the Obama administration gave a fig about deficit spending! The document below shows how easy it is for your government to spend $200 million:

Part VI – Independent Government Cost Estimate

"Source Selection Information – see FAR 2.101 and 3.104"

ASPA is unable to provide a definitive government cost estimate. Campaigns vary is size and scope. Some campaigns involve radio, some TV, and some print. Other campaigns may involve all of those avenues plus on ground events, websites, bus tours, etc. The mix of labor categories and expertise needed for each campaign varies from campaign to campaign.

Based on ASPA's past experience, very large-scale campaigns can cost between five and nine million dollars. Less ambitious campaigns cost three to five million dollars. ASPA is letting this contract in order produce three to four campaigns per year through the life-cycle of the contract. We are requesting a contract with a $200,000,000 maximum.

According to a subsequent March 14, 2011, contract included among the documents, HHS hired the Ogilvy Group "to provide services to design, develop, and execute a multiplatform educational media campaign to promote the new website Healthcare.gov, including the new Spanish language version of the website." The total amount of the contract awarded was $3,998,928. That's a nice little chunk of change for the Ogilvy Group.

The Ogilvy contract "task order" described the purpose of the Healthcare.gov website: "To accompany such a monumental piece of legislation [the Affordable Health Care Act, aka Obamacare], the law charged the Department of Health and Human Services with the creation of a website to aide [sic] Americans about the health insurance coverage options available to them." U.S. senator Charles Grassley rightly deemed the HHS online program "state-sponsored propaganda."

The Ogilvy contract also described the "audiences" that were to receive "targeted messaging" during the campaign: "Hispanic Americans, African Americans, Young People, Women/Mothers," all considered key target demographics for the Obama reelection campaign.

So much for Obama being the president of all Americans. This is pure "divide and conquer."

According to the Ogilvy contract, HHS sought to receive "media training" in the following areas, among others: "controlling your message," "handling hostile interviews," "artful repetition," "identifying loaded questions," and "being persuasive."

Here's how HHS described the key to success for this campaign: "Health and program-related messages are processed by the target audience according to a particular reality, which he or she experiences. Attitudes, feelings, values, needs, desires, behaviors and beliefs all play a part in the individual's decision to accept information and make a behavioral change. It is by understanding the importance of these characteristics that health and program-related messages can be targeted to the beneficiary in effective ways." So, in other words, the Obama administration is paying hired guns a lot of your money to manipulate you into "accepting" the Obama way and "changing" your behavior. There's no other way to put it. Were they aiming these strategies at enemies of the United States, these tactics would rightly be labeled "psychological operations." The Big Brother provision of the Obamacare propaganda campaign is produced below:

C.2.1 Conduct and document consumer research on health and program related messages and materials

The Contractor shall be required to conduct and document consumer research on health and program related messages and materials as described below. Health and program-related messages are processed by the target audience according to a particular reality, which he or she experiences. Attitudes, feelings, values, needs, desires, behaviors and beliefs all play a part in the individual's decision to accept information and make a behavioral change. It is by understanding the importance of these characteristics that health and program-. related messages can be targeted to the beneficiary in effective ways. This information shall be captured via focus groups, professional review, cognitive testing, field tests, quantitative surveys, or individual interviews.

That's certainly what HHS was trying to do with a series of three Medicare television advertisements featuring actor Andy Griffith, a favorite of older Americans. As Judicial Watch uncovered through

FOIA, the Obama administration spent $3,184,000 in taxpayer funds to produce and air the advertisements on national television in September and October 2010.

The administration said it was merely trying to "educate" Medicare beneficiaries, caregivers, and family members "about forthcoming changes to Medicare as a result of the Affordable Care Act." However, according to FactCheck.org, a project of the University of Pennsylvania's Annenberg Public Policy Center—and which site is usually linked to the left side of the political spectrum—the advertisements intentionally misinformed the American people.

There was nothing "educational" about the Griffith ads. They were propaganda. And that was just $3 million. Where did the other $197 million go? These records proved the administration was using taxpayer dollars to manipulate public opinion while at the same time getting a leg up in the reelection campaign by targeting the Obama electoral coalition with positive but misleading messages about the president's "signature policy initiative."

That wasn't the end of the story, either. In the midst of this campaign, the Obama HHS launched an effort to track Internet searches and to use online search engines such as Google and Yahoo to drive traffic to a government website promoting Obama's health-care overhaul. Using "pay-per-click" advertising tools, such as Google AdWords, HHS purposely targeted for influence people searching the term *Obamacare,* a word that has been described as "disparaging" by political agents of the president. According to a budget summary, from October 2010 through February 2011, the Obama administration spent $1,435,009 (or almost $300,000 per month) on these online advertisements alone, including advertising campaigns with Google and Yahoo.

According to a December 10, 2010, email from Margo Gillman, senior vice president of Ogilvy Public Relations, to Jenny Backus, the principal deputy assistant secretary for public affairs and the principal deputy for strategy and planning for HHS, the Obama White House was involved in coordinating the HHS propaganda campaign: "Just a quick note to see if you have any feedback/

direction on how we should proceed with the radio and TV concepts that were presented a few weeks ago. You mentioned on our last call that you were planning to discuss them with the White House on either Friday or yesterday. We would appreciate any guidance that you can provide, so we can determine immediate next steps and a production schedule. Also, we are awaiting your feedback on the overarching strategic campaign plan."

Another HHS internal email dated December 1, 2010, from then–HHS official Jaime Mulligan to agency colleagues references the need to present recommendations to the White House regarding a number of components of the Obamacare campaign, including "a big guerilla campaign splash." (Last I checked, Mulligan was the White House new-media analyst for public health.)

A number of documents address the need to target the Obamacare propaganda campaign to Hispanics, blacks, and women. For example, according to HHS officials on December 16, 2010, summarizing a conference call, "You want to utilize the bulk of their paid media efforts (which would include expenditures for Radio One and Univision) on media that reaches African Americans and Hispanics. The money will go farther and these audiences continue to be a top priority." A January 18, 2011, email from Ogilvy to Director of New Media Communications Julia Eisman of HHS noted with respect to a Spanish banner ad campaign, "I realize we really can't use the blond mom and child for this audience."

An October 25, 2010, email from Eisman suggests changing the online advertising campaign to accommodate Web traffic patterns caused by the midterm elections: "Given the high performance, we're wondering if we should consider reallocating resources from the lesser performing words and put more $$ to 'Obamacare'—at least for the next 7 days," she suggests.

This Big Brother campaign was most certainly underhanded and the government was likely engaging in unlawful domestic propaganda. If Congress was looking for a place to trim the deficit, this was a good place to start. So far, Congress has taken no action on it.

At the same time that Obama spent hundreds of millions to

stump for his new health-care plan, he targeted its opponents and kept its inner workings secret. He borrowed that strategy from—who else?—Hillary and Bill Clinton.

History repeats itself. Remember back in 1993 when Hillary Clinton attempted her government takeover of the nation's health-care system? She failed miserably. But in watching the Obama administration's health-care reform pressure campaign, it is clear that not only did Obama push Hillary-style government-run health-care; he also resorted to the same lowball tactics used by Hillary in 1993.

During the original push for Obamacare, the Obama administration refused to turn over a list of health industry officials who visited the White House;[11] the administration spread disinformation on his proposed plan and mobilized a mob of minions to attack opponents of his health-care plan under the ironic moniker "fight the smears."[12] Most publicly, Obama stonewalled the American people on transparency in health-care reform. According to CBS News:

> President Obama wants the final negotiations on health care reform—a reconciliation of the House and Senate versions of the bill—put on a fast track, even if that means breaking an explicit campaign promise. "The House and Senate plan to put together the final health care reform bill behind closed doors according to an agreement by top Democrats," House Speaker Nancy Pelosi said today at the White House. The White House is on board with that, too, reports CBS News political correspondent Chip Reid. Press Secretary Robert Gibbs stressed today that "the president wants to get a bill to his desk as quickly as possible." During the campaign, though, candidate Obama regularly promised something different—to broadcast all such negotiations on C-SPAN, putting the entire process of pounding out health care reform out in the open. (That promise applied to the now-completed processing of forging House and Senate bills, too.)[13]

Brian Lamb, the founder and CEO of C-SPAN, made a serious effort to force transparency on these proceedings, consistent with President Obama's explicit promise. He wrote a letter to House and

Senate Democratic leaders on December 30, 2009, asking that the network's cameras be allowed into conference committee sessions as the details of this massive health-care bill were being hammered out. Obama and the Democrats said "no deal," prompting the highly respected and usually reserved Lamb to complain, and rightly so, that Obama had used his network as a "political football"[14] during the campaign.

The transparency "bait and switch" on health care was a basic extension of the administration's penchant for conducting the people's business on the most important issues of the day behind closed doors.

These dual strategies of secrecy and targeting of political enemies were nothing new. They should sound familiar to those of you who remember the Clinton years.

In July 2008, Judicial Watch released documents obtained from the Clinton Presidential Library related to Hillary Clinton's health-care campaign. Those documents show a striking resemblance between the Hillary tactics and those of our current White House occupant.

One June 18, 1993, internal memorandum, titled "A Critique of Our Plan" and authored by someone with the initials "P.S.," makes the startling admission that critics of Hillary's health-care reform plan were correct: "I can think of parallels in wartime, but I have trouble coming up with a precedent in our peacetime history for such broad and centralized control over a sector of the economy. . . . Is the public really ready for this? . . . none of us knows whether we can make it work well or at all . . ." Some guessed that the author of this memo was Paul Starr, who served as head of Hillary's Health Care Task Force staff.

A "Confidential" May 26, 1993, memo from Senator Jay Rockefeller (D-WV) to Hillary Clinton, titled "Health Care Reform Communications," criticized the task force as a "secret cabal of Washington policy 'wonks'" that has engaged in "choking off information" from the public regarding health-care reform. The memorandum suggested that Hillary Clinton "use classic opposition research" to attack those who were excluded by the Clinton administration from task force deliberations and to "expose lifestyles, tactics and motives of lobbyists" in order to deflect criticism. Senator Rockefeller also suggested that news organizations "are anxious and willing to receive guidance [from the Clinton administration] on how to time and shape their [news] coverage."

A February 5, 1993, draft memo from Alexis Herman and Mike Lux detailed the Office of Public Liaison's plan for the health-care reform campaign. The memorandum notes the development of an "interest group data base" detailing whether organizations "support[ed] us in the election." The database would also track personal information about interest group leaders, such as their home phone numbers, addresses, "biographies, analysis of credibility in the media, and known relationships with Congresspeople."

Lies, smears, and secrecy. All of these were hallmarks of Hillary Clinton's efforts in 1993. Obama hired many a Clinton hack to work in his White House. So it is no surprise that the Clinton gang's despicable tactics (some of which may have been illegal) are being used by the Obama administration in their aggressive drive for so-cialized health care, or, to quote the Hillarycare memo, "broad and centralized control" over the health-care sector.

Standing Up for "Undocumented Immigrants"

On the immigration issue, President Bush was nearly as bad as President Obama. So it's no wonder that just before leaving office, he extended a helping hand to Obama's family—one of whom was an illegal immigrant.

On November 1, 2008, just a few days before the presidential election, the Associated Press outed Barack Obama's Kenyan aunt, Zeituni Onyango, as an illegal alien who had quietly been living in Boston, evading deportation. Onyango came to the United States in 2000. Her request for asylum was denied by a judge in 2004. She then went into hiding until the AP discovered her in a Boston public housing project.

As surprising as this revelation was at the time, it paled in comparison to what happened next behind closed doors: The Bush administration reportedly ordered immigration officials to effectively freeze all illegal alien deportations for seventy-two hours. According to the Associated Press, the Homeland Security Department distributed "an unusual nationwide directive within Immigration and Customs Enforcement requiring any deportations prior to Tuesday's election to be approved at least at the level of ICE [Immigration and Customs Enforcement] regional directors."

However, immigration officials on the ground said the directive went even further. One ICE official told columnist Michelle Malkin: "The ICE fugitive operations group throughout the United States was told to stand down until after the election from arresting or transporting anyone out of the United States. This was done to avoid any mistakes of deporting or arresting anyone who could have a connection to the election, i.e., anyone from Kenya who could be a relative. The decision was election-driven."[15]

This was just the beginning, however. While the Bush administration was pathetically soft on illegal immigration, the Obama administration made it a point to attack those who wanted to combat illegal immigration. Obama's Justice Department lawyers aggressively targeted states that sought to protect legal citizens and residents from the myriad ills associated with illegal immigration. In short, the Obama administration (and its allies in Congress) cared more about illegal immigrants than it did about Americans.

According to the *Houston Chronicle*: "Several members of a key U.S. House committee called for greater oversight of a controversial federal program that allows local law enforcement to detain suspected illegal immigrants, citing a recent report that questioned its effectiveness. In a hearing Wednesday before the House Committee on Homeland Security, several members of Congress called for Immigration and Customs Enforcement officials to institute improvements. . . . 'The record is incomplete, at best, as to whether or not this program is a success,' said [then] House Homeland Security Chairman Bennie G. Thompson, D-Miss., who also raised concerns about the potential for racial profiling."[16] So according to Thompson—who, it must be reiterated, said this while sitting on the committee to secure *homeland security*—local law enforcement shouldn't be able to detain illegals because doing so would be "ineffective." What would be more effective—*not* detaining them and allowing them to roam free?

This federal program, informally called 287g, specifically trains local law enforcement officers to help enforce federal immigration law. And thanks in part to a public education campaign we designed and ran, the number of local law enforcement agencies participating in the program grew (from twenty-nine participants in 2006 to sixty-seven in 2009). Why did so many local law enforcement bureaus join up? Because, contrary to the brilliant analysis of Bennie Thompson, it works!

To give just one example, the Davidson County, (Nashville) Tennessee, Sheriff's Department significantly reduced crime in the two years after taking advantage of the 287g program. More than four thousand jailed illegal aliens were placed in removal proceedings.

Still, the Obama crowd and their fellow leftists in Congress weren't convinced. And they didn't stop with GAO reports and congressional hearings. They've looked for—and found—a scapegoat. They found him in Maricopa County, Arizona, and his name is Sheriff Joe Arpaio, known as "America's Toughest Sheriff" for his no-nonsense approach to illegal immigration and other crime. (Judicial Watch encouraged Sheriff Arpaio to crack down on illegal immigration in 2007 in Phoenix.)

As the *East Valley Tribune* reported in March 2009, federal investigators, at the behest of top officials in the Obama administration, turned up the heat on Sheriff Arpaio: "[W]ith President Barack Obama's inauguration, and more specifically his nominating Eric Holder as U.S. Attorney General, the federal government is heeding community activists' calls for extensive investigation of Arpaio's office." [17] Even as drug-fueled civil war crept across our border from Mexico, our government investigated one of the few effective lawmen on the front lines! Meanwhile, Nancy Pelosi called the effort to enforce immigration law "un-American." [18]

The "Get Joe Arpaio" effort kicked into high gear when the Obama gang took over the Justice Department in 2009. A multiyear investigation led to vague charges of racism and petulant complaints about Arpaio tactics in a Justice Department report. Arpaio will challenge the allegations in court. In the meantime, the Department of Homeland Security withdrew the 287g authority of Arpaio's deputies to police illegal immigration. The left has got its scalp, courtesy of Holder and Janet Napolitano (the former Arizona governor who now runs DHS)—and the people of Phoenix and Arizona have their safety compromised. And now the Obama administration is proposing to cut $17 million from the 287g program in its latest budget. In the age of trillion-dollar deficits, can anyone believe that the cut to this key immigration enforcement program, out of all the programs in the entire federal government, is anything but part of the Obama crusade against any serious enforcement of our nation's immigration laws?

Their attack on Arizona shows that the Obama administration isn't particularly concerned about the threat of violence on the border. They *were* concerned, however, about another issue of pressing importance: helping "vulnerable and underpaid" illegal alien workers obtain fair wages "regardless of immigration status." The campaign, launched by the Labor Department under the auspices of the Wage and Hour Division in April 2010, encouraged illegal aliens to contact the government for assistance in earning fair wages from employers. According to a Department of Labor press release announcing the We Can Help campaign, "The campaign . . . underscores that wage and hour laws apply to all workers in the United States, regardless of immigration status." The release also indicated that 250 new field investigators had been added to the government payroll to target employers who deny workers their "rightful wage."

In a public service announcement promoting the campaign, available in both English and Spanish, Secretary of Labor Hilda Solis said, "Remember, every worker in America has a right to be paid fairly whether documented or not." She then encouraged workers to contact the government's new toll-free hotline for a "confidential" consultation. The government also has an Internet site dedicated to the We Can Help program and has recruited celebrity spokespersons such as actor Jimmy Smits to help promote the campaign. This is the height of absurdity—while Americans are out of jobs, the administration maintains programs to increase pay for people who are unable to lawfully work in the United States because they *are not in our country legally*!

At least we now knew which side the Obama administration and its allies were on when it came to illegal immigration. And it wasn't our side—the side of law and order.

Even legal immigration is problematic under the Obama administration, which made allowances for illegal alien criminals to legally enter the United States on a far-too-regular basis. We were particularly concerned about the Obama administration's issuance of so-called S Visas, which are granted to alien informants who help U.S. law enforcement officers to investigate and prosecute criminal and terrorist activities.

The S Visa provision was added to the Violent Crime Control and Law Enforcement Act in 1994 in response to the 1993 World Trade Center bombing and allows aliens who possess "critical information on criminal or terrorist organizations to come into the United States in order to provide information to law enforcement officials." Since 1995, the government has issued nine hundred S Visas.

According to the law, two hundred S Visas can be distributed annually for information related to criminal activity (known as S-5 status), while fifty S Visas can be distributed annually for information related to terrorist activity (known as S-6 status). However, there is no cap on the number of family members of informants eligible for S Visa status. S Visas are intended to be temporary, with a maximum stay of three years. However, S Visa holders can achieve *permanent* visa status at the discretion of the attorney general. We got information that the Obama administration was abusing this discretion. From our information, there was very little oversight of this program and even less information available to the public regarding the criteria used to determine who receives an S Visa and under what circumstances. And, as the S Visa requirements would suggest, many of these folks—people who associate with terrorists and criminals—would certainly be suspect!

Even when the Obama administration made noises about being

on our side on the illegal immigration question, they weren't. When it announced a plan to send a few hundred agents to the U.S. border with Mexico to "battle the increasing level of guns, money and drugs trafficked across the border," they said nothing about the unremitting flood of *people* coming across the border with the guns, money, and drugs. As we all know, guns, money, and drugs do not have feet, and do not travel across borders on their own—but according to the Obama administration, we apparently needed more federal agents on the border to prevent Gumby-like bags of marijuana from strolling over to Texas, Arizona, California, and New Mexico.

But at least the Obama administration was calling for more border agents, right? Not exactly. At the same time that the administration announced its plans to put agents on the border, Secretary of Homeland Security Napolitano turned down an offer by the U.S. Senate for more money (about $380 million) to address the problem, despite repeated pleas by members of the Senate Committee on Homeland Defense to use the funds to fix the problem. Simultaneously, the administration also rejected an appeal from Texas governor Rick Perry and Arizona governor Jan Brewer to deploy a thousand National Guard troops to quell the violence associated with drug cartel wars centered in Mexico.

What was going on here? The answer was obvious: just as it did with Obamacare, the Obama White House was attempting to play at moderation in public while secretly pushing radicalism. There was a simple choice: was the administration really interested in dealing with the chaos and drug cartel violence on the border? Or was it interested only in publicity stunts that gave the *appearance* of addressing the border security crisis? The obvious answer was that this was done for appearances. Let's face it—sending three or four hundred federal agents to the border was not by itself going to make much of a difference, especially since the Obama administration had set no timetable, and they were rumored to be removed within months. And while the administration was flexing its border muscles, Secretary of State Hillary Clinton was down in Mexico attacking America and suggesting our Second Amendment was responsible for their civil war (a position that would help explain the Fast and Furious fiasco, which saw the Obama administration sending guns to Mexico in the hopes the guns showed up at crime scenes!).

As Senator Joe Lieberman told Napolitano after she refused the border security money, "I think you're going to need more resources to get the job done. . . . I mean, this is kind of a war."[19] Lieberman was right—as we uncovered through FOIA, U.S. Border Patrol agents have been involved in dangerous confrontations with Mexican government officials *in U.S. territory*, including with members of the Mexican military.

But Napolitano, and her boss in the White House, didn't believe in war—they believed in "man-made catastrophes" and other Orwellian language that undermines our resolve to enforce the law. That's why the Obama gang saved their *real* ammunition not for illegal immigration or the drug cartels, but for Arizona, which had the temerity to fight illegal immigration where the feds wouldn't.

Illegal Immigration Ground Zero

On April 23, 2010, citing the federal government's dismal failure to deal with the illegal immigration crisis, Arizona governor Brewer signed into law a new bill that tried to address the illegal alien crisis that is disproportionately impacting Arizona. The bill, SB1070, was pushed by then–Arizona state senator Russell Pearce (who would soon become a Judicial Watch client). And, as you might expect, the reaction from illegal immigration activists and radical leftists was swift and severe, starting with the Obama White House, which was looking for any opportunity it could to shore up the so-called Hispanic vote.

Obama irresponsibly criticized the legislation as "misguided" and suggested his politically pliant Justice Department would sue the state of Arizona to prevent the law from going into effect. Liberal political leaders immediately called for an economic boycott of the state. Illegal immigration proponents vowed protests across the country.

In his remarks criticizing the Arizona bill, Obama said that the "efforts" in Arizona "threaten to undermine the basic notions of fairness we cherish as Americans." This president evidently learned nothing from the blow-up over his racially charged attack on the Cambridge, Massachusetts, police department after the arrest of Harvard professor Henry Louis Gates Jr.; he wanted another blow-up, this time on behalf of a different racial minority. It was shameful for Obama and his cheerleading section in the liberal press to so readily play the race card in opposing this commonsense law—but shame has never stopped these folks. Nevertheless, maybe transparency and the rule of law would.

With the immigration crisis, there was one thing Americans didn't need: a lecture from Barack Obama on the basic notion of fairness while he prepared to grant amnesty, by hook or by crook, to millions of illegal aliens who reside here in violation of the law.

The most controversial section of the new law simply codified what the police had the inherent power to do anywhere in the United States—investigate the immigration status of individuals in consultation with federal authorities.

We had been on the front lines of this battle in Arizona. Back in 2007, Judicial Watch partnered with local community and business leaders and Sheriff Joe Arpaio on the issue. Our work helped lead to a crackdown on illegal alien criminals, resulting in dozens of arrests. We also launched a comprehensive public education campaign concerning the city of Phoenix's immigration enforcement policies. Several months after we initiated this campaign, then–Phoenix mayor Phil Gordon abandoned his long-held support of his city's sanctuary policy. As a result, even without the new law, everyone arrested in Phoenix was now questioned about his or her citizenship.

In short, we knew what the issues were in Arizona. And we knew that Obama was wrong.

The rampant lawlessness emanating from the unprotected Arizona-Mexico border resulted in the cartels bringing Mexicans illegally across the border and then holding them for ransom in "drop houses" across Phoenix until family members and friends pay to release them from captivity. Rampant crime, violent drug cartels operating with impunity, and human trafficking—this is the reality that Arizona legal residents, both Hispanic and non-Hispanic, face every day. Rather than doing as the law requires—cooperate with state officials to fully enforce our immigration laws—Obama and his "law enforcement" team (to include the ethically challenged Attorney General Eric Holder and the soft-on-border-security Janet Napolitano) attacked Arizona's SB1070 by filing an unprecedented federal lawsuit against the state of Arizona to stop its enforcement.

We immediately got involved in the lawsuit, filing an amicus brief and reaching out to others who wanted to help. Judicial Watch filed a "Motion to Intervene" to defend the law on behalf of Arizona state senator Pearce, the law's author. We also opposed, on behalf of Pearce, the Obama Justice Department's effort in the courts to prevent sections of the law from taking effect as scheduled. We knew that the Obama Justice Department's lawsuit had absolutely nothing to do with the rule of law. The Obama White House was desperate to kill this law because the president knew that if it were allowed to stand, other states would follow suit, and the federal government might finally have to do its job and secure the border. And securing the border is something President Obama was loath to do as he sought to retain and increase his share of political support among Hispanics. President Obama and his appointee Eric Holder let racial politics get in the way of enforcing the rule of law.

To add insult to injury, even as the Obama White House went after the citizens of Arizona, the administration would not go after states and localities that had "sanctuary policies" that frustrated or violated federal immigration law in order to provide sanctuary for illegal aliens. Many big-city police departments prevent, for instance, their police officers from inquiring about someone's immigration status or seeking information about someone's immigration status from ICE.

What makes sanctuary policies illegal? In 1996, Congress enacted legislation that specifies that a "Federal, State, or local government entity or official may not prohibit, or in any way restrict, any government entity or official from sending to, or receiving from, [ICE] information regarding the citizenship or immigration status, lawful or unlawful, of any individual." In other words, if a cop has an inkling that someone—a witness, a suspect, or an arrestee—is an illegal alien, no one can stop him from inquiring with the feds. Again, most major cities violate this law by preventing their police officers notifying federal authorities when they arrest a suspected illegal alien or from even asking federal immigration officials about someone's citizenship or legal status. These "don't ask, don't tell" policies are in place in Los Angeles, San Francisco, Chicago, New York, Washington, D.C., and Houston (to name a few!). Our nation will never secure our borders as long as our major cities put out the "welcome mat" to illegals with these sanctuary policies.

By the way, these sanctuary policies have no public support. They are a product of big-city liberalism. Our most recent national poll on the topic, conducted for us by Harris earlier this year, found that 64 percent of Americans (and 55 percent of Democrats) did not agree with these enforcement-free sanctuary policies for illegal aliens.

However, the Obama administration announced that it will not penalize so-called sanctuary cities, such as Pasadena, that prevent the police from communicating freely with ICE. The contrast with attacks on Arizona's effort to *further* immigration enforcement could not have been more stark.

The Secret Plan on Illegal Immigration, Not So Secret Anymore

As the Obama administration sued Arizona, it planned its real agenda behind the scenes. Conservatives began speculating that President Obama might bypass Congress and grant blanket amnesty by way of executive fiat to millions of illegal aliens currently residing in the United States.

Word of the Obama stealth amnesty plan first leaked out in 2010 when a "draft" report crafted by the U.S. Citizenship and

Immigration Service (USCIS) made its way into the media. The report showed that this lawless Obama administration scheme was far more than mere rumor. It was a detailed and well-thought-out strategy. According to FoxNews.com, "Sen. David Vitter, R-La. . . . said he and his colleagues are still looking for answers on whether the administration has seriously considered mass legalization for illegal immigrants, after an administration memo surfaced outlining ways to grant legalization without going through Congress. The draft memo, first obtained by Iowa Republican Sen. Chuck Grassley's office from the U.S. Citizenship & Immigration Services, outlines ways the administration was exploring to legalize swaths of illegal immigrants 'in the absence of Comprehensive Immigration Reform.' The memo describes how to, 'reduce the threat of removal for certain individuals present in the United States without authorization.' "[20]

The Obama administration quickly tried to downplay the significance of the memo. But these denials rang hollow. And no one could honestly deny the intent of the memo. You don't even have to read past the subject header of the memo to get a clue as to what the USCIS is up to: "Administrative Alternatives to Comprehensive Illegal Immigration Reform." Was there any way to misread the objective here? Clearly the USCIS expended a considerable amount of effort trying to sneak this past Congress in order to implement the president's illegal alien amnesty plan.

But let's take a look at some excerpts from the USCIS document so you can judge for yourself. "The following items—used alone or in combination—have the potential to result in meaningful immigration reform absent legislative action," the memo says. "Allow TPS [Temporary Protected Status] Applicants Who Entered Without Inspection to Adjust or Change Status. . . . USCIS should no longer adhere to the 1990 General Counsel opinions, and instead permit individuals in TPS to adjust or change status. Opening this pathway will help thousands of applicants obtain lawful permanent residence without having to leave the U.S."

How about a few more options? "Expand the Use of Parole-in-Place," suggests the USCIS. "USCIS has the discretionary authority under [federal law] to parole into the U.S. on a case-by-case basis for 'urgent humanitarian reasons' or 'significant public benefit' any applicant for admission. . . . Granting parole to aliens in the U.S. who have not been admitted or paroled is commonly referred to as 'parole-in-place' (PIP). By granting PIP, USCIS can eliminate the need for qualified recipients to return to their home country for consular processing, particularly when doing so might trigger a bar to returning."

And then there's the option listed as "Lessen the Standard for Demonstrating Extreme Hardship," the USCIS report says. "By statute, DHS has discretion to waive these grounds of inadmissibility for spouses, sons, and daughters of U.S. citizens or lawful permanent residents if the refusal to admit these individuals would result in extreme hardship for their qualifying relatives. Generally the 'extreme hardship' standard has been narrowly construed by USCIS. To increase the number of individuals applying for waivers, and improve their chances for receiving them, CIS could issue guidance or regulation specifying a lower evidentiary standard for 'extreme hardship.' "

There was a worse fourth option. "Increase the Use of Deferred Action," the USCIS avers. "USCIS has previously allowed the use of deferred action to provide relief to non-immigrants whose period of admission had expired, or otherwise had failed to maintain lawful immigrant status. . . . While it is theoretically possible to grant deferred action to an unrestricted number of unlawfully present individuals, doing so would likely be controversial, not to mention expensive. . . . Rather than making deferred action widely available to hundreds of thousands and as a nonlegislative version of 'amnesty,' USCIS could tailor the use of this discretionary option for particular groups. . . ."

The memo goes on for about eleven pages with other recommendations, too. I've examined tens of thousands of government documents in my fourteen years here at Judicial Watch. So it is not insignificant for us to say that this memo is about the most brazen and shocking government document I've ever reviewed.

Unfortunately, Congress is once again letting this matter drop.

In 2010, Republican members of the Senate Judiciary Committee wrote to Chairman Pat Leahy demanding the matter be investigated by the committee. "We are very concerned about the options outlined in the memo and are troubled that the executive branch could be engaged in an effort to inappropriately expand its authority to ensure illegal immigrants are not removed from the United States and are given access to various immigration benefits, including potential green card status," the senators stated. But since the November 2010 election, it's only gotten worse. The Obama amnesty scheme is on the verge of being fully implemented as Congress watches haplessly.

Let's sum up. Obama's top political appointees in the agency charged with enforcing our immigration laws are spending their time thinking of ways not to enforce the law and how to bypass the elected representatives of the people to grant mass amnesty through a raw abuse of executive power.

Obama and his appointees are obviously impatient with the niceties of the U.S. Constitution and the rule of law. We already knew they're against the rule of law with their coordinated and dishonest attack on Arizona's SB1070. This memo shows they'd be happy to throw the rule of law out entirely when it comes to immigration.

But that memo was just the beginning. According to the *Houston Chronicle*, "The Department of Homeland Security is systematically reviewing thousands of pending immigration cases and moving to dismiss those filed against suspected illegal immigrants who have no serious criminal records, according to several sources familiar with the efforts. Culling the immigration court system dockets of noncriminals started in earnest in Houston about a month ago and has stunned local immigration attorneys, who have reported coming to court anticipating clients' deportations only to learn that the government was dismissing their cases." [21]

In some instances, the article notes, illegal aliens who have been convicted of crimes will be allowed to stay in the country as long as these crimes do not involve drunk driving, family violence, or sexual assault. But other than those specific circumstances, right now it appears the other deportation candidates are in the clear. (Most of these folks are in the system because they were arrested for committing crimes, so to release those who have only been "convicted" means that illegal alien violent criminals are being set free.)

The court "was terminating all of the cases that came up," said one immigration attorney who was notified that the government requested dismissals in three of his deportation cases. "It was absolutely fantastic." According to ICE memo, this new policy could impact up to seventeen thousand cases.

This activity caused a revolt within ICE. Even the liberals at the *Washington Post* noticed that ICE's front-line immigration enforcement personnel were opposing the nonenforcement program being implemented by Obama political appointees. In a rare action, a major ICE union announced a unanimous vote of "no confidence" in the Obama leadership team at ICE.[22] The detail of the union's complaint was devastating and documented a crisis of law enforcement at ICE. The union noted, for instance, that: "[c]riminal aliens incarcerated in local jails seek out ICE officers and volunteer for deportation to avoid prosecution, conviction and serving prison sentences. Criminal aliens openly brag to ICE officers that they are taking advantage of the broken immigration system and will be back in the United States within days to commit crimes, while United States citizens arrested for the same offenses serve prison sentences. State and local law enforcement, prosecutors and jails are equally overwhelmed by the criminal alien problem and lack the resources to prosecute and house these prisoners, resulting in the release of criminal aliens back into local communities before making contact with ICE. Thousands of other criminal aliens are released to ICE without being tried for their criminal charges. ICE senior leadership is aware that the system is broken, yet refuses to alert Congress to the severity of the situation and request additional resources to provide better enforcement and support of local agencies."[23]

The Houston amnesty program seems to have been a test case for a wider amnesty effort by the Obama administration. ICE went on to test their amnesty schemes in Denver and Baltimore and is expanding it to additional cities. As you read this, Obama stealth amnesty may already be in your city.

What an ugly mess caused by the Obama administration's radical hostility to the rule of law! And U.S. citizens and *legal* alien residents suffer as a result.

Where Health Care Meets Illegal Immigration

In September 2009, President Obama bullied the television networks into covering another of his innumerable joint sessions of Congress. This one was called to make the case for Obamacare. In the middle of the speech, however, when Obama stated that his program wouldn't include coverage for illegal immigrants, Representative Joe Wilson (R-SC) shouted, "You lie!"

The ill-mannered outburst grabbed most of the spotlight. What the media neglected to highlight, however, was that the interjection came after President Obama said that opponents of his plans for health-care takeover had base motives and were liars. But what about Wilson's fundamental charge? Was the president correct when he said his health-care plan wouldn't cover illegals? He was not. Obama was, in fact, lying.

The president pointed out that there was language in Democratic health-care proposals stating that illegal aliens were not entitled to health care. "That idea has never been on the table," the president said in a radio address. However, the fundamental issue regarding whether or not illegals would receive benefits has to do with *verification*. As *National Review Online* blogger (and immigration expert who runs the Center for Immigration Studies) Mark Krikorian pointed out, "The provision of the bill that purports to bar illegals from receiving the insurance subsidy is meaningless, and specifically *intended* to be so; when Rep. Dean Heller (R-Nev.) offered an amendment to require verification of eligibility via the SAVE system (which is used to check applicants for other forms of government assistance), the measure was voted down on party lines. Regarding a different provision of the bill, Rep. Nathan Deal (R-Ga.) offered an amendment to verify the eligibility of applicants for expanded Medicaid, and it too was voted down by the Democrats."[24]

If the president and Democratic leaders in Congress were truly serious about banning illegals from receiving health insurance subsidies, why not legislate the use of the same verification systems already in place for other federal programs?

The answer was easy: the president and liberals *did* want illegals to receive health care under their reform proposals. They were just smart enough to know their health-care takeover proposals would be even less popular with the American people if they were honest about their goals.

The *Washington Post,* for instance, grudgingly highlighted the fact that illegals could buy insurance through taxpayer-subsidized "insurance exchanges" at the heart of Obama's reform plans. One liberal expert admitted to the *Post,* "Will some illegal immigrant get [help]? Probably. Will it be this big problem? Probably not." [25] We beg to differ—*any* illegals getting insurance paid for by taxpayers is a big problem.

Facing the outcry after Wilson's outburst, the White House initially backtracked on illegal aliens and health-care reform. Now the Obama administration said that illegal aliens would not only be ineligible to receive taxpayer-funded subsidies for health care; they wouldn't even be able to purchase health insurance with their own funds in a government-created marketplace.

Of course, the White House claimed this was the Obama policy from the very beginning. Not true. Even congressional Democrats were confused by the switch. "I'm not sure if Gibbs misspoke," Representative Xavier Becerra (D-CA), vice chairman of the House Democratic Caucus, said. [26] Senator Max Baucus (D-MT) immediately seized on the Obama administration's policy reversal, saying that he would include in his bill a provision that would bar illegals from purchasing insurance through these taxpayer-subsidized exchanges, even if illegals were willing and able to pay the full cost. [27]

The restrictions on illegal aliens receiving Obamacare benefits eventually did make their way into the final Obamacare law. But as Senators Tom Coburn and Tom Barrasso point out, illegals still get benefits under Obamacare. In a special report, the senators detail the restrictions:

Some of the inequities in the new federal health care law mean that Americans face more burdensome requirements under the law than do legal or illegal immigrants, according to a recent analysis from the nonpartisan Congressional Research Service (CRS).

Illegal Immigrants Get Free Health Care, but Americans Either Buy Expensive Insurance or Get Taxed

Starting in 2014 [provided that it is upheld by the Supreme Court], Americans will be subject to the individual mandate penalty of $695 annually if they do not purchase federally dictated health insurance. However, under the new federal law, illegal immigrants will not be forced to purchase health insurance, though they will still be able to receive health care—regardless of their ability to pay—in a hospital's emergency department.

According to CRS [the Congressional Research Service], "Unauthorized (illegal) immigrants are expressly exempted from the mandate to have health insurance and, as a result, cannot be penalized for noncompliance." So illegal immigrants get health care without paying for it, but citizens face the choice of either buying expensive health insurance or paying a tax.

The cost of illegal immigrants' health care in the emergency department of hospitals will be shifted to Americans with insurance. As CRS underscored, "the cost of providing uncompensated care to the uninsured was $43 billion in 2008," and, "to pay for this cost, health care providers pass on the cost to private insurers, which pass on the cost to families. This cost-shifting increases family premiums on average by over $1,000 a year.[28]

But now some illegals no longer have to go to emergency rooms to get "free" health care paid for with American tax money. The "ban" is no bother to the Obama administration, which began funneling health-care money to illegals quite brazenly. Our friends over at CNSNews.com found that at least $8.5 million in Obamacare taxpayer funds would go to help community health centers care for "migrant" workers, of which at least 25 percent are illegal. As you might have guessed, these "community health centers" won't be required to confirm the legal status of patients.[29] So despite explicit legal prohibitions against doing so, the Obama administration will use Obamacare tax dollars to help pay for health care for illegal aliens. Joe Wilson, call your office.

Crony Capitalism

This administration has spent more in less than four years than any administration in history. In fact, the Obama administration has increased the national debt by a whopping $4 trillion and has set the nation on the path to fiscal ruin with huge expenses like the stimulus program and the $2 trillion Obamacare program. Too much of the stimulus cash has gone to "stimulus" programs that simply did not stimulate—or, at least, did not stimulate the broader economy. Instead, that cash goes to stimulate friends of the Obama administration.

The most obvious example of crony capitalism was, of course, the government's cram-down of the restructuring of the auto companies. When the government bailed out the auto companies and nationalized Chrysler rather than allowing it to go into normal bankruptcy, simply so that the administration could pay off its union allies, it was just another example of the Obama administration using its power to help its friends. The Obama administration crammed down the deal on bondholders, forcing them to take on the huge financial hit, even though they had recoupment priority over the unions. As Governor Mitch Daniels (R-IN) wrote, "The shock wave through the economic markets from this arbitrary redefinition of 'secured creditors' rights was profound. Could centuries of crystal-clear law really be overthrown by executive fiat? Apparently, yes. The Supreme Court declined to intervene in the takeover. The cost of corporate borrowing was clearly headed upward as the U.S. for the first time imitated those Third World despotisms where economic rules can be changed without warning at the ruler's whim and convenience."[30] In the end, the United Auto Workers, which owned *zero interest* in Chrysler, "were simply handed a 55% interest, a gift valued then at $4.5 billion. . . . After this looting, the legitimate creditors were told to be happy with the remnants. For Indiana's retired teachers and state policemen, this amounted to 29 cents on the dollar, a loss of $6 million versus the purchase price. . . ."[31]

Much of the Obama administration's crony capitalism has been directed at the unions. In April 2011, the National Labor Relations Board filed a complaint against Boeing after the company opened a new plant in South Carolina rather than Seattle, supposedly based on the fact that the Seattle plant has been a repository of union unrest for decades. In fact, the NLRB decided it was a good idea to file a lawsuit against Boeing. We quickly FOIA'd for documents surrounding the decision. Here's what we found:

- A May 5, 2011, email from Barry Kearney, associate general counsel for the National Labor Relations Board, to colleagues at NLRB concerning a press release issued by the International Association of Machinists and Aerospace Workers (IAM) attacking Boeing: "Hooray for the red, white and blue." NLRB attorney Miriam Szapiro responded shortly thereafter, "Good. I like this part [at last they can put it to some good use]: the NLRB's long-term professional Regional Staff, National Office of Advice and General Counsel *reviewed this case for a year. . . .*" (Emphasis in original.)

- A July 12, 2011, email from NLRB regional director Richard Ahearn to NLRB hearing officer Peter Finch, responding to an article in the newspaper the *Hill* about a request from Representative Darrell Issa, chairman of the House Committee on Oversight and Government Reform, seeking documents related to the NLRB Boeing lawsuit: "We will politely decline." (Ahearn signed the NRLB complaint against Boeing.)

- A May 5, 2011, email from NLRB attorney Szapiro warning an unknown recipient (name blacked out) about reading a *Wall Street Journal* article supporting Boeing and criticizing compulsory unionism: "don't look at yesterday's WSJ; you'll puke."

- In response to an April 29, 2011, *Wall Street Journal* article calling on President Obama to explain the NLRB lawsuit against Boeing, NLRB attorney Jayme Sophir issues a one-word email response on May 2, 2011, to NLRB attorney Debra Willen, Division of Advice: "Ugh."

President Obama bypassed the U.S. Senate and used a recess appointment to install Craig Becker as head of the NLRB's five-member board. The Becker appointment was made after the Democratic-controlled U.S. Senate refused to move forward on his confirmation. An ally of ACORN, Becker had previously worked for the Service Employees International Union and the AFL-CIO, major financial backers of Obama and the Democratic Party. Controversially, Becker refused to recuse himself from certain NLRB decisions affecting his former union clients.

Another batch of documents shows the contempt that the Obama NRLB had for Congress and, frankly, America under Becker, who is now gone from the agency:

- On April 22, 2011, acting NLRB general counsel Lafe Solomon sent an email to Wilma Liebman, outgoing chairwoman of the NLRB: "The article gave me a new idea. You go to geneva and I get a job with airbus [French aerospace company that is Boeing's biggest competitor]. We screwed up the us economy and now we can tackle europe." Solomon's comment was in response to an article published in French on the European website Planet Labor noting the devastating potential economic impact on South Carolina if the Boeing plant were to be scuttled: "Two billion dollars were invested in Charleston, 1,000 employees were recruited, and the site was supposed to open in July . . . until the NLRB meddled in." Solomon's "joke" is produced below:

```
-----Original Message-----
From: "Solomon, Lafe E." <Lafe.Solomon@nlrb.gov>
Date: Fri, 22 Apr 2011 08:27:04
To:                         Wilma Liebman
Subject: Re: Boeing

The article gave me a new idea. You go to geneva and I get a job with airbus. We screwed up
the us economy and now we can tackle europe. I didn't read all of the meltwater articles but
some of the headlines tie boeing to craig. Unbelievable.
```

- On April 22, 2011, NLRB attorney Debra Willen received an email in which Republican senator Jim DeMint of South Carolina is ridiculed as "Sen. Dement."

- On May 12, 2011, NLRB deputy assistant general counsel Joseph Baniszewski emailed a political cartoon to Deputy Assistant General Counsel Jennifer Abruzzo mocking the state of South Carolina with regard to the Boeing Company's decision to locate its manufacturing facility in that state.

- On April 28, 2011, Miriam Szapiro sent an email to NLRB attorney Debra Willen commenting on an article in the *Economist* expressing some support for the Boeing lawsuit: "Exactly; it just shows you how incredibly reactionary the US is, that the conservative *Economist* thinks we're Neanderthal."

- On April 20, 2011, Mara-Louise Anzalone, counsel for acting NLRB general counsel Lafe Solomon, took exception to U.S. senator Lindsey Graham's (R-SC) statement, "As Senator, I will do everything in my power, including introducing legislation cutting off funding for this wide [*sic*] goose chase, to stop the NLRB's frivolous complaint [against Boeing]." In an email to NLRB regional attorney Anne Pomerantz, Anzalone writes, "Awesome. Sounds like they're just going to furlough you and me."

I thought it particularly interesting to see a government official complain about "how incredibly reactionary the US is." The term *reactionary* seems straight from Marxist lexicon. There is no other reasonable way to describe it, certainly not in this context. The "reactionary" email appears below:

From: Szapiro, Miriam
Sent: Thursday, April 28, 2011 10:30 AM
To: ▓▓▓▓ *Advice Attorney* ▓▓▓▓ Willen, Debra L
Subject: RE: Boeing's labour problems: Moving factories to flee unions | The Economist

Exactly; it just shows you how incredibly reactionary the US is, that the conservative Economist thinks we're Neanderthal.

From: ▓▓ *Advice Attorney* ▓▓
Sent: Thursday, April 28, 2011 10:28 AM
To: Willen, Debra L; Szapiro, Miriam
Subject: FW: Boeing's labour problems: Moving factories to flee unions | The Economist

Well, who knew the Economist would endorse you?!

Is there any doubt now that the Obama administration's attack on Boeing is irresponsible and politically motivated? Read the documents for yourself. NLRB attorneys come off as juvenile politicos rather than professionals interested in arbitrating a labor dispute. Their utter contempt for congressional oversight shows that the NRLB thinks it is above the law.

According to Boeing, the NLRB's claim "was legally frivolous and represents a radical departure from both NLRB and Supreme Court precedent. Boeing has every right under both federal law and its collective bargaining agreement to build additional U.S. production capacity outside of the Puget Sound region."

Nonetheless, Boeing, facing unremitting hostility from the Obama politicos, has since come to an agreement with its union over the South Carolina plant. Now that the unions have successfully leveraged the NRLB in its contract negations with Boeing, the NRLB has become a lot less interested in Boeing. In fact, the labor board dropped its lawsuit altogether.

The NLRB is supposed to be a neutral arbiter of labor disputes, not a tool for unions. But these days, most of the administration seems to be in the thrall of Big Labor. Now with Obama's unconstitutional appointments to the NRLB, the agency is completely outside the law. You can bet that the agency, now run by constitutional pretenders, won't be able to say the word *union* without a lawsuit challenging its lawfulness (maybe one from Judicial Watch!).

But the NRLB power grab is just the tip of the iceberg. For example, in 2009, the Obama administration announced that the Department of Energy was offering a $528.7 million taxpayer-funded loan for the company Fisker Automotive to buy up a former General Motors plant in Wilmington, Delaware, in Vice President Joe Biden's home state. The company planned to use the plant to produce a new line of hybrid electric vehicles set to launch in 2012.

On October 27, 2009, in a press event announcing the plant reopening, Vice President Biden made news by inadvertently revealing Fisker's undisclosed plans to produce 100,000 plug-in hybrid sedans, coupes, and crossovers. At the conclusion of his speech, Biden told the crowd, made up mostly of UAW members who had previously worked at the plant when it was owned by General Motors, "imagine when this factory, when the floor we're standing on right now is making 100,000 plug-in hybrid sedans, coupes and crossovers every single year."

Fisker's selection of the plant, and the vice president's participation in the press conference announcing the plant reopening as well as his intimate knowledge of Fisker's production plans, raised questions in the auto industry as to whether there was any quid pro quo arrangement with Biden related to the purchase, especially given the fact that a large government loan made the purchase possible. (Moreover, given that the federal government is the majority owner of GM, there were other potential conflicts of interest related to this deal that merit investigation.) We launched a FOIA request at the Treasury Department. They never responded. We're currently in litigation over the stonewalled information. Taxpayers have half a billion dollars at stake in this controversial and expensive business idea. And, now that the federal government has an ownership stake in the auto industry, its decisions must be completely transparent in order to root out any possible corruption.

And what of the cars GM is making? They're being produced abroad.[32]

At the time of the announcement, Secretary of Energy Steven Chu indicated the Fisker loan was "proof positive" that the Obama administration was "putting Americans back to work." However, Fisker came under fire in 2011 for assembling its first line of cars in Finland and for lengthy delays in producing the volume of cars bankrolled, in part, with the Energy Department loan.

Moreover, the company is now beset with massive layoffs in its Delaware and California operations as it seeks additional government funding.

And Judicial Watch seems to be the only one asking any questions. Congress hasn't done anything on this issue and the media is relying on us to get the truth.

Speaking of corruption in the auto industry, the *Washington Post* reported in August 2010 that "General Motors reported making $47,000 in contributions to lawmakers and congressional candidates in July 2010, the first it has made since November 2008. The company stopped giving through its political action committee just as it began to seek government assistance to stay in business. The U.S. government provided support but also steered the company through bankruptcy. Today, the Treasury owns a 60 percent stake in the company, which recently announced plans to go public with a stock sale. GM earlier gave $41,000 to groups and causes associated with lawmakers. The latest contributions were made directly to lawmakers' campaigns."[33]

The *Washington Post* noted the fact that GM was spreading the wealth around to both political parties: $26,000 to Republicans and $21,000 to Democrats. According to the FEC, recipients included Roy Blunt, Sherrod Brown, Dave Camp, Eric Cantor, John Dingell, Amy Klobuchar, Chuck Schumer, and Debbie Stabenow. Do me a favor: if you're reading this book during business hours, put it down and call the U.S. Capitol at 202-224-3121. Ask for any one of these politicians still in office to find out why they think it is appropriate to take campaign cash from a PAC that, for all intents and purposes, is being funded through another Obama power grab, with taxpayer dollars.

It should go without saying that a company that is owned and operated by the government has no business making campaign contributions to members of Congress, no matter how the company tries to spin it. But this is exactly the kind of scuzzy arrangement we can expect now that the government has decided to meddle so obtrusively into the private sector. (Since the bailout, the "Government Motors" PAC has given $754,000 away to politicians.)

We checked with a spokesman for the Corporation for Public Broadcasting (CPB), another "private" corporation funded and controlled by the federal government. He told us that CPB does not have a PAC.

While the political activities of GM were particularly offensive given the government's considerable ownership stake, other companies bailed out with taxpayer dollars also continue to fill the political coffers, according to Fox News: "Several companies that escaped financial failure two years ago through massive taxpayer-funded bailouts are spending millions of dollars to make donations to political causes and even some candidates' campaigns. General Motors, Chrysler, and Citigroup are just three of the biggest bailout recipients who have continued to remain politically active, through their political action committees, federal lobbying or direct donations to the pet projects of lawmakers." [34] This was corruption at its "finest."

Were we being too suspicious? Not if the Obama gang's dealings with Solyndra were any indication. The energy company received a $535 million "stimulus" loan guarantee from the Obama administration in 2009—and then collapsed less than two years later. Solyndra was the poster child for the Obama administration's claim that it could create green jobs with taxpayer money. Now 1,100 more people are out of work and American taxpayers are on the hook for half a billion dollars.

But while this ought to be an abject embarrassment for the dirigistes in the Obama administration, there's a much bigger story behind the Solyndra scandal. It involves a concerted effort by White House officials to improperly rush the Solyndra loan decision for political reasons. The *Washington Post* had the exclusive story:

The Obama White House tried to rush federal reviewers for a decision on a nearly half-billion-dollar loan to the solar-panel manufacturer Solyndra so Vice President Biden could announce the approval at a September 2009 groundbreaking for the company's factory, newly obtained e-mails show. The Silicon Valley company, a centerpiece in President Obama's initiative to develop clean energy technologies, had been tentatively approved for the loan by the Energy Department but was awaiting a final financial review by the Office of Management and Budget [OMB]. The August 2009 e-mails, released exclusively to the *Washington Post,* show White House officials repeatedly asking OMB reviewers when they would be able to decide on the federal loan and noting a looming press event at which they planned to announce the deal. In response, OMB officials expressed concern that they were being rushed to approve the company's project without adequate time to assess the risk to taxpayers, according to information provided by Republican congressional investigators.[35]

The *Washington Post* went on to detail some of these email messages:

"We have ended up with a situation of having to do rushed approvals on a couple of occasions (and we are worried about Solyndra at the end of the week)," one official wrote. That August 31, 2009, message, written by a senior OMB staffer and sent to Terrell P. McSweeny, Biden's domestic policy advisor, concluded, "We would prefer to have sufficient time to do our due diligence reviews."[36]

Now, here's where mere incompetence turns into corruption. Want to guess the name of Solyndra's biggest financial backer? Tulsa billionaire and Obama fund-raiser George Kaiser.

So, in sum, the Obama administration rushed through a half-billion-dollar bailout loan to a now bankrupt alternative energy company bankrolled by one of Barack Obama's top campaign fund-raisers!

Judicial Watch has launched a full investigation of its own. We've already submitted FOIA requests to the Department of Energy, the

OMB, the Treasury Department, and the Government Account-ability Office (GAO) for records related to the loan guarantee, interagency communication regarding the loan, and communications with Solyndra's private financiers. While Judicial Watch's probe is still in its early stages, here are a few things our experienced investigators have already dug up. According to a July 2010 GAO report, "DOE's implementation of the [loan guarantee] program has favored some applicants and disadvantaged others in a number of ways." The GAO cites five companies to which the Energy Department handed conditional financial commitments before receiving reports from external reviewers. Solyndra was one of them.[37]

Argonaut Ventures, LLC, controlled by Obama fund-raiser Kaiser, owns 39 percent of Solyndra. Kaiser, the sixty-fourth-richest person in the world, was an Obama campaign bundler who raised $50,000 for the Obama presidential campaign. He made no fewer than nine visits to the White House between March 12, 2009, and April 14, 2011, including a June 25, 2009, visit with Valerie Jarrett and former White House chief of staff Rahm Emanuel. A number of Solyndra officers have visited the Obama White House as well, including the company's chief executive officer.

Solyndra was never close to solvent. According to a document filed by the company with the Securities and Exchange Commission on March 18, 2010: "We have incurred significant net losses since our inception, including a net loss of $114.1 million in fiscal 2007, $232.1 million in fiscal 2008 and $172.5 million in fiscal 2009, and we had an accumulated deficit of $557.7 million at January 2, 2010. We expect to continue to incur significant operating and net losses and negative cash flow from operations for the foreseeable future. . . ."

The government's interest rate on the Solyndra loan is significantly lower (at least 50 percent lower) than the interest rates given to other beneficiaries of Energy Department stimulus funds. For example Kahuku Wind received an interest rate of 3.406 percent from the federal government. Solyndra's interest rates ranged between 1.025 to 1.515 percent.

During a February 2011 restructuring, the Energy Department weakened its creditor position to benefit Argonaut/Kaiser. According to *Forbes*: "As its finances deteriorated, Solyndra restructured its debt in February. Argonaut Ventures, which owns 38.99% of Solyndra, led a group that agreed to make a $75 million loan available *in exchange for the right to be repaid first if the company failed.* Next in line is the U.S. government—i.e., the taxpayers—who are owed the $527 million given to Solyndra to build the robotic assembly plant known as Fab 2."[38] But under the terms of the loan agreement, the American taxpayers were, by law, first in line for repayment. The payoffs are virtually endless in this administration.

I have an analysis that some Republicans may not like. The Energy Department loan guarantee program has its origins in a horrible law, the Energy Policy Act of 2005, signed by President George W. Bush with the support of most Republicans (and then-senator Obama). This law came out of the secretive Cheney Energy Task Force, which Judicial Watch famously took all the way to the United States Supreme Court in order to expose its inner workings. As I detailed in chapter 2, our investigations did find that the task force was little more than a special interest bazaar through which environmentalists, companies, and industries could make the case for government subsidies of their pet projects and concerns. So it was no surprise that the secretive task force resulted in a law designed to dish taxpayer monies to favored corporations and interests. In our experience, corrupt and secretive government processes lead to corrupt and wasteful legislation. That is true with Obamacare and it is true with the Bush energy law.

So it is also no surprise that a committed socialist like Obama would happily add to the Bush energy law's provisions to spend billions to help companies like Solyndra. Judicial Watch took some flak from some of our conservative friends for opposing the Bush administration over this secret task force. The lesson out of all this for liberals who hate Bush and conservatives who are critical of Obama is, as always, that Big Government, Big Secrecy, and Big Corruption walk together, hand in hand.

THE CORRUPTION CHRONICLES

Fast and Furious:
Obama Appointees Help Kill People?

In October 2009, the Bureau of Alcohol, Tobacco, Firearms and Explosives (ATF) Phoenix Field Division Group VII created a gun-trafficking division for the purpose of funneling weapons illegally to the Mexican drug cartels. According to Frank Miniter, in a piece titled " 'Fast And Furious' Just Might Be President Obama's Watergate" at Forbes.com, "Group VII began using the strategy of allowing suspects to walk away with illegally purchased guns, according to a report from the U.S. House Oversight and Government Reform Committee and the staff of Sen. Charles Grassley (R-Iowa), ranking member of the U.S. Senate Judiciary Committee. The report says, 'The purpose was to wait and watch, in hope that law enforcement could identify other members of a trafficking network and build a large, complex conspiracy case. . . . Group VII initially began using the new gunwalking tactics in one of its investigations to further the Department's strategy. The case was soon renamed 'Operation Fast and Furious.' "

There was one significant issue with Fast and Furious: it didn't catch anybody the feds wouldn't have caught without allowing the guns to flow through to the Mexican cartels. The so-called straw purchasers—the group of buyers who were funneling the weapons to the cartels—were already known to the ATF. So were the gun shops selling the guns. So why allow them to get to the cartels at all? Miniter explains: "As these guns wouldn't be seen again until they resurfaced in crimes (there were no tracking devices installed or other means to trace these guns), the only purpose for letting these guns 'walk' seems to be to back up the president's position that guns used in Mexican crimes mostly come from the U.S."[39] In essence, the government was playing politics with the Second Amendment, trying to undercut it by linking guns to crimes.

Again, only one problem: the crimes had to be committed for the guns to show up at the crime scenes. Well, they did, such as the crime scene of the murdered Border Patrol agent Brian Terry—and countless others in Mexico. Where is the accountability for this reckless insanity?

Once Fast and Furious splashed into the news, the man at the head of ATF, Kenneth Melson, reportedly told Representative Issa that the senior officials at the Justice Department were trying to suppress information about the scandal—an admission that surely earned Melson a transfer to a make-work position at Justice. The U.S. attorney in Phoenix who helped run the operation was forced to resign. And the *Los Angeles Times* reported that two additional high-ranking ATF officials have been demoted as the Justice Department attempts to clean up the mess.

So how is it that Holder, the supervisor of all these men, has kept his job?

Representative Issa, chairman of the House Oversight and Government Reform Committee, subpoenaed Attorney General Holder. "Top Justice Department officials, including Attorney General Holder, know more about Operation Fast and Furious than they have publicly acknowledged," Issa stated. "It's time we know the whole truth."[40]

Why would Representative Issa have reason to believe Holder and his minions at Justice have been less than truthful? After Holder denied knowledge of the Fast and Furious issue, new allegations emerged that Holder lied to Congress about what he knew and when he knew it concerning the operation, prompting calls for a special counsel to investigate.[41]

Here's how Holder got himself into trouble.

On May 3, 2011, in a House Judiciary Committee hearing chaired by Representative Lamar Smith (R-TX), Holder testified: "I'm not sure of the exact date, but I probably heard about Fast and Furious for the first time over the last few weeks." But newly released documents show he was receiving weekly briefings on Fast and Furious as far back as July 5, 2010!

Holder subsequently said he misunderstood the question. Not many are buying that excuse. It is now up to Holder to explain how his own Justice Department can credibly investigate him and his underlings (who for months denied the truth about Fast and Furious) for possibly lying to Congress.

In the meantime, we're trying to obtain correspondence between the ATF and some *Washington Post* reporters who wrote glowing pieces about the ATF gun-busting campaign. We think it is important to find out if the Obama ATF ran the Fast and the Furious operation as part of a press effort to advance their anti–Second Amendment agenda through a liberal media outlet.

And one would suspect that the anti-American Obama administration was desperate to blame "American guns" for the Mexican violence. Not to mention that it all distracts from the fact that one of the key reasons for the drug-gang-fueled violence in Mexico is the unsecured border that allows the drug/human trafficking trade to thrive.

But don't take my word on the human carnage caused by Obama's Fast and Furious guns: the Justice Department's latest admission of crimes associated with Fast and Furious crimes is sickening.

Fast and Furious weapons were likely used to murder U.S. Border Patrol agent Terry in Peck Canyon, Arizona, in mid-December 2010. The guns—assault weapons known as AK-47s—were traced through their serial numbers to a Glendale, Arizona, dealer that led to a Phoenix man the feds repeatedly allowed to smuggle firearms into Mexico.

But details like these have surfaced slowly as the administration scrambles to decide what version of facts it chooses to give Americans. The nation's assistant attorney general for legislative affairs, Ronald Weich, finally admitted that Fast and Furious weapons had been used in at least three violent crimes in the United States and eight others in Mexico.

The crimes were outlined by Weich in a letter, obtained by Judicial Watch to Senate Judiciary Committee chairman Patrick Leahy. It was a response to the Vermont Democrat's months-old request for details of crimes associated with guns from the now infamous operation. Besides the Border Patrol agent's murder, a Fast and Furious firearm (7.62mm Romarm/Cugir) was involved in aggravated assault against a police officer in Arizona, Weich tells Leahy in the letter.

In Mexico the ATF has reported eight events in which guns purchased under Fast and Furious have been recovered in violent crimes, Weich writes. Among them were four firearms used for "kidnap/ransom," two in homicides, and one used during a violent exchange between cartels. A separate stash of Fast and Furious weapons was recovered in various parts of Mexico after being involved in "non-violent crimes," according to Weich's assessment.

For instance, ten guns were retrieved in Atoyac de Alvarez after the Mexican military rescued a kidnap victim. Another ten Fast and Furious weapons were also identified in Durango following a confrontation between Mexico's military and an "armed group." An additional ten rifles were found in Chihuahua after the kidnapping of two people and the murder of a Mexican public official's family member.

We've sued the Justice Department and the ATF to obtain Fast and Furious records. They already refused to answer our very basic requests for documents—we haven't received one document from Justice or the ATF regarding Fast and Furious—which is unusual, even for the secretive Obama administration. Given their dissembling, Justice and the ATF are apparently in cover-up mode. Now they'll have to answer to a federal court for their obfuscation.

Make no mistake: this seems to be one of the most egregious examples of corruption and malfeasance inside the Obama administration that we've seen yet. Holder should resign. But so far, he hasn't. And there are no indicators at this point that he will.

Guantanamo

On the first day of his presidency, President Obama signed an executive order calling for the closing of the terrorist detention facility at the U.S. naval station in Guantanamo Bay, Cuba. Virtually everyone who wasn't an advocate for terrorists would think this a terrible idea. If terrorist enemy combatants would not be held at Gitmo, then where?

But President Obama is an ideologue, and his radicalism trumped whatever modicum of good sense he had when it came to these dangerous terrorists. In March 2009, Obama ditched the term *enemy combatant* altogether. According to Reuters, "The Obama administration stopped calling Guantanamo inmates 'enemy combatants' . . . and incorporated international law as its basis for holding the prisoners while it works to close the facility. The U.S. Justice Department filed court papers outlining a further legal and linguistic shift from the anti-terrorism policies of Republican President George W. Bush, which drew worldwide condemnation as violations of human rights and international law."[42] It should be noted that the "worldwide condemnation" referenced by Reuters was expressed most enthusiastically by terrorist advocates and sympathizers.

According to the Obama Justice Department, "the legal structure for holding the Guantanamo prisoners will now be based on laws passed by Congress and, by extension, international law including the Geneva conventions. . . ."[43]

So in other words, the commander in chief would seek to allow terrorists to be tried in the civilian court system and cater to the anti-American left by suggesting that the Bush administration's treatment of the terrorists was illegal under our international treaty obligations. The terrorist advocates who controlled the media (and legal debate) opposed the "enhanced interrogation techniques" that, for example, led to the killing of Osama bin Laden and to information that has foiled dozens of terrorist attacks around the world. (By "terrorist advocates," I don't mean those who advocate terrorism per se; I mean those who serve as advocates for those terrorists and their allies.)

In August 2009, we obtained a CIA report titled "Khalid Shaykh Muhammad: Preeminent Source on Al Qa'ida," which documented the information gained by interrogations of mastermind Khalid Sheikh Mohammed (KSM): "KSM's decade-long career as a terrorist, during which he met with a broad range of Islamic extremists from around the world, has made him a key source of information on numerous al Qa'ida operatives and other mujahidin. He has provided intelligence that has led directly to the capture of operatives or fleshed out our understanding of the activities of important

detainees, which in turn assisted in the debriefings of these individuals." An earlier, less-redacted version of the report we obtained
added, "Detainee reporting accounts for more than half of all HU-
MINT reporting on al-Qa'ida since the program began. . . ." The
report concluded, "One of the gains to detaining the additional terrorists has been the thwarting of a number of al-Qa'ida operations in
the United States and overseas."

We had to go through hell and high water to get this information—
Obama didn't want to release it, knowing that it showed the efficacy
of harsh interrogation methods against Al Qaeda terrorists. On
March 31, 2009, Vice President Dick Cheney personally issued a
request to the National Archives Presidential Libraries section for
declassification review of this and one other detainee program report. The archives then passed on the request to the CIA for review
on April 8, 2009. We sought these reports after it became clear that
they wouldn't be released by the Obama administration in a timely
fashion.

Here's how perverse the Obama administration's logic was on
treatment of Al Qaeda terrorists and the information surrounding
that treatment. In March 2009, President Obama overruled objections from national security officials and released documents detailing the government's enhanced interrogation program of terrorists
(the so-called torture memos, written during the Bush administration). These memos laid out in stark detail precisely how we interrogate terrorists.

However, President Obama initially withheld information detailing the *results* of this program, including alleged terrorist plots that
the program prevented. Obama didn't care about the results—all he
cared about was being able to score political points at the expense of
the Bush administration (and America's world reputation).

But we went to work—investigated and sued—and found that
all of these CIA documents came to the same conclusion: detainee
interrogations are effective and have helped save lives in the United
States and overseas. If the new restrictions limiting enhanced interrogation had been in place, no such lifesaving intel would ever have
been gathered.

How do we know this? When Obama tried his new "let's read terrorists the Miranda rights" strategy, it failed miserably. By seeking to treat terrorism increasingly as a criminal act, rather than an act of war, Obama turned terrorists into mere criminals rather than threats to the state. This irresponsible policy not only sent a message to our enemies around the world that the United States is soft on terrorism; it also allowed war criminals access to the U.S. court system, providing them the same legal rights as United States citizens.

The most obvious case in point: Umar Farouk Abdulmutallab, aka the Christmas bomber, who attempted to blow up a Northwest Airlines flight by detonating a bomb he had crammed in his underwear on Christmas Day, 2010. Abdulmutallab was read his Miranda rights a few hours after his arrest. He was first interrogated for fifty minutes; doctors stopped the questioning when Abdulmutallab's medical condition reportedly deteriorated. Five hours later, FBI agents attempted to interrogate Abdulmutallab again, without success. After a conference call with officials from four Obama administration agencies (but still not consulting the top national security officials), they gave up and read the terrorist his Miranda rights.

And then, of course, he stopped talking altogether.

Now the administration claims that Abdulmutallab was "Mirandized" only after he had decided not to continue cooperating with the FBI. But this completely misses the point. By treating this terrorist under our civilian criminal law enforcement system, the administration immediately gave him the option to stop talking and let him lawyer up.

And Obama's official position regarding the timing notwithstanding, we know this: before Abdulmutallab was read his Miranda rights he was talking.

Abdulmutallab told the FBI during his initial questioning that he trained as a suicide bomber in Yemen with other English-speaking terrorists. Important information, wouldn't you say? As one FBI official put it: Abdulmutallab is "not the only bullet in the chamber for al Qaeda in the Arabian Peninsula." There are others. And U.S. intelligence officials had an obligation to the American people to find out where they're hiding. If, from the start, Abdulmutallab had been treated as an unlawful enemy combatant according to the law of war, there would have been no "Mirandizing" and more opportunities for intelligence gathering.

Then-senator Kit Bond of Missouri, who was the highest-ranking Republican on the Senate Intelligence Committee, said, "There's no changing the fact that Mirandizing Abdulmutallab gave terrorists a six-week head start to cover their tracks. We will never know what life-saving information on co-conspirators and future plots we missed out on." [44] Vice President Biden admitted that he was "very concerned" about an individual carrying out a terrorist attack in the United States, just like the Christmas bomber. [45] He should be, especially considering the lax Obama-Biden approach to terrorism.

The most disgusting element of this whole debacle was the grandstanding by members of Congress allied with the president. Because of Obama's stated opposition to enhanced interrogation techniques—and even the implication that those who participated as members of the CIA could be prosecuted—many members of Congress, including then–Speaker of the House Nancy Pelosi, suddenly decided to pretend that they had not been properly briefed on enhanced interrogation techniques.

There was only one problem: we uncovered the documents that showed that they had been. We obtained a memo from the CIA marked "Top Secret" that includes a detailed report of a House Permanent Select Committee on Intelligence closed hearing regarding the subject of enhanced interrogation techniques. The memo was dated July 14, 2004, and the testimony therein was provided by Department of Defense official Lieutenant General William Boykin. "General Boykin," the memo summarized, "read a prepared statement to the Committee in which he asserted that interrogation is a critically valuable tool, and, citing observations made by service personnel at Ft. Bragg, said that the most [imp]ortant factor in the capture of Saddam Hussein was interrogation." A member of the Counterterrorism Center stated, "Even today long term detainees like Khalid Shayk Muhammed and [Abu] Zubaydah are providing good information because their histories go back a long way and often a tidbit they provide, while not initially operationally significant, ends up being the piece that completes the puzzle; DC/ CTC closed by noting that he was personally persuaded that detainee reporting has saved lives."

Representative Jane Harman (D-CA) quizzed John Pistole, a witness for the FBI: "What do you think of the value of enhanced techniques?" Said Pistole, "In my view the benefits are huge and the costs are insignificant. Very few detainees don't provide us with good information. . . ."

Representative C. A. "Dutch" Ruppersberger (D-MD) asked, "Are there procedures that we have stopped that should be resumed?" Lieutenant General Keith Alexander, the army G-2, or deputy chief of staff for intelligence (and now director of the National Security Agency), answered, "Yes. Diet and sleep management. Those, plus segregation which is still employed, are key. . . ." General Alexander also testified that field commanders wanted more "97E's" (interrogators), "even to the point of trading off some of their combat troops."

The document also recounts an allegation by Harman that the CIA had not been giving the committee "full and candid testimony on the detainee issue." Testimony also suggests that interrogators at Fort Bragg, in North Carolina, believed that "unobtrusive forms of interrogation are the best."

Here's the bottom line: intelligence officials repeatedly informed members of Congress that enhanced interrogation techniques are effective and save lives. It is little wonder why the Obama administration would try to keep these documents hidden, given the administration's ideological hostility to these effective interrogation techniques."

In February 2010, Judicial Watch released documents, previously marked "Top Secret," showing that, between 2001 and 2007, the CIA briefed at least sixty-eight members of Congress on the CIA interrogation program, including so-called enhanced interrogation techniques. The documents include the dates of all congressional briefings and, in some cases, the members of Congress in attendance and the specific subjects discussed. Nancy Pelosi, who previously denied she was briefed by the CIA on the use of these techniques, is specifically referenced in a briefing that took place on April 24, 2002, regarding the "ongoing interrogations of Abu Zubaydah."

Enhanced interrogation techniques work. And the Obama administration opposed them, covered up their results, and tried to stonewall us when we attempted to show that members of Congress knew full well what was going on.

Where would we house these newly dubbed non–enemy combatants, these "homeless" detainees? At first, the Obama administration considered putting them right here, in the United States. As the *Wall Street Journal* reported, "Attorney General Eric Holder said some detainees being held at Guantanamo Bay, Cuba, may end up being released in the U.S. as the Obama administration works with foreign allies to resettle some of the prisoners. . . . For 'people who can be released there are a variety of options that we have and among them is the possibility is that we would release them into this country,' Mr. Holder said."[46] Does that make you feel any safer? It shouldn't. But one has to wonder whether ideology blinded some in this administration to the safety and security of the United States.

The Obama administration made a habit of treating terrorists like regular captured soldiers or civilian criminals. The soft-on-terrorist approach was even used in the case of Khalid Sheikh Mohammed, the mastermind of the 9/11 attacks. Attorney General Eric Holder decided to grant a civilian criminal trial to him and his cohorts in New York City.

The decision to bring Mohammed and other Al Qaeda terrorists to New York for a civilian criminal trial wasn't Holder's to make. President Obama is the commander in chief and he is ultimately responsible for the safety and security of this county.

There is no question that an unprecedented civilian trial for the 9/11 terrorists would harm our national security, place government officials and civilians at risk, and provide a propaganda platform to rally and recruit terrorists. And it is no small risk that civilian criminal proceedings may result in the release of these terrorists onto American soil. No one elected Eric Holder to make these types of national security decisions. That's why even the persistently deaf

Obama administration retracted the notion of the KSM trial in New York after incredible public outcry. Eighteen senators, including two Democrats, even cosponsored legislation that would have stripped the Obama administration of funding for a civil trial.

We've visited Gitmo, and we've seen the legal proceedings at work. And yes, they work just fine. As Irene Garcia, our correspondent, wrote, "Judicial Watch witnessed a deep commitment to justice by military lawyers as well as [one terrorist's] topnotch capital defense attorney. Even some of the pro [terrorist] civil rights advocates who witnessed the arraignment admitted it was 'well managed' and that they were 'impressed' with some of the questions asked by defense attorneys. . . ."

So, who *was* the administration worried about in terms of national security? The answer became intensely clear when Secretary of Homeland Security Napolitano developed her own, special version of Hillary Clinton's old "vast right-wing conspiracy" theory. In April 2009, Napolitano released a report titled "Rightwing Extremism: Current Economic and Political Climate Fueling Resurgence In Radicalization And Recruitment." Michelle Malkin called the report a "piece of crap" that was nothing more than a "sweeping indictment of conservatives." "The DHS/Office of Intelligence and Analysis (I&A) has no specific information that domestic rightwing[47] terrorists are currently planning acts of violence," said the report, "but rightwing extremists may be gaining new recruits by playing on their fears about several emergent issues. The economic downturn and the election of the first African American president present unique drivers for rightwing radicalization and recruitment."[48] This was absolute sophistry masquerading as policy. It was designed to call Obama's opponents racist, sexist homophobes who hated him personally so much that they truly threatened violence. More than that, it would misdirect America's national security resources away from its true enemies—such as radical Islam—and toward Obama's peaceful and law-abiding domestic political opposition.

The report concluded that the Obama administration's plans to restrict the ownership of firearms would motivate paranoid rightwing extremists to stockpile dangerous weapons in preparation for a violent attack. The report claimed that unrealistic fears of communist regimes and "conspiracy theories" about the government's plan to join a "One World Government" would lead to right-wing violence. Military veterans returning from Iraq and Afghanistan who face challenges "reintegrating" into society may become terrorists or "lone wolf extremists," the report warned under the insulting headline "disgruntled military veterans." The report suggested that right-wing extremists would capitalize on the election of an African-American president to recruit racist members. Finally, the report stated that the economic downturn would turn right-wing extremists into domestic terrorists who attack government buildings, police officers, and other government officials.

The Napolitano report admitted that there were no actual plans for violence but suggested repeatedly that veterans are ripe for recruitment by right-wing extremists. The "assessment" exhibited the typical leftist prejudice against our military and our veterans: that our military turns people into crazed killing machines. And the report assumed that belief in certain conservative values makes one more likely to be an antigovernment terrorist. In fact, the report suggests that if you focus on one conservative public policy issue—such as immigration or opposing abortion—you are especially suspicious. Political scientists might call such citizens "single-issue voters," but the Obama administration thinks such activists are threats to our security.

This document was an attack on the First Amendment and potentially subjected peaceful, conservative Americans to scrutiny by law enforcement at federal, state, and local levels. At least a few sane folks in the Department of Homeland Security had some civil rights concerns about this document,[49] but any concerns were evidently overruled by politician/DHS secretary Janet Napolitano. Isn't it convenient that Napolitano is able to designate opponents of her and Obama's weak immigration policies as terrorists-in-waiting!

Of course, the department did nothing to assess connections between Obama and the Weather Underground terrorists William Ayers and his wife, Bernardine Dohrn. Ayers and Dohrn actually *are* domestic terrorists who *did* participate in violent attacks on innocents. They did nothing to assess any possible Hillary Clinton connections to the FALN terrorists for whom she advocated pardons, or Eric Holder, who worked to pardon terrorists in the Clinton years, and whose former law firm represents Gitmo terrorists.

To be sure, the government also produced a report on specific threats from left-wing extremist groups. The differences were stark. Unlike the right-wing version, this report was fact-based and did not include any political rhetoric.

Even as the Obama administration went after his domestic political opposition, we uncovered documents showing that the Department of Homeland Security held a two-day meeting on January 27 and 28, 2010, between Secretary Napolitano and Arab, Muslim, Sikh, and South Asian "community leaders." The documents included a list of participating individuals and organizations, some with controversial radical ties. Imad Hamad, Midwest regional director of the American Arab Anti-Discrimination Committee, attended the conference. According to investigative reporter and attorney Debbie Schlussel, Hamad is connected to the Marxist-Leninist terrorist group Popular Front for the Liberation of Palestine and has supported the Islamist terrorist group Hezbollah. In a television interview in 2002 on Fox's Detroit affiliate, Hamad supported a Palestinian Authority TV program that urged children to become suicide bombers, calling the program "patriotic."[50]

Another attendee was Salam al-Marayati, founder of the Muslim Public Affairs Council (MPAC). According to press reports, al-Marayati has long been criticized for his extremist views and statements. In 1999 then–House minority leader Richard Gephardt (D-MO) withdrew his nomination of al-Marayati to the National Commission on Terrorism because of al-Marayati's extremist politics. Al-Marayati once said, "When Patrick Henry said, 'Give me liberty or give me death,' that statement epitomized jihad [Islamic holy war]."

One of the organizations that attended the meeting, the Islamic Society of North America (ISNA), was named as an unindicted co-conspirator by the federal government in a plot by the now-defunct Holy Land Foundation to fund the terrorist group Hamas.[51]

In addition to the attendee list and biographies, the documents also included internal Department of Homeland Security (DHS) email correspondence, talking points for Secretary Napolitano, and a meeting agenda. Among the highlights was a Thursday, February 4, 2010, email from David O'Leary, DHS Office of Legislative Affairs, to David Gersten, acting deputy officer for programs and compliance, DHS Office of Civil Rights and Civil Liberties: "Gordon Lederman of Sen. Lieberman's Staff called me asking about the 2-day HSAC meeting last week with American Muslim and Arab groups. He was called by a reporter who told him MPAC (Muslim Public Affairs Council), ISNA (Islamic Society of North America) and Muslim American Society 'rejected the ideas' of soliciting their help with countering violent extremism and were 'angry and indignant.' " But that didn't stop Napolitano and company from cozying up to both groups.

A January 29, 2010, email from Muslim Advocates executive director Khera Farhana to Arif Alikhan, DHS assistant secretary for policy development, noted: "The commitments Secretary Napolitano made to these community leaders include . . . Regular quarterly meetings with the Secretary . . . An honest and full discussion of legitimate grievances from members of these communities about DHS policies that are ineffective and have a deleterious, humiliating impact on Muslim, Arab, Sikh, and South Asian American communities." It wasn't enough to give them face time—now the federal government was going to become a repository for the complaints of Islamic terror-linked groups. How charmingly multicultural!

An internal DHS "talking points" document titled "Community Stakeholder Meeting" stated, "Communicate that DHS understands the need for enhanced partnership with the Muslim, Sikh, South Asian and Arab groups, including those present at the meeting. . . . You should note the importance of sharing information from a policy perspective and on threats to specific Muslim, Arab, South Asian, and Sikh communities."

No one can seriously be opposed to our government working with legitimate "Muslim, Sikh, South Asian and Arab groups," but how did consorting with radicals who had been implicated as terrorist fronts help the Department of Homeland Security protect the United States? It didn't. The Obama administration was bending over backward to cater to radical Muslim organizations in the name of political correctness. While radical Muslims were being granted full access to the White House, some Americans who opposed the Obama agenda on some hot-button issues (such as abortion and gun control) were treated as enemies of the state.

Not only were radical Muslims being treated to White House meetings; the Obama administration was working hard to allow them to build a mosque on the site of the Burlington Coat Factory building destroyed on 9/11, a project known popularly as the Ground Zero Mosque. The outfit behind the mosque, known as the Cordoba Initiative, was led by a radical Islamic extremist who blames America for the terrorist attacks that murdered three thousand innocents on American soil. The mosque had powerful political backers nonetheless, including Mayor Michael Bloomberg, who said that the project would "build a bridge between the West and the Muslim world."

Who was going to lead this new symbol of religious tolerance? Radical Islamic apologist Feisal Abdul Rauf. Here's what Rauf said during a *60 Minutes* interview about the 9/11 terrorist attacks: "I wouldn't say that the United States deserved what happened. But the United States' policies were an accessory to the crime that happened." [52]

He didn't stop there.

When CBS's Ed Bradley then asked, "You say that we're an accessory—how?" Feisal replied: "Because we have been an accessory to a lot of innocent lives dying in the world. In fact, in the most direct sense, Osama bin Laden is made in the USA."

The "center" was no peace-building measure. It was an effort by radical Islamists to build a triumphal monument on the site of the 9/11 atrocity. As you might expect, the majority of Americans were opposed to the Ground Zero mosque. But where did the Obama White House stand on the issue? Then–White House press secretary Robert Gibbs deflected the question when he said the mosque is "rightly a matter for New York City." During a White House dinner celebrating the start of Ramadan (the Muslim month of fasting), President Obama couldn't resist the temptation to weigh in: "Let me be clear: As a citizen and as President I believe that Muslims have the same right . . . to build a place of worship and a community center on private property in Lower Manhattan."

The backlash from families of 9/11 victims was intense and immediate, forcing the president to offer a "retraction" the next day. "I was not commenting and I will not comment on the *wisdom* of making a decision to put a mosque there," President Obama said a day later.[53] But the damage was already done. The president once again demonstrated that he is out of touch when it comes to the concerns of the American people. Heck, even Harry Reid abandoned ship: "The First Amendment protects freedom of religion," said Reid's spokesman in a statement. "Senator Reid respects that but thinks that the mosque should be built someplace else."[54]

Nonetheless, one of the men behind the mosque, Sharif el-Gamal, said this was all news to him and insisted he wouldn't budge: "This is not a debate. This is not a debate. This is us as Muslim Americans giving back to our community."[55]

No, actually. This was a group of Muslim Americans (and their foreign government benefactors) who were trying to force the community to accept something it didn't want. And contrary to Obama's intellectually dishonest remarks, we fail to see how Americans exercising their First Amendment rights to oppose the mosque somehow impinges the First Amendment rights of the mosque proponents. This president likes to apologize to our enemies, but to suggest that opponents of the mosque are opponents of the First Amendment took his anti-Americanism to a new low. Sure enough, Obama's big-government ally Nancy Pelosi said she wanted to investigate the 9/11 families and others opposing the mosque. She said she wanted "transparency."[56] If only her interest in transparency actually extended to all of government, rather than to nongovernmental political enemies.

This was nothing new for the Obama administration, which had reached out directly to Rauf. According to the Associated Press, "The imam behind controversial plans for a mosque near the site of the

Sept. 11 attacks is being sent by the State Department on a religious outreach trip to the Middle East, officials said. . . . The department is sponsoring Imam Feisal Abdul Rauf's visit to Qatar, Bahrain and the United Arab Emirates, where he will discuss Muslim life in America and promote religious tolerance, spokesman P. J. Crowley said. He said the imam had been on two similar trips and that plans for the upcoming tour predated the mosque controversy."[57]

We launched a full investigation of the Ground Zero mosque and sent a detailed open records request to Bloomberg's office for his contacts with the Islamic radicals pushing this outrage. We heard nothing back and were forced to sue. After reviewing the documents, it is no wonder that Bloomberg stalled their release. The documents are an investigative treasure trove of email correspondence between top officials inside the mayor's office and supporters of the Ground Zero Mosque. They show that Mayor Bloomberg's office was working hand in glove with the Muslim activists driving the unpopular Ground Zero Mosque project. Among the highlights:

- A May 10, 2010, email from Daisy Khan, listed as executive director of the American Society for Muslim Advancement, to Fatima Shama, commissioner of the Mayor's Office of Immigrant Affairs: "Is there a good time to chat tomorrow. We need some guidance on how to tackle the opposition."

- A letter supporting the Ground Zero Mosque drafted by Nazli Parvizi, commissioner of the Mayor's Community Affairs Unit, to Julie Menin, chairman of Manhattan's Community Board 1, which had considered a resolution supporting the mosque. Parvizi crafted the letter for Daisy Khan's signature, asking the board to temporarily withdraw the mosque resolution due to public outrage over the project. Parvizi described the purpose of the letter in a May 15, 2010, email: "What the letter will do, I hope, is get the media's attention off everyone's backs and give you guys time to regroup on your strategy as discussed. . . ."

- A legal review of the Menin letter sent to the mayor's office by Rauf on May 15, 2010. The letter contemplates the impact withdrawing the Community Board 1 resolution could have on the effort to de-designate the mosque site as a historical landmark at a June 22, 2010, Landmark Commission meeting, thus allowing the project to move forward: "The Borough President (and Councilmember Chin) have a firm policy at speaking up at public agencies only after the community board has taken a position on an item. So withdrawing the resolution may affect their thinking about how helpful they can be on June 22. That in itself may not be fatal to getting [the site] de-designated but I do know that [Landmark Commission] Chairman [Robert B.] Tierney was looking forward to having the 'political cover' their support would bring him." The Landmark Commission ultimately decided to de-designate the property.

- A May 7, 2010, congratulations email from Shama to Rauf, Khan, and el-Gamal after the Community Board 1 finance subcommittee expressed support for the Ground Zero Mosque project: "Again-congratulations!!! This is very exciting for all of you and the community at large! Daisy, as always—you were AMAZING last night—thank you!"

- A May 7, 2010, email from Khan to Rauf, el-Gamal, and Shama after the finance subcommittee vote: "Just spoke with Commissioner Nazli Parvizi. She will call Julie Mennon [*sic*] to thank them for passing the resolution and ask how she can assist."

- A January 2010 email exchange documenting Shama's successful attempt to expedite a temporary public assembly permit so supporters of the Ground Zero Mosque could conduct prayers at the site.

- A series of email exchanges regarding a September 18, 2009, meeting between Shama, Rauf, el-Gamal, Khan, and others from the Ground Zero Mosque project. A September 22, 2009, follow-up email summarized the meeting: "It was wonderful to be with everyone . . . on Friday night. . . . Fatima mentioned that there are a number of concrete next steps that need to be undertaken re: the Cordoba House. In terms of a point person and centralized contact, please advise Fatima as to whom she should be in direct contact with on these and all other Cordoba House matters moving forward."

- An April 22, 2010, email from Khan to Shama asking Shama to sign a letter of support for the Ground Zero Mosque project. "We have been honored to have developed a relationship with you over the last years. . . . [W]e consider you amongst our closest allies and friends." The email included a draft letter for Shama to sign.

In July 2010, Mayor Bloomberg told reporters it was "un-American" to investigate the individuals behind the Ground Zero Mosque. Rather than slandering Americans exercising their First Amendment rights, Mayor Bloomberg would have been better off not abusing his office to use taxpayer resources to help the Ground Zero Mosque.

The mosque, by the way, opened last year on the ten-year anniversary of the attacks. The "victory mosque" will continue to cause controversy. But at least the controversial Muslim couple originally associated with it, Feisal Abdul Rauf and Daisy Khan, have supposedly been forced out of the project, which is no small victory in the continuing battle against the radical Islamic threat to our nation's security.

Bin Laden Raid Secrecy

President Obama's campaign operation has been trumpeting the military's killing of Osama bin Laden as a reason to reelect the president. Vice President Joe Biden even went so far as to suggest that it was the most "audacious plan" in "500 years."[58] Biden's ridiculous hyperbole aside, one can't blame Obama's campaign advocates for trumpeting the bin Laden raid, as it was a triumphant military success. But when it comes to giving the American people specific documents about the May 1, 2011, raid, the Obama administration has clammed up.

A few days after the raid we filed FOIA requests with the Defense Department and CIA for "all photographs and/or video recordings of Osama (Usama) bin Laden taken during and/or after the U.S. military operation in Pakistan on or about May 1, 2011."

President Obama then told CBS News that he would not release the death photos of Osama bin Laden to the public, saying "we don't need to spike the football" or "gloat."[59] Simply put, those are not lawful reasons for withholding these historic documents. So we sued.[60] This is arguably the most important military operation in our lifetime and we need to complete the public record. Incredibly, given the worldwide interest in this information, ours is the only lawsuit actually seeking these historic photo/video artifacts. The Associated Press called our request "among the most significant of any filed last year under the open records law."[61]

Obama's decision came after heated and confused debate within his administration. Then–defense secretary Robert Gates and Secretary of State Hillary Clinton lobbied against it.[62]

But the then CIA director himself, Leon Panetta, did not seem overly concerned at all about these implications in an interview with NBC's Brian Williams on May 3, 2011, just two days after the raid: "The government obviously has been talking about how best to do this, but I don't think there was any question that ultimately a photograph would be presented to the public."[63] (Panetta is now secretary of defense.)

Not wanting to be seen as "spiking the football" is not a lawful reason to withhold documents under FOIA.

President Obama is seemingly happy to release documents that the left thinks will embarrass and hurt America, but he will stonewall the release of material, like these photos, that reflect well on the ability, heroism, and might of our great nation. (Obama calls that "gloating.")

The Defense Department says it came up empty in response to our request, though I have good reason to believe that the Pentagon didn't look hard enough. But the CIA admitted it found fifty-two responsive records (photos and video). Here's a description of what they found according to the government's court filing:

> These records contain images of Osama bin Laden's body after he was killed. Many are graphic and gruesome, as they depict the fatal bullet wound to bin Laden's head. Some of the images were taken inside the compound in Abbottabad, Pakistan, where bin Laden was killed. Other images were taken as bin Laden's body was transported from the Abbottabad compound to the location where he was buried at sea. Several images depict the preparation of Osama bin Laden's body for the burial as well as the burial itself.[64]

So they have the photos and videos we're after for sure. But the agency refuses to release them to the public. Why? Well, this time they're hiding behind the vague "implications to national security" they claim could result. "The mere release of these images of Osama bin Laden could be interpreted as a deliberate attempt by the United States to humiliate the late al-Qa'ida leader . . . ," the government argued in its brief.[65]

Here's the bottom line. President Obama's decision to keep the bin Laden photos secret is political. It has no basis in law. The government's legal brief incredibly started off by citing Obama's "spiking the football" comment on *60 Minutes*. Most legal briefs cite the law up front, but the Obama Department of Justice cites an interview with the president. The law and the president's own personal views are not necessarily the same thing in our constitutional republic.

And we shouldn't throw out our transparency laws because complying with them might offend terrorists. And regarding implications to national security, FOIA is a disclosure statute, and the public has an affirmative right to know. We're not after legitimate secrets related to operational or intelligence matters. We don't want pictures of SEAL Team Six, their equipment, or other correctly classified material. But the basic historical record of Osama bin Laden's death should be released to the American people as the law requires.

I suspect that the Obama administration doesn't want to release these photos because it is embarrassed both by our victory in killing bin Laden and the subsequent burial at sea.

As I've pointed out, the Obama administration has no problem releasing documents that the left thinks will embarrass the United States—say, for example, Obama's selective release of documents disparaging "enhanced interrogation techniques" over the objections of his own national security officials. But when it comes to documents that show the heroism of our military? No deal.

We should not cower at the possibility that terrorists won't like documentation of our military victory. We cannot subject our Constitution and our rule of law to jihadist blackmail and extortion.

Of course, the professed concern for national security is a big lie. Otherwise, then why release classified information on the raid to a Hollywood producer?

The Obama administration is fighting Judicial Watch tooth and nail to avoid releasing photographs of bin Laden and his burial at sea, citing national security reasons. Yet at the same time, administration officials allegedly leaked information about the bin Laden raid to a Hollywood film director.

That's what press reports seem to indicate. On January 13, 2012, Judicial Watch filed another Freedom of Information Act lawsuit against the Defense Department and CIA to obtain documents regarding meetings and communications between government agencies and Hollywood director Kathryn Bigelow. (Bigelow is the Academy Award–winning director of the military film *The Hurt Locker*. She is also the ex-wife of Hollywood director James Cameron, of *Avatar* and *Titanic* fame.)

At issue is the possibility that the Obama administration selectively leaked information to Bigelow as source material for the making of Bigelow's not-yet-released film, tentatively titled *Killing bin Laden*, while nearly simultaneously declining to release other information about the raid. As is too typical, the Obama administration stonewalled our request for the Bigelow materials for months—hence our lawsuit.

Bigelow's film, in production since 2008, originally intended to document the decade-long hunt for Osama bin Laden. The top-secret Navy SEAL team mission that led to the capture and killing of bin Laden is reportedly the source for the film's new content and conclusion.

As reported by Reuters, "It has been alleged that Bigelow . . . in preparation for the script to their Annapurna Pictures movie about the killing of Osama Bin Laden—received classified information regarding his death." [66]

Now, why would the Obama administration do such a thing?

First, this is an administration that has shown a proclivity to selectively releasing information that helps the "Obama brand" while withholding information that may be harmful or embarrassing.

Second, this is an administration that aggressively uses federal agencies to assist the Obama campaign. (See the lawsuit, recently dismissed, against Boeing in support of Big Labor and the flow of Obamacare waivers to union supporters.)

So it is easy to conclude that the alleged leaking of materials to Bigelow was an effort to boost the Obama 2012 presidential election campaign.

Thank you to liberal *New York Times* columnist Maureen Dowd for alerting us to this abuse:

> The White House is also counting on the Kathryn Bigelow and Mark Boal big-screen version of the killing of Bin Laden to counter Obama's growing reputation as ineffectual. The Sony film by the Oscar-winning pair who made *The Hurt Locker* will no doubt reflect the president's cool, gutsy decision against shaky odds. Just as Obamaland was hoping, the movie is scheduled to open on Oct. 12, 2012—perfectly timed to give a home-stretch boost to a campaign that has grown tougher.
>
> The moviemakers are getting top-level access to the most classified mission in history from an administration that has tried to throw

more people in jail for leaking classified information than the Bush administration.

It was clear that the White House had outsourced the job of manning up the president's image to Hollywood when Boal got welcomed to the upper echelons of the White House and the Pentagon and showed up recently—to the surprise of some military officers—at a CIA ceremony celebrating the hero Seals [*sic*].[67]

In short, if press reports from the liberal media are to be believed, the Obama administration released classified national security information to help Hollywood make a two-hour Obama campaign commercial to be released just weeks before the 2012 elections.

At this point, given the alleged Bigelow leaks, it's hard to put any stock in the claim made by Obama administration officials that their stonewalling of the bin Laden death and funeral photos/video has anything to do with national security.

One might also wonder whether the Obama administration is concerned not so much about enflaming terrorists as it is about outraging Americans. The controversial burial at sea was supposedly done " 'in accordance with Islamic tradition,' meaning within 24 hours of bin Laden's death. No information was available as to whether Muslim prayers were recited or the body was ritually washed, as is usually required by Islamic law. In general, burial at sea means tipping the body overboard—wrapped, likely, in a shroud—after a brief service."[68] When pressed, administration spokesmen would only say that the mass murderer was buried at sea "using the appropriate procedures and rituals."[69]

The intrepid Anneke E. Green of the *Washington Times* asked the inconvenient question about what exactly these "appropriate procedures and rituals" were:

> For those wondering just what an "appropriate" Islamic burial entails, "Navy Military Funerals," created by the Navy to govern laying their dead to rest, is a bit more forthcoming. Their "Service for the committal of a person of the Muslim faith" lays out explicit steps that must be followed in a Muslim sea burial. The body must have

been washed and wrapped "as required for the bodies of Muslims," which refers to ceremonial cleanings that must be done by another Muslim. Those who have gathered to pray at the burial—ostensibly crewmembers since family is not allowed at sea burials—must face Mecca.[70]

Formal funeral prayers must be said—and are specifically listed in the service used by the Navy.[71] In the part of the service in which supplication for the deceased is made, the prayer to be used includes the following:

"O Allah, forgive him, have mercy on him, pardon him, grant him security, provide him a nice place and spacious lodgings, wash him (off from his sins) with water, snow and ice, purify him from his sins as a white garment is cleansed from dirt, replace his present abode with a better one, replace his present family with a better one, replace his present partner with a better one, make him enter paradise and save him from the trials of grave [sic] and the punishment of hell."

As Green points out, "the families of those slaughtered by bin Laden—many of whom were Muslims—might not be happy to learn that the Obama administration may have considered it 'appropriate' to ask Allah to 'pardon' al Qaeda's evil overlord. Or to petition him to not only let him into paradise but give him a nice, big house when he gets there, with a better family and wife (wives?). How will those families feel about the fact that this sociopath got a better burial than many of their dead loved ones, some of whose circumstances of death made them religiously ineligible for the prayers—or 'religious remarks'—he received?"[72]

And as our lawyers point out in the ongoing court fight over the bin Laden documents (the "Defendants" referenced below are the Defense Department and CIA):

Conspicuously absent from Defendants' argument is any proof of how, for example, images of bin Laden's body as it was being prepared for burial at sea or images of the actual burial at sea itself would reveal information about the identities of the members of the U.S. Navy SEAL team that carried out the raid or the tools and equipment used by the SEAL team during the raid. Similarly, Defendants make no effort to describe how images of bin Laden's body taken as it was being transported to the location of its burial at sea would reveal site exploitation tactics, techniques, or procedures employed at bin Laden's compound in Abottabad [*sic*], Pakistan. Obviously, images taken on board the USS *Carl Vinson* of the burial at sea are not going to reveal site exploitation tactics, techniques, or procedures used in the Abottabad compound or even facial recognition techniques or capabilities.[73]

We shouldn't appease our enemies by undermining our nation's core government accountability law—the Freedom of Information Act. We suspect the administration is playing shell games with the bin Laden death and funeral photos. President Obama is asking the court to allow his administration to withhold documents simply because their disclosure may cause controversy. There is simply no legal precedent for this.

President Obama's political calculations are no substitute for the rule of law. The Obama administration has no legal right to withhold this material from the American people, especially now that he is using this military victory in his presidential campaign. The killing of Osama bin Laden is a tremendous historic event. We hope that the courts agree that the law simply doesn't allow President Obama to put the bin Laden photos and video down the memory hole.

PART 3

WATCHING THE FUTURE

8.

HOW TO STEAL AN ELECTION IN PLAIN SIGHT

Back when he was a U.S. senator from Illinois, Barack Obama tried to crack down on voter intimidation. "Both parties at different periods in our history have been guilty in different regions of preventing people from voting for a tactical advantage," he said. "We should be beyond that." [1]

But presidential candidate Obama thought differently. He made no bones about working with questionable groups to win election. He even took cash from overseas.

In office, Obama has only accentuated his seeming pursuit of election fraud. John Fund reported in the *Wall Street Journal* that, for example, Obama's deputy assistant attorney general Julie Fernandes "made a jaw-dropping announcement to attorneys in Justice's Voting Rights section. She said she would not support any enforcement of a key section of the federal 'Motor Voter' law— Section 8, which requires states to periodically purge their voter rolls of dead people, felons, illegal voters and those who have moved out of state." According to J. Christian Adams, a former Justice Department lawyer who served with Fernandes, Fernandes stated, "We're not interested in those kind of cases. What do they have to do with helping increase minority access and turnout? We want to increase access to the ballot, not limit it." [2]

That's the Obama way: more potential for voter fraud. Less honesty, openness, and transparency. For example, the Justice Department stonewalled the independent U.S. Commission on Civil

Rights' investigation of Justice Department decision-making. The Obama Justice Department, the very agency charged with enforcing our civil rights laws, refused to make witnesses available and refused to turn over documents as the law required to a federal government civil rights investigation.[3]

Obama has even pushed legislative measures designed to increase the chances of pro-Democratic voter fraud. John Fund, an elections expert, recently explained that Senator Chuck Schumer (D-NY) and Representative Barney Frank (D-MA) were looking to push a measure called "universal voter registration." What would it do? Says Fund, "It means all of the state laws on elections will be overridden by a federal mandate. The feds will tell the states: 'take everyone on every list of welfare that you have, take everyone on every list of unemployed you have, take everyone on every list of property owners, take everyone on every list of driver's license holders and register them to vote regardless of whether they want to be. . . .' "[4] If that constitutionally suspect and impractical mess of an approach is not a recipe for voter fraud, what is?

And that's only the beginning. President Obama's most favored organization, the ACORN, is still alive and well. Obama loves them. In 1992, he represented ACORN in a lawsuit that forced Citibank to lower its lending standards for unqualified minority borrowers, resulting in the type of "politically correct" lending that has given us our current housing crisis. Obama also served on the board of two foundations where he helped dole millions of dollars in grants to his friends at ACORN.

Now Obama is counting on the ACORN network to help retain office, even as his pliant attorney general refuses to prosecute them for their apparent misconduct.

ACORN Is Growing Again

To understand the challenges to the rule of law and our elections from the ACORN/Obama community organizing ethic, you have to go back more than forty years. ACORN's ideological foundation is rooted in the theory of social change developed by Columbia University sociologists Richard Cloward and Frances Fox Piven. This theory was first articulated and popularized in their 1966 article "The Weight of the Poor: A Strategy to End Poverty," which was published in the *Nation* in 1966.

The "Cloward-Piven" strategy calls for the poor to overwhelm existing public assistance agencies, creating an economic disruption at the state and local levels that would force the federal government to institute a broad new socialist model of wealth distribution. As they wrote: "By the internal disruption of local bureaucratic practices, by the furor over public welfare poverty, and by the collapse of current financing arrangements, powerful forces can be generated for major economic reforms at the national level."

The disruption they call for as a catalyst to political action is described as follows: "By crisis, we mean a publicly visible disruption in some institutional sphere. Crisis can occur spontaneously (e.g., riots) or as the intended result of tactics of demonstration and protest which either generate institutional disruption or bring unrecognized disruption to public attention. Key to implementing this proposed strategy is the concept of 'community organizing.' " Again, quoting from "The Weight of the Poor":

> Advocacy must be supplemented by organized demonstrations to create a climate of militancy that will overcome the invidious and immobilizing attitudes which many potential recipients hold toward being "on welfare." To generate an expressly political movement, cadres of aggressive organizers would have to come from the civil rights movement and the churches, from militant low-income organizations like those formed by the Industrial Areas Foundation (that is, by Saul Alinsky), and from other groups on the Left. These activists should be quick to see the difference between programs to redress individual grievances and a large-scale social-action campaign for national policy reform.

Cloward and Piven are blunt about the racial aspect of their proposed strategy. In an observation that could apply directly to

Obama's radical community organizing efforts, their article concludes with typical liberal contempt for certain minorities:

> Those seeking new ways to engage the Negro politically should remember that public resources have always been the fuel for low-income urban political organization. If organizers can deliver millions of dollars in cash benefits to the ghetto masses, it seems reasonable to expect that the masses will deliver their loyalties to their benefactors. At least, they have always done so in the past.

The Cloward-Piven strategy was put into practice by black organizer George Wiley, whom they recruited to run their new organization, the National Welfare Rights Organization (NWRO), in 1967. The NWRO orchestrated as series of violent welfare rights demonstrations in the late 1960s. On September 27, 1970, the *New York Times* described the organization's tactics as follows:

> There have been sit-ins in legislative chambers, including a United States Senate committee hearing, mass demonstrations of several thousand welfare recipients, school boycotts, picket lines, mounted police, tear gas, arrests—and, on occasion, rock-throwing, smashed glass doors, overturned desks, scattered papers and ripped out phones.

In New York, the strategy was hugely successful and led to the city's bankruptcy in 1975. Journalist Sol Stern wrote in the *City Journal*, "The flooding succeeded beyond Wiley's wildest dreams. From 1965 to 1974, the number of single-parent households on welfare soared from 4.3 million to 10.9 million, despite mostly flush economic times. By the early 1970s, one person was on the welfare rolls in New York City for every two working in the city's private economy."

Mayor Rudy Giuliani also directly attributed the city's financial crisis to the strategy. In a 1997 speech in which he cited "The Weight of the Poor," he said, "This wasn't an accident. It wasn't an atmospheric thing, it wasn't supernatural. This is the result of policies and programs designed to have the maximum number of people get on welfare."

Wade Rathke was an organizer for the NWRO and is frequently described as a "protégé" of Wiley. According to published reports, it was Wiley who sent Rathke to Arkansas to start a new organization based on the NWRO. Rathke's cofounder of ACORN (then the Arkansas Community Organizations for Reform Now), Gary Delgado, was also a lead organizer for the NWRO.

Both tactically and ideologically, the theory and tactics prescribed by Cloward, Piven, and Wiley are clearly evident in the goals and methods of ACORN, Project Vote, and the numerous ACORN organizations that have emerged since ACORN's bankruptcy. "The Weight of the Poor" cites union organization as a model for adopting collectivism over individual economic mobility. As Cloward and Piven wrote,

> If many people in the past have found their way up from poverty by the path of individual mobility, many others have taken a different route. Organized labor stands out as a major example. Although many American workers never yielded their dreams of individual achievement, they accepted and practiced the principle that each can benefit only as the status of workers as a whole is elevated. They bargained for collective mobility, not for individual mobility; to promote their fortunes in the aggregate, not to promote the prospects of one worker over another. . . . That fact has sustained the labor movement in the face of a counter pull from the ideal of individual achievement.

The ACORN network continues to have very close ties with the labor movement, which they see as an economic model for the country as a whole. This is best personified by Patrick Gaspard, who went from the Service Employees International Union (SEIU) to ACORN's Working Families Party, to the White House, to the DNC.

The tactic of overwhelming welfare offices to cause bureaucratic disruption is strikingly similar to the voter registration tactics of ACORN and Project Vote, which regularly "flood" election offices with registration applications as close to the registration dead-line as possible in order to overwhelm election officials and allow fraudulent applications to be accepted. In 1982, Cloward and Piven founded the Human Service Employees Registration and Voter Education Campaign, which lobbied for voter registration at public assistance agencies.

Among their goals, Cloward and Piven include that "adequate levels of income must be assured" and "the right to income must be guaranteed." They assert that "the ultimate objective of their strategy" is to "wipe out poverty by establishing a guaranteed annual income." The demand for "living wage" legislation was a cornerstone of ACORN's platform and resulted in "living wage" ordinances in Chicago, New York, and elsewhere. Many of ACORN's new splinter groups, including New York Communities for Change, continue to lobby for a "living wage."

During the 2008 campaign, President Obama proposed raising the federal minimum wage to $9.50 an hour, saying it would enable workers to "earn a living wage that allows them to raise their families and pay for basic needs such as food, transportation, and housing—things so many people take for granted."

Another goal articulated in "The Weight of the Poor" is "basic assistance for food and rent." ACORN was a strong advocate for public housing assistance, most notably through ACORN Housing/Affordable Housing Centers of America and the Mutual Housing Association of New York (which owns and operates more than 1,200 subsidized low-income housing units).

The tactic of orchestrating crises in order to prompt federal leg-islative action is clearly demonstrated in several of the protests that ACORN successor groups have recently organized and in the "Oc-cupy" movement.

It is also noteworthy that ACORN and ACORN Housing were partly responsible for the housing crisis by supporting federal inter-vention in the housing market and aggressively lobbying for weak-ened underwriting standards for low-income mortgage applicants.

Now that the crisis has been created, ACORN 2.0 groups are supporting new federal measures to forgive delinquent borrowers and increase federal oversight of lenders. Almost overnight, most of ACORN Housing's first-time-homebuyer programs became foreclosure mitigation programs (both funded by the federal government).

In summary, the ideological foundation of ACORN lies in the Cloward-Piven strategy of fomenting social chaos in order to create an environment in which the federal government will implement increasingly socialist policies. Its founders, most notably Wade Rathke, were participants in the first social movements and organizations to adopt this theory, and it is now being implemented in the areas of income redistribution, the collectivization of labor, the electoral system, and the housing market.

This bit of history should help one's understanding that, despite ACORN's claiming to be "a non-profit, non-partisan social justice organization," it was, in fact, a revolutionary activist group that, as a key focus, aggressively sought to register voters who could be counted on to support left-wing issues and candidates. At its peak, the organization had over 400,000 members and 1,200 neighborhood chapters in more than one hundred cities in the United States. (Bertha Lewis was appointed chief executive officer in 2008.)

When ACORN went out of business, it did not go defunct. According to House Oversight chairman Darrell Issa (R-CA), ACORN's successors funded the so-called Occupy movement, which littered American cities with grime, crime, and slime.[5]

We knew ACORN wasn't going away even when it said they were disbanding. The liberal media crafted a pretty compelling obituary for the disgraced "civil rights" organization, declaring the organization bankrupt, disbanded, and out of business. But on February 18, 2010, the House Oversight and Government Reform Committee Republicans, in a staff report, described ACORN's financial management as a "shell game . . . designed to conceal illegal activities, to use taxpayer and tax-exempt dollars for partisan political purposes, and to distract investigators." ACORN officials, however, tried to dupe government officials and the American public through false and misleading claims about ending operations. ACORN officials told the

New York Times that "at least 15 of the group's 30 state chapters have disbanded and have no plans of re-forming." On March 21, 2010, it was reported that the ACORN board met to discuss the closing of state affiliates and field offices.

However, claims that ACORN was disbanding were greatly exaggerated. As ACORN CEO Bertha Lewis told National Public Radio, "[ACORN is] not dead, yet." She added, "these new entities are carrying on ACORN's work of organizing low- and moderate-income folks. . . . [We have created] 18 bulletproof community-organizing Frankensteins that they're going to have a very hard time attacking."[6] A House committee report on ACORN stated, "ACORN's new affiliates have filed corporate registrations in Secretary of State offices throughout the country. . . . Committee investigators found that several new ACORN affiliates maintain the same boards, staff and Employer Identification Numbers as former ACORN offices. This reflects the lack of true change or reform between these new organizations and their predecessors."[7]

Just like a shady operation that goes "out of business" and opens up across the street under a new name, ACORN is attempting to rebrand itself. That's how ACORN Housing Corp. becomes Affordable Housing Centers of America, Arkansas ACORN becomes Arkansas Community Organizations, and Minnesota ACORN becomes Minnesota Neighborhoods Organizing for Change. And so on.

Even ACORN's bankruptcy was suspicious. In the bankruptcy filing dated November 2, 2010, ACORN claimed assets of $114,931.04 and liabilities of $4,092,596.76. The bankruptcy court, however, must have either found the claim to be blatantly false, or else it discovered additional assets. In any case, the court issued a Notice of Discovery of Assets, which notified creditors that there may have been some untruths in the initial filings.[8] Creditors were given a deadline of April 20, 2011, to file claims. Given the significance of the notice, Judicial Watch is investigating the status and results of the "discovery" in terms of net assets. The bankruptcy court has yet to release details.

In October 2009, Louisiana attorney general David Caldwell filed the first of two subpoenas seeking the financial records of ACORN, and in early November 2009, state investigators raided ACORN's office in New Orleans, taking dozens of computers into custody.[9] During testimony before the U.S. House of Representatives Committee on Oversight and Government Reform, Caldwell asked for help from the Obama administration in the investigation.[10] No help has apparently been forthcoming; and the failure by the Department of Justice to conduct its own investigation is a scandal in its own right.

In addition to potentially hiding assets, the evidence suggests, ACORN may have misstated liabilities to "fix" its balance sheet to deny funds to creditors. For example, in its bankruptcy filing, ACORN claimed a debt to the Pennsylvania Bureau of Charitable Organizations in the amount of $750,000. However, the Pennsylvania attorney general's office told Judicial Watch investigators that the state has no record of the debt.[11]

With respect to its assets, the report notes that the New York chapter of ACORN, under the leadership of Lewis, worked quickly to consolidate $20 million from approximately eight hundred bank accounts and an additional $10 million in property. Thus there is no shortage of funds ACORN can use to craft a new image and continue its operations unimpeded. In a letter released to the *New York Times*, ACORN boasted about what it plans to do with all of its riches. "You will continue to hear from ACORN—in the mail, on the Web, and in the media," the letter read. "And we need your continued support to counter the vicious anti-family, anti-minority, anti-immigrant attacks of the Republican right."[12] As of this writing, tens of millions of dollars in ACORN's funds and other assets are unaccounted for—and we're investigating those missing bucks.

Here's a brief rundown on some of the "new" organizations that have coincidentally sprung up in the wake of ACORN's supposed dissolution:

Community Organizations International: ACORN International was rebranded as Community Organizations International (COI) in 2009, though the former name is used interchangeably. In fact, the old ACORN International website now redirects to COI. This name change was the brainchild of Wade Rathke, original ACORN founder, who admits that the change was undertaken to disassociate the organization from the prostitution scandal. Rathke isn't exactly Mr. Clean. His brother, Dale Rathke, embezzled somewhere between $1 million and $5 million from 1999 to 2000 as chief financial officer of Citizens Consulting Inc., the group that managed ACORN's finances.[13] According to the House Representatives Committee on Oversight and Government Reform, Wade knew about the theft for more than eight years and reportedly kept it quiet, except for discussions with legal counsel and ACORN's management council. The extent of the cover-up included filing bogus reports with the IRS and the U.S. Department of Labor. After Wade Rathke was forced to step down as the chief organizer of ACORN, ACORN senior staff members, including Bertha Lewis, continued to keep the embezzlement from the full board and from law enforcement authorities. Though terminated from ACORN, Rathke managed to retain his position for a time with ACORN International.[14]

ACORN International operates as an ongoing concern. ACORN employees who knew about the embezzlement still have positions of authority in ACORN's spin-off state organizations. The organization has offices in ten countries, but apparently none in the U.S. (For a time, however, ACORN International listed a New Orleans address.)

Affordable Housing Centers of America: This is the former ACORN Housing. Except for the name, it's the same organization. Former ACORN Housing president Alton Bennett has retained the same position with AHCOA, as has executive director Mike Shea and vice president Dorothy Amadi (who was also the former president of the Mutual Housing Association of New York). Public affairs director Bruce Dorpalen was formerly ACORN Housing's loan director. Shea was a member of the ACORN executive council that chose to cover up the Rathke embezzlement. AHCOA's headquarters are located in Chicago at 209 West Jackson Boulevard, the former headquarters of ACORN Housing, and its fourteen field offices were the former locations of ACORN Housing. The new corporation also adopted the same employee identification number.

ACORN Housing received a great deal of its funding from federal sources in recent years. In fiscal years 2008 and 2009, the organization reported total revenues of $30.5 million. During the same time frame, HUD granted the organization over $3.25 million, and NeighborWorks—a congressionally funded nonprofit—awarded over $25 million in federal funds. Since March 1, 2011, the Affordable Housing Centers of America has received three grants totaling $729,849 from the Department of Housing and Urban Development.[15] It bears repeating that this is an outrage.

Despite an explicit federal funding ban, Obama has turned the taxpayer-funded spigot back on for his old buddies at ACORN Housing.

Judicial Watch uncovered documents in the summer of 2011 proving that Obama appointees are apparently violating the "De-fund ACORN Act" and other laws by sending a $79,819 grant from the Department of Housing and Urban Development (headed by fellow Chicagoan and longtime Obama and ACORN ally Shaun Donovan) to a renamed ACORN affiliate, the "Affordable Housing Centers of America."

Our investigators then confirmed reports of two more grants from HUD to AHCOA, one for $300,000 and another for $350,000, pushing the total amount of taxpayer funds given to AHCOA well past the $700,000 mark.

Make no mistake, AHCOA is ACORN. And ACORN is AHCOA.

Although the Government Accountability Office (GAO) issued a ridiculous advisory opinion in September 2010 stating that AHCOA is not an "allied organization" of ACORN and is therefore not subject to the federal funding ban, the government's own website listing federal expenditures had identified the organization receiving the first grant I mentioned as "ACORN Housing Corporation Inc." and listed ACORN's New Orleans address.

Moreover, AHCOA maintains the same board of directors, executive director, and offices as its predecessor, ACORN Housing

Corporation Inc.—whose very employees had been caught on tape offering advice on how to break the law.

Federal investigators have documented fraudulent activity by ACORN Housing/AHCOA. For example, a September 21, 2010, Department of Housing and Urban Development (HUD) inspector general report notes that ACORN Housing is "now operating as Affordable Housing Centers of America"; the organization misappropriated funds from a $3,252,399 federal grant. The inspector general concluded that ACORN Housing/AHCOA had charged salary expenses to the HUD grant that "were not fully supported." The organization also continued to pay its counselors even after they were terminated, did not meet federal procurement standards, and allegedly destroyed documents to conceal the fraudulent activity. The inspector general articulated a number of benchmarks that must first be met by AHCOA before the organization can begin receiving any future federal funds, including reimbursing the government the misappropriated funds.[16]

A separate report in November 2010 by the HUD inspector general documented additional fraudulent activity by ACORN/AHCOA. A December 2010 internal audit by NeighborWorks America found that ACORN Housing funneled $6.1 million in grant funding it received to ACORN via noncompetitive vendor contracts. The audit also questioned whether it was truly a separate entity from ACORN, noting "significant relationships between ACORN and AHC, which calls into question the validity of the arms-length transaction."

Despite the fact that AHCOA is nothing more than ACORN Housing with a new name, HUD ruled on June 1, 2010 that the company was not subject to the ACORN funding ban. According to documents obtained by Judicial Watch pursuant to a FOIA request, that decision was made by HUD general counsel Helen Kanovsky. Kanovsky is an Obama appointee who, before her nomination, was the chief operating officer and general counsel of the AFL-CIO Housing Investment Trust. Previously, she was the chief of staff to Senator John Kerry. On September 29, 2010, the Government Accountability Office issued a highly controversial decision that the federal ban on funding for ACORN and its affiliates (as articulated in Section 418 of the 2010 Transportation, Housing and Urban Development Appropriations Act of 2010) was not grounds for withholding federal funding from AHCOA.[17] In February 2011, the House Financial Services Committee proposed defunding NeighborWorks, but that good idea has evidently gone nowhere.

But ACORN not only has a friend in Obama. As reported by the *New York Times* in 2009, "perhaps no administration official has had more interaction with Acorn [*sic*] than [Shaun] Donovan," who is Obama's secretary of housing and urban development. The *Times* notes that Donovan "worked closely" with ACORN's politically powerful New York housing affiliate when he was a New York City housing official. And now he's helped secure a nice chunk of change for ACORN from HUD's coffers.

ACORN's ties to Obama and Donovan run deep. So it is no surprise they would illegally continue to dole out tax dollars to an ACORN affiliate with a documented history of fraudulent activity. This is another instance of President Obama's appointees stubbornly refusing to follow the law by not denying funding to this crooked organization.

And I have to ask the question: is the Obama gang ensuring that ACORN is around to help them again in 2012?

By the way, in 2011, HUD provided $40 million in grants to 108 "fair housing" organizations, representing a $13.2 million increase over the 2010 award. According to HUD's press announcement, the general purpose of these grants is "to educate the public and combat housing and lending discrimination." This funding of activist groups like ACORN Housing helped lead to our housing crisis. These socialist revolutionaries leveraged your tax dollars to press for government and mortgage policies that gave housing loans to people who couldn't afford them. That led to the ongoing mortgage crisis (and a federal government takeover, more or less, of the private mortgage market).

You can see that the Obama administration is doing several bad things at once—funding a group barred by law from receiving funds, funding a group that has a record of fraud, and funding a group and policies that have helped destroy the housing market (and depressed our economy).

ACORN's officers have found soft landings, too:

The Black Institute: Bertha Lewis now heads up the Black Institute, an organization supposedly concerned mainly with immigration reform. The new organization is a 501(c)(3) charitable organization, receiving "fiscal sponsorship" from the Association for the Rights of Citizens (ARC). What is ARC? It's an affiliate organization of ACORN, providing a direct link between the Black Institute and ACORN.[18] Notably, Lewis signed the articles of incorporation for the Black Institute on February 17, 2010, *more than a month before* she announced that ACORN would be closing its doors.

The Advance Group: Scott Levenson, former national spokesman for ACORN, became the president of the Advance Group, which does PR for the Black Institute. Rachel Mann, who produced ACORN's 25th Anniversary Gala, is the group's chief operating officer. Secretary of the Advance Group is Arthur Z. Schwartz, who was formerly the secretary/treasurer and general counsel for ACORN and the person who filed ACORN's bankruptcy papers.[19] He was also on Obama's New York City field team and a delegate to the Democratic National Convention. Michael Gaspard is counsel for the Advance Group. Gaspard is the brother of Patrick Gaspard, one of the founders of the Working Families Group, a group occasionally associated with ACORN activities. Patrick Gaspard was also the political vice president of SEIU 1199, as well as a former White House political director and is currently the executive director of the Democratic National Committee.[20]

ACORN remains alive and kicking in multiple states. It has newly renamed branches in:

- Arkansas
- California

- Delaware

- Louisiana

- Minnesota

- Missouri

- New England

- New York (where its affiliates act as a shell corporation for the mother ship)

- Pennsylvania

- Texas

- Washington

- North Carolina

- Washington, D.C.

- Florida

- New Mexico

In multiple states, ACORN remains under investigation, including:

- Colorado

- Connecticut

- Missouri

- Nevada

- New Jersey

- Texas

- Florida

- Indiana

- Pennsylvania

Most of these investigations surrounded voter registration fraud. Overall, seventeen states launched criminal investigations of ACORN. Prosecutions led to convictions of ACORN workers in some of these states. And in August 2011, a Nevada judge handed down the maximum fine to an ACORN affiliate for its role in a massive violation of voter registration laws. The crimes were so serious that at sentencing the judge said that if an individual, instead of a corporation, had been hauled before him he would have handed down a ten-year prison sentence. "And I wouldn't have thought twice about it," he said.[21]

He's exactly right. Using FOIA we obtained documents of an investigation in Missouri in 2007, for example, in which the FBI found that people working for Project Vote and ACORN sought to "cause confusion on election day to keep polls open longer . . . [and] allow people who can't vote to vote, and allow people to vote multiple times." You can bet those false votes didn't go to conservatives.[22]

As if that weren't enough, ACORN spin-off groups in several states were active in coordinating the Occupy protests in several cities:

- **Boston:** New England United for Justice was part of the coalition organizing the "Take Back Boston" protests that led to dozens of arrests;

- **New York:** New York Communities for Change was caught paying staff and homeless people ten dollars per hour to attend Occupy Wall Street;

- **Orlando:** ACORN spin-off Organize Now coordinated and publicized the Occupy Orlando protests;

- **California:** The Alliance of Californians for Community Empowerment (ACCE) organized joint protests with Occupy Oakland.

An ACORN by any other name stinks as much.

Meanwhile, the Obama administration is running a protection racket for Obama's personal community organizing group. In March 2010, we obtained documents from the FBI about investigations into the corrupt activities of ACORN. The documents referenced serious allegations of corruption and voter registration fraud by ACORN as well as the Obama administration's decision to shut down a criminal investigation without filing criminal charges.

Some of this material were FBI documents related to the 2007 investigation and arrest of eight St. Louis, Missouri workers from the "community organization" ACORN for violation of election laws and voter fraud. The documents include handwritten notes from FBI investigators interviewing, among others, canvassers working with Project Vote. Among the shocking details from the FBI's interview notes: "ACORN HQ is wkg for the Democratic Party." That particular note is reproduced below:

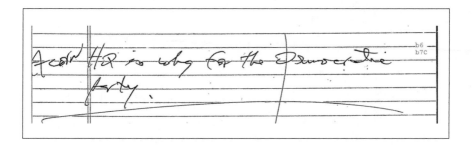

Here are a few other verbatim quotes from these these FBI interview notes.

- [ACORN] "Told employees not to talk to the FBI. 'FBI trying to intimidate you.' "

- Fraudulent cards:
  - To cause confusion on election day to keep polls open longer
  - To allow people who can't vote to vote.
  - To allow to vote multiple times.

- Project Vote will pay them whether cards fake or not—whatever they had to do to get the cards was attitude.

- Constantly threatened

- Staff restricted on what to say to FBI

- "Poverty pimpin" [sic] ACORN

- PV [Project Vote] pays ACORN $6.00 per card . . . Said "You treat the cards like (cash) $"

- Some [names] went right from the phone book and made up the rest.

- Canvassers: homeless, volatile, drug users, drunks . . .

- Anyone who was against PV (Project Vote) or ACORN's goals "right wing"

- She thought if she used a completely fake name it would be less like ID theft . . .

- "Yeah, it's against the law, I know."

In April 2008, all eight ACORN employees involved in the St. Louis scandal pled guilty to voter registration fraud.

In March 2010, Judicial Watch obtained a separate batch of FBI documents detailing a federal investigation into alleged ACORN corruption and voter registration fraud in Connecticut. The FBI and Department of Justice initiated these investigation. However, the Obama Justice Department, while noting that ACORN had engaged in "questionable hiring and training practices," closed down the investigation in March 2009, claiming ACORN broke no laws.

I followed up by calling the Connecticut voting official referenced in the documents to ask about what had happened. He was upset that there were no prosecutions, because honest elections officials worked hard to make sure the rolls were correct just prior to the election. Then an organization like Project Vote dumps thousands and thousands of voter registrations on the last day. And these registrations are mostly garbage. But the net effect is it disrupts the system and not only provides an opportunity for voter fraud, it also makes it more difficult for people wanting to vote legally. Cloward-Piven would be proud.

Given all of this evidence, much of it contained in the files of various government agencies, why has there been no comprehensive Obama Justice Department investigation of an organization deemed by at least one congressional report to be a "criminal enterprise"?

Voter Fraud?

So, what does ACORN's continued activity mean for the 2012 election? Our investigations have uncovered a shocking partnership between the Justice Department and ACORN-connected Project Vote to use the National Voting Rights Act to register more individuals on public assistance, widely considered a key voting demographic for the Obama 2012 campaign. As you'll recall, this relationship goes way back—Obama previously ran Project Vote. In fact, Obama acted as a lawyer for ACORN in a suit against Illinois after Governor Jim Edgars refused to implement the motor-voter law according to ACORN's radical specifications, a law that critics believe promotes voter registration fraud and outright vote fraud. Actually, Obama did more than that—he teamed up with the Clinton Justice Department, letting "the heavy-hitters at the Justice Department make the arguments." [23]

On August 19, 2011, we filed a FOIA request asking for records surrounding communications between the Justice Department and Estelle Rogers, director of advocacy for Project Vote. The documents we uncovered leave no doubt that a suspiciously close relationship between Project Vote and Justice is developing behind closed doors. Our friend J. Christian Adams observed, "Project Vote appears to be directing DOJ resources toward particular states; is having meetings with DOJ staff; and is even recommending lawyers to work in the Justice Department Voting Section that will oversee the 2012 presidential election." [24]

Now, let's review what we know about Rogers.

As director of advocacy for Project Vote, Rogers—a former attorney for ACORN—is a primary contact person on policy matters at Project Vote on both state and federal levels and has been actively involved in voter registration issues. By threatening lawsuits under Section 7 of the National Voting Rights Act, Project Vote has aggressively sought to force election officials in various states to increase the registration of people receiving public assistance.

So how involved was the Obama Justice Department in this scheme? According to the records we uncovered, "civil rights groups" met with Associate Attorney General Thomas J. Perrelli on March 17, 2011 to specifically discuss Section 7 of the National Voting Rights Act (NVRA), which requires states to offer voter registration services at all public assistance agencies. The groups included Project Vote, American Association of People with Disabilities, Demos, League of Women Voters, Lawyers' Committee for Civil Rights Under Law, Brennan Center for Justice, Fair Elections Legal Network, NAACP Legal Defense Fund, and Paralyzed Veterans of America.

On March 29, 2011, Rogers and the "undersigned voting rights groups" that met with Perrelli sent detailed recommendations to the associate attorney general for strengthening "compliance with the NVRA." Forwarded to Perrelli by Rogers, the recommendations stated "we are grateful that you have invited us to continue this dialogue on the Department's role in providing guidance to states, and we would be happy to supply any additional information you need."

So, in short, the Justice Department invited Project Vote (and other leftist groups) to help provide guidance to states regarding the enforcement of the NVRA. If that sounds good to you, check with a mental health specialist—Project Vote, a leader in suspected voter fraud, is advising the Obama administration on how to register voters.

The records also detail an effort by Rogers to secure jobs for three individual applicants for positions with the Civil Rights Division's Voting Section, the department within Justice responsible for enforcing the NVRA. In a February 23, 2010, email to the chief of the Justice Department's Voting Section, Rogers wrote, "I want to heartily recommend two candidates to you." In an email a month later, Rogers wrote, "I look forward to continuing to work with you. . . . And please let me know if you need any more feedback regarding hires." As if that weren't enough, in December 2010 she wrote, "the main reason I called is that you have an applicant for the [REDACTED] position [REDACTED] qualifies her beautifully for your position, and I hope you will give her every consideration. [REDACTED] So she would be a great fit, and I recommend her without reservation. Please let me know if I can tell you more. And give me a call if you possibly can."

Personnel is policy. To install ACORN/Project Vote ideological clones in the Justice Department's Civil Right Division is to invite chaos and corruption. Which is, of course, precisely what Obama and his cronies want.

The cooperation between Project Vote and Justice runs even deeper. If you look at the timeline of the NVRA lawsuits that have already been filed, it's clear that Project Vote and the department have implemented a joint litigation strategy in the run-up to the 2012 election.

The connection, we've discovered, runs through the Obama White House.

A second batch of documents that has come as this book is being finalized closes the loop on the conspiracy. The additional documents provided in response to our FOIA lawsuit detail more email communications between Rogers and high-ranking officials, such as the notorious Cecilia Muñoz, from the Obama White House and Justice Department:

- On April 27, 2009, Estelle Rogers wrote to Deputy Assistant Attorney General Sam Hirsch regarding an upcoming meeting on April 30, 2009. In addition to Rogers and Hirsch, other attendees included: Nicole Kovite, director of Public Agency Project for Project Vote; Spencer Overton, deputy assistant attorney general in the Office of Legal Policy; and two officials from the Obama White House: Celia Muñoz, then–director of intergovernmental affairs and recently promoted to director of the Domestic Policy Council; and Tino Cuellar, special assistant to the president for justice and regulatory policy.

In her email, Rogers references documents she forwarded in preparation for the upcoming meeting on the National Voter Registration Act (NVRA), to which Hirsch replies that he looks forward to "reading these materials" and to "seeing everyone on Thursday."

- On February 23, 2011, Rogers wrote to Associate Deputy Attorney General Robert Weiner, asking him to "make some headway with Attorney General [Eric] Holder in enforcing Section 7 of the NVRA." The email notes that the Justice Department had not yet filed any Section 7 lawsuits, which Rogers dubbed "deeply disappointing." The first such Justice Department lawsuit (against Rhode Island) was filed on March 18, 2011, less than one month later. Of particular note is Rogers's comment, "We have received oral assurances from [Assistant Attorney General Thomas] Perez on several occasions that enforcement action was imminent," suggesting that Rogers was privy to internal discussions inside the Justice Department regarding pending legal action.

- On March 29, 2011, Rogers wrote to Associate Attorney General Thomas Perrelli, urging him to review and "make improvements" to a document she was sending following another meeting held on March 17, 2011, between Project Vote and the Justice Department on Section 7 compliance with the NRVA. Accompanying the document was a previous letter she had sent to the Civil Rights Division plus "additional comments on the Q and A."

Once again, these documents raise fundamental questions about the politicization of the Justice Department under Eric Holder and demonstrate that the ACORN-connected Project Vote is throwing its weight around the Justice Department and driving the agency's "voting rights" agenda. And evidently the Obama White House is now directly implicated in this growing scandal. It is now clear that Project Vote and the Obama/Holder Justice Department are conspiring to file Justice Department lawsuits to help reelect Barack Obama. This collusion between Project Vote and the Obama administration is a significant threat to the integrity of the 2012 elections. To have Project Vote involved in voting rights enforcement at the Justice Department is like having the Mafia run the FBI. At least now we know why the Obama/Holder Justice Department never bothered to fully investigate voter registration fraud by Project Vote/ACORN. They are in cahoots.

Project Vote hasn't cleaned up its act. On August 4, 2011, Judicial Watch released documents obtained from the Colorado Department of State showing that ACORN and Project Vote successfully pressured Colorado officials into implementing new policies for increasing the registration of public assistance recipients during the 2008 and 2010 election seasons. Following the policy changes, the percentage of invalid voter registration forms from Colorado public assistance agencies was four times the national average. You read that right—thanks to the Justice Department and Project Vote, invalid voter registration in Colorado was *quadruple* the national average.

Project Vote has also sought a "legislative fix" to allow people without a driver's license or state identification to register to vote on-line. In addition to pursuing public agency registration cases in Missouri, Ohio, Indiana, Georgia, and New Mexico, Project Vote and the NAACP filed a lawsuit on April 19, 2011, against the state of Louisiana alleging violations of the NVRA. Less than three months later, on July 12, the department's Civil Rights Division/Voting Section sued Louisiana on the same grounds, claiming that "Louisiana officials have not routinely offered voter registration forms, assistance and services to the state's eligible citizens who apply, recertify or provide a change of address for public assistance or disability services."

The Justice Department also sued the state of Rhode Island, on March 11, 2011, alleging violations of the NVRA. The lawsuit led to policy changes intended to increase the number of voter registration applications processed by "public assistance and disability service officers." These two lawsuits, filed within five months of each other, are the first such lawsuits filed by the department since 2007. Coordination, or coincidence? You be the judge.

As we've already discussed, Project Vote and ACORN have both been linked to massive voter registration fraud. As documented in a July 2009 report by the House Committee on Oversight and Government Reform, of the 1.3 million registrations that Project Vote/ACORN submitted in the 2008 election cycle, more than one-third were invalid. The congressional report also noted that a total of seventy ACORN/Project Vote employees in twelve states have been convicted of voter registration fraud.

And yet nobody is pointing out this glaring problem. That's why what we do at Judicial Watch is perhaps the only firewall standing between the Obama administration and a deeply corrupt 2012 election.

Judicial Watch to States: Clean Up the Voting Rolls

Here's the harsh reality:

- The liberal national media routinely ignores Obama administration secrecy, corruption, and potentially criminal acts. They are as much "in the tank" for Barack Obama today as they were when he first ran for president in 2008;

- Corrupt organizations like those in the ACORN network that are part of the Obama machine's election conspiracy will be backing Barack Obama with massive amounts of money and "volunteers";

- Although Republicans will attack Obama for short-term partisan gain, their own history of corruption and government secrecy gives no guarantee that they will seriously challenge the underlying corrupt culture of the Obama gang.

Besides already being on the front lines in this battle against Obama administration corruption, Judicial Watch is working on a new national voter registration accountability program that could include court action to ensure that the voting rolls in 2012 are clean and accurate, a direct pushback to the ACORN network's penchant for voter registration fraud and the related voter fraud threat. This effort is part of our comprehensive 2012 Election Integrity Project.

I've described above how the Obama Justice Department's focus, after consulting with the Obama White House and the criminal ACORN network, is on enforcing Section 7 of the National Voting Registration Act—the section of the law that allows public assistance agencies to register voters. Nothing wrong with that in theory—but in practice, the Obama/ACORN method for registering Obama's "Food Stamp Army" is a recipe for fraud and abuse.

The obvious risk of fraud and abuse that comes with having every government welfare agency under the sun register voters was supposed to be balanced by the NVRA's Section 8, which requires states and localities to make "a reasonable effort to remove the names of ineligible voters from the official lists of eligible voters." In other words, they are supposed to make a reasonable effort to ensure that the voting rolls are kept up to date and correct. For instance, states and localities are supposed to take steps to remove dead people from the rolls and remove ineligible voters (such as those who have moved out of a voting district and, in most states, felons).

Section 8 of the NVRA is an important counterpart to Section 7. It represents a carefully crafted compromise in Congress to increase voter registration but also protect voter roll integrity.

Leftist ideologues and partisans at the Obama Justice Department simply will not enforce this provision requiring accurate voting rolls. The Obama crowd, through ACORN/Project Vote, may be happy to allow fraudulent names to get on the voter rolls but it has no interest in taking them off the rolls. The longer these names and the names of the dead remain on the voting rolls, the more chances for voter fraud. For example, in South Carolina (where, as in Texas, the Obama Justice Department is outrageously challenging another voting ID law), it is believed that over nine hundred "dead people" may have voted.[25] Of course, if many jurisdictions don't bother to remove the deceased from the rolls, dead voters can become a real live voting bloc for fraudsters.

Thankfully, the law allows Judicial Watch to go to court on behalf of those who want the rule of law enforced. If the Obama Justice Department and the ACORN voter registration fraud crowd don't want free and fair elections, then we must step up to the plate.

In the autumn of 2011, we conducted an analysis of all available census and voter registration data. We uncovered that many key states have counties where more than 100 percent of their voting age population registered to vote! That's obviously an indication that those states are not scrubbing their voter lists as Section 8 requires. Our expert analysis found that problem states include Alabama, California, Colorado, Florida, Indiana, Iowa, Mississippi, Missouri, Ohio, Pennsylvania, Texas, West Virginia.

Let me be perfectly clear: Judicial Watch does not endorse or oppose candidates for public office. Judicial Watch is nonpartisan. Judicial Watch *does* want elections to be honest, open, and free of fraud. Indeed, the states and localities that do not maintain their voting rolls properly are run by both Republican and Democratic officeholders. No matter which politician is responsible, allowing the names of ineligible voters to remain on the voting rolls harms the integrity of the electoral process and undermines voter confidence in the legitimacy of elections. As the U.S. Supreme Court has stated, "[P]ublic confidence in the integrity of the electoral process has independent significance, because it encourages citizen participation in the democratic process."

We have already alerted most of the affected jurisdictions to the problem and, if they don't take action, we will sue where we can in federal court.

You can see how the corruption described here harms our republic. The Obama administration's alliance with the voter registration fraud-tainted ACORN/Project Vote, its hostility to voter ID laws, its refusal to take steps to clean up the voting rolls, and its desire to keep illegal aliens in the United States during the upcoming election season lead me to one conclusion—the Obama machine is prepared to "steal" the November elections, if necessary.

So it would not surprise me if our nonpartisan, anti-corruption efforts are opposed in court by both the ACORN network and the Obama campaign (or the Justice Department, which is a front for them both). It may result in pitched legal battles but it will be worth the effort, considering that the integrity of our national elections is at stake—not only in 2012 but beyond.

Epilogue

MAINTAINING TRANSPARENCY

These *Corruption Chronicles* show that Washington is embroiled in a corruption crisis. This administration, building on awful legacies of its predecessors, has grown government beyond accountability; it is simply unknowable to the average American. Congressional oversight has not kept pace with the growth of government. Our debt stands at $16 trillion and counting. It was $10 trillion when Obama took his presidential oath of office.

The media is a lapdog not only to President Obama but to the oblivious political class whose idea of "ethics" wouldn't allow a normal person to sleep at night. With a liberal media pathologically incapable of questioning the inherent wrongs and corruption of big government, a compromised and political legislature, and an executive branch almost gleeful in its willingness to break the rules and violate the U.S. Constitution to stay in power and "remake" America, it's no wonder our system of government is off the rails and out of control. And no wonder the job of serious oversight in Washington falls in no small measure to our group of investigators and litigators. We ask the tough questions and go to court so the American people are educated with the information necessary to meaningfully exercise their God-given right of self-government.

Americans feel that they have lost control of their government. Our government is, in our civic dreams, supposed to be of the people, by the people, and for the people; instead, it's become a government that is of, by, and for the politicians and their allies in the government bureaucracies. We live in an era of big government, full of big secrets. And with this big secrecy comes big corruption.

Big government, big secrecy, and big corruption walk hand in hand through presidential administration after presidential administration. Recently, each presidential administration seemed to compete with the next in terms of corruption and its kissing cousin, nontransparency. From the impeachment of Bill Clinton to the "secrecy as policy" of President Bush, by the time the 2008 election rolled around, Americans were tired of presidencies that seemed hostile to public concern about ethics and transparency.

And then Barack Obama was elected.

In too many ways, the Obama administration represents the apex of government secrecy—and, not coincidentally, it represents the apex of government growth and corruption. Virtually every day, the regulatory thickets that entangle the American people grow; virtually every day, the government bureaucracy that encroaches on American freedom expands. This expansion has come with a startling lack of transparency, oversight, and accountability. And if the American people can't find out what their government is up to, then their government will be up to no good.

The Obama administration has hidden broad swaths of federal spending from public accountability, despite candidate Obama's promises (which are still repeated by the administration ad nauseam) to restore openness to government. The Obama administration has covered for its political allies—some of whom committed massive voter registration fraud—to get him reelected in 2012. The Obama administration has appointed nonaccountable czar after nonaccountable czar to lord over the American people. And that's just the beginning.

The story didn't begin with the Obama administration, and it will not end there. The story includes the administrations of President Bill Clinton and President George W. Bush and their cabinet officers. It includes major American regulatory bodies. Government secrecy is not only anathema to our republican form of government; it threatens to swamp America's economy and her foreign policy in ways that put our treasure and safety at risk.

America's Founding Fathers believed that sunlight was the best disinfectant, because they recognized that those who served in the government were as prone to error and corruption as anyone else—in fact, many times more so. In Federalist 51, James Madison, the chief author of the Constitution, famously wrote:

> If men were angels, no government would be necessary. If angels were to govern men, neither external nor internal controls on government would be necessary. In framing a government which is to be administered by men over men, the great difficulty lies in this: you must first enable the government to control the governed; and in the next place oblige it to control itself.

One of those "auxiliary precautions" is the checks and balances among the three branches of our government; another is the expectation that the people will have the ability to see what is going on inside the government itself.

This was not a minor concern for Madison or any of the other Founders. They saw government transparency as the key to good government. Thomas Jefferson and John Adams didn't agree on much—their 1800 election was about as ugly an election as there has ever been—but they agreed that the public had a right to full information about their government. Said Jefferson, "Wherever the people are well-informed, they can be trusted with their own government." And again: "If we are to guard against ignorance and remain free, it is the responsibility of every American to be informed." Adams agreed and said freedom of information about our government is a God-given right: "Liberty cannot be preserved without a general knowledge among the people, who have a right . . . an indisputable, unalienable, indefeasible, divine right to that most dreaded and envied kind of knowledge, I mean, of the characters and conduct of their rulers." George Washington himself also knew the value of pursuing knowledge: "Truth will ultimately prevail where there is pains taken to bring it to light."

Other Founding Fathers agreed that the best insurance for good government is an informed populace that fights for its right to information. Samuel Adams, father of the Sons of Liberty, rightly stated, "No People will tamely surrender their Liberties, nor can any be easily subdued, when knowledge is diffused and Virtue is preserved." "A nation of well informed men who have been taught to know and prize the rights which God has given them cannot be enslaved," said Benjamin Franklin. "It is in the region of ignorance that tyranny begins."

But it was Madison who was the most resolute on this point— he thought that transparency was the crucial bulwark against governmental oppression. "A popular Government," he wrote in 1822, "without popular information, or the means of acquiring it, is but a Prologue to a Farce or a Tragedy; or perhaps both. Knowledge will forever govern ignorance: And a people who mean to be their own Governors, must arm themselves with the power which knowledge gives." [1]

In this era of Bailout Nation, Solyndra, Obamacare, congressional corruption, and government overreach, government operations unfortunately are well into realm of farce and tragedy. Few Americans have any idea what goes on inside the government they elect, to which they pay their taxes, and to whose authority they are subject each and every day. Maybe they don't want to know. But they need to know.

Much of the public ignorance, which the government is happy to further, is a direct by-product of government's growth. When Jefferson, Adams, and Madison wrote their words, in the aftermath of the Revolutionary War, total federal debt constituted 35 percent of gross domestic product; by the 1830s, our young nation (despite having been almost strangled in its crib in the War of 1812) had this debt paid off. During the Civil War, federal debt was just 33 percent of GDP. Again, it was paid off, by the year 1900. Today, in an era in which we have fought no wars of any such scale for nearly seventy years (Iraq and Afghanistan look like mere battles compared to the carnage of the World War II), the federal debt amounts to well over 100 percent of our GDP. When it comes to the federal budget, the numbers are even more stark. In 1800, the federal government spent $11 million, or about $2 per person. By 1900, that number had climbed to $521 million, or about $7 per person.[2] This year, President Obama proposed a $3.7 *trillion* budget—a budget 336,363 times bigger than that of 1800 and 7,101 times larger than that of 1900, or about $12,022 per person.

In 1901, excluding defense and the post office, there were almost 59,000 federal employees; by 1999, there were 1,685,000;[3] today, there are over 2.7 million federal civilian employees. Government is growing exponentially, and with that growth comes a massive army of bureaucrats dedicated to protecting their agencies' power, their taxpayer-financed bloated budgets, and, most importantly, their high-paying jobs.

One cannot separate the Founders' desire for transparent government from their desire for smaller government. Yes, they wanted the people to know what was going on, but they weren't pure democrats—they wanted a representative republic that would allow elected leaders discretion to do their jobs. So why the focus on transparency? Because our Founders knew that transparency could keep government in check by allowing Americans to check if each action by the government encroached on liberty in some way. Transparency gives Americans an external check on their government to prevent their freedoms from being smothered.

There's a reason that Thomas Jefferson's first inaugural address called for both limited and transparent government. In that speech, he championed "a wise and frugal government, which shall restrain men from injuring one another, which shall leave them otherwise free to regulate their own pursuits of industry and improvement, and shall not take from the mouth of labor the bread it has earned. This is the sum of good government." He simultaneously recognized the need for transparency to make that "good government" possible, calling for "the diffusion of information and the arraignment of all abuses at the bar of public reason."

Unfortunately, both Jefferson's transparency and his small government have gone the way of the dodo bird. By 1974, the Senate openly recognized that the size and scope of government made the Madisonian vision untenable: "Today the very vastness of our Government and its myriad of agencies makes it difficult for the electorate to obtain that 'popular information' of which Madison spoke. But it is only when one further considers the hundreds of departments, branches, and agencies which are not directly responsible to the people, that one begins to understand the great importance of having an information policy of full disclosure."[4]

The words of that Senate report ring hollow. Today's politicians are more interested in nontransparency than ever—and that desire for secrecy can't be separated from their desire for an ever-growing federal government that is corruptly at odds with the public interest.

Our politicians are clever, though. This present administration, in particular, has figured out how to dissemble about openness, first pretending to advocate for transparency, then entering office and growing government while stifling transparency. Politicians of both parties consistently pay homage to the need for transparency, even as they undercut it.

President Clinton attributed his election wins in 1992 and 1996 to his willingness to "be held accountable for results"—but he was unwilling to be held accountable for anything at all. President Bush promised a restoration of honest and open government to the White House, while almost immediately stifling investigations and openness.

If Clinton and Bush both touted their dedication to "open government," President Obama has made it his personal mission to push the notion that he is transparent and accountable while doing everything in his power to prevent both transparency and accountability. During his campaign, Obama pledged "an unprecedented level of openness in Government" and said that he would "establish a system of transparency, public participation, and collaboration."[5] On his first day in office, Obama sent a memo promising that all agencies would "adopt a presumption in favor of disclosure, in order to renew their commitment to the principles embodied in [the Freedom of Information Act], and to usher in a new era of open government. The presumption of disclosure should be applied to all decisions involving FOIA." President Obama said that "[a] democracy requires accountability, and accountability requires transparency. . . . [FOIA] encourages accountability through transparency."

The Obama memo stated that FOIA "should be administered with a clear presumption: [i]n the faceoff doubt, openness prevails," and that agencies should "take affirmative steps to make information public and not to wait for specific requests from the public."[6]

Obama, taking a swipe at the Bush administration, went even further, saying that agencies shouldn't withhold information "merely because public officials might be embarrassed by disclosure, because errors and failures might be revealed, or because of speculative or abstract fears. . . . [Agencies should respond to requests] promptly and in a spirit of cooperation."[7] (Judicial Watch had already figured out Obama's transparency lies by then, so we were a bit skeptical of his FOIA rhetoric.) Yet incredibly, in Obama's first full year in office, his administration denied 70,779 FOIA requests, as opposed to 47,395 times in Bush's last year. According to the Associated Press, seventeen major agencies denied FOIA requests almost 500,000 times, a jump of nearly half from the Bush years.[8]

Yet in July 2011, Obama created a Government Accountability and Transparency Board—an oxymoron if ever there was one. "Cutting waste, fraud and abuse has been something Washington has talked about for decades," said Vice President Joe Biden, "but now more than ever, what the American people need is action. . . . With our nation's top watchdogs at the helm, we will deliver the kind of transparency and accountability for Federal spending that the public deserves and expects." As you'd expect, other federal officials with an interest in secrecy have pretended that the Obama administration's dismal record on transparency is in fact glowing. "From the first day of this administration, the president and the vice president have outlined a vision of government that is more open and more accountable to the American people," said federal chief performance officer Jeffrey Zients.[9] Even Obama's supporters are disappointed by his performance on this score. University of Chicago law professor and Obama backer Geoffrey R. Stone wrote in the *New York Times*, "The record of the Obama administration on this fundamental issue of American democracy has surely fallen short of expectations. This is a lesson in 'trust us.' Those in power are always certain that they themselves will act reasonably, and they resist limits on their own discretion. The problem is, 'trust us' is no way to run a self-governing society." [10]

Stone is absolutely right. Truth fears no inquiry. That's why so many in the government fear inquiry—they have something to hide.

So Judicial Watch stands in the gap on behalf of the American people. We use the open records and freedom of information laws to uncover corruption from federal, state, and local governments. And when government agencies don't follow the law and turn over documents as they are supposed to—we sue in court to get them. Democrat or Republican administrations—if we think you have something to hide about government corruption, our lawyers will see you in court.

And when it comes to vindicating the rule of law, Judicial Watch will try to do the job that the Justice Department won't do. As part of the Election Integrity Project, Judicial Watch is prepared to sue in federal court up to a dozen states that have dirty voting rolls. We know who they are. We've warned state and local officials to clean up the rolls to protect the integrity of the elections. And if they don't, we'll do what Eric Holder won't: go to court.

It is simply impossible to have any faith in the integrity of an election where dead people remain on the voting rolls. This is a recipe for voter fraud and stolen elections. So you can see how Judicial Watch is your watchdog in Washington. I encourage you to join our grassroots movement.

We are here to help you. We are here to defend you. We are here to represent you in Washington and wherever else the rule of law is under attack from politicians who think they are above the law. Our motto: "Because no one is above the law!"

APPENDIX:

The New Millennium's Ten Most-Wanted Corrupt Politicians

We've spent nearly two decades fighting corrupt politicians. And we've encountered many who abuse their office and the public trust to line their own pockets and those of their friends, or aid certain special interest groups, or push particularly radical policies. In 2006, we began compiling an annual list that has set many politicians on edge: Washington's Ten Most-Wanted Corrupt Politicians. Since the turn of the millennium, we've fought too many of these opponents to count. But there are some who stand out. So, special to *The Corruption Chronicles*, here's our list of the New Millennium's Ten Most-Wanted Corrupt Politicians:

Hillary Clinton. Now that she's legitimized herself by spending an uncontroversial several years as secretary of state, it's easy to forget just how corrupt Hillary Clinton is. Remember, she's the only First Lady to have ever testified to a grand jury. From Whitewater to her scandalous days in the White House as First Lady to her corrupt and venal (and successful) attempts to manipulate her Senate election in 2000, from her corrupt Senate election fund-raising operation (which was fined $35,000 by the FEC for improprieties) to her attempts to block release of her official White House records, from her association with felon and erstwhile fugitive from justice Norman Hsu to her assumption of the office of secretary of state despite her constitutional ineligibility, Hillary proves that corrupt politicians never die—they just fade away. And maybe, just maybe, fade back in.

President Barack Obama. We have devoted almost an entire book to the corruption and unlawfulness of the Obama administration, but it's worth noting once again that Obama, personally, is one of "the worst of the worst" in Washington. In 2011, President Obama made Judicial Watch's "Ten Most-Wanted" list for the fifth consecutive year. (The former Illinois senator was also a "Dishonorable Mention" in 2006.) And when it comes to Obama corruption, it may not get any bigger than Solyndra. Solyndra was once known as the poster child for the Obama administration's massive "green energy" initiative, but it has become the poster child for the corruption that ensues when the government meddles in the private sector. Solyndra filed for bankruptcy in September 2011, leaving 1,100 workers without jobs and the American taxpayers on the hook for $535 million, thanks to an Obama administration stimulus loan guarantee. Whether it's the Chicago way, the Solyndra scandal, his continued funding of the newly rebranded ACORN, his attempts to hide the Secret Service White House visitors logs, his attempts to stack the National Labor Relations Board illegally, or his attempt to use that same board to shut down private industry, this is a politician with serious abuse of power issues. And all of those problems occurred in 2011. President Obama remains the supreme example of what can happen after two decades of escalating unaccountability at the very highest levels of government.

Eric Holder. President Obama's attorney general operates the most politicized and ideological Department of Justice (DOJ) in recent history. Revelations from the Operation Fast and Furious scandal suggest that programs approved by the Holder DOJ may have resulted in the needless deaths of many, including a federal law enforcement officer. Holder's DOJ has covered up the voter intimidation of the New Black Panthers. In February 2011, Holder announced that DOJ lawyers would not defend the constitutionality of the Defense of Marriage Act. Holder's DOJ continues to stone-wall the release of information regarding Supreme Court justice Elena Kagan's participation in Obamacare discussions when she served as solicitor general. In addition to forcing Judicial Watch to file a lawsuit to obtain this information, Holder's DOJ thumbed its nose at Congress by failing to release this material to the Senate Judiciary Committee during Kagan's judicial confirmation hearing. Holder continues to personally resist requests from Judicial Watch and Congress for additional information on this controversy.

Most recently, Judicial Watch obtained shocking documents showing how the Holder DOJ is conspiring with scandal-ridden Project Vote (President Obama's former employer and ACORN front) to use the National Voter Registration Act to increase welfare voter registrations. One former ACORN employee (and current Project Vote director of advocacy), Estelle Rogers, is even helping to vet job candidates for the Justice Department's Voting Rights Division! (ACORN and Project Vote have a long record of voter registration fraud.) Eric Holder is the worst attorney general since John Mitchell.

Tom DeLay. DeLay (R-TX) was forced to step down from his position as House majority leader and resign from Congress. He has been embroiled in a series of scandals from bribery to influence-peddling, and was indicted twice by grand juries in Texas. He was deeply involved with corruption magnet Jack Abramoff. His corruption was so bad it arguably led to the Democrats being able to take back control of the House by running against DeLay-type corruption in 2006. And, of course, DeLay wasn't alone in Congress— Representative Duke Cunningham (R-CA) pled guilty in 2005 to conspiracy to commit bribery, mail fraud, wire fraud, and tax evasion. Cunningham got eight years in prison and was ordered to pay $1.8 million in restitution in March 2006. Delay faces three years in prison in Texas after being convicted on violations related to state campaign finance laws.

Charles Rangel. Representative Rangel (D-NY) is one of the most corrupt congressmen to sit in the chamber in modern memory.

In 2010, the House voted to censure Rangel for corruption; now those same congresspeople who censured him stand by his side. He was never properly punished for failing to pay taxes on $75,000 in income, misusing his congressional office, staff, and resources to raise money for his private Rangel Center for Public Service, misusing his apartment as a campaign headquarters, and failing to report $600,000 in income on his official financial disclosure forms. He remains defiant. And why not? His congressional colleagues gave him a slap on the wrist for conduct that would have landed a regular American in jail.

Alcee Hastings. In 2011, we launched a lawsuit against Representative Hastings (D-FL). Hastings allegedly sexually harassed our client Winsome Packer, a female government employee, then proceeded to engage in a cruel campaign of retaliation when she rebuffed his advances. The harassment and retaliation began in 2008 when Hastings (formerly an impeached federal judge) served as chairman of the Organization for Security and Co-operation in Europe. His alleged victim served as his employee; Hastings allegedly told her that he would advance her career in return for sexual favors. Hastings also apparently abused his office by using government travel as a cover for sightseeing and by soliciting gifts and campaign contributions from congressional staff.

It's worth pointing out that Hastings isn't alone here. Representative Anthony Weiner (D-NY) was forced to resign from Congress after Andrew Breitbart revealed that Weiner had been tweeting pictures of his genitals to female admirers; Representative Mark Foley (R-FL) left Congress after it came out that he was propositioning male pages; Senator Larry Craig (R-ID) was soliciting people in airport bathrooms. When it comes to sexual corruption (which usually involves abusing one's office to cover it up), Congress takes the cake.

Nancy Pelosi. No need to rehash most of Nancy Pelosi's sins here. Suffice it to say that she has been one of the most corrupt House leaders in recent memory, from Air Pelosi (the abuse of the perk of military luxury travel) to the insider trading scandal that exploded into the news in November 2011: as it turns out, she and her husband bought shares in Visa in 2008 just before legislation was killed that would have hurt the credit card giant. Over the next two months, the shares more than doubled. And that's just the tip of the iceberg from the San Francisco politician.

Maxine Waters. Representative Waters (D-CA) is one of the most senior and one of the most outspoken members of Congress. She is also one of the most corrupt. In August 2010, an investigative subcommittee of the House Ethics Committee charged Waters with three counts of violating House rules and ethics regulations in connection with her use of power and influence on behalf of OneUnited Bank. That wasn't all. According to the *Washington Times*: "A lobbyist known as one of California's most successful power brokers while serving as a legislative leader in that state paid Rep. Maxine Waters' husband $15,000 in consulting fees at a time she was co-sponsoring legislation that would help save the real-estate finance business of one of the lobbyist's best-paying clients. . . ." "Real-estate finance businesses," such as the one helped by Waters's influence, were labeled a "scam" by the IRS in a 2006 report.

Barney Frank. Representative Frank (D-MA) has always portrayed himself as an honest defender of the little guy. But he's always been one of the most corrupt politicians in Congress—and, overall, one of the most corrupt politicians in American history. Leave aside his involvement in the OneUnited Bank scandal. Leave aside his failure to monitor Fannie Mae and Freddie Mac while taking campaign contributions from them, and installing his boyfriend as an executive there (Frank received $42,350 in campaign contributions from Fannie Mae and Freddie Mac between 1989 and 2008). This goes all the way back. In 1990, the House voted to reprimand him after he used his office to fix parking tickets for Stephen Gobie, an acknowledged male prostitute and former boyfriend of Frank who had been running a gay prostitution ring from the congressman's apartment. Corrupt politicians don't change their stripes. Barney Frank never has. Frank admitted in the book *Reckless Endangerment* that he helped yet another boyfriend gain a lucrative position with Fannie and Freddie, which is yet another abuse of office. When confronted on the controversy, Frank said, "If it is a [conflict of interest] then much of Washington is involved in [conflicts]." That might be the most factual statement Barney Frank has ever made.

Rod Blagojevich. It took more than two years and two trials, but disgraced former Illinois governor Rod "Blago" Blagojevich was finally brought to justice on June 27, 2011, for a number of crimes, including his efforts to "sell" President Obama's vacant Senate seat to the highest bidder. He became the state's fourth governor, and one of at least seventy-nine Illinois public officials, to be found guilty of a crime since 1972, proving that Illinois has certainly lived up to its reputation as a cesspool of corruption.

As the trial unfolded, it became clear that many hands were dirty in the Blago scandal, including Chicago mayor and former Obama chief of staff Rahm "Rahmbo" Emanuel, who was finally forced to testify during this second Blago trial—for a whopping five minutes—and President Obama himself, who was interviewed by the FBI in the scandal even before he took office.

This list could go on and on: John Ensign, Bill Clinton, "No Controlling Legal Authority" Al Gore, Bob Ney—a top-ten list of corrupt politicians could easily turn into a dirty dozen to a corrupt score. The good news is that most of these corrupt politicians have been exposed and face some measure of accountability. As one group, we've gone to court to expose and confront many of these individuals. That is one of the most wonderful things about this country and our republican form of government. The rule of law matters and citizens and civic society can still use the laws (and free speech) to hold government and our political leaders accountable for corruption and abuse.

NOTES

Introduction: The Mission of Judicial Watch

1. Thomas Blanton, "Freedom of Information at 40," George Washington University National Security Archive Electronic Briefing Book No. 194, http://www.gwu.edu/~nsarchiv/NSAEBB/NSAEBB194/index.htm.

Part One: Judicial Watch Before Obama

1. *The Clinton Machine*

1. "Western Journalism Center to sue IRS," WND.com, May 8, 1998, http://www.wnd.com/?pageId=3230, accessed October 2011.
2. "IRS smoking gun documents: White House tied to improper political audit of Western Journalism Center," JudicialWatch.org, July 20, 1999, http://www.judicialwatch.org/archive/1999/262.shtml, accessed October 2011.
3. Mary Matalin and James Carville, *All's Fair: Love, War, and Running for President* (New York: Simon & Schuster, 1995), 112–14.
4. George Lardner Jr., "IRS Audit of Paula Jones Is 'Harassment,' Adviser Says," *Washington Post*, September 15, 1997.
5. Eric Breindel, "Is the IRS targeting Clinton's foes?" JewishWorldReview.com, February 22, 1998, http://www.jewishworldreview.com/cols/breindel022298.html, accessed October 2011.
6. Joseph Farah, "Clinton's IRS Gestapo," WND.com, March 19, 1999, http://www.wnd.com/news/article.asp?ARTICLE_ID=14702, accessed October 2011.
7. Robert Novak, "IRS Reveals Smoking Gun," *Chicago Sun-Times*, February 2, 2002.
8. Complaint, *Judicial Watch, Inc. v. Clinton, et al.* (D.D.C. 2002) (No: 1:02CV 1633).
9. David Limbaugh, *Absolute Power: The Legacy of Corruption in the Clinton-Reno Justice Department* (Washington, DC: Regnery, 2001), 169.
10. Ibid., 171.
11. Ibid., 179–90.
12. Ibid., 194–212.
13. Ibid., 217, 239.
14. Ibid., 239–41.
15. *Meng, et al. v. Schwartz, et al.*, Amended Complaint (Filed September 10, 2001), Case No. 01-cv-01715 (RCL). The complaint resides on our Internet site at: http://www.judicialwatch.org/archive/ois/cases/chinagate-loral/amendcomp-loral.htm.

16. *Meng, et al. v. Schwartz, et al.*, Amended Complaint (Filed August 8, 2001), Case No. 01-cv-01715 (RCL).

17. *Meng, et al. v. Schwartz, et al.*, Amended Complaint (Filed September 10, 2001), Case No. 01-cv-01715 (RCL).

18. http://www.loral.com/inthenews/020109.html.

19. Toni Locy, "For White House Travel Office, a Two-Year Trip of Trouble," *Washington Post*, February 27, 1995, http://www.washingtonpost.com/wp-srv/politics/special/whitewater/stories/wwtr950227.htm, accessed October 2011.

20. Timothy J. Burger with Kenneth R. Bazinet, "Bill Rips Foes Of House Scheme," *New York Daily News*, October 1, 1999, http://articles.nydailynews.com/1999-10-01/news/18120828_1_washington-president-clinton-chappaqua-larry-klayman, accessed October 2011.

21. "Spitzer: U.S. sues Deutsche Bank for lying about home loans while Americans suffered," CNN.com, May 4, 2011, http://inthearena.blogs.cnn.com/2011/05/04/spitzer-u-s-sues-deutsche-bank-for-lying-about-home-loans-while-americans-suffered/, accessed October 2011.

22. Steven A. Holmes, "Fannie Mae Eases Credit to Aid Mortgage Lending," *New York Times*, September 30, 1999, http://www.nytimes.com/1999/09/30/business/fannie-mae-eases-credit-to-aid-mortgage-lending.html, accessed October 2011.

23. "Terrorism/Usama bin Ladin: Who's Chasing Whom," State Department, July 18, 1996, http://www.judicialwatch.org/archive/2005/Usama.pdf, accessed October 2011.

24. Press Office, "Judicial Watch Obtains Newly Declassified Information from State Department regarding Osama bin Laden," Judicial Watch, August 20, 2008, http://www.judicialwatch.org/news/2008/aug/judicial-watch-obtains-newly-declassified-information-state-department-regarding-osama, accessed October 2011.

25. http://www.imdb.com/title/tt0120885/.

26. State Department, "Senior Executive Intelligence Brief," September 21, 1998, http://www.judicialwatch.org/cases/78/iraq.jpg, accessed October 2011.

27. http://www.nytimes.com/2001/02/22/us/a-clinton-in-law-received-400000-in-2-pardon-cases.html?pagewanted=all&src=pm.

28. http://www.judicialwatch.org/press-room/press-releases/judicial-watch-uncovers-new-photos-from-clinton-presidential-library-linking-hillary-clinton-to-controversial-clinton-presidential-pardons/.

29. *Judicial Watch, Inc. v. Department of Justice*, 365 F.3d 1108 (D.C. 2004)

30. http://www.judicialwatch.org/archive/2005/pardondocs.pdf.

2. *The Bush Fog*

1. "Bush rules out pre-emptive pardon for Clinton," CNN.com, January 8, 2001, http://articles.cnn.com/2001-01-08/politics/bush.pardon.clinton_1_president-clinton-independent-counsel-robert-ray-bush-rules?_s=PM:ALLPOLTICS, accessed October 2011.

2. "Clinton aide denies reports of White House vandalism," CNN.com, January 26, 2001, http://articles.cnn.com/2001-01-26/politics/whitehouse.pranks.02_1_offices-prank-cnn?_s=PM:ALLPOLITICS, accessed October 2011.

3. Christopher Newton, "No evidence White House was vandalized," Associated Press, May 19, 2001.

4. George Lardner Jr., "Clintons Shipped Furniture Year Ago," *Washington Post*, February 10, 2001.

5. "Remarks by the President and Secretary of Commerce Donald Evans at Swearing-In Ceremony," White House Transcript, February 5, 2001.

6. Editorial, "Mr. Clinton's Next Move," *New York Times*, February 14, 2001.

7. "Remarks by the President to Pool Aboard Air Force One," White House Transcript, February 13, 2001.

8. Robert L. Jackson and Richard A. Serrano, "U.S. Atty. Launches Inquiry of Rich Case," *Los Angeles Times*, February 15, 2001.

9. Mark Hosenball and Michael Isikoff, "Clinton's Designing Women," *Newsweek*, March 12, 2001. (Retrieved April 6, 2012 via Lexis.)

10. Jim Burns, "Reaction Mixed to Reno's Decision Not to Investigate Gore," CNSNews.com, August 23, 2000, http://cnsnews.com/news/article/reaction-mixed-renos-decision-not-investigate-gore.

11. William Safire, "Exegesis of Acceptance," *New York Times*, August 7, 2000.

12. William Safire, "Riady Cops a Plea," *New York Times*, January 15, 2001.

13. http://www.washingtonpost.com/wp-srv/politics/special/campfin/stories/cf02 1098.htm.

14. http://archives.cnn.com/2002/BUSINESS/asia/01/09/china.loral/.

15. http://www.washingtontimes.com/news/2001/jan/24/20010124-020849-36 66r/print/.

16. http://www.washingtonpost.com/wp-srv/politics/special/campfin/stories/cf02 1098.htm.

17. "New Attorney General FOIA Memorandum Issued," Justice.gov, October 14, 2001, http://www.justice.gov/archive/oip/foiapost/2001foiapost19.htm, accessed October 2011.

18. "Federal Advisory Committee Act (FACA) Management Overview," GSA.gov, September 2, 2011, http://www.gsa.gov/portal/content/104514, accessed October 2011.

19. Paul Krugman, "A Vision of Power," *New York Times*, April 27, 2004, http://www.nytimes.com/2004/04/27/opinion/27KRUG.html, accessed October 2011.

20. Dick Cheney, *In My Time: A Personal and Political Memoir* (New York: Threshold Editions, 2011), 317–18.

21. Michael Abramowitz and Steven Mufson, "Papers Detail Industry's Role in Cheney's Energy Report," *Washington Post*, July 18, 2007, http://www.washingtonpost.com/wp-dyn/content/article/2007/07/17/AR2007071701987.html?hpid=topnews, accessed October 2011.

22. Ibid.

23. Carl Limbacher, "Don't Blame Me, FBI Failure Freeh Whines," Newsmax.com, October 8, 2002.

24. Lacey Phillabaum, "When Exemptions Become the Rule," Coalition of Journalists for Open Government, http://www.cjog.net/documents/Exemptions_Study.pdf, accessed October 2011.

25. Jim VandeHei, "Wealthy Tribes Give More to GOP as Desire for Tax Breaks Increases," *Wall Street Journal*, April 11, 2002.

26. Michael Weisskopf, "The Man to See on Indian Affairs?" *Time*, April 22, 2002.

27. John Ydstie, "Sen. Burns Scrutinized for Earmark Tied to Abramoff," NPR, March 27, 2006; Jeffrey H. Birnbaum and Derek Willis, "Democrats Also Got Tribal Donations," *Washington Post*, June 3, 2005.

28. "Freedom of Information Act Request," Judicial Watch, January 20, 2006, http://www.judicialwatch.org/archive/2006/wh-travel-foia.pdf, accessed October 2011.

29. Pete Yost, "Lawyer: Cheney Visitor Logs Not Recorded," *Washington Post*, May 29, 2007, http://www.washingtonpost.com/wp-dyn/content/article/2007/05/29/AR2007052901508.html, accessed October 2011.

30. *U.S. v. Biaggi, et al.*, 853 F.2d 89, 97 (2nd Cir. 1988).

31. "Complaint Against Representative Tom DeLay (R) of Texas," Judicial Watch, April 10, 2001, http://www.judicialwatch.org/cases/75/delay/DeLayComplaint.htm, accessed October 2011.

32. Larry Bivens, "White House Briefings, Dinners to Be Used to Raise Campaign Money," Judicial Watch, April 28, 2001.

33. Dori Meinert, "Fitzgerald, Hastert Distance Themselves from GOP Fundraising Tactics," Judicial Watch, May 9, 2001.

34. "Complaint Against the National Republican Senatorial Committee, et al.," Judicial Watch, May 21, 2001, http://www.judicialwatch.org/cases/75/FECcomplreNRSC.htm, accessed October 2011.

35. Timothy Noah, "Defendant DeLay?" *Slate*, October 1, 2004, http://www.slate.com/articles/news_and_politics/chatterbox/2004/10/defendant_delay.html, accessed October 2011.

36. http://www.politico.com/news/stories/0111/47384.html.

37. "House Vote on Passage: H. Res. 1031 [110th]," GovTrack.us, March 11, 2008, http://www.govtrack.us/congress/vote.xpd?vote=h2008-122&sort=vote, accessed January 2012.

38. "Referrals," Office of Congressional Ethics, http://oce.house.gov/disclosures.html, accessed January 2012.

39. http://www.thegrio.com/politics/why-cant-the-congressional-black-caucus-catch-a-break.php.

40. http://www.nytimes.com/2010/06/02/us/politics/02ethics.html.

41. http://www.washingtontimes.com/news/2012/mar/19/small-office-has-big-job-monitor-ethics-house/?page=1.

3. *The Financial Meltdown: From Clinton to Bush to Obama*

1. http://www.ritholtz.com/blog/2011/12/bailout-total-29-616-trillion-dollars/.
2. Michael McAuliff, "Bailout watchdog barks over $24 trillion," *New York Daily News*, July 21, 2009, http://www.nydailynews.com/new-york/bail out-watchdog-barks-24-trillion-article-1.429994, accessed November 2011.
3. Steven A. Holmes, "Fannie Mae Eases Credit to Aid Mortgage Lending," *New York Times*, September 30, 1999, http://www.nytimes.com/1999/09/30/ business/fannie-mae-eases-credit-to-aid-mortgage-lending.html, accessed November 2011.
4. http://www.politico.com/news/stories/0708/11781.html.
5. Lisa Lerer, "Fannie, Freddie spent $200M to buy influence," *Politico*, July 16, 2008, http://www.politico.com/news/stories/0708/11781.html, accessed November 2011. http://www.politico.com/news/stories/0908/13270.html.
6. Alex Pappas, "Watchdog group: Boxer not transparent over all Country-wide mortgages," *Daily Caller*, October 12, 2010, http://dailycaller.com/20 10/10/12/watchdog-group-boxer-not-transparent-over-all-countrywide-mort gages/, accessed November 2011.
7. Bill Sammon, "Lawmaker Accused of Fannie Mae Conflict of Interest," FoxNews.com, October 3, 2008, http://www.foxnews.com/story/0,2933 ,432501,00.html, accessed November 2011.
8. Donovan Slack, "Stance on Fannie and Freddie Dogs Frank," *Boston Globe*, October 14, 2010, http://www.boston.com/news/politics/articles/2010/10/ 14/frank_haunted_by_stance_on_fannie_freddie/?page=1, accessed November 2011.
9. Ibid.
10. http://www.pbs.org/newshour/bb/business/july-dec11/fanniefreddie_11-16 .html.
11. Lindsay Renick Mayer, "Update: Fannie Mae and Freddie Mac Invest in Lawmakers," OpenSecrets.org, September 11, 2008, http://www.opensecrets .org/news/2008/09/update-fannie-mae-and-freddie.html, accessed January 2012.
12. Gretchen Morgenson, "Mortgage Giants Leave Legal Bills to the Taxpayers," *New York Times*, January 24, 2011, http://www.nytimes.com/2011/01/24/ business/24fees.html?_r=1, accessed November 2011.
13. http://money.cnn.com/2008/03/28/magazines/fortune/boyd_be ar.fortune/.
14. Slack, "Stance on Fannie and Freddie Dogs Frank."
15. http://www.google.com/hostednews/afp/article/ALeqM5jyyKrPjYt7VhpS8G8 DrRkr18B0hA.
16. http://articles.cnn.com/2008-10-17/politics/ron.paul.qa_1_bailout-monetary -system-inflation?_s=PM:POLITICS.
17. *McKinley v. Federal Deposit Insurance Corporation*, No. 10-420, Mem. Op. (D.C. December 23, 2010).

18. http://www.sigtarp.gov/reports/audit/2011/Extraordinary%20Financial%20 Assistance%20Provided%20to%20Citigroup,%20Inc.pdf.

19. "Bear Stearns: Government Emails on Takeover," CNBC.com, February 20, 2009, http://www.cnbc.com/id/29300204, accessed November 2011.

20. Press release, "Answers to Frequently Asked Investor Questions Regarding the Bear Stearns Companies, Inc.," Securities and Exchange Commission, March 18, 2008, http://www.sec.gov/news/press/2008/2008-46.htm, accessed November 2011.

21. http://money.cnn.com/news/storysupplement/economy/bailouttracker/.

22. http://money.cnn.com/2009/01/16/news/economy/fdic_tlgp/index.htm.

23. http://www.newhavenregister.com/articles/2009/03/20/opinion/doc49c2ce5 4e5064525023132.txt.

24. Trish Turner, "Sen. Dodd Admits Adding Bonus Provision to Stimulus Package," FoxNews.com, March 18, 2009, http://www.foxnews.com/politics /2009/03/18/sen-dodd-admits-adding-bonus-provision-stimulus-package/, accessed November 2011.

25. http://www.newhavenregister.com/articles/2009/03/20/opinion/doc49c2ce5 4e5064525023132.txt.

26. "Quarterly Report to Congress," Office of the Special Inspector General for the Troubled Asset Relief Program, April 21, 2009, http://www.sigtarp.gov/ reports/congress/2009/April2009_Quarterly_Report_to_Congress.pdf, accessed November 2011.

27. http://www.sigtarp.gov/investigations.shtml.

28. John Carney, "GAO Audit Reveals Fed Played Fast and Loose with Loan Rules," CNBC.com, July 22, 2011, http://www.cnbc.com/id/43855944, accessed November 2011.

29. "TARP Tracker," Treasury.gov, http://www.treasury.gov/initiatives/financial -stability/results/Pages/TarpTracker.aspx, accessed January 2012.

30. "Federal Reserve Rescue Efforts," Money.cnn.com, http://money.cnn.com/ news/storysupplement/economy/bailouttracker/#SECTOR, accessed March 2012.

31. http://www.ritholtz.com/blog/2011/12/bailout-total-29-616-trillion-dollars/.

32. R. Jeffrey Smith, "Federal examiners protested help for politically connected bank, e-mails show," *Washington Post*, April 6, 2011, http://www.washington post.com/politics/federal-examiners-protested-help-for-politically-connected -bank-e-mails-show/2011/03/31/AF99aloC_story.html, accessed November 2011.

33. Susan Schmidt, "Waters Helped Bank Whose Stock She Once Owned," *Wall Street Journal*, March 12, 2009, http://online.wsj.com/article/SB123682571 772404053.html, accessed November 2011.

34. Michelle Malkin, "Maxine Waters: Banking on Hypocrisy," Creators Syndicate, March 13, 2009, http://townhall.com/columnists/michellemalkin /2009/03/13/maxine_waters_banking_on_hypocrisy/page/full/, accessed November 2011.

35. Damian Paletta and David Enrich, "Political Interference Seen in Bank Bail-

out Decisions," *Wall Street Journal*, January 23, 2009, http://finance.yahoo.com/news/pf_article_106471.html, accessed January 2012.

36. Wendell Cochran, "Bank in Waters case was weakest TARP recipient," Investigativereportingworkshop.org, August 9, 2010, http://banktracker.investigativereportingworkshop.org/stories/2010/aug/09/bank-waters-case-was-weakest-tarp-recipient/, accessed January 2012.

37. Smith, "Federal examiners protested help for politically connected bank, e-mails show."

38. Beth Healy, "OneUnited Bank gets poor marks on lending," Boston.com, January 10, 2012, http://articles.boston.com/2012-01-10/business/30607940_1_community-reinvestment-act-boston-bank-lending, accessed January 2012.

39. "Report and Findings," Office of Congressional Ethics, United States House of Representatives, August 6, 2009, http://ethics.house.gov/sites/ethics.house.gov/files/documents/Waters%20OCE%20Report.pdf, accessed January 2012.

Part Two: Judicial Watch and the Obama Administration

4. Introducing Barack Obama

1. David Jackson, "The Obama-Rezko Connection," *Chicago Tribune*, April 7, 2008, http://www.chicagotribune.com/news/local/chi-obamarezko-connect.swf,0,4929416.flash, accessed November 2011.

2. http://articles.chicagotribune.com/2008-03-16/news/0803150403_1_house-purchase-tony-rezko-answers.

3. John Fund, "Obama Should Come Clean on Ayers, Rezko and the Iraqi Billionaire," *Wall Street Journal*, August 30, 2008, http://online.wsj.com/article/SB122005063234084813.html, accessed November 2011.

4. Jackson, "The Obama-Rezko Connection."

5. Tim Novak, "Obama's letters for Rezko," *Chicago Sun-Times*, June 13, 2007.

6. Stanley Kurtz, "Obama and Ayers Pushed Radicalism on Schools," *Wall Street Journal*, September 23, 2008, http://online.wsj.com/article/SB122212856075765367.html, accessed November 2011.

7. Rich Noyes, "Barack Obama and Bill Ayers: Stanley Kurtz Makes the Connection," Newsbusters.org, September 23, 2008, http://newsbusters.org/blogs/rich-noyes/2008/09/23/barack-obama-bill-ayers-stanley-kurtz-makes-connection, accessed November 2011.

8. "Report Your Call to WGN," MyBarackObama.com, http://my.barackobama.com/page/s/WGNstandards, accessed November 2011.

9. Ben Smith, "Obama camp blasts National Review writer as 'slimy character assassin,'" *Politico*, August 27, 2008, http://www.politico.com/blogs/bensmith/0808/Obama_camp_blasts_National_Review_writer_as_slimy_character_assassin.html, accessed November 2011.

10. Chuck Neubauer and Tom Hamburger, "Obama donor received a state

grant," *Los Angeles Times*, April 27, 2008, http://www.latimes.com/news/printedition/front/la-na-killerspin27apr27,0,7173710.story, accessed November 2011.

11. Todd Spivak, "Barack Obama and Me," HoustonPress.com, February 27, 2008, http://www.houstonpress.com/2008-02-28/news/barack-obama-screamed-at-me/full/, accessed November 2011.

12. Mike McIntire and Christopher Drew, "In '05 Investing, Obama Took Same Path as Donors," *New York Times*, March 7, 2007, http://www.nytimes.com/2007/03/07/us/politics/07obama.html?pagewanted=print, accessed November 2011.

13. Ken Timmerman, "Hillary Backers Decry Massive Obama Vote Fraud," Newsmax.com, October 27, 2008, http://www.newsmax.com/InsideCover/obama-voter-fraud/2008/10/27/id/326134, accessed November 2011.

14. "Obama and Acorn," *Wall Street Journal*, October 14, 2008, http://online.wsj.com/article/SB122394051071230749.html, accessed November 2011.

15. Warner Todd Huston, "New York Times Killed Stories of Obama's Links to Vote Fraud/ACORN During Campaign," CanadaFreePress.com, April 1, 2009, http://canadafreepress.com/index.php/article/9830, accessed November 2011.

16. Pamela Geller, "Foreign Contributions: Investigating Obama," BigGovernment.com, http://biggovernment.com/pgeller/2010/10/11/foreign-contributions-investigating-obama/, accessed November 2011.

17. Pamela Geller, "Obama's Foreign Donors: The media averts its eyes," AmericanThinker.com, August 14, 2008, http://www.americanthinker.com/2008/08/obamas_donor_contributions_sil.html, accessed November 2011.

18. Chelsea Schilling, "Black Panthers 'intimidate' voters at polls," WND.com, November 4, 2008, http://www.wnd.com/?pageId=80036, accessed November 2011.

19. "The U.S. Department of Justice and the New Black Panther Party Litigation," U.S. Commission on Civil Rights, http://www.usccr.gov/NBPH/USCCR_NBPP_report.pdf, accessed January 2012.

20. Jerry Markon and Krissah Thompson, "Dispute over New Black Panthers case causes deep divisions," *Washington Post*, October 22, 2010, http://www.washingtonpost.com/wp-dyn/content/article/2010/10/22/AR2010102203982.html?sub=AR, accessed November 2011.

21. Michael Luo, "Group Plans Campaign Against G.O.P. Donors," *New York Times*, August 7, 2008, http://www.nytimes.com/2008/08/08/us/politics/08donate.html, accessed November 2011.

22. Jim Kuhnhenn, "Obama seeks to silence ad tying him to 60s radical," Associated Press, August 25, 2008, http://www.breitbart.com/article.php?id=D92PL7400, accessed November 2011.

5. Obama's Picks

1. "Obama Nominee Runs Into New Lobby Rules," *Washington Post*, January 23, 2009, http://voices.washingtonpost.com/washingtonpostinvestigations/2009/01/president_barack_obamas_strict.html, accessed November 2011.

2. Kenneth P. Vogel and Mike Allen, "Obama finds room for lobbyists," *Politico*, January 28, 2009, http://www.politico.com/news/stories/0109/18128.html, accessed November 2011.

3. "Profile: Rahm Emanuel, Barack Obama's new enforcer," *Telegraph* (London), November 6, 2008, http://www.telegraph.co.uk/news/newstopics/profiles/3392848/Profile-Rahm-Emanuel-Barack-Obamas-new-enforcer.html, accessed November 2011.

4. Bob Secter and Andrew Zajac, "Rahm Emanuel's profitable stint at mortgage giant," *Chicago Tribune*, March 26, 2009, http://www.chicagotribune.com/news/politics/obama/chi-rahm-emanuel-profit-26-mar26,0,5682373.story?page=1, accessed November 2011.

5. http://thehill.com/homenews/administration/52045-white-house-eases-stimulus-lobbyist-restrictions.

6. Michelle Malkin, "What the NYT's 8,100-Word Valarie Jarrett Profile Didn't Tell You," July 27, 2009, MichelleMalkin.com, http://michellemalkin.com/2009/07/27/what-the-nyts-8100-word-valerie-jarrett-profile-didnt-tell-you.

7. http://www.judicialwatch.org/news/2008/nov/obama-advisor-valerie-jarrett-linked-real-estate-scandals.

8. http://www.judicialwatch.org/press-room/press-releases/jw-will-file-foia-lawsuit-against-chicago-mayor-daleys-office-obtain-records-related-o/.

9. http://www.judicialwatch.org/press-room/press-releases/judicial-watch-obtains-documents-revealing-cost-of-barack-and-michelle-obamas-failed-bid-to-bring-2016-olympics-to-chicago/.

10. Murray Weiss and Deborah Orin, "FALN Crew No Innocents: Report," *New York Post*, August 31, 1999.

11. Terry Frieden, "Justice blocks FBI testimony at FALN clemency hearing," CNN.com, September 14, 1999, http://cgi.cnn.com/US/9909/14/fbi.faln/, accessed November 2011.

12. John Henry, "Clinton snubs Congress in clemency investigation," *Houston Chronicle,* September 17, 1999, retrieved from Lexis, May 2012.

13. Josh Meyer and Tom Hamburger, "Eric Holder pushed for controversial clemency," *Los Angeles Times*, January 9, 2009, http://articles.latimes.com/2009/jan/09/nation/na-holder9, accessed November 2011.

14. David Kirkpatrick, "Obama's Pick of Daschle May Test Conflict-of-Interest Pledge," *New York Times*, November 20, 2008, http://www.nytimes.com/2008/11/20/us/politics/20daschle.html?_r=1&pagewanted=print, accessed November 2011.

15. Ceci Connolly, "Daschle Pays $100K in Back Taxes Over Car Travel," *Washington Post*, January 30, 2009, http://voices.washingtonpost.com/44/

2009/01/30/daschle_pays_100k_in_back_taxe.html, accessed November 2011.

16. Toby Harnden, "Barack Obama nominees forced to quit over taxes," *Telegraph* (London), February 3, 2009, http://www.telegraph.co.uk/news/worldnews/barackobama/4450211/Barack-Obama-nominees-forced-to-quit-over-taxes.html, accessed November 2011.

17. Amie Parnes, "Clintonites jostle for jobs at State," *Politico*, February 10, 2009, http://www.politico.com/news/stories/0209/18642.html, accessed November 2011.

18. http://www.house.gov/coxreport/.

19. Dan Frosch and James C. McKinley Jr., "Political Donor's Contracts Under Inquiry in New Mexico," *New York Times*, December 18, 2008, http://www.nytimes.com/2008/12/19/us/politics/19richardson.html?_r=1, accessed November 2011.

20. "Richardson withdrawal leaves cabinet gap," MSNBC.com, January 6, 2009, http://www.msnbc.msn.com/id/28493919/#.Tr2UavTiGU8, accessed November 2011.

21. Darren Samuelsohn, "Obama's pick for EPA deputy administrator withdraws," *New York Times*, March 25, 2009, http://www.nytimes.com/gwire/2009/03/25/25greenwire-obamas-pick-for-deputy-administrator-with draws-10304.html, accessed November 2011.

22. Kathy Shaidle, "Ron Bloom: Another White House Insider Praises Mao (video)," *Washington Examiner*, October 20, 2009, http://www.examiner.com/x-722-Conservative-Politics-Examiner-y2009m10d20-Ron-Bloom-another-White-House-insider-praises-Mao-video.

23. Amanda Carpenter, " 'Diversity Czar' Takes Heat Over Remarks," *Washington Times*, September 23, 2009, http://www.washingtontimes.com/news/2009/sep/23/diversity-czar-takes-heat-over-remarks //print.

24. Colin Sullivan, "Vow of silence key to White House–Calif. fuel economy talks," *New York Times*, May 20, 2009, http://www.nytimes.com/gwire/2009/05/20/20greenwire-vow-of-silence-key-to-white-house-calif-fuel-e-12208.html, accessed November 2011.

25. Maxim Lott, "Critics Assail Obama's 'Safe Schools' Czar, Say He's Wrong Man for the Job," FoxNews.com, September 23, 2009.

26. Mark Tapscott, "Obama Appointee Lauded NAMBLA Figure," *Washington Examiner*, October 1, 2009, http://washingtonexaminer.com/politics/beltway-confidential/2009/10/obama-appointee-lauded-nambla-figure/9800.

27. David D. Kirkpatrick, "53 Republicans Seek Ouster of Obama Schools Official," *New York Times*, October 15, 2009.

28. "US Regulatory Czar Nominee Wants Net 'Fairness Doctrine,' " WND.com, April 27, 2009.

29. Ibid.

30. Benjamin Lesser and Greg B. Smith, "Buildings Sprang Up as Donations Rained Down on Bronx Borough President Adolfo Carrin" New York *Daily News*, March 1, 2009, http://www.nydailynews.com/ny_local/

bronx/2009/02/28/200298_buildings_sprang_up_as_donations_rained_.html
?print=1&page=all.

31. Robert Gearty and Greg B. Smith, "Probers Looking at Whether Adolfo
Carrin Got a Steep Discount on Home Renovations," New York *Daily News,*
March 23, 2008, http://www.nydailynews.com/ny_local/2009/03/23/2009
-03-23_probers_looking_at_whether_adolfo_carrin.html?print=1&page
=all.

32. "Obama's Chief Techie: Big Plans, and an Old Shoplifting Rap," http://
abcnews.go.com/Technology/story?id=7154315&page=1#.T5_rAGA0Px4,
March 24, 2009.

33. "Cisco CCNA—Yusaf Acar Busted by FBI as Perp in Federal Bribery Sting,"
NetworkWorld.com, March 12, 2009; "Barackistan Scandal of the Day:
More Vivek Kundra," March 17, 2009, http://therealbarackobama.word
press.com/2009/03/17/barackistan-scandal-of-the-day-more-vivek-kundra.

34. "Rattner Resigns as Obama's Point Man on the Auto Industry," *Washington
Post,* July 14, 2009.

35. David P. Caruso, "Ex-Car Czar Rattner Settles NY Probe for $10M," *Seattle
Times,* December 30, 2010.

36. John Crudele, "Car Czar's Roundabout Ties to General Motors," *New York
Post,* November 3, 2009.

37. Micheline Maynard and Michael J. de la Merced, "A Cliffhanger to See if a
G.M. Turnaround Succeeds," *New York Times,* July 25, 2009.

38. http://www.youtube.com/user/JudicialWatch#p/a/u/1/CFPZ0xn8G7E.

39. Byron York, "Obama: 'I'd like to work my way around Congress,'"
Washington Examiner, September 15, 2011, http://campaign2012.wash
ingtonexaminer.com/blogs/beltway-confidential/obama-id-work-my-way
-around-congress, accessed January 2012.

6. Let the Stonewalling Begin

1. Presidential Memorandum for Heads of Executive Departments and
Agencies Concerning the Freedom of Information Act, 74 Fed. Reg. 4683
(January 21, 2009).

2. "Promises, Promises: Little Transparency Progress," Associated Press, March
14, 2009, http://abcnews.go.com/Politics/wireStory?id=13129681#.Trxw
-PTiGU8, accessed November 2011.

3. Editorial, "On FOIA, Obama wants a license to lie," *Washington Examiner,* October 30, 2011, http://washingtonexaminer.com/opinion/editori
als/2011/10/foia-obama-wants-license-lie, accessed November 2011.

4. "Obama says lobbyists have been excluded from policy-making jobs,"
PolitiFact.com, January 27, 2010, http://www.politifact.com/truth-o-meter/
statements/2010/jan/27/barack-obama/obama-says-lobbyists-have-been-ex
cluded-policy-mak/, accessed November 2011.

5. Carol D. Leonnig, "More than 300 public-records lawsuits filed in Obama's
first year," *Washington Post,* January 27, 2010, http://www.washingtonpost

.com/wp-dyn/content/article/2010/01/26/AR2010012602048.html?hpid=top news, accessed November 2011.

6. "The White House Fires a Watchdog," *Wall Street Journal*, June 17, 2009, http://online.wsj.com/article/SB124511811033017539.html, accessed November 2011.

7. "White House Staff Cut Short Interview Regarding Conflicting Statements Made About Firing of Inspector General," House Committee on Oversight & Government Reform, http://oversight.house.gov/index.php?option=com_content&task=view&id=446&Itemid=29, accessed November 2011.

8. Byron York, "Gerald Walpin loses appeal; court guts protections for agency watchdogs," *Washington Examiner*, January 4, 2011, http://washingtonexaminer.com/blogs/beltway-confidential/2011/01/gerald-walpin-loses-appeal-court-guts-protections-agency-watchdog, accessed November 2011.

9. Matthew Boyle, "Scandal-plagued Americorps loses inspector general funding," DailyCaller.com, January 12, 2012, http://dailycaller.com/2012/01/12/americorps-ig-loses-funding-after-obama-fired-previous-chief-during-investigations-into-admin-corruption/, accessed January 2012.

10. http://www.pogo.org/resources/good-government/go-igi-20120208-where-are-all-the-watchdogs-inspector-general-vacancies1.html#permanent.

11. Jeff Coen, Rick Pearson, and David Kidwell, "Blagojevich arrested," *Chicago Tribune*, December 10, 2008, http://articles.chicagotribune.com/2008-12-10/news/chi-rod-blagojevich-1209_1_blagojevich-and-harris-political-corruption-crime-spree-first-lady-patricia-blagojevich, accessed November 2011.

12. "Final Report of the Special Investigative Committee," State of Illinois 95th General Assembly, House of Representatives Special Investigative Committee, January 8, 2009, http://www.impeachment.senategop.net/Assets/HouseImpeachReport.pdf?utm_source=EmailDirect.com&utm_medium=Email&utm_campaign=December+9+Weekly+Update, accessed January 2012.

13. "Illinois State Legislators Call for Burris Resignation Over Wiretapped Conversations," FoxNews.com, May 28, 2009, http://www.foxnews.com/politics/2009/05/28/illinois-state-legislators-burris-resignation-wiretapped-conversations/?test=latestnews, accessed November 2011.

14. Michael D. Shear, "A Blagojevich retrial? Don't expect smiles from White House," *Washington Post*, August 18, 2010, http://www.washingtonpost.com/wp-dyn/content/article/2010/08/18/AR2010081801131.html?hpid=topnews, accessed November 2011.

15. Carol E. Lee and David Catanese, "Andrew Romanoff: W.H. offered three jobs," *Politico*, June 2, 2010, http://www.politico.com/news/stories/0610/38064.html, accessed November 2011.

16. Brody Mullins and T. W. Farnam, "Lawmakers' Global-Warming Trip Hit Tourist Hot Spots," *Wall Street Journal*, August 8, 2009, http://online.wsj.com/article/SB124967502810515267.html, accessed November 2011.

17. John Fund, "Air Congress Hits Turbulence," *Wall Street Journal*, August 12, 2009, http://online.wsj.com/article/SB10001424052970204251404574344672056749360.html, accessed November 2011.

18. Joe Curl, "The cost of a NYC weekend," *Washington Times*, June 1, 2009, http://www.washingtontimes.com/news/2009/jun/01/curl-cost-nyc-weekend/, accessed November 2011.

19. Stephanie Strom, "Funds Misappropriated at 2 Nonprofit Groups," *New York Times*, July 9, 2008, http://www.nytimes.com/2008/07/09/us/09embezzle .html?_r=1, accessed November 2011.

20. "White House Voluntary Disclosure Policy Visitor Access Records," White-House.gov, http://www.whitehouse.gov/VoluntaryDisclosure/, accessed January 2012.

21. Fred Schulte and Viveca Novak, "White House visitor logs riddled with holes," IWatchNews.org, April 13, 2011, http://www.iwatchnews.org/2011/ 04/13/4115/white-house-visitor-logs-riddled-holes, accessed January 2012.

7. Remaking America

1. Mark Steyn, *After America: Get Ready for Armageddon* (Washington, DC: Regnery, 2011), 22.

2. Matthew Mosk, "EXCLUSIVE: Democratic donors rewarded with W.H. perks," *Washington Times*, October 28, 2009, http://www.washingtontimes .com/news/2009/oct/28/democratic-donors-rewarded-with-wh-perks/?feat =home_cube_position1, accessed November 2011.

3. http://us-code.vlex.com/vid/sec-place-solicitation-19191050.

4. "Labor leaders back at the W.H.," *Politico*, January 13, 2010, http://www .politico.com/livepulse/0110/Labor_leaders_back_at_the_WH.html, accessed November 2011.

5. Holly Rosenkrantz, "Trumka Has Detractors, Not Opponents, in AFL-CIO Bid," Bloomberg.com, June 8, 2009, http://www.bloomberg.com/apps/news ?pid=newsarchive&sid=aXDR8281bQlw, accessed November 2011.

6. Lori Montgomery and Michael D. Shear, "White House, unions reach deal on taxing insurance coverage," *Washington Post*, January 14, 2010, http:// voices.washingtonpost.com/44/2010/01/white-house-unions-reach-deal.html, accessed November 2011.

7. Lexie Hemesath, "Obama Returns to Iowa," MyDUHawk.com, April 7, 2010, http://www.myduhawk.com/2010/04/07/obama-visits-iowa/, accessed November 2011.

8. Karl Rove, "ObamaCare Rewards Friends, Punishes Enemies," *Wall Street Journal*, January 6, 2011, http://online.wsj.com/article/SB10001424052748 7044057045760638924687795556.html?mod=WSJ_hpp_sections_opinion, accessed November 2011.

9. "Annual Limits Policy: Protecting Consumers, Maintaining Options, and Building a Bridge to 2014," Center for Consumer Information and Insurance Oversight, http://cciio.cms.gov/resources/files/approved_applications_for_waiver .html, accessed January 2012.

10. Terence P. Jeffrey, "What Did Kagan Tell Her Deputy About Winning the Health-Care Case? DOJ Won't Say," CNSNews.com, April 26, 2011, http://

cnsnews.com/news/article/what-did-kagan-tell-her-deputy-about-winning
-health-care-case-doj-won-t-say, accessed November 2011.

11. Vincent Rossmeier, "Obama adopts Bush's arguments for secrecy," *Salon*, July 22, 2009, http://www.salon.com/2009/07/22/citizens/, accessed November 2011.

12. Ben Smith, " 'Fight the Smears' (Health Care edition)," *Politico*, August 4, 2009, http://www.politico.com/blogs/bensmith/0809/Fight_The_Smears_Health_Care_edition.html, accessed November 2011.

13. Chip Reid, "Obama Reneges on Health Care Transparency," CBSNews.com, January 7, 2010, http://www.cbsnews.com/stories/2010/01/06/eveningnews/main6064298.shtml, accessed November 2011.

14. "C-SPAN CEO: Obama Used Us as 'Political Football,' " FoxNews.com, January 7, 2010, http://www.foxnews.com/politics/2010/01/07/c-span-ceo-obama-used-political-football/?test=latestnews, accessed November 2011.

15. Michelle Malkin, "Obama's illegal alien auntie: The rest of the story," Creators Syndicate, November 12, 2008, http://michellemalkin.com/2008/11/12/obama%E2%80%99s-illegal-alien-auntie-the-rest-of-the-story/, accessed November 2011.

16. Susan Carroll, "Lawmakers worry as local police take on immigration," Chron.com, March 5, 2009, http://www.chron.com/news/houston-texas/article/Lawmakers-worry-as-local-police-take-on-1729478.php, accessed November 2011.

17. Ryan Gabrielson, "Changes in D.C. put Arpaio on hot seat," *East Valley Tribune*, March 14, 2009.

18. William Lajeunesse, "Pelosi Tells Illegal Immigrants That Work Site Raids Are Un-American," FoxNews.com, March 18, 2009, http://www.foxnews.com/politics/2009/03/18/pelosi-tells-illegal-immigrants-work-site-raids-are-un-american/, accessed November 2011.

19. Jordy Yager, "Napolitano says thanks but no thanks, DHS has funds," *Hill*, March 25, 2009, http://thehill.com/homenews/news/18924-napolitano-says-thanks-but-no-thanks-dhs-has-funds, accessed November 2011.

20. Heidi Noonan, "GOP Senators Want Answers on Amnesty Memo," FoxNews.com, August 1, 2010, http://liveshots.blogs.foxnews.com/2010/08/01/gop-senators-want-answers-on-amnesty-memo/, accessed November 2011.

21. Susan Carroll, "Feds moving to dismiss some deportation cases," *Houston Chronicle*, August 24, 2010, http://www.chron.com/news/article/Feds-moving-to-dismiss-some-deportation-cases-1706119.php, accessed November 2011.

22. Andrew Becker, "Tension over Obama Policies Within Immigration and Customs Enforcement," *Washington Post*, August 27, 2010, http://www.washingtonpost.com/wp-dyn/content/article/2010/08/26/AR2010082606561.html, accessed November 2011.

23. "Vote of No Confidence in ICE Director John Morton and ICE ODPP Assistant Director Phyllis Coven," ICEUnion.org, June 25, 2010, http://www

.iceunion.org/download/259-259-vote-no-confidence.pdf, accessed November 2011.

24. Mark Krikorian, "Now He Really Is Lying," NationalReview.com, August 25, 2009, http://www.nationalreview.com/corner/186044/now-he-really-lying/mark-krikorian, accessed November 2011.

25. Alec MacGillis, "Rep. Wilson's Yell Draws Attention to Issue of Coverage for Illegal Immigrants," *Washington Post*, September 11, 2009, http://www.washingtonpost.com/wp-dyn/content/article/2009/09/10/AR2009091004276.html?hpid=topnews&sub=AR, accessed November 2011.

26. Suzanne Gamboa, "Democrats question White House stand excluding undocumented from health care exchanges," Associated Press, September 15, 2009, http://www.startribune.com/templates/Print_This_Story?sid=59405307, accessed November 2011.

27. David M. Herszenhorn, "Baucus Bill Would Bar Illegal Immigrants from Insurance Exchanges," *New York Times*, September 14, 2009, http://prescriptions.blogs.nytimes.com/2009/09/14/baucus-bill-would-bar-illegal-immigrants-from-insurance-exchanges/, accessed November 2011.

28. Senator Tom Coburn, M.D., Senator John Barrasso, M.D., "Bad Medicine: A check-up on the new federal health law," United States Senate, July 2010, http://www.coburn.senate.gov/public/index.cfm?a=Files.Serve&File_id=722faf8b-a5be-40fd-a52b-9a98826c1592, accessed January 2012.

29. Matt Cover, "HHS: Obamacare-Funded Health Centers for 'Migrants' Won't Check Immigration Status," CNSNews.com, August 10, 2011, http://cnsnews.com/news/article/hhs-obamacare-funded-health-centers-migrants-wont-check-immigration-status, accessed January 2012.

30. http://howeypolitics.com/main.asp?SectionID=10&SubSectionID=20&ArticleID=5943.

31. Mitch Daniels, "Hoosiers vs. Crony Capitalism," *Wall Street Journal*, July 8, 2011.

32. See, for example, Mike Colias, "GM to build Cadillacs outside the U.S.," AutoWeek.com, June 7, 2011, http://www.autoweek.com/article/20110607/CARNEWS/110609894, accessed January 2012.

33. T. W. Farnam and Dan Eggen, "GOP bringing in the bucks for House midterms," *Washington Post*, August 26, 2010, http://www.washingtonpost.com/wp-dyn/content/article/2010/08/25/AR2010082507029.html, accessed November 2011.

34. Stephen Clark, "Bailed Out Firms Spend Millions on Political Causes, Federal Lobbying," FoxNews.com, August 6, 2010, http://www.washingtonpost.com/wp-dyn/content/article/2010/08/25/AR2010082507029.html, accessed November 2011.

35. Joe Stephens and Carol D. Leonnig, "Solyndra loan: White House pressed on review of solar company now under investigation," *Washington Post*, September 13, 2011, http://www.washingtonpost.com/politics/white-house-pushed-500-million-loan-to-solar-company-now-under-investigation/2011/09/13/gIQAr3WbQK_print.html, accessed November 2011.

36. Ibid.

37. "Department of Energy: Further Actions Are Needed to Improve DOE's Ability to Evaluate and Implement the Loan Guarantee Program," U.S. Government Accountability Office, July 2010, http://www.gao.gov/new .items/d10627.pdf, accessed November 2011.

38. Todd Woody, "Solyndra: Pay Some Investors Before Taxpayers in Solar Flame Out," Forbes.com, September 6, 2011, http://www.forbes.com/sites/todd woody/2011/09/06/solyndra-pay-some-investors-before-taxpayers-in-solar -flame-out/, accessed November 2011.

39. Frank Miniter, " 'Fast and Furious' Just Might Be President Obama's Watergate," Forbes.com, September 28, 2011.

40. "Issa Issues Subpoena to Holder in Fast and Furious Investigation," FoxNews .com, October 12, 2011, http://www.foxnews.com/politics/2011/10/12/issa -issues-subpoena-to-holder-in-fast-and-furious-investigation/, accessed No-vember 2011.

41. "House Republicans Request Special Counsel to Probe Holder on 'Fast and Furious,' " FoxNews.com, October 4, 2011, http://www.foxnews.com/ politics/2011/10/04/house-republicans-to-request-special-counsel-to-probe -holder-on-fast-and/, accessed November 2011.

42. Randall Mikkelsen, "Guantanamo inmates no longer 'enemy combatants,' " Reuters, March 14, 2009, http://www.reuters.com/article/2009/03/14/us -obama-security-combatant-idUSTRE52C59220090314, accessed Novem-ber 2011.

43. "Department of Justice Withdraws 'Enemy Combatant' Definition for Guan-tanamo Detainees," U.S. Department of Justice, March 13, 2009, http:// www.justice.gov/opa/pr/2009/March/09-ag-232.html, accessed November 2011.

44. Evan Perez, "Abdulmutallab Resumes Talking to Federal Agents," *Wall Street Journal*, February 2, 2010, http://online.wsj.com/article/SB1000142405274 8704022804575042000390632726.html, accessed November 2011.

45. "Biden Fears Terror Hit by Individual," CBSNews.com, February 17, 2010, http://www.cbsnews.com/stories/2010/02/17/earlyshow/main6215792.shtml, accessed November 2011.

46. Evan Perez, "Guantanamo Detainees May Be Released in U.S.," *Wall Street Jour-nal*, March 19, 2009, http://online.wsj.com/article/SB123741378746277081 .html, accessed November 2011.

47. The text of the report details the asterisk as follows: "Rightwing extremism in the United States can be broadly divided into those groups, movements, and adherents that are primarily hate-oriented (based on hatred of particular religious, racial, or ethnic groups), and those that are mainly antigovernment, rejecting federal authority in favor of state or local authority, or rejecting government authority entirely. It may include groups and individuals that are dedicated to a single issue, such as opposition to abortion or immigration." http://www.fas.org/irp/eprint/rightwing.pdf.

48. "Rightwing Extremism: Current Economic and Political Climate Fueling Resurgence in Radicalization and Recruitment," U.S. Department of Homeland Security, April 7, 2009, http://www.fas.org/irp/eprint/rightwing.pdf, accessed November 2011.

49. Audrey Hudson, "Homeland issued 'extremism' report despite objections," *Washington Times*, April 17, 2009, http://www.washingtontimes.com/news/2009/apr/17/homeland-security-got-internal-flags/, accessed November 2011.

50. Debbie Schlussel, "Schlussel Stops FBI Award to Terrorist Supporter," DebbieSchlussel.com, September 18, 2003, http://www.debbieschlussel.com/6282/schlussel-stops-fbi-award-to-terrorist-supporter-the-column-that-started-it-all/, accessed November 2011.

51. http://www.investigativeproject.org/2340/federal-judge-agrees-cair-tied-to-hamas.

52. Noel Sheppard, "Ground Zero Mosque Imam's Controversial Post-9/11 60 Minutes Interview," Newsbusters.org, August 19, 2010, http://newsbusters.org/blogs/noel-sheppard/2010/08/19/ground-zero-mosque-imams-controversial-60-minutes-interview, accessed November 2011.

53. "Obama on Islamic Center: Not commenting on 'wisdom of making a decision,'" CNN.com, August 14, 2010, http://religion.blogs.cnn.com/2010/08/14/obama-on-islamic-center-not-commenting-on-wisdom-of-making-a-decision/, accessed November 2011.

54. Stephanie Condon, "Harry Reid: Ground Zero Mosque 'Should be Built Some Place Else,'" CBSNews.com, August 16, 2010, http://www.cbsnews.com/8301-503544_162-20013773-503544.html, accessed November 2011.

55. Grace Rauh, "NY1 Exclusive: Developer Won't Budge on Mosque Location," NY1.com, August 17, 2010, http://www.ny1.com/content/123896/ny1-exclusive—developer-won-t-budge-on-mosque-location, accessed November 2011.

56. Jake Sherman and Andy Barr, "Pelosi wants mosque 'transparency,'" *Politico*, August 18, 2010, http://www.politico.com/news/stories/0810/41204.html, accessed November 2011.

57. Matthew Lee, "US govt sending ground zero mosque imam to Mideast," Associated Press, August 10, 2010, http://www.boston.com/news/nation/washington/articles/2010/08/10/feds_send_ground_zero_mosque_imam_to_mideast/, accessed November 2011.

58. http://www.politico.com/politico44/2012/03/biden-bin-laden-killing-most-audacious-plan-in-years-117961.html.

59. http://www.cbsnews.com/8301-503544_162-20059739-503544.html?tag=cbsContentWrap;cbsContent.

60. http://www.judicialwatch.org/cases/judicial-watch-v-u-s-department-of-defense-central-intelligence-agency/.

61. http://www.google.com/hostednews/ap/article/ALeqM5hCJU5RbH3YQeV0agFaNT11sMXEIg?docId=ec15acc54eed444fb76d9c15c7eaf8f9.

372   *Notes*

62. http://abcnews.go.com/blogs/politics/2011/05/gates-clinton-advising-presi
    dent-to-not-release-obl-photograph-obama-increasingly-concerned-no-good-/.
63. http://thepage.time.com/2011/05/03/panetta-public-likely-to-see-obl-pic
    ture/.
64. http://www.judicialwatch.org/files/documents/2011/Osama_Photos_SJ_Mo
    tion.pdf.
65. Ibid.
66. http://www.reuters.com/article/2012/01/17/idUS349735306920120117.
67. http://www.nytimes.com/2011/08/07/opinion/sunday/Dowd—The-Down
    grade-Blues.html?_r=3&ref=opinion.
68. http://www.washingtonpost.com/politics/osama-bin-laden-is-killed-by-us-for
    ces-in-pakistan/2011/05/01/AFXMZyVF_story.html.
69. http://www.washingtontimes.com/news/2011/may/6/obama-allah-pardon
    -osama/.
70. Ibid.
71. http://factcheck.org/UploadedFiles/2011/10/NAVPERS-15555D-Navy-Mil
    itary-Funerals1.pdf.
72. http://www.washingtontimes.com/news/2011/may/6/obama-allah-pardon
    -osama/.
73. http://www.scribd.com/JWatchDC/d/86245994-81046072-OBL-Reply#full
    screen.

Part Three: Watching the Future

8. How to Steal an Election in Plain Sight

1. John Fund, *How the Obama Administration Threatens to Undermine our Elections* (New York: Encounter Books, 2009), 1.
2. John Fund, "Who Will Investigate the Investigators?" *Wall Street Journal,* July 8, 2010, http://online.wsj.com/article/SB10001424052748703636404575353052562578046.html, accessed January 2012.
3. "Race Neutral Enforcement of the Law? DOJ and the New Black Panther Party Litigation," U.S. Commission on Civil Rights, November 23, 2010, http://www.usccr.gov/NBPH/CommissionInterimReport_11-23-2010.pdf, accessed January 2012.
4. James Simpson, "What the Dems Know: Universal Voter Registration," AmericanThinker.com, January 6, 2010, http://www.americanthinker.com/2010/01/what_the_dems_know_universal_v.html, accessed January 2012.
5. Ben Smith, "ACORN heirs deny funneling cash to Occupy Wall Street," *Politico,* November 7, 2011, http://www.politico.com/news/stories/1111/67793.html, accessed November 2011.
6. Cynthia Gordy, "Bertha Lewis on Life After ACORN," *The Root,* May 16, 2011, www.theroot.com/views/bertha-lewis-life-after-acorn?GT1=38002.
7. "Issa Releases Investigative Report Finding ACORN Still Alive and Well,"

House.gov, http://oversight.house.gov/index.php?option=com_content&view
=article&id=647:issa-releases-investigative-report-finding-acorn-still-alive
-and-well&catid=22, accessed January 2012.

8. "Notice of Discovery of Assets, Notice to Debtor(s), Creditor(s) and Interested Parties," United States Bankruptcy Court, re: Association of Community Organizations for Reform Now, Inc. (aka ACORN), Case No.
1-10-50380, January 20, 2011.

9. Brendan McCarthy, "State Investigators Taking Dozens of Computers from
ACORN Office on Canal Street," November 6, 2009, http://nola.com/
crime/index.ssf/2009/11/attorney_general_serves_search.html.

10. Testimony of David Caldwell for the U.S. House of Representatives
Committee on Oversight and Government Reform and the Judiciary
Regarding the ACORN Forum, December 1, 2009.

11. Telephone conversation between Sean Dunagan of Judicial Watch and the
Pennsylvania attorney general's office on May 23, 2011. Dunagan was also
informed that investigation of ACORN is continuing and is being handled
by the Charitable Trust Section.

12. Ian Urbina, "Acorn Says It Continues Its Work," *New York Times*, April 2,
2010, http://www.nytimes.com/2010/04/03/us/politics/03acorn.html?hp,
accessed November 2011.

13. "ACORN Missing Money Could Top 5 Million Dollars," KPLC 7 and the
Associated Press, October 8, 2009, www.kplctv.com.

14. "Is ACORN Intentionally Structured as a Criminal Enterprise?" U.S. House
of Representatives Committee on Oversight and Government Reform Staff
Report, July 23, 2009, 8–9, 16–23.

15. "Obama Administration Issues $79,819 Grant to ACORN Offshoot in
Apparent Violation of ACORN Funding Ban," Judicial Watch news release,
July 5, 2011, www.judicialwatch.org.

16. ACORN Housing Corporation, Inc., Evaluation of HUD Housing Counsel-
ing Grant Expenditures, U.S. Department of Housing and Urban Development (HUD), Inspector General Report, IED-10-002, September 21, 2010,
www.hud.gov/offices/oig/ied/10-002.cfm.

17. Letter, Lynn H. Gibson, Acting General Counsel for U.S. Government Accountability Office, to Jeffrey T. Bryson, General Counsel, NeighborWorks
America, September 29, 2010.

18. IRS Form 1023, Application for Recognition of Exemption Under Section
501(c)3 of the Internal Revenue Code, filed by Black Institute, Inc.

19. Voluntary Petition, Association of Community Organizations for Reform
Now, Inc. (ACORN), Chapter 7 Filing, United States Bankruptcy Court,
November 2, 2010.

20. "Gaspard to DNC, Dillon to Re-elect," *Politico*, January 20, 2011.

21. Francis McCabe, "Judge fines ACORN $5,000 for voter registration scheme,"
Las Vegas Review Journal, August 10, 2011, http://www.lvrj.com/news/judge
-fines-acorn-5-000-for-voter-registration-scheme-127467598.html, accessed
January 2012.

22. Chelsea Schilling, "FBI Report: ACORN 'Poverty Pimpin' for Democrats," WND.com, June 9, 2010, http://www.wnd.com/2010/06/164621/, accessed January 2012.

23. James Simpson, "What the Dems Know: Universal Voter Registration," AmericanThinker.com, January 6, 2010, http://www.americanthinker.com/2010/01/what_the_dems_know_universal_v.html, accessed January 2012.

24. J. Christian Adams, "Documents Reveal Coordination Between ACORN Affiliate and Justice Department Voting Section," BigGovernment.com, December 14, 2011, http://biggovernment.com/jcadams/2011/12/14/documents-reveal-coordination-between-acorn-affiliate-and-justice-department-voting-section/, accessed January 2012.

25. Noelle Phillips, "S.C. DMV chief: 900 dead people may have voted," CharlotteObserver.com, January 12, 2012, http://www.charlotteobserver.com/2012/01/12/2918973/sc-dmv-chief-900-dead-people-may.html, accessed January 2012.

Epilogue: Maintaining Transparency

1. Pat Gleason, "Public Disclosure: A Founding Principle That Boosts Accountability Today," *Journal of the James Madison Institute* 40 (Fall 2007), 44–45.

2. Allen Schick and Felix LoStracco, *The Federal Budget: Politics, Policy, Process* (Washington, DC: Brookings Institution, 2000), 12.

3. Michael B. Katz and Mark J. Stern, *One Nation Divisible: What America Was and What It Is Becoming* (New York: Russell Sage Foundation, 2006), 42.

4. Suzanne J. Piotrowski, *Governmental Transparency in the Path of Administrative Reform* (Albany: State University of New York Press, 2007), 3.

5. William Fisher, "Obama's Pledge of Transparency Remains Largely Unfulfilled," *Public Record*, June 22, 2009, http://pubrecord.org/politics/2056/obamas-pledge-of-transparency-remains-largely-unfulfilled/.

6. http://www.whitehouse.gov/the_press_office/Freedom_of_Information_Act.

7. Presidential Memorandum for Heads of Executive Departments and Agencies Concerning the Freedom of Information Act, 74 Fed. Reg. 4683 (Jan. 21, 2009).

8. Andrew Malcolm, "A little secret about Obama's transparency," *Los Angeles Times*, March 21, 2010, http://articles.latimes.com/2010/mar/21/nation/la-na-ticket21-2010mar21.

9. Office of the Press Secretary, "White House Launches Government Accountability and Transparency Board to Cut Waste and Boost Accountability," WhiteHouse.gov, July 28, 2011, http://www.whitehouse.gov/the-press-office/2011/07/28/white-house-launches-government-accountability-and-transparency-board-cu.

10. Geoffrey R. Stone, "Our Untransparent President," *New York Times*, June 26, 2011, http://www.nytimes.com/2011/06/27/opinion/27stone.html?pagewanted=all.

ACKNOWLEDGMENTS

The material in this book is the result of years of dedication and persistence by dozens of Judicial Watch employees. And none of their work would have been possible without the generous help of nearly 800,000 Judicial Watch supporters over the years. Paul Orfanedes, our Director of Litigation, and Chris Farrell, our Director of Research and Investigations, have helped develop a formidable and effective watchdog organization. And I know I speak for all of the Judicial Watch staff as we say a special thanks to our families, who patiently support our passionate commitment to our cause. To those of you who worked with me directly on the development of *The Corruption Chronicles,* you know who are, and I thank you for your help and advice.

INDEX